Views From Inside

Languages, Cultures, and Schooling
for K–12 Educators

A Volume in
Literacy, Language, and Learning

Series Editor:
Wen Ma, *Le Moyne College*

Literacy, Language, and Learning

Wen Ma, Series Editor

*The Perfect Norm: How to Teach Differentially, Assess Effectively, and Manage
a Classroom Ethically in Ways That Are "Brain-Friendly"
and Culturally Responsive* (2009)
By Sharon L. Spencer and Sandra Vavra

*African-American Middle-Income Parents: How Are They Involved
in Their Children's Literacy Development?* (2007)
By Ethel Swindell Robinson

*Closing the Gap: English Educators Address the Tensions
Between Teacher Preparation and Teaching Writing in Secondary Schools* (2007)
Edited by Karen Keaton Jackson and Sandra Vavra

Research and Reflection: Teachers Take Action for Literacy Development (2006)
Edited by Andrea Izzo

*ABC's of Cultural Understanding and Communication National
and International Adaptations* (2006)
Edited by Patricia Ruggiano Schmidt and Claudia Finkbeiner

*Preparing Educators to Communicate and Connect
With Families and Communities* (2006)
Edited by Patricia Ruggiano Schmidt

*Reading and Writing Ourselves Into Being:
The Literacy of Certain 19th Century Young Women* (2004)
Edited by Claire White Putala, SUNY Oswego

*Reconceptualizing Literacy in the New Age
of Multiculturalism and Pluralism* (2001)
Patricia Ruggiano Schmidt and Peter B. Mosenthal

Views From Inside

Languages, Cultures, and Schooling
for K–12 Educators

Edited by

Joy Egbert and Gisela Ernst-Slavit
Washington State University

Information Age Publishing, Inc.
Charlotte, North Carolina • www.infoagepub.com

Library of Congress Cataloging-in-Publication Data

CIP data for this book can be found on the Library of Congress website:
http://www.loc.gov/index.html

Paperback: 978-1-64113-019-6
Hardcover: 978-1-64113-020-2
E-Book: 978-1-64113-021-9

Printed in the United States of America

CONTENTS

SECTION 8:   EUROPEAN REGION

SECTION 9:   UNITED STATES

DEDICATIONS

As always, for Princess J and DavetotheMax—thanks for your patience and hugs; George M. Egbert, Jr. (aka Poppy), for his bravery and support (you go, Dad!); Dr. Gisela Ernst-Slavit, whose voice in my head makes me think harder and better; and Mom, whom I miss every day but who I know would be proud.

For Hubert and Luchita, whose goal was to raise worldly trilingual children. For Dave, Max, and Arthur, whose multiplex and multicultural lives sustain me every day in every way. And for Marina Astorga Retamozo, Guillermina Rosales de Morales, Elsa Leon Iglesias, and Dr. Cecilia Thorne de Trelles, outstanding Peruvian educators who inspired me to learn and teach about our world.

ACKNOWLEDGMENTS

Special thanks to graduate student Steve Morrison for his thorough and timely assistance in the final editing stages. Also thanks to the amazing graduate students in the College of Education at WSU, who are ever willing to question, learn, and create, and, in doing so, teach us to understand the world.

PREFACE

Joy Egbert
Washington State University

The goal of this text is to help readers understand the importance of students' cultures, languages, and previous schooling to curriculum development, assessment, and student achievement. Readers will learn about aspects of specific cultures and language that are important to their understanding of diverse students, and they will discover that cultures that are often considered similar (or different) may not be so (and why). Overall, the text focuses on how educators can address languages and cultures in classrooms and schools and how they might account for students' backgrounds and funds of knowledge.

We developed this book because we saw a need for our pre- and inservice teachers, administrators, and faculty in higher education (particularly those in teacher education programs) across the United States to have a resource that provided information about cultures and languages from those who have lived within them. There is a lack of texts for educators in this area that present the information in ways that are accessible, useful, and engaging. We believe that this text fills this need. This book can also be used for teacher development programs, teacher education classes, book groups, and other communities of practice. Because the text is not discipline-specific, it can be tapped across content areas. Educators may also be interested in sharing this book with parents as a resource text.

The text starts with an introduction chapter that presents definitions, describes contexts, and explains why learning about cultures, languages, and schooling matters. The main body of the book comprises 25 chapters written by natives from the languages and cultures under discussion who also have experience in U.S. schools and with U.S. culture. All of the

Views From Inside: Languages, Cultures, and Schooling for K–12 Educators
pp. xiii–xvi
Copyright © 2018 by Information Age Publishing
All rights of reproduction in any form reserved.

authors are in some way experts in education, whether through advanced study or extensive experience, and the information they include in each section was chosen by them. As we edited this book, we tried to honor both the language and the style of the authors, revising only for clarity; any atypical word uses or grammatical constructions are those of the authors and help to share their insider status. We also worked as a group to try to avoid paternalism/prescription (i.e., saying what teachers *should* or *must* do), but all of the authors in this book are passionate about meeting the needs of diverse children, so sometimes this tone comes through.

Each chapter starts with a school scenario that actually occurred in a U.S. school. The purpose of this scenario is to help readers understand the contexts and challenges that students from the title culture may experience as they participate in education in the United States. The chapter then presents information that can help educators address these challenges. To do so, the second part of each chapter includes background data on the country, which, according to the authors' perceptions of what U.S. educators should know, may include demographics, geography, and historical events and other foundational aspects that may have an impact on immigrant students and their families. Each chapter also includes a section on the culture(s) of the nation(s), which may include famous people, contributions to the world, personal characteristics, important religious information, focal customs, family relations, and other aspects that are important to the cultural insiders who wrote the chapter. The language and literacy section in each chapter may address how the language relates to the culture, a number of words that teachers can learn, how it is different from *and* similar to English, and what those differences and similarities might mean for English language learners from that culture. In this section, words foreign to U.S. English are italicized (e.g., *maestro* ["teacher" in Spanish]), and capital letters are used to show word stress in transliterations (e.g., ma-EH-stro). Some of the authors have used symbols from the International Phonetic Alphabet (IPA) to help readers understand exact pronunciations of unfamiliar words; Table P.1 shows some of the IPA symbols and related sounds for reference. The final part of each chapter comprises advice, resources, and ideas for educators (for example, if it is an oral culture, the teacher might consider working with students on oral storytelling before transitioning to written stories, or incorporate both using technology). Each chapter also contains additional recommended resources and short tasks for teachers that extend the chapter information. We hope that readers will carefully explore each chapter not only for what is included, but for what the authors have left out, as this omission may also provide a glimpse into the culture(s) being addressed.

Table P.1.   Some IPA Symbols and Sounds

Consonants		Vowels	
IPA	*Examples*	*IPA*	*Examples*
b	buy, cab	ʌ	cup, gun, luck
d	did, Dad, do	ɑ:	arm, father
ð	this, breathe, father	æ	tap, cat, black
dʒ	giant, bridge, major	ɛ	met, dress, men
f	fan, fish, phi	ə	other, comma
g	game, bag	ɪ	hit, sit, inch
h	help, ahead	i:	see, neat
hw	why	ɒ	hot, rock
j	yes, hallelujah	ɔ:	call, hawk
k	sky, crack	ʊ	put, book
l	lip, slip, grill	u:	soup, food
m	my, smile, come	aɪ	five, eye
n	night, snoop, can	aʊ	now, owl
ŋ	sing, sink, stinger	eɪ	pay, eight
θ	think, math	oʊ	go, know
p	pin, spy, mop	ɔɪ	boy, joint
r	rip, trap, very		
s	sight, miss		
ʃ	ship, rash, potion		
t	tip, stop, pit, atoll		
tʃ	china, patch		
v	vest, cave		
w	went, swore		
z	zip, has		
ʒ	equation, measure, vision		
x	ugh, loch, Chanukah		
ʔ	Glottal stop (a release of air after a full stop) as in "uh-oh" [ˈʌʔoʊ]. In some American dialects, words like kitten will have a stop instead of the "tt" sound (e.g., kʔn)		

Readers of this text should understand that each chapter provides the perceptions and ideas of its authors, and that other members of the culture might choose to provide different information; the authors might also disagree with information written in other chapters. Therefore, the chapter information can be considered a starting point for cultural and linguistic understandings, and educators are encouraged to make their own decisions about what to do with this information and how to extend their own and their students' knowledge.

SECTION 1

INTRODUCTION TO CULTURE AND LANGUAGE

CHAPTER 1

UNDERSTANDING CULTURE AND LANGUAGE IN EDUCATION

Gisela Ernst-Slavit
Washington State University Vancouver

WHAT IS CULTURE?

"Culture" is a notoriously difficult term to define, although it seems definite and its use pervasive in anthropology, education, sociology, business, health, industry, and other areas. However, a close examination of the concept reveals its elusiveness. Different folks perceive it and define it differently. This is not surprising, since definitions are influenced by disciplinary stances, worldviews, and political perspectives.

The concept of culture has changed over time. Its Latin roots are connected with cultivating and facilitating growth. In addition, it has also been used to refer to the level of refinement of a person in terms of their education, manners, and interest in the arts. In classical German, the term *Kultur* was used to refer to the spiritual comradeship of people in a community. In French, *Kultur* was contrasted with *Zivilisation* (civilization) to refer to knowledge and traits that can be acquired through education (e.g., manners, arts, literature, science). Similarly, in English, the term "culture" has been used in relation to manners, arts, and other sophisti-

Views From Inside: Languages, Cultures, and Schooling for K–12 Educators
pp. 3–24

cated pursuits of an educated upper class. However, as anthropology has expanded in reach from just studying faraway exotic communities to heavy infiltration in industry, social sciences, and education, the term has been adopted to describe groups and communities.

In their now famous *Culture: A Critical Review of Concepts and Definitions* (1952), anthropologists Kroeber and Kluckhohn compiled a list of over 160 different definitions for culture. During the next 50 years, additional definitions of culture were offered without experts reaching consensus. So, while there is no clear agreement regarding the nature of culture, many define it as a total way of life, including ways of perceiving and behaving (Valentine, 1968), as exhibiting structure and organization, while at the same time demonstrating local uniqueness (Spindler, 1974), or as a system of knowledge that includes beliefs, values, and ways of doing things that are transmitted to groups and individuals by others (Spradley & McCurdy, 1971). More recently, definitions of culture view the concept as fluid, dynamic, and ever-changing (D'Andrade & Strauss, 1992).

Erickson, in his 2011 chapter entitled "Culture," offers a view of culture that can serve us well in the field of education. Erickson summarizes culture not as a complex unit, but,

> As clusters of parts, all in trajectories combining continuity with change. If we think of culture as the organization of the conduct of everyday life, then the locus of culture as experience, as learned and enacted, is the local community of practice. It follows that to be human is to be multicultural, to be engaged continually in new culturing activity, because it appears that all humans participate in multiple local communities of practice and take action opportunistically within them. Thus, within the conduct of their everyday lives, humans develop personal repertoires of practice that are multiplex and dynamically changing, rather than participating in a single, unitary cultural entity and following passively a single system of cultural rules. (pp. 31–32)

The notion that every individual is multicultural deserves attention. People are born into certain groups based on their personal, social, geographical, and cultural surroundings. People also join different groups based on their occupations, interests, relationships, or goals. Each group has its own culture, its own way of doing things. Thus, every individual is multicultural because he or she participates in many cultures (Pollock, 2008) and is influenced by many groups (Erickson, 2006; Goodenough, 1976).

For this volume, we build on Erickson's view of culture and define it as *a complex set of values, beliefs, cognitive constructs, behaviors, interactions, and affective understandings that are learned through an ongoing process of socialization.* These shared views and behaviors identify the members of a culture group while distinguishing those of another group. However, culture is not static. Humans are constantly entering and leaving different communities of practice and are influenced and in turn influence their communities.

Children in school, then, belong to various groups or communities of practice. For example, an eighth grader in the Pacific Northwestern United States is part of a bicultural family of four, attends a public middle school, and belongs to a soccer team. In addition, this student is part of several other communities of practice such as an online gaming group, a neighborhood group of BMX bikers, and a rock band directed by his guitar teacher. As this eighth grader grows up and traverses different cultural groups, each group will influence him and, at the same time, he will bring new conceptualizations and behaviors to his other groups.

To better understand the concept of culture, it is helpful to examine its characteristics. Table 1.1 presents key characteristics of culture with explanations and relevant examples.

HOW DO CLASSROOMS REFLECT CULTURE?

The K–12 population in the United States is becoming increasingly diverse. The U.S. Census Bureau, based on the 2010 census, reported that Hispanic and Asian populations grew faster than any other group between 2000 and 2010. The same report projects that by the end of this decade, no single racial or ethnic group will constitute a majority of children under 18 (Humes, Jones, & Ramirez, 2011). This means that schools will continue to experience rapid growth in the number of ethnically and linguistically diverse students. In addition, data suggest growth in the number of students from low-income families. These rapidly changing demographics demand that educators learn about the students they teach and reexamine and adapt their pedagogy and practices to the needs and characteristics of these students.

Educators often hear comments such as "that's a multicultural classroom" in reference to a classroom with students from diverse backgrounds. However, a cursory look at the classroom shows that, aside from the diversity provided by students' physical presence, very little in the classroom reflects the spectrum of cultures, languages, and traditions of the students. In fact, the classroom's physical organization, the artifacts, the interactions among participants, and the curriculum and materials may all reflect a monocultural and even ethnocentric perspective. If the school and classroom do not include features of the students' traditions, homes, and communities in the learning experience, students may feel excluded from the learning experience. Furthermore, if teachers do not understand the cultural ways that guide students' thinking, behaviors,

Table 1.1.   **Characteristics of Culture**

Characteristic	*Explanation*	*Example*
Culture is an adaptive mechanism	Culture has been a highly successful mechanism for the survival of the human species.	Humans cannot survive outside of the warmer regions of the planet without the aid of culture and technology.
Culture is based on symbols	A symbol is something that represents something else. Symbols vary from culture to culture and are arbitrary. Language is the most important symbol.	Japanese believe that the chrysanthemum is a symbol of the sun and of happiness. In some European and Latin American countries, the chrysanthemum symbolizes bereavement.
Most people are not aware of their culture	Like fish, perhaps not aware of water, we are unaware of our culture. Our culture seems "natural" to us and different ways of doing things may appear to be odd or wrong.	Dogs are pets in many countries. However, in areas of Asia and Southeast Asia, dogs are a source of food for humans.
Culture changes	No culture ever remains constant or changeless. It is subject to slow but constant change. An account of a cultural group is a type of snapshot view of one particular moment in time.	Hunting and gathering skills have been replaced in some areas by skills such as driving a car, using a computer, and using home appliances.
Culture affects behavior and interpretations of behavior	Although some aspects of culture are visible, their meaning can be invisible or are visible only to "insiders."	While dining in an Afghan home, a visitor's plate will be filled up constantly. The visitor may be unaware that if food is not left on the plate it will keep getting filled.
Culture is transmissive	Culture is transmitted from one generation to another. Observation is another way in which culture is learned.	Parents and elders pass on habits, traditions, values, and ways of doing things to their children and they, in turn, to their children.
Culture is learned, not inherited	Culture is not inherited biologically; it is derived from one's social environment.	Eating from a plate or a leaf with your hands, chopsticks, or a fork are all learned behaviors.
Culture influences biological processes	Most of our conscious behavior is acquired through observing, learning, and interacting with other members of our group.	All humans need to eat to subsist. However, what we eat, how, and when will often depend on a combination of individual and cultural influences.
Culture is associated with social groups	Everyone is simultaneously a member of several different cultural groups and has multiple cultural memberships.	Individuals belong to different cultural groups—nations, regions, neighborhoods, families, friends, sporting clubs, hobby clubs, religious groups, classes in school, colleagues at work, and gender and age groups.

(*Table continues on next page*)

Table 1.1.   (Continued)

Characteristic	Explanation	Example
Culture is both an individual and a social construct	While the rules of any group should be relevant to all people within that group, it is also true that those rules will be relevant in different degrees for different people.	Just because many Asian students exhibit numerous polite behaviors (e.g., bowing, attentive listening, speaking indirectly, being deferential), it does not mean that some students are not polite because they do not display all of those behaviors.
Group members are unlikely to share identical sets of attitudes, values, and beliefs	Because individuals have different cultural affiliations (e.g., school, neighborhood, age, religion, gender, sports, hobby, occupation), no two individuals will share identical sets of perspectives and views.	Despite having the same genetic makeup and being raised in the same household, many sets of identical twins have separate cultural affiliations and distinctive personalities.
The various parts of a culture are to some degree interrelated	Cultures are coherent systems with their constituent parts interrelated with one another. A change in one part of the system is likely to produce changes in other parts of the system.	For several years, an elementary school might be very active in promoting the arts. Many students would stay after school for guitar, drawing, painting, and dance lessons. When a new principal and a new PTA board come along, the emphasis may switch from the arts to sports.
Culture is a descriptive, not an evaluative, concept	Descriptions of cultures are not value-laden; it is not that some cultures are more advanced than others. Rather, cultures are similar to or different from each other.	Handshakes, bows, hugs, or giving one, two, three or even four kisses on the cheek are different ways to greet people. No one way is better than the others; they are just different.
Cultures no longer exist in isolation	Even isolated tribal societies are integrated in some manner into the global economy.	A few of the last isolated tribal societies in the Amazon jungle were unaware of the outside world until the 1950s. Today, members of these societies are learning about other cultures via radios and other technologies.

and ways of knowing, they may not understand what students know and what their needs and strengths are.

Embracing cultural diversity assumes the belief that cultural identities should not be abandoned or ignored but rather recognized, affirmed, and celebrated. The assumption is that different cultures have made unique and substantial contributions that have enriched America throughout history. While it is important to celebrate diverse groups (e.g., Black history in February, women's history in March, Native American month in October), the goal is to celebrate and affirm the contributions of each group throughout the school year.

LANGUAGE AS A MIRROR OF CULTURE

In most grocery stores in the U.S., eggs are graded jumbo, extra-large, large, and medium. Why are there no "small" eggs? Why is the official grading of egg sizes tilted towards bigger, and why do most U.S. recipes mostly call for "large" eggs? It's easy to assume that this grading is the result of a marketing device, but the labeling of eggs in the U.S. may also reflect some cultural traits in American society that favor bigger, higher, stronger, and faster. While language can be defined differently by different people, most will agree that language can be seen as a reflection of culture and vice versa. Language provides many of the categories we use for expression of our thoughts and feelings. In other words, our thinking is influenced by the language we use, while the values and customs in the region or country we grow up in shape the way in which we think about the world. Boroditsky (2010) describes how in a remote Aboriginal Australian community speakers do not use the terms "right" and "left." Instead, orientation is talked about in terms of absolute cardinal directions (north, south, east, west). For example, speakers would say things like:

> "There's an ant on your southwest leg." To say hello in Pormpuraaw, one asks, "Where are you going?" and an appropriate response might be, "A long way to the south-southwest. How about you?" If you don't know which way is which, you literally can't get past hello. (Boroditsky, 2010)

Further, in many collectivist cultures, that is, cultures that prefer a tightly knit arrangement where members of a group look after each other and are loyal to each other, students would not say "my teacher," "my school," or "my street." Instead, they would talk about "our teacher," "our school," "our street." In fact, in many languages in collectivist societies, the pronoun for the first person singular "I" is dropped, as in the following example:

> *En la mañana voy al colegio.*
> In the morning [I] go to school.

As in the above example, in Spanish, the first person singular, *yo*, is often omitted because the ending of the verb indicates who does the action. In collectivist societies, found in many Asian, Latin American, and African countries, social ties are paramount, and the languages in these contexts reflect the emphasis on the group, on the "we." On the other hand, in individualist societies, such as those in North America, Australia, and Northern Europe, the emphasis is on the individual and his or her independence. A reflection of this focus is made clear in how the first person pronoun, "I," in English, is capitalized. Interestingly, few other languages capitalize the first person pronoun. Clearly, language and culture are integrated in complex and important ways.

LINGUISTIC DIVERSITY IN THE U.S.

The number of people 5 years old and older who speak a language other than English at home has more than doubled in the last 30 years, according to a U.S. Census Bureau report (Shin & Kominski, 2010). During that time frame, the percentage of speakers of languages other than English grew by 140% while the nation's overall population grew by 34%. Spanish and Vietnamese speakers were the groups with the largest percentage increase; the Vietnamese-speaking population had the largest percentage increase of 511% (1 million speakers) over the same period of time.

The report, *Language Use in the United States: 2007*, identifies the most commonly spoken languages other than English (Shin & Kominski, 2010). These are listed in Table 1.2. Salient information about these language speakers reported by the Census Bureau is included below (for more information see, Shin & Kominski, 2010):

- Twenty percent of the 281 million people 5 and older in the United States in 2007 reported speaking a language other than English at home.
- Three hundred and eighty-one different languages were reported.

Table 1.2.   Most Commonly Spoken Home Languages Other Than English in the United States

Languages Spoken at Home	Number of Speakers
Spanish	34.5 million
Chinese	2.5 million
Tagalog	1.5 million
French	1.4 million
Vietnamese	1.2 million
German	1.1 million
Korean	1.1 million

- Some of the most commonly spoken languages other than English, and the states with the highest concentrations of speakers include Spanish (Texas, California and New Mexico), French (Louisiana and Maine), German (North Dakota and South Dakota), Slavic languages (Illinois, New York, New Jersey, and Connecticut), Chinese (California, New York, Hawaii, and Massachusetts) and Korean (Hawaii, California, and New Jersey).

- Among people who spoke a language other than English at home, a majority reported speaking English "very well."

- The largest group of English-only speakers (78.3 million) were 41 to 64 years old, compared with 42.3 million speakers from 5 to 17 and 72.4 million speakers aged 18 to 40. Over 32.5 million monolingual English speakers were 65 and over.

- Among Spanish speakers, nearly as many were native-born as foreign-born—17 million versus 17.5 million, respectively. This was not the case for the other three major language groups (Chinese, Tagalog, and French)—all three had sizably more foreign-born speakers.

- Not all languages have grown in use over the years: Italian, Yiddish, German, Polish, and Greek were spoken at home by fewer individuals in the United States in 2007 than in 1980.

While the Census Bureau reports numbers of speakers and languages in neat categories, demarcations of languages and their speakers are seldom that clear. If you attended a gathering at the home of a bilingual family, you might only use English while you were there. However, different family members might use different languages for multiple purposes. For example, if you visit an Indian family (from southeast Asia), you might find grandma busy in the kitchen pulling pans out of the oven and reading recipes in Hindi while the kids are playing video games in English. Mom, Dad, and guests may be speaking mostly in English. However, when Dad speaks to the children, he does so in Urdu. And then, there is grandpa, watching a Bollywood movie in Urdu that includes regional variants such as Gujarati and Punjabi. What you would be observing here is translanguaging in action, as a family uses their many linguistic resources in their everyday lives. While Urdu might be the home language mentioned in the census or in the children's school records, in reality there is not one home language but a full range of language practices used fluidly according to the speaker, purpose, and context.

The term *translanguaging* was originally used by Williams (1996) to refer to a pedagogical practice where Welsh students would receive information in one language (e.g., through reading) and then use it in another language (e.g., by writing). Later, the term was expanded by García (2009) to refer to the language practices of people who speak more than one language. In education, translanguaging can be understood as the "constant adaptation of linguistic resources in the service of meaning-making and in tending to the singularities in the pluralities that make up multilingual classrooms" (García & Sylvan, 2011, p. 385). Translanguaging is not code-switching; it is not just going from one language to another. The notion of code-switching assumes the alternation of separate languages in the context of a single conversation (e.g., "*Yo quiero una* red bike," where the child uses the first words in Spanish to mean "I want"). Translanguaging, rather than looking at two separate languages, affirms that "bilinguals have one linguistic repertoire from which they select diverse features strategically to communicate effectively" (García, 2011, p. 1).

WHY CULTURE AND LANGUAGE
ARE IMPORTANT FOR TEACHERS TO KNOW ABOUT

As discussed earlier, current demographic data indicate a rise in the number of non-White students and students for whom English is an additional language. Demographers project that by the year 2025, 25% of all school-aged children in the U.S. will be speakers of a language other than English at home. Similar projections indicate that by 2100, the U.S. minority population will become the majority, with non-Hispanic Whites making up to 40% of the U.S. population (Humes et al., 2011). These numbers suggest that educators and school personnel need to be adequately prepared to teach in linguistically and culturally diverse classrooms and schools, and the need will only grow greater over time.

In our teacher education classes we often hear students say, "I don't see color, I only see children," or "I just want to teach students and don't care what they look like or what languages they speak." While these comments show a level of caring, they can also reflect a certain level of naïveté. Nieto (2000) considers that this kind of colorblindness may mask negative assumptions about differences. She notes,

> Being color-blind can mean being *nondiscriminatory* in attitude and behavior, and in this sense color blindness is not a bad thing. But color blindness may result in *refusing to accept differences* and therefore accepting the dominant culture as the norm. It may result in denying the very identity of our students, thereby making them invisible. (Nieto, 2000, p. 138)

Stated differently, seeing all kids as alike overlooks their uniqueness, their individual strengths and particular needs. For example, not acknowledging that Geoffrey has two mothers, that Katia just came from the Ukraine, that Humberto is a whiz in mathematics, that on occasion Tony uses a wheelchair, and that Roxana's parents are in danger of being deported might impede their teachers' understanding of their individual circumstances. More specifically, not knowing students' individual biographies, trajectories, needs, and strengths can effectively negate needed accommodations and access to the whole array of opportunities offered by their school. In other words, teachers need both linguistic and cultural competence to work with all students effectively.

Cultural Competence

Cultural competence refers to the ability to work effectively and to interact with people from cultures different than our own. The National Education Association (NEA) considers cultural competence as the "key to thriving in culturally diverse classrooms and schools—and it can be learned, practiced, and institutionalized to better serve diverse students, their families, and their communities. Cultural competence is the ability to successfully teach students who come from a culture or cultures other than our own" (NEA, n.d., para. 1).

Becoming culturally competent does not happen after attending a 3-hour professional development workshop, taking a college class, or reading two books. Rather, becoming culturally competent is a lifelong process that includes *becoming culturally aware* (i.e., developing a general understanding of our own group and what another group is like and how it functions), *developing cultural sensitivity* (i.e., learning to accept and appreciate the differences that exist between cultures without assigning judgments to those differences), and *acquiring cultural knowledge* (i.e., becoming familiar with selected cultural traits, histories, value systems and behaviors of another group). Cultural competence allows educators to confront deep-seated stereotypes, ask questions about their practice, build relationships based on trust with students and their families, and better serve the students they teach.

Equal or Equitable?

By becoming culturally competent—in other words, by recognizing and learning about the pivotal role that cultural differences may have in student learning—educators can plan and implement a variety of "promising pedagogical and curricular adaptations" (Nieto 2000, p. 139) that tap into students' gifts and address their unique needs. In education, the concepts of *equality* and *equity* have important implications into how services and funds are allocated to students. While all students should have equal access to resources, not all students will need the same kind of resources. The following example might shed some light on the difference between these two terms: A family of five is having pizza and salad for dinner. *Equality*, in this case, means that everyone in the family—mom, dad, teenage son, 5-year old daughter and 2-year old toddler—would get the same amount of salad and the exact same amount of pizza. *Equity*, on the other hand, means that the amount of salad and pizza is given according to individual needs. In this particular case, chances are that the younger children will need much less pizza and salad than their teenage brother and parents.

According to Nieto (2000), there are three important implications of teaching equitably. First, it means acknowledging the differences that children bring to school, such as their race, ethnicity, gender, language, and social class, among others. Second, it suggests that teachers must understand the possibility that students' identities may influence their learning process. Differences should not be seen as problematic, but rather that one size does not fit all. Finally, accepting differences demands making provisions for them. That means that, for example, Humberto needs to be placed in advanced math classes while Oksana can benefit from having some language support as she learns language and content simultaneously. In other words, providing the same services to all children will not necessarily lead to equality; in fact, "it may end up perpetuating the inequality that already exists" (Nieto, 2000, p.139). Teachers who understand these ideas can make sure that a student like Humberto has an opportunity to be challenged and supported in an area in which he excels and that Katia will not be placed in a sink-or-swim environment without any support for her incipient English language skills.

PROMISING APPROACHES AND PEDAGOGICAL PRACTICES THAT AFFIRM CULTURAL DIVERSITY

Culture and language are central to learning. Early life experiences, values, and traditions all affect both students' orientations to learning and their processes of learning. For many students, some of the behaviors and discursive practices required in school (e.g., "eyes on me," sitting in rows, centers) and types of classroom discourse (e.g., "Who can tell me where the median is here?," "One at a time, please," "The point of the story is…") may very well be different from the ones used at home. To increase opportunities for student success, educators need to create instructional environments that minimize students' alienation as they attempt to learn how to "do" school (Ernst-Slavit & Mason, 2011; Ernst-Slavit & Poveda, 2011; Heath, 1996; Lucas & Villegas, 2002). A pedagogy that acknowledges, responds to, affirms, and celebrates diverse cultures and languages affords all students equitable access to education. All school personnel—from principals and teachers to administrative assistants and bus drivers—should have some basic knowledge of students' cultures and languages. This knowledge will allow school personnel to adequately understand what it takes to be a language and culture learner (Ernst-Slavit & Wenger, 2006).

However, pedagogies throughout the history of the United States have been based on an imbalance of power between the "majority" culture and "other" cultures. This has resulted in decades of misunderstandings, conflict, antagonism, and resistance. This is changing; a recognition that cultural differences are an asset rather than a liability is increasingly permeating all segments of society from education to health and industry. For example, the majority of workplaces have policies on equal opportunities that are meant to (a) protect employees from discrimination (e.g., age, disability, race, religion, sexual orientation), (b) promote diversity in the workplace (e.g., by encouraging and managing diversity), and (c) respond to changing demographics and work patterns (e.g., using flexible schedules to respond to both customer and employee needs).

In education, several models and approaches are used to enhance the educational opportunities of diverse students. These approaches acknowledge and build on students' cultural knowledge, prior experiences, and ways of thinking and acting to make teaching and learning processes more appropriate and beneficial for all students. Three such approaches are discussed below: culturally responsive teaching, funds of knowledge, and multicultural education. Although there are differences among these three different approaches, there are also several commonalities, including:

- valuing students' cultures and backgrounds
- communicating high expectations
- integrating those into the teaching and learning process by involving parents and community
- differentiating instruction by building on what students bring
- advocating for students, their families, and their communities

Multicultural Education

Definitions of multicultural education abound. This term is used to refer to any form of education that incorporates the histories, values, beliefs, and perspectives of people from different cultural backgrounds. For example, in the classroom, a teacher may modify lessons to affirm and reflect the cultural diversity of the students. The following description of multicultural education is based on the expanded definition given by the National Association for Multicultural Education (NAME, 2003) on their website.

Multicultural education is built on the ideals of freedom, justice, equality, equity, and human dignity. It affirms our need to prepare students for their responsibilities in an interdependent world and recognizes the role schools can play in developing the attitudes and values necessary for a democratic society. Multicultural education values cultural differences and affirms the diversity that students, their communities, and teachers reflect.

> Multicultural education is a process that permeates all aspects of school practices, policies and organization as a means to ensure the highest levels of academic achievement for all students. It helps students develop a positive self-concept by providing knowledge about the histories, cultures, and contributions of diverse groups. It prepares all students to work actively toward structural equality in organizations and institutions by providing the knowledge, dispositions, and skills for the redistribution of power and income among diverse groups. Thus, school curriculum must directly address issues of racism, sexism, classism, linguicism, ableism, ageism, heterosexism, religious intolerance, and xenophobia.

Multicultural approaches place students' experiences and trajectories at the center of the teaching and learning process while at the same time encouraging and affirming multiple ways of thinking. In addition, multicultural education challenges all forms of discrimination in schools and society through the promotion of democratic principles of social justice.

Culturally Responsive Teaching

Gay (2000) defines *culturally responsive teaching* as using the cultural knowledge, prior experiences, and performance styles of diverse students to make learning more appropriate and effective for them; it teaches to and through students' strengths. Although called by different names, including *culturally responsive, culturally relevant, congruent, reflexive,* and *centered,* features of culturally responsive teaching include:

- communicating high expectations;
- actively engaging students in learning;
- understanding the gifts and talents that students' families bring to their parenting;

- anchoring curriculum in the everyday lives of students;
- selecting participation structures for learning that reflect students' ways of knowing and doing;
- sharing control of the classroom with students;
- engaging in reflective thinking, writing, and teaching;
- acknowledging membership in different groups;
- visiting students' homes and communities; and
- exploring personal and family histories.

While this list is not exhaustive, it provides a starting for point for conceptualizing culturally responsive teaching. If what happens in the classroom reflects the cultural and linguistic values and practices of only one set of students, then the other students are denied equal opportunity to learn. Culturally relevant pedagogy is instruction that recognizes the importance of including students' cultural references in all aspects of learning (Ladson-Billings, 2009).

The Funds of Knowledge Approach

Funds of knowledge are not to be confused with background knowledge or prior knowledge. While there might be some overlap with these terms, funds of knowledge are the skills and knowledge that have been developed historically and culturally to enable an individual household to function within a given culture. This perspective implies that integrating funds of knowledge into classroom activities generates a richer and more highly scaffolded learning experience for students (Moll & Gonzalez, 2004).

When educators study their students' funds of knowledge, they are thinking like anthropologists. They are observing the ways in which people live, how they know what they know, and how they interact with each other. When teachers are willing to become learners of their students, they can come to know their students and their families in new and distinct ways. With this new knowledge, they can begin to see that the homes and communities of their students contain rich cultural and cognitive resources and that these resources can and should be used in their classroom to provide culturally responsive and meaningful lessons that tap students' prior knowledge. Information that teachers learn about their students in this process is considered the students' funds of knowledge.

USEFUL TERMINOLOGY

In talking about the issues discussed in this book, it is important that all stakeholders share a general understanding of some of these multifaceted and multilayered concepts. We do not expect that any one definition of these complex terms will satisfy all specialists or fully escape the ambiguities that seem an inevitable part of the study of culture, language, and schooling.

Acculturation

Acculturation is a process in which members of one cultural group adopt the cultural traits of another group. Acculturation can be the result of two cultures in close contact for a long period of time. Acculturation may occur in such a way that the recipient cultural group does not significantly alter its own culture (e.g., Japan adopting Chinese characters in their writing system). Acculturation can also have devastating consequences (e.g., the imposition of Spanish and Catholicism by Spain on the Americas). At the individual level, acculturation can be an adaptive strategy to retain the home culture while adopting traits from the new culture (e.g., in school, students learn to take a critical perspective, while at home, they do not question parents' actions).

Cultural Assimilation

Cultural assimilation is the process whereby individuals' traditions, values, and beliefs are replaced by new ones. This change can happen at the individual or group level and often involves gradual change. A case in point are the many Americans who have parents and grandparents born and raised in other countries, yet they do not speak the language of these previous generations nor share their traditions. Assimilation can be voluntary (e.g., an Eastern European family escaping from religious persecution) or involuntary (e.g., during the first half of the 20th century, the Australian government sought to create a single uniform culture by forcing aboriginal populations to acquire the White society's customs and beliefs).

Cultural Determinism

Cultural determinism is the belief that the ideas, meanings, beliefs, and values people learn as members of a community shape human nature. In other words, humans are what they learn from the context they inhabit. Throughout history, there have been many examples of cultural determinism. Ancient Greeks, for example, thought that only those who understood Greek could understand their thoughts, arts, and political views. Those who did not understand Greek were called barbarians.

Cultural Pluralism

Cultural pluralism refers to the harmonious coexistence of several cultures and value systems in a diverse society. Within this context, different groups keep their distinctive sets of cultural traits while coexisting together with the dominant group (e.g., the Pennsylvania Dutch of Lancaster County run their own schools, farms, banks, and stores and travel by horse and buggy even though they are surrounded by and have business relationships with technology-based communities).

Cultural Relativism

Cultural relativism is the idea that different cultural groups differ in their values, beliefs, and ways of behaving. However, there is no scientific standard for considering one group as intrinsically superior or inferior to another. What is considered moral in one society may be considered immoral in another. Studying cultural differences among groups and societies presupposes a position of cultural relativism. For example, in places in China there is a cat and dog market where customers buy dogs and cats not as pets but for food. From a cultural relativist perspective, the practice of eating cats and dogs is neither good nor bad. The consumption of cat and dog meat is part of some Chinese cuisine; it is simply the result of separate socialization.

Culture Shock

Culture shock is the feeling of unbalance and disorientation that may happen when a person encounters different values, customs, traditions, and practices that are very different from their own. Culture shock can be the result of traveling to another country, being in a new social environment, or pursuing another type of life. Culture shock can also be understood as part of a process that proceeds through several steps: the honeymoon (i.e., moving to a new place is filled with excitement and optimism); shock (i.e., differences between the new and old culture become apparent and feelings of frustration, information overload, loneliness, and homesickness take over); adjustment (i.e., the individual negotiates ways of becoming accustomed to the new culture); and acceptance (i.e., when the home and host cultures are reconciled and allow the individual to participate productively in the new environment).

Cultural Universals

Cultural universals can be described as elements, traits, or institutions found in virtually all human cultures. Anthropologists have developed lists of cultural universals that include language, symbolism, taboos, peer and kin groups, family, gender roles, rites of passage, incest prevention, conflict, marriage, beliefs about death, narratives, music, play, rituals, and several others. Although these elements appear in all cultures, their form and manifestation may look very different across cultures.

Ethnicity

Ethnicity refers to the common cultural characteristics of a group of individuals that distinguish them from most other people in the larger society. Ethnicity is based on common ancestry, memories of shared historical past, culture, language, nationality, or religion, or a combination of these elements. Biological characteristics such as skin color, facial features, and other anatomical traits may or may not play a role in the formation or definition of an ethnic group. Ethnic groups are self-conscious populations who see themselves as distinct. For example, siblings Sarah and Levi were born in a traditional Jewish family living in a Jewish neighborhood in Long Island. Yet, while Sarah decidedly embraced Jewish values, customs, and religious practices, Levi moved to a rural town in Colorado, married a non-Jewish woman, and with his wife is raising their family as non-Jewish, both in terms of religious and cultural traditions. Although Levi is still ethnically Jewish, he chose not to embrace his ethnicity in the same way his sister did.

Ethnocentrism

Ethnocentrism is judging another culture based on one's own values and beliefs. This view presumes that one's own culture is superior to other cultures. Ethnocentric individuals judge other groups relative to their own particular ethnic group or culture, especially regarding language, behavior, customs, and religion. Examples of ethnocentric comments include:

"Hebrew is written backwards," instead of, "Hebrew is written from right to left"; "That's so weird, the steering wheel is on the wrong side," instead of, "the steering wheel is on the right side"; or, "They are so primitive, they eat with their hands," instead of, "They have different customs, they use their hands to eat their food."

Hidden Curriculum

The hidden curriculum refers to the unwritten and unofficial sets of rules, values, and perspectives that students learn in school. While the overt curriculum consists of the classes, lessons, practices, and learning activities students participate in, as well as the knowledge and sets of skills educators teach to students, the hidden curriculum consists of the unspoken academic, social, and cultural messages that are communicated to students while in school. These ways of communicating, thinking, and acting are called "hidden" because they usually go unexamined by students, school personnel, and the larger community. In some schools, for example, the expectation is that recent immigrant students learn English as soon as possible, even though there may not be any policy or document at the school or district level that outlines that expectation. However, the school systematically forbids the use of the home language at school, does not provide translation services, and only purchases library materials in English. Those actions are ways of enacting a hidden curriculum that expects immigrant students to assimilate into American culture.

Hybridity

Basically, hybridity refers to mixture. In cultural studies, hybridity has been dominant in conceptual discussions of mixed identities. The popularity of the term can be explained because it challenges fixed and separate identities such as territories, languages, cultures, and ethnicities. As such, the concept of hybridity allows us to understand cultural identities not as fixed, but in transition, between different positions, and as more complex and fragmented, due in part to international migration and cultural globalization. A case in point is Carlos, born in Tijuana and a resident of Los Angeles. At 17, after being rejected by his family for being gay, Carlos came to the United States without the appropriate paperwork. Ten years later, Carlos is a successful hairdresser who owns several properties and is part of a group of upwardly mobile gay and straight Angelinos. Carlos has not assimilated. In fact, he has kept his Mexican traditions, speaks English with a thick accent, and is still undocumented.

School Culture

School culture generally refers to the beliefs, perceptions, relationships, attitudes, rituals, and written or unwritten rules that shape and influence every aspect of the school. A school culture is the result of both conscious and unconscious values, beliefs, discourse, and practices and is shaped by a school's history and trajectory. The school culture is often invisible, hard to grasp, dynamic, and filled with rituals and traditions. For example, having children line up to go to recess, using bells to mobilize students from one place to another, having the principal at the helm, and organizing instruction by age level all add to the school culture.

Syncretism

Syncretism is an umbrella-like term that refers to a wide variety of strategies and processes, both conscious and unconscious, by which cultures, practices, religions, or schools of thoughts adapt to one another. A historical example of cultural syncretism is the way Christianity incorporated many of the celebrations and rituals encountered by Christian missionaries in other religions. The best cases of cultural syncretism are those where both cultural groups benefit from the process or amalgamation.

Transculturality

The concept of transculturality is built on the assumption that cultures are not homogeneous units with clear borders. Boundaries for nations, ethnicity, religion, cultures, and so on are not stable. Instead, they evolve, change, and shift as people become linked with one another. Transculturality is the merging of diverse cultures and the creation of new cultural phenomena. Lifestyles are no longer limited or delineated by nation-state cultures. Traditional categories and distinctions such as "foreign" and "familiar" are becoming obsolete in an age of globalized economic and communication systems. Transculturation can often be the result of colonization, as in the case of the impact of Spanish colonialism on Cuba's indigenous peoples.

CONCLUSIONS

The remainder of the chapters in this book discuss aspects of specific languages, cultures, and education systems and how they may hinder or enhance learning in U.S. classrooms. The inclusion of examples like the ones provided above will also bring clarity to educators who may be wondering, for example, why a student is not using the first-person pronoun in her essay. Vignettes and examples discussed may be:

- of a sociolinguistic nature (e.g., in some societies small children are spoken about rather than spoken to);
- related to language transfer (e.g., learning an additional language is influenced by the languages that the learner already knows);
- due to cultural differences (e.g., some languages have specific words for concepts, whereas other languages have to use multiple words to refer to that same concept);
- attributed to teaching and learning styles (e.g., in some cultures children learn by observing while in others they learn through verbal instruction);
- related to other aspects of language, culture, and schooling; and
- regardless of the specifics, as demographics, cultures, and education change, the underlying concept of this book will not; educators need to learn about cultures and languages in order to be prepared to address the needs of all of their students in the most effective ways possible.

ADDITIONAL RESOURCES

Ernst-Slavit, G., & Mason. M. (2012). Making your first ELL home visit: A guide for classroom teachers. *Colorín Colorado*. Retrieved from http://www.colorin-colorado.org/article/making-your-first-ell-home-visit-guide-classroom-teachers
> This article provide practical tips for home visits with English language learners. Learn about your diverse students by making a home visit.

Ferlazzo, L. (2010, August 11). The best sites for learning about the world's different cultures. Retrieved from http://larryferlazzo.edublogs.org/2010/08/11/the-best-sites-for-learning-about-the-worlds-different-cultures/
> Helpful compilation of sites to learn about the geography, languages, data and other information about different countries around the world.

Gorski, P. C. (2016). Critical multicultural pavilion. *EdChange Project*. Retrieved from http://www.edchange.org/multicultural/arts/songs.html.
> A wealth of resources about diversity, equity, social justice, and multicultural education.

Johnson, E. (2016). *Funds of knowledge and home visit toolkit*. Migrant and Bilingual Education. Office of the Superintendent of Public Instruction. Retrieved from http://www.k12.wa.us/MigrantBilingual/HomeVisitsToolkit/default.aspx

A wealth of resources and practical information for educators on the topics of funds of knowledge and home visits.

Kottak, C., & Gezon, L. (2013). *Culture* (2nd ed.). New York, NY: McGraw-Hill. This text will enhance readers' basic anthropological understandings of culture. Written simple and engagingly in a kind of magazine format, it provides an overview for readers unacquainted with the foundations of culture.

TASKS FOR EDUCATORS

1. Work with your peers to add to the list of important terminology presented in this chapter. You may want to start a personal dictionary to help you remember specific terms—this could include pictures, text, graphics, or other supports.

2. Have you ever experienced any of the topics or issues discussed in this chapter? Write or draw an anecdote that you would be willing to share with peers.

3. Think about the culture of one of your communities—can you describe it? What about other communities that you belong to? Do the cultures of any of them conflict? In what ways?

REFERENCES

Boroditsky, L. (2010, July 23). Lost in translation. *The Wall Street Journal*. Retrieved from http://www.wsj.com/news/articles/SB10001424052748703467304575383131592767868

D'Andrade, R., & Strauss, C. (Eds.). (1992). *Human motives and cultural models*. New York, NY: Cambridge University Press.

Erickson, F. (2006). Culture in society and in educational practices. In J. Banks & C. M. Banks (Eds.), *Multicultural Education: Issues and Perspectives* (3rd ed., pp. 31–60). Hoboken, NJ: John Wiley–Jossey Bass.

Erickson, F. (2011). Culture. In B. A. U. Levinson & M. Pollock (Eds.), *A companion to the anthropology of education* (pp. 25–33). West Sussex, UK: Blackwell Publishing Ltd.

Ernst-Slavit, G., & Mason, M. (2011). "Words that hold us up": Teacher talk and academic language in five upper elementary classrooms. *Linguistics and Education, 22*, 430–440.

Ernst-Slavit, G., & Poveda, D. (2011). Teacher knowledge and minority students: The potential of *saberes docentes*. *Pedagogies: An International Journal, 6*(1), 1–15.

Ernst-Slavit, G., & Wenger, K. (2006). Teaching in the margins: The multifaceted work and struggles of bilingual paraeducators. *Anthropology & Education Quarterly, 37*(1), 62–82.

García, O. (2009). *Bilingual education in the 21st Century: A global perspective*. Oxford, UK: Wiley-Blackwell.

García, O. (2011). Educating New York's bilingual children: Constructing a future from the past. *International Journal of Bilingual Education and Bilingualism, 14*(2), 133–153.

García, O., & Sylvan, C. E. (2011). Theorizing translanguaging for educators. In C. Celic & K. Seltzer (Eds.), *Translanguaging: A CUNY-NYSIEB Guide for Educators* (pp. 1–6). New York, NY: CUNY-NYSIEB, The Graduate Center.

Gay, G. (2000). *Culturally responsive teaching: Theory, research, and practice.* New York, NY: Teachers College Press.

Goodenough, W. (1976). Multiculturalism as the normal human experience. *Anthropology & Education Quarterly, 7*(4), 4–7.

Heath, S. B. (1996). *Ways with words: Language, life and work in communities and classrooms* (11th ed.). Cambridge, UK: Cambridge University Press.

Humes, K. R., Jones, N. A., & Ramirez, R. R. (2011, March). Overview of race and Hispanic origin: 2010 (2010 Census Briefs #C2010BR-02). Washington, DC: U.S. Census Bureau. Retrieved from http://www.census.gov/prod/cen2010/briefs/c2010br-02.pdf

Kroeber, A. L., & Kluckhohn, C. (1952). Culture: A critical review of concepts and definitions. *Peabody Museum of American Archaeology and Ethnology Papers, 47*(1).

Ladson-Billings, G. (2009). *The dreamkeepers: Successful teachers of African-American children* (2nd ed.). San Francisco, CA: Jossey-Bass.

Lucas, T., & Villegas, A. M. (2002). Preparing culturally responsive teachers: Rethinking the curriculum. *Journal of Teacher Education, 53*(1), 20–32.

Moll, L. C., & Gonzalez, N. (2004). Engaging life: A funds of knowledge approach to multicultural education. In J. Banks & C. McGee Banks (Eds.), *Handbook of research on multicultural education* (2nd ed., pp. 699–715). San Francisco, CA: Jossey-Bass.

National Association for Multicultural Education. (2003). Multicultural education. NAME Position Statements. Retrieved from http://www.nameorg.org/name_position_statements.phpl

National Education Association. (n.d.). Diversity toolkit: Cultural competence for educators. Retrieved from http://www.nea.org/tools/30402.htm

Nieto, S. (2000). *Affirming diversity: The sociopolitical context of multicultural education* (3rd ed.). New York, NY: Longman.

Pollock, M. (2008). From shallow to deep: Toward a thorough cultural analysis of school achievement patterns. *Anthropology & Education Quarterly, 39*(4), 369–380.

Shin, H. B., & Kominski, R. A. (2010). *Language use in the United States: 2007 American community survey reports, ACS-12.* Washington, DC: U.S. Census Bureau. Retrieved from http://www.census.gov/prod/2010pubs/acs-12.pdf

Spindler, G. D. (1974). *Education and the cultural process.* New York, NY: Rinehart and Winston.

Spradley, N. A., & McCurdy, D. W. (1971). *Conformity and conflict.* Boston, MA: Little, Brown.

Valentine, C. (1968). *Culture and poverty.* Chicago, IL: University of Chicago Press.

Williams, C. (1996). Secondary education: Teaching in the bilingual situation. In C. Williams, G. Lewis, & C. Baker (Eds.), *The language policy: Taking stock* (pp. 63–78). Llangefni, UK: Canolfan, Astudiaethau Iaith.

SECTION 2

ARAB AND PERSIAN REGION

CHAPTER 2

THE GULF REGION

Abir El Shaban
Washington State University

Rana Raddawi
American University of Sharjah, United Arab Emirates

Jacqueline Tanner
University of Siegen in Germany

Mohammed, an international student in the U.S., is from Saudi Arabia. He feels his lack of vocabulary, linguistic fluency, and familiarity with U.S. customs not only affects his understanding of class discussions but his self-esteem as well. He often does not understand the humor and the responses of his American classmates, and this hinders his interactions with them. He told his teacher, "Almost in every class, they [his classmates] share some jokes, and they all start laughing, except me. Because sometimes the jokes contain cultural references and the phrases are difficult, I feel embarrassed and stupid, so I just smile pretending that I understand what they say." However, Mohammed maintains a positive attitude toward American people. He elaborated, "I like my American friends. They are so helpful and friendly. I decided to avoid interacting with my old friends (co-nationals) and spend more time with my American colleagues to understand their culture better."

Hanof is from Saudi Arabia, and she explains that most females from the Gulf region avoid communication with males. In their home country,

Views From Inside: Languages, Cultures, and Schooling for K–12 Educators
pp. 27–44
Copyright © 2018 by Information Age Publishing
All rights of reproduction in any form reserved.

they are used to studying in segregated schools where the males and females are separated. Therefore, she experiences difficulties communicating with classmates of the opposite gender in American classrooms. If she *must partner with a male classmate, though, she prefers an American male rather than one from her native country or the Gulf region.*

BACKGROUND

The Gulf region is known by Iranians as the Persian Gulf and by Arabs as the Arabian Gulf region (the naming conventions are a hot topic in the region). The Gulf Cooperation Council (GCC) countries formed a union in 1981. These six countries (i.e., Saudi Arabia, United Arab Emirates [UAE], Kuwait, Bahrain, Qatar, and Oman) are the focus of this chapter. They are located on the west side of the Gulf and are a part of the Arabian Peninsula. In addition to security interests, they share a common religion (Islam), a common language (Arabic), and a common culture (Arabian), as well as common standards and traditions (Dadush & Falcao, 2009). The discovery of oil in the middle of the 20th century initiated the countries' civil and political evolution; these countries control 40% of the world's oil assets. This has resulted in prosperity that allows for free healthcare and education for their citizens. The Gulf countries are among the richest countries in the world.

The Kingdom of Saudi Arabia (KSA)

The Kingdom of Saudi Arabia (KSA) is the largest of the GCC countries, with a population of more than 32 million people (Population Pyramids of the World from 1950 to 2100, 2016). Riyadh is its capital. KSA Arabs first originated in the area now occupied by Saudi Arabia on the Arabian Peninsula, most of which the KSA occupies. The Red Sea and the Gulf of Aqaba are to the west and the Arabian Gulf is to the east. Muslims consider the Kingdom the homeland of Islam because the two holy pilgrimage cities, Mecca and Medina, are located there. *Al Sharia* (Islamic jurisprudence) is the main law of this country, which supports the Wahhabi sect of Sunni Islam.

Saudi Arabia was a complete monarchy until 1992, when the royal family of Saud instituted the Kingdom's first constitution (Constitute Project, 2016). In 2009, King Abdullah decided to restructure his administration. For instance, he dismissed provocative officials, some of whom were the conservative religious leaders of the land, and replaced them with more moderate clerics. In addition, he assigned the first five female ministers to the KSA Ministry of Education.

The United Arab Emirates

The United Arab Emirates (UAE) is a federation of seven emirates. These are Abu Dhabi, Dubai, Sharjah, Ajman, Ras Al-Khaimah, Fujairah, and Umm Al-Quwain. The state of Abu Dhabi is the capital of the UAE. The population of the UAE is 9,479,536 people (estimated in 2014) with less than 20% of the population being native citizens. The rest are Southeast Asians, Iranians, Westerners and other Arabs. The majority of Emiratis are Muslim, and Arabic is the Emirates' official language. However, due to the more than 200 nationalities that coexist in the UAE, English has become the lingua franca in the country, and the medium of instruction in most schools and all universities (Raddawi & Meslem, 2015). The Emirates is in the southeast region of the Arabian Peninsula and shares borders with the Gulf of Oman and the Arabian Gulf. Each emirate has its own leader, a separate ruler who runs the emirate's government under the leadership of the federation (Al Abed, 1997).

Kuwait

Kuwait, with its capital, Kuwait City, boasts a population of approximately 2.9 million people. The country has one of the highest standards of living in the world, with an income of approximately $48,900 per capita per year (BBC News Middle East, 2016b). Most of its oil income is devoted to Kuwait's citizens, supporting free healthcare and the education system. During Abdullah El Salem Al Sabah's reign in 1950, Kuwait witnessed not only a renaissance in its economy and politics, but also its transition to a democratic state. The process began with the issuance of a permanent constitution for the country (National Assembly, 2011).

In 2009, Kuwait witnessed the first three female parliament members and, in the same year, women obtained another victory, allowing them to own passports without their male guardians' permission. They were also granted the choice whether or not to wear a *hijab* (head scarf).

The Kingdom of Bahrain

The name Bahrain means "two seas." Al-Manámah is its capital. Its population is half of Kuwait's, or about 1,248,348 people. The Al-Khalifah family has controlled the wealth and power in the kingdom since 1783

(BBC News Middle East, 2016a). Although Bahrain was one of the first GCC countries to discover and benefit from oil in the 1930s, its production is relatively small compared to that of Saudi Arabia and Kuwait. In 1961, Sheik Isa bin Sulman al-Khalifah set rules for expanding his state's economy, turning it into a strategic financial center. The Bahraini people enjoy free healthcare and education. In 2001, women were permitted to vote for the first time. Furthermore, the kingdom became a constitutional monarchy with an elected legislative parliament in 2002.

Qatar

Qatar is the richest country in the Gulf region. It is on a tiny peninsula that borders the Gulf to the east, Saudi Arabia to the west, and the United Arab Emirates to the south. Its people enjoy one of the highest gross domestic products (GDP) in the world at $103,000 U.S. per capita (United Nations Development Program, 2010). Also, Al-Jazeera, a popular TV and news channel in the Arab world, is broadcast from Qatar. Qatar is a constitutional monarchy.

The Sultanate of Oman

Muscat is the capital of Oman. The country has a population of three million people. It is located in the southeast area of the Arabian Peninsula and shares its borders with the United Arab Emirates, Saudi Arabia, and Yemen. Oman is an Islamic state whose majority shows allegiance to the Ibadi branch of Islam and rejects both the Sunni and the Shiite branches. However, there are no political conflicts between the Ibadis and the Sunnis, who constitute 10% of the entire population. Like other Gulf countries, oil is an important aspect of the Omani economy; however, Oman's production of oil is relatively low compared with other states in the region. Therefore, the people are also dependent on farming and fishing for their livelihood. The Sultanate of Oman's governmental system is a monarchy. In 1997, its ruler, Sultan Qaboos, approved women's rights to participate in the country's consultative body elections.

CULTURE, LANGUAGE, ISLAM, AND THE GCC

Regardless of GCC modernization, the Arab world in general and the GCC in particular are still based on tribalism and remain highly conservative countries. Islam has guided their culture, establishing their customs, traditions, and values. It is more than a simple religion; Islam's teachings and principles nourish these Arab societies' cultures. Religion is a regulator of the Arab culture at the personal, social, political, and economic levels.

Islam

Islam was first initiated in the Arabian Peninsula in the area now known as Saudi Arabia. It is a "monotheistic religion characterized by the acceptance of the doctrine of submission to God and the belief that Mohammad is the messenger and last prophet of God" (Islam, 2015, n.p.). For Sunni Muslims, Mohammad is the final prophet chosen by God (*Allah*) after Jesus, Moses, Abraham, and the other prophets. Muslims also believe in Judaism and Christianity and recognize Jews and Christians as the people of the Bible. Islam is a religion of peace, mercy, and forgiveness that expressly condemns certain kinds of violence, especially against seniors, women, and children in time of war. For instance, verse 32 of chapter five of the Islamic holy book, the Quran, says the following:

> That was why We laid it down for the Children of Israel that whoever killed a human being, except as a punishment for murder or for spreading corruption in the land, shall be regarded as having killed all mankind, and that whoever saved a human life shall be regarded as having saved all mankind. Our messengers came to them with clear signs, but many of them continued to commit excesses in the land. (Khan, p. 81)

The most recognized religious holidays that GCC countries and the whole Muslim world celebrate are Eid Al-Fitr, which follows the last day of Ramadan (the month of fasting), and Eid Al-Adha, which occurs two months and 10 days after Eid Al-Fitr. These holidays are explained more in detail in the chapter on North Africa.

Social Relations

To appreciate and better understand Gulf culture, it is important to consider its people's perceptions and priorities. Family bonds and the respect of their conservative values are the foundation of the identity of the Gulf peoples. They also value the ties that dictate their social interactions. The Arab culture can be considered as collectivist (Jandt, 2016). Hence, mutual trust, respect, and harmony among group members are the main values that predict the continuous success of any sort of relationship.

The Arab Gulf Traditional Customs

The imagery of Gulf people usually portrays women wearing black robes (*abaya*) with a veil covering their heads (*sheyla*) and sometimes veils covering their faces (*burqa*) and men wearing white robes with white head-scarves (*dishdasha*), as in Figures 2.1 and 2.2. However, this is not always the case. Women in Kuwait and Bahrain tend to dress in conservative Western styles, such as in long blouses with medium-to-long sleeves and trousers or skirts, although some still wear beautifully ornamented *abayas* just like most Emirati and Qatari women. In all GCC countries except for Saudi Arabia, women have the choice to wear the *hijab* (head scarf) and *abaya* or not. However, the majority of local women do wear the *abaya* and the veil by tradition and due to family pressure, rather than by force. However, in Saudi Arabia, Saudi women must cover their bodies and faces, and females from other countries are also obliged to wear *abayas* and cover their hair.

In the GCC, tourists and visitors are expected to follow laws setting out a dress code that does not violate the conservative culture of these states. For example, visitors should read signs at the entrances of public places

Figure 2.1.   Example of men's traditional Khaliji dress.

Figure 2.2.   Example of men's traditional
Khaliji dress.

that require them to not wear skirts or shorts that are above the knee and
other signs that prohibit public displays of affection. Nevertheless, the
governments, except in the Kingdom of Saudi Arabia, are often flexible
with such laws.

Omani women tend to be slightly different from women in the other
GCC states. In Oman, "women's dress reflects tribal associations, settlement, and traditions that draw from India, eastern Africa, and Yemen"
(Torstrick & Faier, 2009, p. 96). Generally, Omani Khaliji women tend to
cover their hair and dress in loose clothing that hides their body shapes.
However, they are fashionable, owning some of the most famous brands
such as Prada and Chanel.

Traditional Food

Traditional food reflects an important trait of any nation's cultural heritage. As mentioned earlier, Islam influences the culture of GCC coun-

tries, and it even impacts Arabs' eating habits. Muslims in general are obliged to eat permissible (*halal*) food. Pork and alcohol, for instance, are completely prohibited in Islam, and any animal eaten should be slaughtered based on Islamic rituals in order to be considered *halal*. Otherwise, it is considered to be *haram* (forbidden) and thus cannot be eaten. The Gulf countries share most of the same dietary habits, with slight variations from state to state.

The lifestyle of the GCC countries has been greatly influenced by the rapid growth experienced by these countries, which has helped to shape their nutritional needs and patterns (Musaiger, 1993). Standard foods such as milk, dates, bread, fish, and seafood have been the basis of the GCC diet for centuries. However, the modern diet of the GCC also contains a mixture of dishes from around the world. Breads such as date bread (*khoubez* al-tamer), thin pan bread (*al-rigag*), and flat bread (*tanoor*) are commonly consumed in GCC countries. Also, rice is considered a staple food for the entire region and it can be cooked for both lunch and dinner. Lamb and mutton are consumed more than beef. One of the most common dishes, served on many different occasions, is *al mansaf*. It consists of roasted lamb and rice with herbs.

Arab cuisine is known for its aromatic food; this is because, "for centuries, even before the birth of Christ, Arab merchants controlled the spice trade" (Salloum, 2006, para. 8). Moreover, Arabian or Gulf bitter coffee (*gahwa khalijia*) is a hospitable traditional drink available on all occasions. It is served from a pot (*dallah*) in small handleless cups with no sugar added. Coffee is usually served with dates.

Music

Most of the Gulf region shares not only language but music as well. Khaliji music is common throughout the area due to cultural relationships and collaborations among the countries of the Gulf region. This kind of music is easy for other Arabs to recognize; it contains a combination of Indian, African, and Arabic pitches, rhythms, attitudes, and melodies (Saeed, 2012).

ARABIC LANGUAGE

As noted previously, the Gulf people share a common language that is spoken with some dialectical variations. This is the language of the Quran, also discussed in other chapters in this section. Interestingly, Christopher Columbus, in his attempt to reach India sailing westward, had an Arabic-speaking interpreter with him because, at that time, Europeans thought that Arabic was the sole trading language of the world (Salloum, 2006).

The Arabic language is very different from English. Arabic is a member of the Semitic language family. Although it has a standard writing form (*Al foss'ha*), vocal Arabic has dialectical variations. In the GCC region it is known as the Gulf or Khaliji dialect, and some know it as "Gulf Arabic." It is native to Saudi Arabia, the United Arab Emirates, Kuwait, Bahrain, Qatar, Oman, and Southern Iraq.

Arabic is read from right to left. Its alphabet has 28 letters, comprising 25 consonants and 3 vowels; this is in addition to another three marks that function as short vowels. All the letters are written the same size; there is no distinction between capital and small letters. Phonologically, due to the limited set of vowels in Arabic, learners of English tend to face difficulty reading and pronouncing many words correctly. This also includes some consonants that do not exist in Arabic such as /p/, /ch/, and /v/ and others that look the same but might be produced differently, such as /th/. In terms of vocabulary, there are few English/Arabic cognates. Arabic is grammatically different from English, too. For instance, there is neither the auxiliary verb "to be" in Arabic nor any modal verbs (i.e., should, could, can, might). Furthermore, unlike English, Arabic has only one present and one past tense.

Generally, Arab learners of English experience interference from their first language when speaking or writing in English. Arab learners of English might get confused with the use of punctuation, and teachers should not feel surprised with their frequent use of run-on sentences—this is acceptable in the Arabic language. Similarly, redundancy is another technique that writers in Arabic use to emphasize an idea, while this is not welcomed in formal English writing. Additionally, word order in English sentences differs from Arabic; in English, adjectives precede the noun they qualify, but in Arabic the adjective follows the noun. For instance, Arab learners of English might say "apple red" instead of "red apple."

Some of the recommended words and phrases for foreigners to learn are: *harAM* (forbidden) and *haLAL* (permissible). This is in addition to some other common words such as:

- *SHOkran*, meaning thank you;
- Ala, meaning hello;
- alHEEN meaning now;
- elYUM, meaning today;
- WAYn, meaning where; and
- SaYArah, meaning car.

The pronunciations of these words are similar in the Arabic dialects of the GCC countries.

EDUCATION AND SCHOOLING IN THE GULF REGION

Education in all GCC countries was historically an informal learning process taking place mainly in *kuttab* (Quranic schools) and in corners of mosques or *mutawas'* (religious scholars') houses (Al Hebsi, Pettaway, & Walker, 2015). This education started in the late 19th century and continued up to the first quarter of the 20th century. Learning at that time comprised mainly religion, Arabic, and basic math. All schools were historically segregated by gender.

Since the 1950s and the oil boom, GCC countries shifted from the religious schooling system to more modern schooling that includes geography, history, and the sciences. Education consisted of 4 cycles and 12 levels: 2 levels of preschool, levels 1–6 in primary, 7–9 in intermediate school, and 10–12 in high school. Free public schools were and continue to be restricted to local citizens, and if expatriates from other countries want to attend, they have to pay for their seats (Abu Dhabi Education Council, 2016).

Since the 1970s, the Gulf States, with profits from their natural resources (primarily petroleum), have been investing large amounts of money in various areas to improve their futures, including education. The region witnessed a significant influx of immigrants who came to work in different fields, one of which is education. Because of educational development, literacy rates in the United Arab Emirates, for example, have risen from 48% in the 1970s to over 93% at the current time (Crown Prince Court, 2012). The presence of diverse ethnicities in the Gulf countries, especially in the 1990s, required a common language for these multilingual and multicultural communities to communicate. Thus, English became the lingua franca in most of these countries except for Saudi Arabia, paving the way for private international schools to open. Private schools started operating mainly with British- and American-based curricula. Class size varies between 30–35 in public schools and 15–30 in private institutions. Public schools remain segregated by gender in all GCC countries up to today, although some private schools have been mixed since their inception.

In the last decade, education in the Gulf States has been undergoing many reforms. Such reforms include introducing English to public schools by teaching math and sciences in English, while Arabic and Islam are taught in Arabic (Gallagher, 2011). The system does not only focus on content area subjects but also addresses students' mental development.

For example, student growth, activity, behavior, interaction, and participation all account for around 50% of their grade (UNESCO, 2011). In all GCC countries, elementary and intermediate (junior school) education is compulsory. However, many students in high school, especially in public schools where the majority (around 95%) are local citizens, do not have the motivation to continue to study in higher education. This is because boys have jobs waiting for them in the army or police upon completing high school (grade 12), and girls are expected to get married.

Expectations of Educators in the GCC

In Gulf countries, educators need to follow some rules. For example, if it is suspected that a student could be injured or offended by a peer or a teacher, they are required to inform authorities. Also, sexual relationships with students are not acceptable, in or out of the class or on the school premises. Touching within the same gender is fine but very sensitive when it comes to the opposite gender. For disciplinary purposes, verbal harassment, anything that causes physical or emotional pain to students, and corporal punishment are all unacceptable. Also, punishing the group on account of one's mistake, giving extra work, preventing the student from going to the bathroom or from eating or praying, and making fun of the student are all banned punishments. All public schools in the GCC have prayer rooms or corners for students of both genders.

Further, educators are not allowed to smoke or drink on school property. Regarding the dress code, educators who are locals typically wear their traditional clothes, while those who are expatriates wear formal and modest attire. Students have school uniforms that are gender specific (Zaman & Sabry, 2014). Educators in the GCC should make sure that only the subject matter is being discussed and prevent students from asking about controversial issues during group discussions. Teachers are not allowed to engage students in conversations about issues of politics and religion if they are not part of the curriculum. Main taboo subjects in GCC classrooms, whether in public or private schools, include but are not limited to sex, dating, contraceptives, dancing, pork, homosexuality, politics (such as the Palestinian–Israeli conflict), atheism, horoscopes, alcohol, and drugs.

Students with special needs can enroll in any school that is near to them upon availability of seats, and if seats are not available, they enroll in the nearest available school. However, depending on the kind of disability, some of the children are asked to go to centers for special needs. Usually physically challenged students are fine, but learners with advanced mental illnesses cannot be admitted because they need shadow teachers that the public schools cannot provide.

Relationships of educators with parents vary between public and private schools. In the former, parents are almost absent in their students' school lives, while in the latter the relationship between teachers and guardians is mostly confined to the regular meetings held at school throughout the year. Furthermore, Arab learners in general tend to be conservative in dealing with teachers and this is due to the fact that Arabs belong to a high context culture where respect and harmony within the hierarchy is of high importance.

In the last two decades, there has been a movement to employ more Arab teachers in educational settings in the GCC. This was easy to do in kindergarten and primary schools but harder to achieve in intermediate and secondary schools. This means that education in the Gulf still relies heavily on foreign labor. In public schools, Arab teachers mainly teach subjects like sciences, information technology, English, and Arabic. In private schools, Western teachers are dominant in teaching English but share the teaching task for other subjects with colleagues of other nationalities. Only Arabs teach Arabic and religion.

Teaching methods still rely heavily on the rote-learning and memorizing process in GCC countries, although there have been calls by scholars and authorities in some Gulf states for educational reforms to use more modern strategies. Sheikh Mohammed bin Rashid Al Maktoum, the vice president and prime minister of the United Arab Emirates (UAE) and ruler of Dubai, for example, has emphasized the necessity to support critical thinking skills for youth through language and technology education: "For that reason, the UAE Vision 2021 National Agenda emphasizes the development of a first-rate education system, which will require a complete transformation of the current education system and teaching methods" (UAE Vision 2021, 2016, para. 1).

Education in the GCC has resulted in greater openness and better understanding between men and women and has empowered women in all aspects of life; they are now more aware of what is happening around them regarding healthcare, job rights, personal status, and political participation. Women in the GCC have made significant advances in the areas of literacy and university education (Al Gharaibeh, 2015) that have allowed them to be more involved in the labor market and business world; they are also among the most educated in the Arab world. Women nowadays seem to be more interested in studies than men, which is seen through their higher university enrollment in almost all countries of the region (Gladys-Jakóbik & Górak-Sosnowska, 2007). With these changes, it is expected that there will be many future opportunities for GCC women to work, manage, and lead in a variety of settings (Madsen & Cook, 2010).

However, women still face cultural obstacles. As noted above, countries in the Gulf region are considered to be very conservative due to their desire for preservation of their traditions and to religious rules that limit women from contact with the opposite gender (Gladys-Jakóbik & Górak-Sosnowska, 2007). Many Arabs are concerned about maintaining their cultural identity and their independence from the West (Najjar, 2005). This also explains the existing gap between the high number of educated women and the much lower rate in the workplace. This gap is also due in part to the fact that parents in general would allow their daughters (and husbands their wives) to study since education is segregated, but they might have second thoughts when it comes to mixed workplaces.

IDEAS FOR EDUCATORS

Based on the information in this chapter, we recommend a focus for U.S. educators on intercultural communication, awareness, and sharing.

- Workshops could be held to promote interaction between American teachers and GCC students that would allow better understanding of each other's culture and also enhance students' proficiency in English. Further, this kind of training can focus on intercultural communication to avoid cultural shock, which would make it easier for students to adapt to the United States and its culture.
- GCC students could be assigned same-sex academic partners. Research studies dealing with international students' cultural adjustments consider, in general, the students' attitudes, norms, and values that might be different from the host country's; therefore, they emphasize the importance of social interaction with American friends in order to more easily shift to the new cultural environment (Ahmed, 2015; Kagan & Cohen, 1990; Shaffer & Harrison, 2001).
- A program could be developed to teach female students self-defense in order to avoid any harassment, assault, threat, or theft to which they may be exposed in the United States.
- Teachers can make a point to be aware of the cultural regulators of their GCC students, mainly language, religion, and traditions. Honoring their students' cultures and languages can help educators contribute to a friendly learning environment and to the academic success of the students. For example, the teacher can remember some of the commonly used words of the students' first

language, and the teacher can have an awareness of the taboos and the topics that are culturally sensitive to Gulf students.

- For issues related to sex, male/female relations, alcohol, pork, and drugs, educators can mention to all students that, while some cultures do not honor or accept these taboos, the U.S. society in general does.

- Teachers can explain that, in order to learn a language, students can also try to understand U.S. culture. If Gulf students know that understanding other cultures helps enhance intercultural communication and might help promote peace and harmony among nations, this will help them accept the exposure to and discussion of taboo topics and other culturally based issues.

- Teachers might also want to incorporate some elements into the curriculum that encourage the students to share aspects of their cultures with their peers, such as food, family habits, and their country's history.

- Teachers can be open to using online dictionaries or a thesaurus to find the meaning of some words in the students' native language and never feel embarrassed to pronounce those words with the students' assistance.

- Teachers might consider providing Arab learners with enough time to share their thoughts without interrupting them.

- The teacher of Arab students needs to be aware that the majority of students are taught in classes that are more teacher-centered and that the students might struggle at the beginning in student-centered classrooms; it may be difficult for them to cooperate and rely on themselves or trust their peers.

- Because Arab learners in general come from an oral culture, teachers can take advantage of this trait by first engaging them in interesting listening and speaking activities and topics that relate to the students' own culture and experiences before asking them to read and write.

Other Points for Educators to Consider

- GCC and other Arab learners are influenced by their traditional way of learning. The majority of them will not volunteer, so call upon them to respond to a question.

- GCC students learn to copy down everything written on the blackboard. Although their listening skills tend to be better than their writing, free lecturing might frustrate them. Therefore, it is highly recommended to highlight the main point on the board until they get used to the system.

- Allow GCC students to feel more comfortable by calling you "Ms. X" or "Mr. X" rather than by the first name.
- It is acceptable in the GCC culture to ask personal questions about such topics as salary, relationship status, weight, and religion, so do not be surprised if students do so. Do, however, let them know that it is inappropriate to ask such questions to many Americans.
- Some parents of GCC students would expect a lot of homework to be sent and done at home on a daily basis. Also, they might wonder why their children do not have textbooks, so teachers should be prepared to answer questions during the first conference.
- Plagiarism is an issue that some GCC students may not be aware of. Teachers should make sure to inform them about the concept and its common practices. Likewise, cheating is understood differently in GCC countries and warrants an exploration by students and educators. Teachers can use strategies such as randomizing exam questions to get the students used to the system in the United States and learn to be independent learners.
- Most GCC students may be surprised with some teachers' and students' behaviors, such as eating and drinking in class, sitting on the desk (e.g., feet on desk), asking them to call you by name, and dressing casually (e.g., shorts, jeans, short skirts). They will probably need time to get used to the new environment.
- Male teachers are advised to avoid asking personal questions related to their male students' female relatives such as mothers, wives, or sisters. This can cause offense. However, female teachers may do so with no problem.

CONCLUSIONS

GCC countries situated in the Arabian Gulf as described in this chapter have their own "regulators of culture" that can be summarized as language, religion, and history. For teachers of Arab students, cultural competence entails that they know the culture of their learners, celebrate diversity in the classroom, tolerate cultural differences related to rituals and learning abilities, and choose a curriculum that considers cultural representation of this diversity. Educators who empower their GCC students by embracing their work and culture will have students who do their best to impress them and succeed.

ADDITIONAL RESOURCES

Arabian tales for kids. (2016). Retrieved from http://www.kidsgen.com/stories/arabian_tales/
> A variety of enchanting tales for younger readers.

Gulf Arabic. (2016). Learn the spoken Arabic of the Gulf countries. Retrieved from http://www.gulfarabic.com/
> Lessons to learn the Arabic language variant spoken from the locals of the United Arab Emirates, Qatar, Kuwait, Bahrain, parts of eastern Sauid Arabia, most of Southern Iraq, and to a lesser extent, Oman.

Haase, F-A. (2014). Contrastive studies in communication styles of Gulf Arab business culture and Western business communication cultures. Retrieved from http://dx.doi.org/10.2139/ssrn.1937092
> Research paper discussing the expression "Arab business." Author explains how this term is an inaccurate metaphor constructed by the Western world.

TASKS FOR EDUCATORS

1. We, the foreigners, are afraid to participate in class because we feel we are less advantaged than American students." Do you agree or disagree with this student's opinion? What would you do to encourage your students to feel safer and have a voice in your class?

2. To what extent might the cultural differences between Americans and GCC students affect the learning environment for Arab learners?

3. Consider whether you have experienced any of the cultural issues presented at the start of this chapter that affected Mohammed and Hanof. Share some ideas for how to address these issues with your peers.

4. What are the elements that you like most about the GCC culture? Do you have a similar tie or cultural regulator in your culture?

5. Using a Venn diagram, list the differences and the similarities between your culture and the GCC.

6. Work with a partner and try to recall as many Arabic words and phrases as possible.

REFERENCES

Abu Dhabi Education Council. (2016). Expats students. Retrieved from https://www.adec.ac.ae/en/students/ps/pages/expats-students.aspx

Ahmed, K. (2015). Intercultural communication and Muslim American youth in U.S. school contexts. In R. Raddawi (Ed.), *Intercultural communication with Arabs* (pp. 127–140). New York, NY: Springer.

Al Abed, I. (1997). The historical background and the constitutional basis to the federation. In E. Ghareeb & I. Al Abed (Eds.), *Perspectives on the United Arab Emirates* (pp. 99–122). London, UK: Trident Press.

Al Gharaibeh, F. (2015). An exploration of the evolution of women's roles in societies of the Gulf Cooperation Council. *Social Development Issues, 37*(3), 22–44.

Al Hebsi, A., Pettaway, L., & Walker, L. (2015). A history of education in the United Arab Emirates and trucial sheikdoms. *The Global Elearning* Journal, *4*(1). Retrieved from http://research.aurak.ac.ae/wp-content/uploads/2015/11/a-history-of-education-in-the-united-arab-emirates-and-trucial-sheikdoms.pdf

BBC News Middle East. (2016a). Bahrain Profile. Retrieved from http://www.bbc.com/news/world-middle-east-14540571.

BBC News Middle East. (2016b). Kuwait Country Profile. Retrieved from http://www.bbc.com/news/world-middle-east-14644252.

Constitute Project. (2016). Saudi Arabia's Constitution of 1992 with amendments through 2005. Retrieved from https://www.constituteproject.org/constitution/Saudi_Arabia_2005.pdf

Crown Prince Court. (2012). *United Arab Emirates: 40 Years of Progress.* Retrieved from https://www.cpc.gov.ae/sitecollectiondocuments/40%20years%20book%20english.pdf

Dadush, U., & Falcao, L. (2009). Regional arrangements in the Arabian Gulf. Carnegie Endowment for International Peace: Policy Outlook. Retrieved from carnegieendowment.org/files/gcc1.pdf

Gallagher, K. (2011). Bilingual education in the UAE: Factors, variables and critical questions. *Education, Business and Society: Contemporary Middle Eastern Issues, 4*(1), 62–79.

Gladys-Jakóbik, J., & Górak-Sosnowska, K. (2007). Women of the gulf: The situation in the labour market and business. *Kobieta i Biznes, 1*(4), 17–25.

Islam. (2015). In *The free dictionary.* Retrieved from http://www.thefreedictionary.com/Islam

Jandt, F. E. (2016). *An introduction to intercultural communication: Identities in a global community* (8th ed). Thousand Oaks, CA: SAGE.

Kagan, H., & Cohen, J. (1990). Cultural adjustment of international students. *Psychological Science, 1*(2), 133–137.

Khan, W. M. (2010). *The Quran.* New Delhi, India: Goodword Book.

Madsen, S. R., & Cook, B. J. (2010). Transformative learning: UAE, women, and higher education. *Journal of Global Responsibility, 1*(1), 127–148.

Musaiger, A. O. (1993). *Traditional foods in the Arabian Gulf Countries.* Bahrain, UAE: Arabian Gulf University. Retrieved from http://www.acnut.com/v/images/stories/pdf/publications/traditional_foods_in_the_agc.pdf

Najjar, F. (2005). The Arabs, Islam and globalization. *Middle East Policy, 12*(3), 91–106.

National Assembly. (2011). *The progress of democracy in the state of Kuwait*. Kuwait City: Studies and Research Department, National Assembly of Kuwait.

Population pyramids of the world 1950 to 2100. (2016). Retrieved from http://www.populationpyramid.net

Raddawi, R., & Meslem, D. (2015). Loss of Arabic in the UAE: Is bilingual education the solution? *International Journal of Bilingual and Multilingual Teachers of English, 3*(2), 85–94.

Saeed, S. (2012). Music of the Arab world: The history and development of Khaleeji music. *The National.* Retrieved from http://www.thenational.ae/arts-culture/music/music-of-the-arab-world-the-history-and-development-of-khaleeji-music

Salloum, H. (2006). Foods of the Arabian Gulf countries. *ThingsAsian.* Retrieved from http://www.thingsasian.com/stories-photos/3726

Shaffer, M. A., & Harrison, D. A. (2001). Forgotten partners of international assignments: Development and test of a model of spouse adjustment. *Journal of Applied Psychology, 86*(2), 238.

Torstrick, R., & Faier, E. (2009). *Culture and customs of the Arab Gulf states*. London, UK: Greenwood Press.

United Nations Development Program. (2010.) *Arab human development report: Building a knowledge society.* New York, NY: UNDP Regional Bureau for Arab States.

UAE Vision 2021. (2016). *UAE vision: First-rate education system.* Retrieved from https://www.vision2021.ae/en/national-priority-areas/first-rate-education-system

United Nations Educational, Scientific, and Cultural Organization (UNESCO). (2011). *World data on education: Qatar* (7th ed.). Retrieved from http://www.ibe.unesco.org/sites/default/files/Qatar.pdf

Zaman, S., & Sabry, S. (2014). Abu Dhabi school pupils wear a whole new look. *Gulf News.* Retrieved from http://gulfnews.com/news/uae/education/abu-dhabi-school-pupils-wear-a-whole-new-look-1.1380600

CHAPTER 3

THE MIDDLE EAST

Raed Alsawaier
Washington State University

Mrs. Lee is a new 4th grade teacher in an elementary school in the U.S. Pacific Northwest and has many students of Arabic descent, mainly from the Middle East. She addresses one of the students, Saeed, who does not seem to follow instructions. Her concern turns into frustration as she tries to explain to the student that he needs to follow directions like everyone else in the class. She feels offended. Saeed just smiles at her. She takes that as a sign of disrespect. She reports the case to the principal and sends a long email to the parents about what happened, requesting their help in addressing their son's behavior issue. Saeed's father gets upset and talks with Saeed about his behavior; in return, Saeed explains to his father that he could not follow the teacher's instructions. He only smiled because he felt embarrassed in front of the class and meant no disrespect. Saeed's father remembers that he used to do that in front of his teacher and father when he felt bad. The fake smile was a culturally accepted way to cover his feelings of pain and embarrassment.

BACKGROUND

The term "Middle East" was created by the British Empire as a name to describe the area between the British mainland and the Far East (China). The people who live in the vast territories that the term "Middle East" encompasses never call themselves Middle Eastern, except maybe when

Views From Inside: Languages, Cultures, and Schooling for K–12 Educators
pp. 45–58

they move to Western countries. This can be understood by considering the diverse countries, cultures, languages, and religions that flourished throughout history and continue to exist today in the Middle East region. As Minor (1961) noted, "The Middle East is a vast and critical area of the world, a composite of ancient and modern cultures, disparate races and religions, and uneven historical and natural influences" (p. 86).

Zubaida (2015) notes that "the Middle East is that part of Western Asia extending from the eastern Mediterranean coast of Turkey and Syria, through the desert to Iraq and Arabia" (p. 1). However, this chapter will focus on four main countries: Egypt, Jordan, Lebanon, and Syria. The reason this chapter will only discuss these four countries is for practical reasons related to the commonalities among them, which are in some ways generally representative of other countries and cultures in the Middle East. For example, Palestinian culture and education are historically intertwined with Jordanian culture. On the other hand, the Jewish culture, represented by Israel, has not been listed here, although it is an essential part of Middle Eastern history and culture, because of the considerably low percentage of Israeli elementary students in the U.S. school system and the uniqueness of the Jewish culture.

DEMOGRAPHICS AND GEOGRAPHY

Egypt is the largest Arab country in terms of population, estimated at 93 million in 2015 (Worldometers, 2015). Egypt is part of North Africa and is not geographically connected to Jordan, Lebanon, and Syria. The populations of Jordan, Lebanon, and Syria have been radically transformed recently due to the Syrian refugee crisis following the civil war in Syria. Because of the shared borders between Jordan, Lebanon, and Syria, millions of Syrian refugees fled to Jordan and Lebanon, among many other countries, causing the population of Syria to drop dramatically. The population of Jordan jumped from 7 million to over 8 million following the large influxes of Syrian refugees. The population of Lebanon also increased by a million due to the refugee crisis, to become over 7 million. The current population of Syria is almost impossible to know; recent satellite images show vast Syrian territories with no human activity due to refugee displacement (Data Team, 2015). More than 50% of the Syrian population (approximately 4.5 million) are refugees in other countries (Amnesty International, 2016). The Obama administration has pledged to resettle 10,000 refugees in the United States (many children of school age) (Sengupta, 2016), but with an incoming administration with different ideas, it is unclear if this will happen. Close to 30% of the population in

Egypt, Jordan, Lebanon, and Syria is between 15–29 years old (Youth Policy, 2016).

MIDDLE EASTERN CULTURES AND HISTORY

The main components that Middle Eastern cultures share are language, religion as the source of ideas and beliefs, and behavior in terms of morals and folkways. For example, Arabic is the main language of communication in education, although English is more prevalent in academic settings; however, Lebanon and Syria have more communication in French as a result of past French colonization. The majority of the population in the Middle East is Muslim, with a significant number of Christians, especially in Lebanon.

Religion

Egypt
The largest Arab country in the Middle East by land area is Egypt, which also has the largest Coptic Christian population, estimated at approximately 8 million. Christianity in Egypt dates back to the Roman era when Alexandria was an early center of Christianity. Egypt is truly an amalgamation of cultures and religions, although dominantly Islamic Arab. One researcher acknowledged that Egyptian culture, just like other world cultures, has been affected by a "hybridization process" (Gregg, 2005, p. 4).

Lebanon
Lebanon has the most diverse culture in the Arab world, with multiple religious groups and ethnicities. Lebanon has a considerable population of Christians, estimated at 38.22%, although the number is decreasing for sociopolitical reasons (Lebanese Information Center, 2013); many Christian Lebanese, with strong European influences, choose to have one or two children, whereas the Muslim population does not limit the number of children in the same way.

Jordan
Jordan has one of the oldest Christian populations in the world and many consider it, including the West Bank of the Jordan River, to be the birthplace of Christianity. The percentage of Christians in Jordan is 6% and is dropping due to the small family size many Christians choose to have, in addition to emigration to Western countries (BBC, 2011). The

relationship between Christians and Muslims in Jordan is largely peaceful, with many Christians serving in key government positions and in the parliament.

Syria

The majority of the population in Syria is Muslim (87%), with 10% Christians in addition to other minorities (Mundi, 2016). These other religious minorities include Alwayites, Duruuz, and Jews; however, the religious and ethnic shape of modern Syria has been changed due to the current civil war. Estimated between 175,000 and 200,000, the last Jews from the city of Aleppo escaped to Israel following the intense fighting (Kaplan, 2015). Furthermore, much of the Sunni population has been displaced due to attacks by the Shiite-supported regime.

Literacy and Reading

The four Middle Eastern countries (Egypt, Jordan, Syria, and Lebanon) have succeeded in lowering the illiteracy rates in their populations. Based on United Nations Educational, Scientific and Cultural Organization (UNESCO) statistics, Jordan has a literacy rate of 99.1%; Egypt 86%; Syria 96%; and Lebanon 98% (Kanalan & Celep, 2011; UNICEF, 2013).

In a report that was attributed to UNESCO (2003), Arabs were found to read less than six minutes per year; this was reported widely in Arab and international news. Caldwell (2015) described this six-minute-a-year figure as a myth and conducted her own investigation. She could not find this statistic in the original UNESCO report. In 2007, a Bulgarian-based research institute conducted a survey on 1,000 Egyptians to study their reading habits. Of the total number of participants, 800 reported reading 54 minutes a day (Caldwell, 2015). However, this 54-minute reading per day is mainly focused on recitation of the Quran; the 6-minutes idea may be based on other kinds of reading, such as science fiction, which are not popular in these countries. There is no information on the reading habits in Jordan, Lebanon, and Syria. However, these three countries have higher literacy rates than Egypt, and it is possible that they have higher reading time per day than Egypt. For example, historically, Lebanon has always been a publication epicenter for the entire Arab world. Translations and different literature in Arabic often can be found to have a Beirut (the capital of Lebanon) stamp on them.

Another misconception regarding the reading habits of the Arabs is that all they read is the Quran. It is true that the Quranic schools were the only ones that provided education up to the middle of the 19th century (Akkari, 2004). Furthermore, research has indicated that the Quran has contributed in promoting literacy skills among Arabs through its own writing and recitation systems (Neuwirth, Sinai, & Marx, 2010). However, to assume that the Quran is the only book Arabs read is an inaccurate overgeneralization. As colonial powers controlled the Middle East from the middle of the 19th century to the first half of the 20th century, they imposed their own educational systems on the countries they occupied. After the departure of colonizers, modern secular education was introduced and funded by the governments of Egypt, Jordan, Lebanon, and Syria. Gradually, these Quranic schools disappeared except in Islamic institutions and universities and were substituted by Western-style schools and curricula. This created an atmosphere where Arabs were exposed to reading on different subjects necessary for their education and for leisure as well. As noted below, however, Arab students, who often read the news and other informational texts, may not often read fiction and other related genres because they come from traditionally oral cultures.

The Schooling System

The schooling systems in Jordan, Egypt, Syria, and Lebanon are similar in many ways. Like in the majority of Arab countries, the governments strongly control the educational systems, the content, and the curricula in the schools. The enrollment rate is high but is still behind world enrollment rates (Kanalan & Celep, 2011). The school day usually consists of 8 hours, where the students study different topics including math, English, science, and other topics, including Islamic studies. There are several private Christian schools that teach according to their own curricula and are open to Christians and Muslims as well (Kanalan & Celep, 2011). One major difference between American and Arab schools is that all schools in Arabic countries have curricula in the form of books that both teachers and students must adhere to. As noted in the previous chapter, when Arab students join the American school system, their parents usually raise questions about how they can help their children without designated textbooks. American teachers could solve this dilemma by explaining to the parents how the American school system works and the fact that many teachers have books they keep in the classroom from which they copy selected materials for the convenience of the students.

Morals and Folkways

The behavior component of culture in the four countries of Egypt, Jordan, Lebanon, and Syria is quite similar in many ways. They share the idea of respecting the teacher who, in most cases, will be like a "sage on the stage" with complete power and control of the classroom learning experience. The majority of teachers in Middle Eastern schools "tend to use direct lecturing, illustrating concepts and reading from textbooks. Moreover, assessment relies almost entirely on examinations" (Derderian-Aghajanian & Cong, 2012, p. 174). Summative assessment is essential in Middle Eastern cultures, where teachers evaluate their students based on their scores on examinations and not on authentic, formative assessments or overall language development. Similarly, parents will judge their students' progress based on their final scores, which will determine, in their opinion, their child's future and level of social acceptance. It is important for American teachers to understand that the score they assign to students of Middle Eastern origin may carry a lot more weight culturally and socially than for other students. During teacher–parent meetings, teachers could explain to the parents why and how their children are being assessed in order to address their concerns.

LANGUAGE

Classic (or "standard") Arabic is used in all forms of formal communication and is widely understood by the majority of the Arabic-speaking population, including Middle Easterners. This is because classic Arabic is the language used in the writing of the Quran, the holy book for Muslims, and the *hadith*, the sayings of the Prophet Mohammad, which all Muslims study. Colloquial Arabic has more vowel and sound combinations than standard Arabic. For example, whereas in standard Arabic there are 28 consonants and 6 vowels (3 long and 3 short), Syrian Arabic slang uses 11 vowels total (Shafiro, 2013). This can be explained in part due to foreign language influences such as English and French, introduced during British and French colonization of the region. This influence was exerted more on colloquial Arabic because of its use in everyday communication, while standard Arabic is used mainly in writing. In spite of the variation between classic Arabic and colloquial versions of the Arabic language, they both originate from the same phonological system.

One of the main problems that Arabic ELLs face is the absence of some of the common vowels that are widely used in the English language (Table 3.1 shows a list of Arabic vowels and how they are pronounced in English words). Arabic ELLs have a tendency to replace the consonants and vowels not used in their native language (L1) with the closest sounds to be able to communicate in English. The /tʃ/ sound not used in standard Arabic, as in the word "tea*ch*er," will be replaced by many Arabic learners with the sound / ʃ/ as in the word "*sh*ape" (see Table 3.2). Even Arabic students

Table 3.1.   Arabic Vowels With English Pronunciations

ء	/a/	As in the English article *a*
ٱ	/a:/	m*a*n
ٱ	/u/	t*o*
او	/u:/	t*oo*
ٳ	/i/	*i*nn
إي	/i:/	m*ee*t

Table 3.2.   English Vowels Not Used in Arabic

/ei/	vowel combination	as in b*ai*t
/ɛ/	forward vowel	as in b*e*t
/ai/	vowel combination	as in b*y*
/au/	vowel combination	as in h*ou*se
/ju/	vowel combination	as in ab*u*se
/ɔi/	vowel combination	as in b*oy*
/ʌ/	vowel	as in r*u*n
/ɛə/	vowel combination	as in b*ea*r
/ɔə/	vowel combination	as in b*oa*r

Table 3.3.   English Consonants Not Used in Arabic Language

/t͡ʃ/	consonant	as in *ch*air
/v/	consonant	as in *v*ote
/p/	consonant	as in *p*en
/ʒ/	voiced sibilant	as in sei*z*ure
/ŋ/	velarnasal	as in si*n*g

with relatively good English language skills exhibit this tendency occasionally. Similarly, the consonant /v/, which does not exist in the Arabic alphabet, will be often substituted with the consonant /f/ (see Table 3.3). It is not unusual for Arabic students, especially at the beginning level, to say "fery (very) good!" The most commonly misused consonant by Arabic students is /p/, which only exists in the Arabic alphabet as a strong voiced /b/ sound. Some English teachers will try to help these students pronounce the /p/ sound with a piece of paper close to their mouths to illustrate the tiny current of air associated with it.

English vowel combinations present challenges for Arabic learners. Due to the limited number of vowels in the Arabic language, more complex English vowel combinations need extra effort on the part of teachers and the learners as well. Although the Arabic language is complex and rich, the vowel limitations could be attributed to the fact that "the Arabic writing system was originally consonantal" (Alotaiby, 2014, p. 810).

IDEAS FOR EDUCATORS

Understanding the cultural variations between the Middle East and the United States could aid American educators in terms of teaching methodology and content. Although teachers in the U.S. school system have to comply with state standards and curriculum requirements, there is still some room for them to modify their teaching techniques and slightly alter the learning content.

Pedagogy

Once they come from their countries overseas, the immersion of Middle Eastern students is instant, but their assimilation into American culture is slow. It will take longer for Arabic students coming from this background to "break the ice" and become actively involved in class participation and activities. It is not uncommon for Arabic students, especially at the elementary level, to show their embarrassment by smiling, which could be interpreted in Western society as a sign of disrespect (as in the scenario with Mrs. Lee in the beginning of the chapter). One approach educators can use is to limit initial involvement in classroom activities to pair work or even individual work to gradually help the students of Arabic descent to overcome their social anxiety.

Relevant Learning Content

Storytelling, which is an essential part of elementary school pedagogy in the United States, is not so for students of Middle Eastern origins. Although Arabic culture is very rich with fictional literature, bedtime stories and children's stories are simply not part of the culture. In a similar vein, students of Middle Eastern origin do not read, in most part, as often as students in other cultures. However, when Arab American children are exposed to stories translated into English from Arabic, they are able to make connections to their own heritage and establish cultural identity in terms of their experiences and self-esteem (Al-Hazza & Bucher, 2008). When teenage Arab American (born in the Middle East) students were interviewed about their experience as children exposed to different kinds of literature, they "remembered many favorite European American, Hispanic American, and African American children's stories, but no stories that reflected their own Middle Eastern culture" (Al-Hazza & Bucher, 2008, p. 210). One approach that U.S. teachers can use to make sure Middle Eastern students are not alienated from the classroom experience is to diversify the literature sources and include translations of Arabic stories into English. Another more creative and student-centered approach is to involve the students in introducing stories from their own cultural backgrounds and writing or translating them for their peers in class.

Establishing Connections

Although culture shock can have a significant impact on Middle Eastern students, especially when they first move into the United States, studies have shown that they generally have "healthy self-esteem" (Alkhateeb, 2014, p. 805). However, their acculturation and assimilation into the U.S. educational system may take some time and can be dependent on a number of factors. These factors include the time the students need to master English and the support the students get from their parents and the local Arab community. In the case of Syrian refugee children, war trauma and the loss of close family members could delay their full involvement in the school system and possibly impact their overall performance. One method U.S. teachers can use to facilitate Middle Eastern students' engagement is to know some basic Arabic words and phrases. Using simple words of greetings and phrases communicating basic messages could have a tremendous effect on the psychological readiness of students to get involved. Table 3.4 presents a list of basic words and phrases in classic Arabic (understood by all Arabic speakers of all backgrounds) and their transliteration/translation into English. Note that the stressed syllables are in capital letters.

Culturally Sensitive Topics

There are a number of subjects considered to be cultural taboos that Middle Eastern students deliberately ignore or were never exposed to in their home countries. Topics such as sexual education, sexual orientation, and atheism, in addition to other culturally sensitive topics, are rarely, if ever, addressed or discussed openly in any classroom setting in Middle Eastern countries. Generally speaking, culturally acceptable or inacceptable topics are decided based on the idea of *halal* (Islamically permissible)

Table 3.4.   Common Arabic Phrases

Hello—Peace'Assalāmu'alAYkum-marHAban السَّــلام عَلَيْكُــم - مَرْحَبًــا

(To which the reply is): Hello—peace Wā'alAYkumus-salām-marHAban وعَلَيْكُـــم السَّـــلام - مَرْحَبًــا

Welcome 'ahlAn أهْلاً

Goodbye ma'As-salAma مَع السَّلامَة

Good morning! sabA?u khAIr! صَـــباحُ الخَيْــر!

Good evening! masA'ul-k?AIr! مَســاء الخَيْــر!

Good night! (to a male) tusbIH'alakhAIr! تُصـــبح علــى خَيْـــر!

Good night! (to a female) tusbiHI'alakhAIr! تُصـــبحينَ علــى خَيْـــر!

How are you? kAifaalhAl ? كَيْفَألْحَــال؟

What's your name? māismUk? مَاأَسْمُك؟

My name is … Ismi …اسْمِي

I don't speak Arabic. Lā'ataḥ Addaṭul-'arabiyyAH. لا أَتَحَـــدّثُ الْعَرَبِيَّـــة.

I speak English. ataḥAddaṭual-ingilīziyYAh. أتحـــدث الإنجليزيـــة.

Source: Pimsleur Approach (2015).

or *haram* (Islamically prohibited), which affects many students coming from Muslim backgrounds. Cultural taboos have been connected in many studies to religious prohibitions (Fowles, 2008). However, as discussed earlier in the chapter, not all Middle Eastern students are Muslim, which is essential for American teachers to know. Culturally inappropriate topics can be defined as the ones "which may contradict the 'common sense' of the local society [of a native country] including authorities, peers, and even teachers" (Gitsaki, 2011, p. 82). American teachers should consider the sensitivity of these kind of topics before presenting them to students of Middle Eastern descent. Some schools in the United States give the option for parents to provide sexual education for their children as a way to show cultural discretion in handling culturally sensitive topics. Another approach is to present these topics strictly from a scientific basis and not to expose students of Middle Eastern descent to discussion or questions that could cause embarrassment. For example, showing the anatomy or the biology of the human body could be more culturally acceptable than discussing ways of having protected sex.

CONCLUSIONS

Understanding Middle Eastern cultures can help American teachers adjust their pedagogy to fulfill the needs of Middle Eastern students. In this chapter, some important information on the Middle East has been presented: its history, demography, folkways, language, literacy, and ideas for educators in the U.S. context. If you are an American teacher with students from the Middle East, please allow the students to consult with an Arabic dictionary if they want to; to read stories translated from Arabic to English if this promotes their engagement; to speak a little Arabic among themselves if that facilities comprehension. Learn a few words in Arabic; they could make a huge difference and make the Middle Eastern students feel more at ease and more receptive to learning.

ADDITIONAL RESOURCES

Cleveland, W. L. (2004). *A history of the modern Middle East.* Boulder, CO: Westview Press.
> Examines the modern history of the Middle East in light of the relationships between the Middle East and Western powers including the U.S.

Gregg, G. S. (2005). *The Middle East: A cultural psychology.* Oxford, England: Oxford University Press.
> Offers the reader a good background on the culture, values, and individual variations between men and women in the Middle East.

Peterson, M. A. (2011). *Connected in Cairo: Growing up cosmopolitan in the modern Middle East.* Bloomington, IN: Indiana University Press.
> Focuses on Egypt, the largest Arab country, and describes the social factors that contribute to creating both the individual Arab and class identity.

TASKS FOR TEACHERS

1. What does the literature say about first language support for second language learning? How would you respond if you see some of your students consulting an Arabic-English dictionary to help them do an activity or understand instruction?

2. Teachers often send books home with students to read with the help of the parents; however, some students of Middle Eastern descent may not complete the assignment. Why do you think some students of Arab descent fail to do the assigned readings?

3. Give your students of Middle Eastern descent some stories from Arab culture translated into English. If you do not have any in your classroom, you can always refer them to websites where Arab stories translated into English are available. Ask your students to write a summary of the story and share it with the class. Websites where popular Arab stories could be found include:

o Worldstories. (n.d.). Joha and his donkey. *Worldstories.* Retrieved from   www.worldstories.org.uk/stories/story/9-joha-and-his-donkey

o Resources to learn Arabic language. (2010, April 22). 36 Arabic stories for kids (for learning of Arabic) [Blog post]. Retrieved from http://toolstolearnarabic.blogspot.com/2010/04/pdf-36-arabic-stories-for-kids-for.html

o Children's Library. (n.d.). Simple search: Arabic. Retrieved from http://www.childrenslibrary.org/icdl/SimpleSearchCategory?langid=309

REFERENCES

Akkari, A. (2004). Education in the Middle East and North Africa: The current situation and future challenges. *International Education Journal, 5*(2), 144–153.

Al-Hazza, T. C., & Bucher, K. T. (2008). Building Arab Americans' cultural identity and acceptance with children's literature. *The Reading Teacher, 62*(3), 210–219. Retrieved from http://doi.org/10.1598/RT.62.3.3

Alkhateeb, H. M. (2014). Self-Esteem and Arab-American elementary students. *Psychological Reports, 115*(3), 805–809. doi: 10.2466/07.11.PRO.115c27z9

Alotaiby, F. F. (2014). Arabic vs. English: Comparative statistical study. *Arabian Journal for Science and Engineering, 39*(2), 809–820.

Amnesty International. (2016, February). Syria's refugee crisis in numbers. *Amnesty International.* Retrieved from https://www.amnesty.org/en/latest/news/2016/02/syrias-refugee-crisis-in-numbers/

British Broadcasting Corporation (BBC). (2011). Guide: Christians in the Middle East. Retrieved from http://www.bbc.com/news/world-middle-east-15239529

Caldwell, L. (2015, March 6). The Arab reader and the myth of six minutes. *Al-Akhbar English.* Retrieved from http://english.al-akhbar.com/node/3168

Data Team. (2015). Daily chart: Syria's drained population. *The Economist.* Retrieved from http://www.economist.com/blogs/graphicdetail/2015/09/daily-chart-18

Derderian-Aghajanian, A., & Cong, W. (2012). How culture affects on English Language Learners' (ELL's) outcomes, with Chinese and Middle Eastern immigrant students. *International Journal of Business and Social Science, 3*(5), 172–180.

Fowles, S. M. (2008). Steps toward an archaeology of taboo. In L. Fogelin (Ed.), *Religion, anthropology and the material world* (pp. 15–37). Carbondale, IL: Southern Illinois University Press.

Gitsaki, C. (2011). *Teaching and learning in the Arab world.* Berne, IN: Peter Lang AG.

Gregg, G. S. (2005). *The Middle East: A cultural psychology.* Oxford, UK: Oxford University Press.

Kanalan, E., & Celep, C. (2011). A glance to education in the Middle East under the shadow of politic and ethnic conflicts in the region. *Procedia—Social and Behavioral Sciences, 15*, 2864–2868. doi: 10.1016/j.sbspro.2011.04.204

Kaplan, M. (2015, November 8). Last Jews of Aleppo escape Syria and head for Israel with help from American businessman. *International Business News.* Retrieved from http://www.ibtimes.com/last-jews-aleppo-escape-syria-head-israel-help-american-businessman-2174714

Lebanese Information Center. (2013). *Lebanese demographic reality.* Beirut, Lebanon: PAPEC.

Minor, H. B. (1961). The peculiarities of geography: The Middle East. *The ANNALS of the American Academy of Political and Social Science, 335*(1), 86–90. doi: 10.1177/000271626133500113

Mundi, I. (2016). *Syrian demographic profile.* Retrieved from http://www.indexmundi.com/syria/demographics_profile.html

Neuwirth, A., Sinai, N., & Marx, M. (2010). *The Qur'ān in context: Historical and literary investigations into the Qur'ānic milieu.* Boston, MA: Brill.

Pimsleur Approach. (2015). Common Arabic words and phrases. Retrieved from http://www.pimsleurapproach.com/resources/arabic/articles/common-arabic-phrases/

Sengupta, S. (2016, May 10). U.S. has taken in less than a fifth of pledged Syrian refugees. *The New York Times.* Retrieved from http://www.nytimes.com/2016/05/11/world/middleeast/us-has-taken-in-less-than-a-fifth-of-pledged-syrian-refugees.html?_r=0

Shafiro, V. L.-D. (2013). Perceptual confusions of American English vowels and consonants by native Arabic bilinguals. *Language and Speech, 56*(2), 145–161.

UNESCO. (2003). *Literacy and adult education in the Arab world.* Hamburg, Germany: United Nations.

UNICEF. (2013, December 24). Egypt / Statistics. *UNICEF.* Retrieved from http://www.unicef.org/infobycountry/egypt_statistics.html

Worldometers. (2015). Egypt population. *Worldometers.info.* Retrieved from http://www.worldometers.info/world-population/egypt-population/

Youth Policy. (2016). *Middle East and North Africa: Youth Facts.* Retrieved from http://www.youthpolicy.org/mappings/regionalyouthscenes/mena/facts/

Zubaida, S. (2015, December). *Encyclopedia of food and culture.* Retrieved from http://www.encyclopedia.com/doc/1G2-3403400421.html

CHAPTER 4

ISLAMIC REPUBLIC OF IRAN/PERSIA

Seyed Abdollah Shahrokni
Washington State University

Navid has recently immigrated to the U.S. from Iran through the U.S. government's Diversity Visa program. He has a four-year-old daughter, Maryam, who is very verbal when it comes to Persian, speaking in her sweet, playful way. There is a problem, though. When in Iran, she was very sociable, always willing to make new friends and participate in the games played by children her age, both in the daycare center and at family social events; however, she has changed—Maryam is not a happy, lively little girl anymore. Instead of playing with the kids in the neighborhood, her parents say that she mostly plays games on her tablet computer and uses social media applications to connect to her family and friends back home. Her parents have recently put Maryam in a daycare center, hoping that it will help their daughter recover from her isolation and, in addition to learning English, be the happy girl she once was.

BACKGROUND

The media seems to be replete with Iran-related news, from nuclear energy to terrorism. It seems that Iran, a country that many U.S. adults cannot locate on a world map (Lukinbeal & Craine, 2008), is the center of

Views From Inside: Languages, Cultures, and Schooling for K–12 Educators
pp. 59–73

every global issue. In an op-ed published in the English-language outlet *Russia Today*, Marandi (2016) captured this irony by stating that the only thing Iran has not been blamed for is global warming, and only because it is technically "global." However, the blame for so many problems that is directed towards Iran obscures her colorful history, culture, and heritage under a heavy cloud of world politics.

Geography

Located in Western Asia (also known as the Middle East), Iran is officially known as the Islamic Republic of Iran and historically known as Persia. Iran has a land area of 636,400 square miles, and it is the world's 18th largest country (Avery, Afray, & Mostofi, 2016). The country borders Turkey, Azerbaijan, and Armenia to the northwest; Russia through the Caspian Sea in the north; Turkmenistan to the northeast; Afghanistan and Pakistan to the east; Iraq to the west; and the Arab states of the Persian Gulf (Kuwait, Bahrain, Iraq, Oman, Qatar, Saudi Arabia, and the United Arab Emirates) through the Persian Gulf and the Gulf of Oman in the south. Iran is made up of 31 provinces and 268 cities, with Tehran, the capital, being the most populous. Iran is home to a population of 75,149,669 people from diverse ethnic, linguistic, and religious backgrounds (Iran National Statistics Center, 2010). Contrary to the popular belief that Iran is an Arab country because of its location, it is not, although the country is home to a population of citizens with Arab ethnicity.

Ethnicity

Due to its geopolitical position (that is, mediating Central Asia, Turkey, and Europe) and historical stretching or shrinking of the territories owned by the Persian Empire, Iran enjoys a diverse ethnic composition. Ethnicities include Persian, Arab, Azeri, Kurd, Lur, Bakhtiyari, Balouch, Qashqai, Turkmen, Gilaki, Mazandarani, Talysh, and other ethnic minorities such as Assyrians, Armenians, Georgians, Circassians, and Mandaeans.

Religion

Based on the national census carried out in 2010, the country's religious architecture comprises 74,682,938 Muslims, 117,704 Christians,

8,756 Jews, 25,271 Zoroastrians, and 315,000 people of other religious orientations (Iran National Statistics Center, 2010). Although 90–95% of the country's population follows the Twelver School of Shia Islam, other religious orientations, including the four schools of Sunni Islam (Hanafi, Shafi'i, Hanbali, and Maliki), the Zaidi school of Shia Islam, Christianity, Judaism, and Zoroastrianism, are constitutionally legal and practiced throughout the country. The followers of these religious orientations also possess reserved seats in Iran's parliament.

Flag

Since 1980, there have been three colors in the Iranian flag: green, white, and red. Green symbolizes prosperity and Islam; white, peace and purity; and red, the country's defenders' (martyrs') blood. In the center of the white stripe sits the emblem of the Islamic Republic of Iran, a stylized Persian writing of the Arabic word *Allah* (God). Furthermore, in the margins of the red and green stripes, the Arabic phrase *Allahu* Akbar ("God is greater than can be described") is written 11 times in each panel and 22 times in total. This symbolizes the 22nd day of the 11th Iranian month (*Bahman*) in which the 1979 Iranian Islamic Revolution, led by Grand Ayatollah Rouhollah Khomeini, emerged victorious over the royal Pahlavi dynasty under Mohammad Reza Shah Pahlavi (known to Westerners as the "Shah of Iran").

History

Iran is an ancient country with over 5,000 years of civilization (Mojtahed-Zadeh, 2007). Civilization on the Iranian Plateau dates back to the Neolithic Era in the vicinity of the Zagros and Elborz mountains. Archeological explorations of the historical sites belonging to this era have uncovered crafts dating back to the 5th century BC.

The migration of Indo-Iranian (Aryan) people to the Iranian Plateau started in the 2nd century BC. Of course, before the arrival of Aryans to this area, there were other dwellers, mostly Caspian, who farmed in the fertile lands of Persia. From the three migrant ethnic groups, the Parthians resided in northeast, the Medes in the west, and the Persis (Persians) in the south. Subsequently, the Median Empire was formed. Around 128 years later, the Median Empire was overthrown and the Achaemenid Empire was founded by Cyrus the Great. This was the first Persian Empire, and it is known as the largest empire in ancient history. The present day historical sites of Persepolis and Pasargadae, which are also two main tourist attractions, are remains of that era. Around 220 years later, the Achaemenid Empire was ousted by Alexander the Great, and Persepolis was set on fire. After the death of Alexander the Great, Seleucus I Nicator founded the Seleucid Empire in Persia. About 310 years later, the Parts in the Northeast rose to power and founded the Parthian Empire, which lasted for 471 years. In 224 AD, the last Iranian empire before the rise of Islam, the Sasanian Empire, ruled over Persia for over 400 years. From the ancient history of Iran, in addition to Persepolis and Pasargadae, a dozen historical sites remain.

In the middle of the 7th century AD, the Muslim conquest of Persia led to the overthrow of the Sasanian Empire. This new era brought about fundamental changes in the social, political, religious, and governmental conditions of Iran. In Persia's multiethnic melting pot, the new rulers of Persia used Iran's bureaucratic system but rendered Islam and Arabic as the official religion and language, respectively. With the Umayyad and Abbasid caliphates in power, many national uprisings led to the dominance of other Central Asian ethnicities over Iran, such as Turkic Seljuq, Mughals, and Timurid. In this era, the Persian language and culture were adopted and practiced by the new rulers.

At the time of the Safavid dynasty, the second largest Iranian empire was founded. One of the most focal changes of this era was the conversion of Iranians to the now dominant Shia branch of Islam, holding the belief that, after the Prophet, the Islamic nation needs to refer to the son-in-law of the Prophet, Ali ibn Abi Talib, and his descendants as Imams—infallible religious leaders chosen by God. Although the two main sects of Islam (i.e., Sunni and Shia) have different interpretations of who should have followed the Prophet as the leaders of the religion, they have generally similar principles to observe, and the two communities practice their religious obligations freely in Iran today (PressTV Documentaries, 2014).

This basic account of Iranian history tends to suggest how the outlines of modern Iran were drawn. For a language teacher who wants to work with Iranian children, it is important to realize that they come from one of the oldest civilizations in the world that incorporates diverse ethnic, linguistic, and religious backgrounds.

CULTURE

National Traditions

Iran embraces several traditions rooted in centuries of civilization that grant the country her national and ethnic identity. Such traditions, rituals, and festivals, rooted in the country's multilayered ethnic, linguistic, and religious composition, have been brought about through decades of historical diversification. Three important national traditions and ceremonies held in modern day are *Yalda Night*, *Nowruz*, and *Muharram*.

Yalda Night

Yalda Night celebrates the advent of winter in the northern hemisphere. In the Syriac language, *"yalda"* means "birth," and here it refers to the birth of the sun. *Yalda Night* is the longest night of the year, when darkness dominates the earth, but the sun prevails and light triumphs over the darkness the next day. This natural occurrence gives the Iranians a time to celebrate. Although this tradition has gone through some historical changes, the essence has been kept and is celebrated by all Iranian ethnic groups. People keep vigil during this night, with family members and friends gathering together. Among the rituals of the night are making and eating trail mix, sweets, watermelon, pomegranates, and other fruits symbolizing prosperity, health, and happiness. Other special activities of the night include fortune-telling through choosing random verses in a collection of poems by the famous Persian poet Hafez Shirazi, storytelling (especially by grandparents), and playing music.

Nowruz

Nowruz (meaning "New Day") is the Iranian New Year. The Iranian New Year is celebrated on the first day of spring. This joyous time of year lasts for 13 days and is celebrated not only in Iran but also in other countries in the region and beyond. This holiday has also been recognized by the United Nations as the "International Day of Nowruz," inspiring other nations to observe the goodwill and peace it has spread (United Nations, 2010).

One of the joyful traditions of *Nowruz* is keeping a *Haft Seen* table for the first 13 days of spring. Literally meaning "seven 's'es," *Haft Seen* refers to the arrangement of seven fixed items starting with "s" on a tabletop specially designed for Nowruz. These seven items include *sabze* (wheat sprouts grown in a dish symbolizing rebirth and solidarity with nature), *samanu* (a sweet Iranian pudding symbolizing birth and wealth), *senjed* (dried silverberry, symbolizing love), *seer* (garlic, symbolizing medicine and health), *seeb* (apple, symbolizing health, love, and beauty), *somaq* (sumac fruit, symbolizing the color of sunrise, a new day), and *serkeh* (vinegar, symbolizing patience, old age, and affluence). In addition to these fixed items, people usually add other items to the table: holy books, for instance the Quran for Muslims or the Bible for Christians (for blessing), Persian poetry books, Hafez's *Diwan* and Ferdowsi's *Shahnameh*; a goldfish bowl (symbolizing light and life); a mirror (symbolizing light); candles (symbolizing light); painted boiled eggs (symbolizing birth and a colorful life); and *esfand* (wild rue, symbolizing purity and good omens), sweets, fruits, and nuts. Overall, in addition to the seven fixed items, people may place the items they like on the tabletop so as to have them blessed when the year changes. Traditionally, reading verses of holy books and/or poetry precedes the moment the New Year begins.

Muharram

Muharram is the first month of the Arab calendar. This month constitutes a period of mourning for Shia Muslims. In this month, Iranians mourn the martyrdom of the third Shia Imam, Hussain ibn Ali, the prophet's grandson, along with his companions and family members. The peak of mourning is the 9th (*Tasua*) and 10th (*Ashura*), when Hussain ibn Ali and his companions, 72 in number, were killed in the Battle of Karbala (680 AD), refusing to pledge allegiance to the then-ruler of the Muslim world, Yazid, whom they considered unjust.

In this month, especially on *Ashura* and *Tasua*, people across the country embark on several mourning traditions in harmonious combination: establishing mourning sites (*tekyeh*); composing elegiac poems (*marsiya*), laments (*noha*) and mournful martial music; performing passion plays (*ta'zieh*); marching in massive parades; self-flagellation (beating on the chest with hands as a sign of mourning, or the shoulders and backs using specially woven light metal chains) in harmonious choral practice; raising mourning banners; and distributing donations. Likewise, it is customary that people wear black shirts and/or trousers in mourning rituals.

Besides patriotism, the *Muharram* mourning tradition, with the motto "every day is *Ashura*; every place is Karbala," has given the nation a doctrine not to succumb to injustice. A case in point is resisting and thwarting the fierce military invasion of Iran by the former Iraqi regime in the 1980s, the 20th century's longest conventional war. The war did not lead to any border changes and was terminated with the acceptance of UN Resolution 598 in 1988.

Literature

Before Islam, Persian literature mostly included poems. The oral poems, handed down through decades, later formed parts of *Avesta*, the Zoroastrian collection of sacred texts. Of course, there are other texts in nonliterary genres such as history and the sciences that are now preserved as classics. In the Islamic era, Persian literature was influenced by Arab poetry; Persian poetry was known beyond the borders of the country. However, the epitome of Persian poetry and writing was in the Samanid Empire, when poets and writers such as Ferdowsi, Hafez, Nezami, and

Omar Khayam gained global fame. Great literary works by Persian poets such as Rumi have survived the passage of time, spreading the message of peace, love, and prosperity in the world as depicted in *Saadi*'s well-known poem inscribed at the United Nations:

> *The sons of Adam are limbs of each other,*
> *Having been created of one essence.*
> *When the calamity of time affects one limb,*
> *The other limbs cannot remain at rest.*
> *If you have no sympathy for the troubles of others,*
> *You are unworthy to be called by the name of a Human.* (Burton, 1928, p. ix)

Science and Technology

Persian scholars have played a significant role in laying out the foundation of most of today's sciences. Many of these advances were made during the Islamic era, when the country's official language was Arabic. Advances were made in mathematics, physics, astronomy, philosophy, geology, logic, psychology, chemistry, anthropology, theology, poetry, history, and medicine by such great scholars as Khwarizmi, the Persian mathematician, astronomer, and geographer (see the chapter on North Africa for more detail); Avicenna, a polymath; and Omar Khayyam, a seminal mathematician, astronomer, philosopher, and poet.

Modern-day Iran is considered to be a developing country, with many top universities. Likewise, Iranian students, both in Iran and abroad, have constantly startled the world by their achievements. For instance, in 2003, the administrators of Stanford University's Electrical Engineering Department reported being surprised when a group of Iranian students from Sharif University of Science and Technology excelled in the department's notoriously difficult exam, achieving some of the highest scores ever ("Surprising success of Iran's universities," 2008). Furthermore, Iran ranked 16th in the world scientific arena in 2015 (SJR, 2015), with some fields having a faster pace of development and progress. For instance, Iran's nanotechnology ranked 6th globally in 2016 (StatNano, 2016).

Arts

The Persian/ Iranian artistic heritage has historically been depicted in such influential forms as painting, pottery, weaving, enamel, mosaic, metalworking, ceramics, miniatures, calligraphy, sculpture, and music; each era is noted for the flourishing of its specific types of art. Nowadays, such forms attract art lovers worldwide.

EDUCATION

The Iranian educational system is divided into three separate but connected levels: primary, secondary, and tertiary. The first two levels, primary and secondary, form K–12 education and are supervised by the Ministry of Education. The tertiary level, on the other hand, forms higher education, which is supervised by the Ministry of Science, Research, and Technology. Education in Iran is considered public and, hence, free; however, there are also private and semiprivate institutes that some people prefer because of the higher quality of education they provide.

Elementary Education

Iranian students start kindergarten, or preprimary (*pish-dabestani*), at the age of 5. This grade is a one-year optional period preceding the mandatory primary level (*dabestan*), starting at the age of 6. Primary education lasts for 6 years, targeting eight educational goals: instructional, moral, religious, artistic, social, political and governmental, economic, and living. Therefore, the subjects taught at this level aim to develop students' general knowledge and skills to function properly in the society through development of language and cultural skills; knowledge of civilization through geography, history, sociology, and literature; instruction on hygiene, ethics, safety, social norms and laws; and knowledge of religion.

Secondary Education

Secondary education (*dabirestan*), spanning grades 6–12, covers two merged sublevels, with grades 6–8, lower-secondary (*rahnamaei*), being mandatory. This level, which is equivalent to the U.S. middle school, aims to guide students' talents and potential in the later selection of fields in upper secondary school. This level covers similar content area subjects plus foreign languages (English and Arabic) and technical as well as vocational skills.

At the upper-secondary level, which is equivalent to the U.S. high school, the students will choose their specialties based on their test scores and interests. There are three tracks: theoretical, technical-vocational, and work and knowledge. Under the theoretical branch, the students can choose from three fields: literature and humanities, empirical science, and physics and mathematics. The subjects taught at this level correspond to the students' chosen fields. Under the technical-vocational and work and knowledge tracks, the students will train to be skilled and semiskilled professionals entering directly into the work market in a variety of fields.

In addition, parallel to regular public and private schools dedicated to literacy practices, gifted education has its own system. The entrance to gifted schools is based on participation in a highly competitive nation-wide examination administered by the National Organization for Development of Exceptional Talents (NODET), which is also a branch of the Ministry of Education. These schools admit applicants at the secondary level.

LANGUAGE

Because Iran is a large country with many ethnic groups, more than 75 languages and dialects are spoken, among which Farsi (*Parsi*), Turkish, Kurdish, Turkmen, Gilaki, Mazanderani, and Khalaj are the most notable based on the number of speakers. However, based on the Iranian constitution, the official language and writing system of Iran is Farsi. Although formal education is in Farsi, using and teaching ethnic languages are constitutionally legal.

Farsi is considered a classical language, one with an ancient history and a rich literature (Katzner, 2002). In addition to Iran, it is the official language of Afghanistan (referred to as Dari Persian) and Tajikistan (referred to as Tajik Persian), and it is spoken in other Persianate societies—those influenced by Persian language, culture, art, and identity (Arjomand, 2008). Farsi is classified as a Western Iranian language within the Indo-Iranian branch of the Indo-European language family. Due to geopolitical changes in the region throughout different historical eras, as well as the mixed ethnic composition of Iran, Persian has many loanwords from different languages, including Arabic, Turkish, and Kurdish.

Persian Alphabet

Since the 9th century of the current era, the Persian alphabet, which is a writing system based on Arabic script (see other chapters in this section for more details), has been used to write Farsi. However, the writing system includes four more letters compared to the Arabic alphabet [پ = p], [چ = tʃ], [ژ = ʒ], and [گ = g], and it does not quite read like Arabic, as the two languages belong to different language families. Furthermore, there are morphemes in the written language that have only one corresponding phoneme in Farsi. For instance, the sound /s/ has three corresponding morphemes [س], [ص], and [ث]. These incongruities arise from the imposition of the Arabic script on Parsi (even the lack of the sound /p/ in Arabic changed *P*arsi to *F*arsi) during the rule of Islamic Arab conquerors over Persia. There have been calls to change the writing system to a new optimal form; however, as there is a fear of disconnecting from the historical, the system with Arabic letters is still practiced.

A FEEL FOR IRAN

Although Iran is a diverse land and people from each ethnic background may have some unique traditions and customs, there are some principles that are shared by almost all. Similarly, there are some issues that are considered normal in Iran but may be different overseas. The following briefly explains some typical Iranian cultural aspects.

Hospitality

Generally, Iranians are hospitable people. They love receiving guests and do their best to make sure they have a good time. This might range from preparing different colorful and tasty Iranian dishes to insisting on them staying overnight, which is sometimes hard to decline unless you make it clear that you definitely need to go back home.

Ta'arof (Politeness)

This is considered an Iranian system of valuing others' wants and likes in a polite way, by either assigning humbleness to their own actions or praising another's. Of course, this is done in a reciprocally professional way that both parties in the conversation are aware of. There are some automatic expressions that cannot be translated into English literally but are exchanged just to help create an intimate atmosphere between people. For instance, when somebody does something invaluable, they know they have done so, and they are praised for that deed, they may say "I've done nothing" as a way to show modesty, or they may assign the praise to God and say, "God empowered me to do it." Another example of *ta'arof* is when someone is invited to a party and offered a host of different dishes nonstop. When the guest seems not to be able to continue eating, the host will automatically say, "Oh, don't practice *ta'arof* (that is, being polite), eat something; you haven't eaten anything." In that case, the guest will either need to continue and risk overeating or just tell the host that it is impossible to go on. Of course, being frank can be appreciated when it comes to daily conversations, but being polite may also maintain rapport with others. The system of *ta'arof* requires some practical experience to master.

Family

Iranians are generally very family oriented. The parents try to provide the children, as they do anywhere else, with the best available opportunities. Family support is particularly evidenced at major social undertakings: making friends, finding a job, and getting married. It is usually the case that children do not leave home unless they marry, are admitted to a university, or find a job in a different city.

Respect for Parents and Elders

Iranians generally feel indebted to their parents and consider it part of their moral responsibility to listen to their advice and attend to their needs in old age. Accordingly, most families look after their aging parents instead of placing them in a retirement home. This can extend to nonfamilial elders, too. Iranians usually address senior citizens as "Mother" or "Father," and they are prepared to carry their shopping bags or give them their seats in a crowded bus or metro.

Islamic Regulations

Iranian life is informed by Islam in two ways. First, Islam is the country's official religion, requiring people to observe certain Islamic rules in public dress and interactions. Accordingly, both men and women must abstain from dressing in an immodest way. As for food and drinks, Iran has almost everything except alcoholic drinks and pork.

Second, as Islam, like other religions, encourages peace, beauty, wisdom, and goodness, it is generally advised that people's lives reflect Islamic teachings. Iranians living in the U.S., however, may not observe the *hijab* (women's head-covering) rule, either because of practicing faiths other than Islam or believing that the *hijab* was for the security of women and not required overseas. Of course, many Iranian Muslim women living overseas still willingly observe *hijab*.

Socialization

When it comes to greetings in public, there are certain things to know when meeting an Iranian for the first time. The first meeting is usually considered a formal one, where the Iranian party usually dresses formally and addresses you by your title and last name out of respect. Second, as in Western countries, men shake hands with men, but, contrary to the norms in Western countries, men usually kiss on the cheeks and hug each other. Although an Iranian in the U.S. will probably not do the same when meeting a non-Iranian for the first time, if it happens, Americans should understand it as the norm in Iran and not be upset. Likewise, Iranian women usually do the same for women, that is, they shake hands, kiss on the cheeks, and hug. However, men and women usually do not do the same when meeting people of the opposite gender. Although this is the normal procedure, people interacting with Iranians can experience otherwise because Iran is so diverse in religious and cultural backgrounds.

When it comes to parties, Iranians usually go out of their way to make sure the guest has a good time. To begin with, when entering an Iranian's house, it is customary to take off shoes at the door unless the host is wearing shoes. As with other aspects of Iranian culture, Iranian cuisine is a conglomerate of different ethnic dishes, which are usually tasty and colorful. The food is usually served either on the floor on a beautiful tablecloth with people sitting around it or on a table. Unlike some cultures in the area, Iranians generally use spoons and forks unless they are having a special dish requiring a certain way of eating or dining among an ethnic community practicing different local norms.

Learning Skills to Achieve Individual Success

Iranians work hard at acquiring multiple skills and talents, including learning how to fix things, developing artistic and musical talents, speaking foreign languages, and gaining high-tech skills. There are two basic reasons for this. First, it is usually the family's obligation and expectation to raise a fully developed child, while the children are usually prepared to do their best. Therefore, the instruction phase usually starts from a young age when the children go to different classes parallel to their regular schooling or during summer breaks. Second, these skills are required to compete in a multiskilled society. In general, Iranians are considered individual achievers; that is, they may tend not to participate as willingly in teamwork activities (Javidan & Dastmalchian, 2003; Nejati, Nejati, & Nami, 2010). However, they can also be successful group members.

Living in the United States

Homesickness may cause Iranians in the United States to delve into Persian literature, watch Iranian TV channels, follow Iran-related news, and call home regularly. There is much to see and experience in the United

States, and once children begin to explore the new culture with support from parents and teachers, they can overcome their culture shock. However, Iranians do not generally have a hard time adapting to new cultures. Although the process of acculturation and adaptation comes at some obvious costs, such as possible depression, isolation, and homesickness, the diversity of the new culture can allow for the immigrants' smooth integration.

IDEAS FOR EDUCATORS

Language plays a very important role in the process of integration. As was stated in the opening scenario about Maryam, failure to interact effectively with the peer group partly resulted in her isolation from the society, leading her towards using virtual forms of communication and engagement. Likewise, parents with limited language proficiency may find it hard to integrate into the new culture. Accordingly, English teachers are advised to be aware of the hard time immigrant families on the whole, and students in particular, experience in positioning themselves within the new community. For example, when a Persian student stands up from his seat every time the teacher walks into the classroom, the teacher needs to be aware that the student is being polite, and this simple cultural mismatch may isolate him if not properly addressed. Similarly, Iranian students may be perceived as silent listeners in a typical class in the United States; however, if such a case happens, it could be due to the students being polite, as they respect teachers and do not interrupt them unless they are addressed. For Iranians, teachers are highly respected; therefore, they believe they need to listen carefully to teachers and follow their examples. Likewise, the use of titles for teachers in the Iranian culture is the norm, so it may take a while for a student to adapt to the fact that such a level of formality is often not required in the United States.

CONCLUSIONS

Although the governments of Iran and the U.S. do not always agree, there is much that the people can learn from each other and that they share. Observing even small but important aspects of culture can help U.S. teachers to create an equitable teaching and learning environment for all students.

ACKNOWLEDGMENTS

I would like to thank my friends and colleagues, Kourosh Amirkhani, Ali Talaeizadeh, and Muhammad Jahanshaiyan, who kindly provided me with invaluable feedback on an earlier version of this chapter.

ADDITIONAL RESOURCES

Ministry of Culture and Islamic Guidance. (2016). Retrieved from http://www.far-hang.gov.ir/en/home

> This is the official website of Iran's ministry of culture.

Islamic Republic of Iran: Ministry of Science, Research, and Technology. (2016). Retrieved from http://en.msrt.ir/en

> This is the official website of Iran's ministry of science, research, and technology, which supervises higher education.

Ministry of Education. (2016). Retrieved from http://www.medu.ir/portal/home.php?ocode=100010876

> This is the official portal of Iran's ministry of education, which supervises K–12 education.

Iranian Institute of Anthropology and Culture. (2016). Retrieved from from http:// anthropology.ir/

> A rich collection of articles on a wide range of Iranian cultural topics, including humanities, sociology, politics, economics, art, literature, architecture, history, and so on.

Iran Chamber Society. (2016). Available from http://www.iranchamber.com/

> A rich collection of articles on Iran's history, culture, language, art, and heritage.

Richard Frye Organization. (2016). *Richard N. Frye.* Retrieved from http://rich-ardfrye.org/

> The website of the late Dr. Richard Nelson Frye, who spent over six decades researching and teaching the cultural and ancient history of Iran, Central Asia, and the Near East.

REFERENCES

Arjomand, S. A. (2008). From the editor: Defining Persianate studies. *Journal of Persianate Studies, 1*(1), 1–4.

Avery, P. W., Afray, J., & Mostofi, K. (2016). Iran. *Encyclopedia Britannica online.* Retrieved from https://www.britannica.com/place/Iran

Burton, R. S. (1928). *Tales from the Gulistan* or rose garden of the Sheikh *Sa'di* of Shiraz. London, England: Philip Allan & Co.

Iran National Statistics Center. (2010). *Census 2011.* Retrieved from http://iran.unfpa.org/Documents/Census2011/census-90-results(3).pdf

Javidan, M., & Dastmalchian, A. (2003). Culture and leadership in Iran: The land of individual achievers, strong family ties, and powerful elite. *The Academy of Management Executive, 17*(4), 127–142.

Katzner, K. (2002). *The languages of the world.* London, England: Routledge.

Lukinbeal, C., & Craine, J. (2009). Geographic media literacy: An introduction. *GeoJournal, 74*(3), 175–182.

Marandi. (2016, January 1). The only thing Washington has not blamed Iran for is global warming. *Russia Times.* Retrieved from https://www.rt.com/op-edge/327666-iran-washington-global-sanctions/

Mojtahed-Zadeh, P. (2007). Iran: An old civilization and a new nation state. *FOCU.S. on Geography, 49*(4), 20–32.

Nejati, M., Nejati, M., & Nami, B. (2010). Teamwork approach: An investigation on Iranian teamwork attitudes (Approche de travail d'équipe: Une enquête sur les attitudes de travail d'équipe iraniennes). *Canadian Social Science, 6*(3), 104.

PressTV Documentaries. (2014, December 20). *Sunnis in Iran (How Sunni Muslims live in a Shiite country?)* [Video File]. Retrieved from https://www.youtube.com/watch?v=3B6MGqWkpMk

SCImago Journal Rank. (2015). SJR—International Science Ranking. Retrieved from http://www.scimagojr.com/countryrank.php?year=2015

StatNano. (2016). *Nano statistics: Report: ISI indexed nano-articles*. Retrieved from http://statnano.com/report/r60

Surprising success of Iran's universities. (2008, August 8). *Newsweek*. Retrieved from http://www.newsweek.com/surprising-success-irans-universities-87853

United Nations. (2010). *International Day of Nowruz, 21 March*. Retrieved from http://www.un.org/en/events/nowruzday/

SECTION 3

NORTH/CENTRAL AMERICAN REGION

CHAPTER 5

MÉXICO

María Isabel Morales
The Evergreen State College

Brenda L. Barrio
Washington State University

Oscar is a sixth grader in Mrs. Schmidt's math class. Although he is a well-behaved student, at times Oscar seems distracted and unengaged even though math is his favorite subject. The first day of math class, Mrs. Schmidt placed Oscar in the remedial level because she believed it would be more useful for him, as she understood English to be Oscar's second language. While Mrs. Schmidt knows that Oscar loves and understands math well, she believes his disconnect is due both to his lack of English skills and to what she sees as a lack of engagement from his parents. She has sent many letters home requesting parent meetings and has received no response. To give him a community of support, Mrs. Schmidt constantly groups Oscar with three other Hispanic students in the class that she knows speak Spanish. What Mrs. Schmidt is not aware of is that Spanish is not Oscar's first language; Oscar's family speaks Mixtec—an indigenous language from Oaxaca, México. His parents speak no English and very little Spanish, and they depend on Oscar and his sister Yuli to translate between the languages. Unlike Mrs. Schmidt's belief that they do not care about their children's education, Oscar's parents use their own stories of struggle to teach their children lessons of the importance of education. Oscar is very aware of his parents' challenges living as underrepresented indigenous people in Mexico, their ordeal to cross the border, and now their struggles as agricultural workers in the U.S. He is determined to finish school and attend a university to fulfill his dream of being a medical doctor, but his placement in remedial math could be a roadblock on the way to this dream.

Views From Inside: Languages, Cultures, and Schooling for K–12 Educators
pp. 77–98
Copyright © 2018 by Information Age Publishing

77

BACKGROUND

Mexican people are perhaps one of the most misconstrued communities in the United States. The relationship between these two bordering nations is long and complicated and has resulted in a diverse range of lived experiences and identities for communities of Mexican descent. From generational differences to language fluency, the experience of Mexican American students in the United States is anything but homogenous. To understand this diversity of experiences, it is important to begin with recognizing Mexico as a nation of diverse cultures, languages, and ethnicities. Like many colonized Latin American countries, Mexico is indigenous land and home to communities like Oscar's *Mixteco* family from the state of Oaxaca. The immigration experience is part of the reality of many students like Oscar, but not all Mexican American people residing in the United State are "new" immigrants. In fact, many citizens have been part of the U.S cultural, political, and social fabric for generations.

This chapter seeks to illuminate the diversity and complexity of Mexican American student experiences with an illustration of major historical events, culture, and traditions. We hope that after reading this chapter, teachers have a more holistic understanding of how to support students from Mexican American families. We draw from a framework that recognizes Mexican American student stories and experiences as funds of knowledge (Moll & Gonzalez, 2004) that educators like Mrs. Schmidt can draw from for culturally relevant teaching that gives Mexican American students "a more positive frame of reference for success in the public education system" (Godina, 2003, p. 142). This is an important step towards the reduction of the opportunity gap (Contreras & Stritikus, 2008) between Mexican American children and their White counterparts. According to Contreras and Stritikus (2008), Mexican students in the U.S. have the lowest educational attainment compared to other Latina/o subgroups, as well as the lowest high school completion rates, at 26.7% (Kiyama, 2010). The latter is a crucial point, considering that Mexican immigrants constitute about 65% of the Latina/o population (Brown & López, 2013; Suarez-Orozco & Paéz, 2002). For these reasons, it is pivotal that researchers and practitioners move towards more culturally responsive curricula that honor student backgrounds, experiences, and cultures and that hold educational systems accountable for doing the same.

Furthermore, there is urgency to build bridges of understanding and solidarity with Mexican American communities as a result of the growing anti-Latina/o sentiments and xenophobia disseminated in political debates, social media, and the news. While many of the arguments in the political sector are full of historical, cultural, and political inaccuracies (i.e., negative attitudes towards Mexican people [see Hee Lee, 2015]), they have incidentally shed light on the prevalence of xenophobia and racism in society's understandings (or lack of) of Latina/o people in the United States, particularly of Mexican American people. This chapter urges teachers to understand and dismantle dehumanizing stereotypes and erroneous beliefs of Latina/o people—specifically Mexican communities, because these "anti-immigrant ideologies" enter our classroom spaces and affect children's educations (Catalano, 2013) and relationships to schooling.

IDENTITY AND TERMINOLOGY

To begin, it is important to understand the various identity terms—the "standardized terminology" (Gimenez, 1997)—that are often used. When referring to people south of the U.S./Mexican border, common terms used are: Hispanic, Latina/o, Chicana/o, Mexican, or Mexican American. Hispanic, a term coined and imposed in the 1970s by President Nixon, describes all people of Spanish-speaking descent (González & Gándara, 2005), including people from Spain. Iglesias and Valdez (1998) problematize "Hispanic" as a noninclusive Eurocentric term that fails to acknowledge the African and indigenous roots of peoples in Latin America. In México, for example, many communities like Oscar's family self-identify as indigenous and speak an indigenous language as a first language. The term "Hispanic" also fails to recognize Latin American countries that do not hold Spanish as their main language, such as Brazil. Although this is the case, many Mexican Americans prefer to use the term Hispanic for self-identification.

Latina or Latino (or Latina/o), on the other hand, tends to be more widely used in scholarship and accepted by communities (this varies by region). It is an umbrella term used to describe all people of Latin America. While the term is seen as more inclusive than "Hispanic" at acknowledging non-European ancestry, the umbrella term marginalizes the diverse experiences of communities who become a monolithic group under this label. For example, both Cubans and Mexicans are considered "Latina/os," but they have very different historical trajectories and experiences in the United States. Thus, it is important that educators are cognizant of the different identity labels and the ways such umbrella labels may marginalize particular experiences. When working with Mexican American students, we invite teachers to begin by asking students what they are more comfortable with (self-identification is critical). If teachers have Latina/o students from different countries/regions, teachers need to be aware that their experiences cannot be described by one identity label (whether it be Latino/a or Hispanic). In this chapter, we use Mexican American and will use "Latina/o" or "Hispanic" only when citing specific research.

Furthermore, many communities from Mexican American backgrounds prefer to self-identify as Chicana/o. This identity is both a political identity with ties to the Chicano civil rights movement(s) (Acuña, 2011) and a term historically used to describe U.S.-born descendants of Mexican communities. Other important terms to understand are "immigrant children" and "children of immigrants." The former strictly refers to foreign-born children who migrated to the U.S and the latter refers to both U.S-born (second-generation) students and foreign-born children (Suárez-Orozco & Suárez-Orozco, 2001, p. 1).

Although it cannot be assumed that all Mexican American students are immigrants, immigration is a part of the experience of many students in our classrooms. In fact, 20% of the student population in school districts nationwide are children of immigrants (Fix & Passel, 2003). While it is beyond the scope of this chapter to fully examine the complexity of immigration, including the pull and push factors that lead families like Oscar's to immigrate to the United States (and which subsequently affect their relationship to/in school), it is important to name parts of the unique experiences of children of immigrants in schools. For example, acculturation and shifts in identity are woven throughout the generations, and studies expound a significant correlation between acculturation and achievement in school. Suárez-Orozco and Suárez-Orozco (2001) explain that "for many immigrant groups, length of residency in the United States is associated with declining health, school achievement, and aspirations" (p. 4). Compared to recent immigrants, second-generation children of immigrants and later generations have poor achievement in schools and have a higher dropout rate or "push out rate" as Valenzuela (1996) describes. This research is important for teachers to understand because it begs the question: What is happening to children that is leading to decreases in motivation and achievement in schools?

Unlike deficit theories that blame students' academic struggles on their culture (Valencia, 2010; Valencia & Black, 2002), research suggests that poor student achievement is highly affected by schooling and structural barriers and is not a cultural "deficit." For example, a study conducted with Mexican immigrant students in California (Suárez-Orozco & Suárez-Orozco, 2001) indicated that Latina/o adolescents in the United States were highly motivated, but their expectations for success were negatively affected by experiences of societal hostility and discrimination as well as a lack of cultural responsiveness from schools and teachers.

Another aspect of immigration that is important to note is that of being undocumented, or unauthorized. While not all Mexican students are undocumented as common stereotypes portray, according to the Pew Research Center (2015) about 7% of K–12 Mexican American students have at least one parent who is undocumented. Among these students, close to 80% are U.S. citizens, which means that many U.S. citizen children live in a "mixed status family," where some members are documented and others are not (Brabeck & Xu, 2010). Moreover, about 1.4% of the K–12 student population is also undocumented. Therefore, it is important that teachers are aware that an unclear legal status may be a fact of their students' lived experiences and one that might have an effect on their engagement (or lack of) in school. According to Brabeck and Xu (2010), the fear of detention and deportation has a significant effect on children's emotional wellbeing and academic performance.

Brief History of Mexico

The first evidence of humans in Mexico was around 12,000 B.C. when the Tepexpan man, an early human, resided in its territory (Michael, Meyer, & Beezley, 2000). Agriculture was established around 9000 B.C., and the domestication of corn began. Corn was essential to the development of indigenous peoples in Mesoamerica. Around 7000 B.C. people began establishing communities and becoming sedentary. Cultures and civilizations such as the Olmec, Maya, and Aztec flourished around 2000 B.C., creating artwork, architecture, writings, and calendars (see Figure 5.1 for an example of a complex Mogollon culture site in Northern Mexico). Mesoamerica consisted of a major part of what Mexico is today.

Source: Photo taken by Brenda L. Barrio.

Figure 5.1. Paquime archaeological zone, Casas Grandes, Chihuahua.

The Aztec Empire fell to the Spanish in 1521, two years after their takeover of Tenochtitlan (the capital of the Aztec Empire). For the next 300 years, Spain exploited Indian and African labor to accumulate wealth (Acuña, 2011) in *New Spain,* the name given to the territory by Charles (Carlos) the 5th, King of Spain. With this proclamation, he established his rule and governance over the land and its people. It was not until September 16, 1810 that Mexico's people declared a war of independence in the city of San Miguel de Allende, in the state of modern day Guanajuato. The war of independence lasted over 11 years until in 1821, Iturbide (a Mexican army general and politician) and the popular military took over Mexico City and the country.

The years 1846 through 1848 marked a pivotal part of Mexico's history as Antonio Lopez de Santa Ana led the famous Mexican American War between Mexico and the United States—a war that many Mexican people call *"La intervención Norteamericana"* (North American intervention) (Ryal Miller, 2006). The Treaty of Guadalupe Hidalgo, signed in 1848, ended the Mexican American War and forced Mexico to cede 55% of its territory to the U.S. (i.e., present-day Arizona, California, New Mexico, and parts of Colorado, Nevada and Utah) (Acuña, 2011).

In 1858, Benito Juarez became the first president of Mexico from an indigenous background. Although he was a prodemocratic president, a three-year war with Spain, Great Britain, and later the French destroyed all of his efforts, and an empire was again declared by the French monarch Maximiliano de Habsburgo from 1864–1867. In 1884, Porfirio Diaz took control of the country with a dictatorship that lasted three and a half decades. In 1910, the *Revolucion* Mexicana (Mexican Revolution) broke out and President Diaz was taken down by efforts led by well-known revolutionaries such as Pancho Villa and Emiliano Zapata. Emiliano Zapata, an indigenous *campesino* (peasant), continues to be an iconic symbol of cultural identity and resistance for Mexicans. The revolutionary war lasted until 1920, when a prodemocratic government was established that continues until today.

Mexican American History

While over half of Mexican Americans in the United States were born in Mexico and the group continues to grow, the label includes a large number of people whose American roots go back many generations (Gómez, 2007). Important historical events have shaped the unique relationship between these two neighboring nations and their people in society and schools. Unlike common misconceptions often state, Mexican people are not a "new" group of recent immigrants (Gómez, 2007); Mexican Americans have been a significant part of U.S society since the late 18th century. In fact, over 115,000 Mexican Americans joined the United States nation "involuntarily, not as immigrants, but as people conquered in war" (Gómez, 2007, p. 2).

Many Americans of Mexican background and culture are the descendants of the early Mexicans whose lands were conquered during the Mexican American War of 1848. Thus, when working with these communities, it is important to consider generational differences. For example, a third- or fourth-generation Mexican American may or may not speak Spanish or have connections with family or communities in México. In fact, many of these generations may self-identify as Chicana or Chicano instead of Mexican American (for a more detailed history of Chicana/os in the U.S, see Acuña, 2010). It cannot be assumed that students who self-identify as Chicana/o speak Spanish or are connected with Mexican culture.

Other important generational differences are those between 1st and 2nd generation Mexican Americans. First generation are immigrants that came to the United States as adults, while the term "1.5 Generation" is used to describe children that left México at a young age and were brought up in American society—in other words, they were *made* in Mexico but were raised in the U.S. (Rumbaut, 2004). These experiences are different than their counterparts born and schooled in Mexico, or those born in the U.S. (Gonzales, 2010; Rumbaut, 2004); they have characteristics of both first- and second-generation immigrants (Rumbaut & Ima, 1988). Unlike students who have lived or been schooled in Mexico, the 1.5 Generation students may not have memories of living there. They might have limited to no proficiency in the Spanish language. This generation's experiences that support their senses of identity and belonging might be split between Mexico and the United States. Another term used to describe this generation of immigrant students (but more specifically undocumented immigrant students) is *Dreamers*—a term that comes from the U.S.'s proposed D.R.E.A.M. Act (Development, Relief, and Education for Alien Minors).

Along with the history of colonization of Mexican lands and subsequent involuntary immigration, the Mexican American experience is also marked by voluntary immigration and migration within U.S. borders for employment. According to a Farmworker Justice report (2015), there are close to 2.5 million farmworkers in the United States, out of which 76% identify as Hispanic or Latino. Migrant and seasonal farmworkers are an important part of U.S. history, economy, and culture. Activists like Dolores Huerta and Cesar Chávez were and continue to be leaders in the struggles for social, economic, and political justice for the millions of farmworkers in the country.

Mexican American people have been affected by political and economic pull and push factors. For example, the labor shortages during World War I and World War II led to guest worker programs that attracted thousands of Mexican nationals for labor (i.e., the Bracero Program in 1942). After the need for labor ended, mass deportations sent millions back to Mexico—including the many U.S. citizens who were sent back during Eisenhower's Operation Wetback in 1954. The term "wetback" is a derogatory term that makes reference to the crossing of the border by swimming through the Rio Grande. It assumes that all Mexican people crossed the border illegally.

In 1994, the controversial North America Free Trade Agreement (NAFTA) was signed between Canada, the United States, and Mexico, devastating the livelihoods of many poor rural communities in Mexico—an event that contributed to an increase in immigration to the U.S. (Varsanyi, 2008). NAFTA also increased migration (especially of women) from central and southern Mexico to the border towns to work in U.S.-owned *maquiladoras,* modern-day sweatshops. Although migration from Mexico has slowed significantly in recent years (Passel & Cohn, 2012), the history and complexity of pull and push factors are important to be aware of in order to fully understand the lived experiences of Mexican American children in U.S. classrooms.

CULTURE

People

The people in Mexico are rich in culture, traditions, and deep roots from their ancestors (Arizpe, 2011; INEGI, 2004). Their everyday lives are based on their cultural and historical backgrounds. Its people pride themselves on their modernization and technological advances while at the same time retaining their historical cultural traditions in ancestral lands. Contrary to what Hollywood or other media in the U.S. depict people of Mexico to look like, there is rich diversity in culture, traditions, mixture of ethnic backgrounds, and even the latest fashions.

After being colonized by the Spanish, the *mestizaje,* or mixing of races, created what is now a wide range of ethnic and cultural backgrounds (Arizpe, 2011), a mix of Europeans, Natives, Africans, and people from other parts of the world. In the north of Mexico, European descendants (e.g., German, Spanish, and Dutch communities) are more prominent than in the south, where there is a larger native Mayan or Nahuan community. In the west, Asian backgrounds, such as Chinese, are observed in large communities. Finally, in the eastern part of the country, a large French and Spanish influence continues to be felt.

Indigenous Peoples

Over 60 indigenous languages are still spoken in Mexico (Navarrete Linares, 2010). Indigenous people in Mexico mostly speak Nahuatl (2.4 million), Maya (1.475 million), Zapoteco (777,000), and Mixteco (726,000). A total of more than 10 million people are considered to be indigenous and speak their native languages (INEGI, 2000; Navarrete Linares, 2010). It is important to understand that Mexico continues to have many indigenous communities because students like Oscar have yet another level of cultural diversity that shapes their experiences in school. For example, indigenous people in Mexico continue to live in close communities, speaking the same language, and sharing similar thoughts, ideologies, and customs (Navarrete Linares, 2010). Along with their specific cultural traditions and values, indigenous people face issues like extreme poverty and discrimination in Mexico as they continue to be oppressed in the country. In fact, many indigenous communities lack the basic needs to live, such as clean running water, housing, accessible food, and education. This discrimination against indigenous peoples (and Black Mexican people as well) is an example of internalized racism that began during the colonial times in Mexico.

Race and Ethnicity as Discussion Topic

Although people in Mexico are as mixed in races and ethnicities as people in the U.S., ethnicity and race are not discussed in the same way in Mexico as in the U.S. The exception is for rights of the indigenous peoples, who to this day continue to be underrepresented and underserved in every aspect of society (e.g., education, politics, economy). Instead, Mexico's society focuses more on the separation of its people by their income level. The disparity among socioeconomic classes is often larger than those in the U.S., making it very difficult for people in poverty to have similar opportunities to those with higher socioeconomic status.

Family Structure

The structure of the family continues to change in Mexico, but for the majority of the population, the traditional family is large and is made up of the father, mother, and children, with input from grandparents, aunts, uncles, cousins, and other relatives (CDC, 2008). Although *machismo*, or patriarchy, is not as prominent as it used to be, many households in Mexico still rely on the male figure to be the breadwinner. Although this is the case, in Mexican society the mother figure typically has the most power when it comes to decision making in the household. In the end, the entire family provides input in the decision-making process.

Identity

The identity of people from Mexico is as unique as other cultures/ nations. Whether they remain in the country or move to another to seek better opportunities, they continue to have and show their rich values, traditions, and customs that are part of their Mexican roots. For example, immigrant communities in the United States often live in small enclaves where they create Spanish radio, TV, and community organizations to maintain their cultural traditions. Both in Mexico and the United States, the state/region is an important part of the way people identify. Often times, rather than saying "I'm Mexican," people will say "I'm *Michoacana/o*" (from the state of Michoacan).

States and Regions

Mexico is composed of 31 states and one federal district, Mexico City, similar to what Washington, DC is for the United States. Mexico's landscape is especially unique, with deserts, mountains, tropical forests, jungles, and more. Mexico is considered the 4th most biodiverse country in the world (Arizpe, 2011). The northern part of Mexico is dry and warm. Central and southern Mexico are wet but sunny and a bit more humid. Because of the differences in landscape and climate, each region has different strengths. For example, the south is known for its fruit production because of its tropical landscape. The north is known for its cattle and agriculture. The central part of the country is rich in lumber, and the east and west have abundant seafood and oil.

Educational Systems and Practices

The constitution of Mexico states that every child has the right to a free basic education (i.e., preschool–9th) and most recently, to secondary education (i.e., grades 10-12) (Secretaría de Educación Pública, 2014). In addition, public universities are often very accessible for most of the population as their costs are very low (e.g., $200 U.S. for a year) or free with scholarships from the government. The educational system in Mexico varies depending on the setting. For example, in urban settings there is a wide range of options for students, with federal (10.1%) and state (71.1%) public schools, autonomous schools supported by universities (5.3%), as well as the option for private secular, international, or nonsecular schools

(13.5%; Secretaría de Educación Pública, 2014). In contrast, rural areas have a more limited range of educational options, with federal and state public schools as often the only choices. As typical in the U.S. and around the world, urban schools have more resources than those in rural areas, in which poverty levels are higher than the norm. The lack of educational opportunities in many high-poverty areas, along with the lack of economic growth, is often a reason why people immigrate to the U.S. and other areas of Mexico.

One important aspect of the educational system in Mexico is that teachers are often seen as the educational experts; therefore, they make most of the decisions regarding children's schooling. Parents of students in Mexico believe that the experts should make the decisions. Therefore, it is important for teachers in the U.S. to understand that the possible disconnect between parents and schools is not because they do not care, but rather because they respect teachers as the experts and let them make the decisions regarding their students. A solution is to ask the parents for their input and make them feel comfortable getting involved.

In addition, the collectivistic value system in the Mexican family can conflict with the individualistic values in the U.S. educational system and society, and they can often be a source of stress for students (Greenfield & Quiroz, 2013). For example, students from Mexico or of Mexican ancestry may be more inclined to excel in group work rather than independent or individual work.

Traditions and Customs

Mexico and its people continue traditions and customs from centuries ago. From their native ancestors to the mixture of migrant communities, the traditions and customs are important in their everyday lives.

Food is often at the center of every gathering and it is as traditional and modern as the Mexican culture (see Figure 5.2 for examples of spices). Traditional dishes such as *mole*, *chiles rellenos*, and *pozole* have been staples in Mexican cuisine for centuries (Dragonné & Méndez, 2011) thanks to the rich number of local spices and ingredients. Depending on the region, food can vary, including "specialty" foods such as chocolate-covered *chapulines* (grasshoppers).

Music in Mexico is a national and international tradition. From the well-known Mariachi to Banda and Cumbia, music can be a strong connection to their homeland for many Mexican immigrants around the world. Just as the food in Mexico does, music has strong indigenous, European, and African influences.

Clothing can come in different forms and shapes. From the latest fashions in the U.S. and Europe to more traditional clothing from indigenous

Source: Photo taken by Brenda L. Barrio.

Figure 5.2.   Rich local spices.

or ancestral communities, people in Mexico for the most part dress like other Western societies. The traditional clothing is often used for celebrations, festivals, or historical reenactments.

Values

The core values of people from Mexico are based on its collectivist society as well as the importance of hard work and honesty in their everyday lives (De las Heras Aguilera, 2009; Figueroa Rodriguez, Figueroa Sandoval, Figueroa Rodriguez, & Hernandez Rosas, 2012). Although some values continue to change with new generations, the core values continue to hold strong. Some of these core values include:

- Mexico's society is collectivist in nature; therefore, family is a priority in most households.
- Respect, hospitality, and generosity are central to its people and communities.
- Honesty and sincerity are key in everyday life.
- Hard work is a value as important as family is to the people of Mexico.
- Solidarity is their motto.

- Passion is at the core of everything they do.
- Religion continues to be important and their lives follow Catholic teachings.

Unacceptable Behaviors in Mexico

Just as in many other collectivist societies, some unacceptable behaviors are related to people. For example:

- Calling an adult by their first name without knowing them. Out of respect, use Mr. or Ms./Mrs. and their last name. Be careful though, when using Mrs., as you cannot assume all women are married.
- Rushing or cutting meetings, lunches, or visits short. These behaviors are often seen as rude or as if the person is not enjoying the company. To approach this in a culturally responsive manner, teachers could inform parents of the time limit in advance. For example, when scheduling a parent–teacher conference, teachers can let the parents know their time is only 30 minutes, for example from 3:00 p.m. to 3:30 p.m., because other parents are visiting next.
- Punctuality is not expected; therefore, try to be flexible with your timing. Following the example above where you schedule a 30-minute conference, teachers can allow themselves to see the next set of parents at 3:40, rather than right at 3:30. This way, it gives everyone more flexibility in the time and teachers can avoid misinterpretations of behaviors.
- Avoid discussing topics such as politics, immigration, the Mexican American War, or comparisons between the U.S. and Mexico in negative ways. Most recently, avoid discussing issues of violence, criminal activity, and safety in the country.
- Eye contact can be a sign of challenge in certain communities (CDC, 2008); therefore, if a parent or student does not look straight into your eyes, do not see it as a sign of disrespect.

Impact of Religion on Culture

About 89% of the population in Mexico still identifies itself as Catholic, although a number of people are recently identifying themselves as Protestants (6%) (CDC, 2009). A small portion of the population also practices other religions such as Judaism, Islam, and Buddhism. In Mexico, religion is at the center of families and communities and their everyday lives. Often, these religious beliefs can be combined with indigenous spiritual beliefs from centuries ago when it comes to topics such as healing and illness. For example, many communities continue to have home remedies that have been passed down from generation to generation. This can help teachers understand if students seem hesitant to visit a nurse or a hospital. Involving parents in an initial conversation to explain the processes to students can prove useful.

Important Days and Holidays

In order to better understand Mexico and its people, it is imperative to learn about the important days, holidays, and traditions as they continue to be a large part of people's everyday lives wherever they may go in the world.

Independence Day in Mexico is celebrated on September 16th, starting with *El Grito de Independencia* (the Independence Yell) at midnight. Contrary to what people in the U.S. may think about *Cinco de Mayo* (May 5th), people in Mexico celebrate Independence Day as the most important federal holiday. Festivities usually begin the night of September 15th with fireworks and *El Grito* and continue the next day with parades and festivals. Many communities in the U.S. hold special festivals to celebrate this day. Teachers can include activities in their classrooms for students to understand the historical significance of this day in order to disrupt the stereotype that *Cinco de Mayo* is Mexican Independence Day.

Dia de *los Muertos,* or Day of the Dead, is celebrated every November 2nd. *Dia* de *los Muertos* is a celebration of those people, especially family members, who have passed away. Traditionally, families, including children, build *altares* (altars) with *papier mache*, food, and pictures of the person or people whose lives are being celebrated. *Calaveras* (skulls) made out of sugar and *pan* (bread) are made specifically for this celebration. The modern-day celebration holds influences from the Spanish Catholic church as well as indigenous spiritual beliefs.

In Mexico, Three Kings Day is celebrated on January 6, the original day on which children receive presents from the three wise men based on Christian (Catholic) beliefs. The day begins with the traditional eating of the *rosca* de *reyes*, a specialty bread only made for this festivity, in which a figurine of a baby Jesus is hidden. The tradition states that whoever gets the baby Jesus in their piece of bread must have a tamale party on February 2nd (the Feast of the Presentation of the Lord). This tradition has slowly faded due to the melding of the American culture into the Mexican culture and celebrating Santa Claus during Christmas. This celebration and tradition continues to be more prominent in the central and southern parts of the country.

Birthdays, weddings, and *quinceañeras* are seen as important days for the majority of the population, who celebrate them for a day, weekend, or several days. As part of the collectivist society, these celebrations are focused on festivities involving families, friends, and the community and are often based on Catholic practices (e.g., saying mass before each party). *Quinceañearas* are major celebrations to honor the 15th birthday of Mexican girls, for it is believed that this is the year that marks their shift from girlhood to young adulthood.

LANGUAGES AND LITERACIES

Today in Mexico, there are over 110 linguistic groups, with over 364 variations of languages, including Maya, Nahuatl, Zapoteco, and Mixteco (Arizpe, 2011; CDC, 2008). In addition, for centuries, languages such as Spanish, English, German, Yiddish, Chinese, and African languages (e.g., Bantu and Wolof) have been spoken in this country. The official language in Mexico is Spanish, with over 90% of the population speaking the language; about 8% of the population speaks a native or indigenous language (CDC, 2008). Communication in the Mexican culture is important, although verbal communication is not the only way of communicating, as nonverbal communication is as key in everyday relationships. For example, greetings are often in the forms of hugs or kisses on the cheek. This is a form of nonverbal communication in Mexican culture that demonstrates a positive interaction between people.

Characteristics of the Spanish Language

Although Spanish is spoken in many Latin-American countries as well as in Spain, every country has a different way of speaking it. The Spanish language in Mexico has been transformed through the decades by the use of slang and "Spanglish" (the combination of Spanish and English). Also, phonological differences can be heard. For example, in the north the sound of the *ch* can sound like a typical *ch* or a *sh* sound (Mackenzie, 2013). The *x* can be said as *x, j,* or *h*. A complete guide for how each letter in the Spanish alphabet sounds is found in Table 5.1. Moreover, in Spanish, words are pronounced how they look rather than as they sound, so English learners may want to do the same in English. This is useful for teachers to know because oftentimes students can get confused when words that are almost the same in Spanish and English have different meanings (e.g., Spanish "molesté," disturb, can be mistaken for "molest," or "physically abuse" in English).

Spanglish has been a phenomenon for decades now. In Mexico, the U.S., and in other Spanish-speaking nations, the use of words in English and Spanish intertwined in the other language is common. For example,

Table 5.1.   Spanish (Mexico) Alphabet With English Letter Names

A	B	C	Ch	D	E	F
a	bé	sé	ché	dé	eh	efe
G	H	I	J	K	L	LL
jé	aché	ee	jota	ka	elle	eyé
M	N	Ñ	O	P	Q	R
eme	ene	eñe	ó	pe	koo	erré
RR	S	T	U	V	W	X
dobleerré	ese	té	oo	oo bé	doble oo	ekees
Y	Z					
eegriega	seta					

the word "chocolate" comes from Nahuatl, and "patio" and "mosquito" come from Spanish and are now part of the English language. Today, words such as "OK," *troca* (truck), "sandwich," "ticket," and "shopping" are words that are often used in Mexico. More common and useful phrases can be found in Table 5.2.

A challenge for those who speak Spanish and English, or only Spanish, is that cultural norms can often degrade the use of the Spanish language. For example, there is a historical belief that if you live in the U.S., English should be the only language spoken, making many migrant families and students suppress their native language. To the contrary, research suggests that bilingualism or multilingualism is an asset for a child's or person's intelligence, skills, and opportunities (Office of Head Start, 2015).

IDEAS FOR EDUCATORS

Home/school Relations

Deficit thinking models have been used to explain the school failure of poor students of color (Valencia, 1997) including Mexican students (Wortham, Mortimer, & Allard, 2009). These deficit views linger in the literature and media and are the basis for the myth that Mexican families do not value education (Valencia & Black, 2002). According to Valencia and Black (2002), "the argument goes as follows: Given that Mexican Americans (allegedly) do not hold education high in their value hierarchy, this leads to inadequate familial socialization for academic competence, which in turn contributes to the school failure of Mexican American children and youths" (p. 83). However, dominant understandings of "involvement"

Table 5.2. Common Phrases in Spanish (Mexico)

English	Context	Transliteration	Literal Meaning
Nice to meet you	When you first meet people	Mucho gusto (MUcho GUsto)	Much pleasure
Hello	When answering the phone	Bueno (BWAYno)	Good
Hopefully	To confirm an appointment or any future plan	Si Díos quiere (Si DIos kiEray)	If God wills
What's your name?	Before you call someone by their first name	Como se llama? (COmo se YAma)	How are you called?
Good morning		Buenos días (BWAY nos DIas)	
How are you?		Como está? (Formal) Como estas? (Informal) Como están? (More than one person) (COmo esTAS)	
Goodbye		Adios (Ádios) Hasta luego (HAsta LUAYgo) Nos vemos (VEmos)	Goodbye See you later See ya!
I understand		Entiendo (No) Entiendo (enTIENdo)	I understand I don't understand
Excuse me	When you are trying to get by	Con permiso (perMIso)	With permission
	When you are trying to get someone's attention	Disculpe (disCULpe)	Forgive me

often exclude the internal ways that many Mexican parents are engaged in their children's education. Many families (for one reason or another) are not able to be involved "externally" in events such as meetings with schoolteachers or administrators but *do* care about their children's education. For example, Morales (2016) demonstrates the *consejos* (advice) that children learn from the stories and experiences of their familial or communal spaces, which come with them into the classroom and serves as motivation to do well in school. For example, Oscar's teacher made assumptions about Oscar's family based on their lack of what she considered involvement. If she were to provide opportunities for Oscar to share his stories, Mrs. Schmidt would learn that Oscar's family does not respond because of the language barriers. She would learn that while his family is not attending parent–teacher meetings, they sit with Oscar and Yuli every night to share *consejos* of hard work and dedication to teach him the value of *si se puede* ("it is possible"), a strong part of their view of *educación*.

According to Godinez (2006), for many Mexican families *educación* involves much more than the literal translation of "education"—*educación* is for them "the daily teachings and lessons most often related to behavior/ actions with illustrative examples based on the elder's life experiences" (p. 31). Providing opportunities for students to share their cultural knowledge can help teachers understand how families and communities are involved in their children's learning. Culturally responsive teachers seek multiple ways to involve families "externally" but also acknowledge and validate the "internal" forms of involvement that Valencia and Black (2002) summarize as: "Such actions as telling family stories about school experiences and making sure children arrive at school on time each day are examples of parents' involvement with school *internally*, that is, through private, family behaviors within the home" (p. 97).

CONCLUSIONS

It is vital that teachers do not make assumptions about the cultural backgrounds and experiences of Mexican American students, their families, and communities. As discussed earlier, not all Mexican students are immigrants—many are second, third, or fourth generation whose lived experiences differ greatly from what stereotypes often state. Moreover, not all students of Mexican background are undocumented or unauthorized. The experiences of those students who are first, second, or 1.5 generation children of immigrants are not homogenous. Mexico, like the United States, is a country with diverse ethnicities and languages and vernaculars spoken. Mexican students living and/or studying in the U.S may or may not speak Spanish. Their Spanish might differ from other Spanish-speaking Mexican students, depending on the region. To avoid making dangerous assumptions about Mexican students, teachers need to provide opportunities in their curriculum for students and their families to share their own stories.

In the opening narrative, Mrs. Schmidt acted with good intentions trying to provide a safe space for Oscar. However, she worked on assumptions that were counterproductive and further marginalized Oscar. She unintentionally questioned Oscar's learning intellect by conflating Oscar's language proficiency with his cognitive ability to do well in other subjects. Culturally responsive teachers constantly check their biases when (re)creating more inclusive and respectful classroom spaces that honors all student experiences, identities, histories, cultures, and knowledge systems.

ADDITIONAL RESOURCES

Graham, A., Reynolds, K., & St. Pierre, L. (2014, April 9). *Film school shorts: "Dia de los muertos"* [Video file]. Retrieved from http://www.pbs.org/video/2365218406/
>   Animated video of a young girl who visits the land of the dead to experience the Mexican holiday Dia de los Muertos.

Time for Kids. (2016). Around the world: Mexico. *Time for Kids*. Retrieved from http://www.timeforkids.com/destination/mexico
>   Quick research guide for students.

Reading Rockets. (2016). Available from http://www.readingrockets.org/spanish
>   For literacy activities for the classroom.

WETA. (2015). Colorín Colorado. Available from http://www.colorincolorado.org
>   A site for educators and families of English language learners.

WETA. (2015). Reading rockets: Launching young readers. Available from http://www.readingrockets.org/spanish
>   This site offers literacy activities in English and Spanish.

TASKS FOR EDUCATORS

1. Reflect on these questions:
    o   What might the history of Mexican American communities in the U.S. mean for students coming into U.S. schools? What should teachers consider when working with Mexican American children?
    o   With what you now know about the people of Mexico, their traditions, customs, and values, how is your perception about them? Has your perception changed? How can you celebrate and incorporate these traditions, customs, and values in your classroom without the possibility of stereotyping? How can you better build relationships with your students' families based on this information?
    o   What does the importance of bilingualism or multilingualism mean to you? Are you enhancing your students' bilingual skills or suppressing them? How can you celebrate the importance of literacy in school and home based on the students' culture?
2. Explore your students' backgrounds and family histories by inviting a family member as a storyteller for your class.
3. Build one or more literacy nights to share with parents the different strategies on how to improve literacy skills for their students in both English and Spanish, using books that relate to them and their culture.

4. Attend an activity, event, or festival in your student's community to learn more about their culture, traditions, and customs.

REFERENCES

Acuña, R. (2011). *Occupied America: A history of Chicanos.* London, UK: Pearson.

Arizpe, L. (2011). Cultura e identidad, Mexicanos en la era global. *Revista de la Universidad de Mexico, 92,* 1–7. Retrieved from http://www.revistadelauniversidad.unam.mx/9211/arizpe/92arizpe.html

Brabeck, K., & Xu, Q. (2010). The impact of detention and deportation on Latino immigrant children and families: A quantitative exploration. *Hispanic Journal of Behavioral Sciences, 32*(3), 341–361.

Brown, A., & López, M. H. (2013). *Mapping the Latino population by state, county, and city.* Pew Research Hispanic Trends Project. Retrieved from http://www.pewhispanic.org/2013/08/29/mapping-the-latino-population-by-state-county-and-city/

Catalano, T. (2013). Anti-immigrant ideology in U.S. crime reports: Effects on the education of Latino children. *Journal of Latinos and Education, 12*(4), 254–270.

Center for Disease Control (CDC). (2008). *Promoting cultural sensitivity: A practical guide* for tuberculosis programs that provide services to persons from Mexico. Atlanta, GA: U.S. Department of Health and Human Services. Retrieved from http://www.cdc.gov/tb/publications/guidestoolkits/ethnographicguides/mexico/chapters/mexico.pdf

Contreras, F. E., & Stritikus, T. (2008). *Understanding opportunities to learn for Latino students in Washington.* University of Washington, College of Education, Services.

De las Heras Aguilera, S. (2009). Una aproximación a las teorías feministas. *Universitas: revista de filosofía, derecho y política, 9,* 45–82.

Dragonné, C. & Méndez, E. (2011). *Gastronomía Mexicana: Una historia que se cuenta por tradiciones.* Retrieved from http://lossaboresdemexico.com/gastronomia-mexicana-una-historia-que-se-cuenta-por-tradiciones/

Farmworker Justice. (2015). *Selected statistics on farmworkers.* Retrieved from https://www.farmworkerjustice.org/sites/default/files/NAWS%20data%20factsht%201-13-15FINAL.pdf

Figueroa Rodríguez, K. A., Figueroa Sandoval, B., Figueroa Rodríguez, B., & Hernández Rosas, F. (2012). Análisis de los valores que construyen la identidad del mexicano. *Culturales, 8*(16), 7-32. Retrieved from http://www.scielo.org.mx/scielo.php?script=sci_arttext&pid=S1870-11912012000200001&lng=es&tlng=es.

Fix, M., & Passel, J. S. (2003). *U.S. immigration: Trends and implications for schools.* Washington, DC: The Urban Institute.

Gimenez, M. E. (1997). Latino/"Hispanic"—Who needs a name? The case against standardized terminology. In A. Darder, R. D. Torres, & H. Gutíerrez (Eds.), *Latinos and education: A cultural reader* (pp. 225–238). New York, NY: Routledge.

Godina, H. (2003). Mesocentrism and students of Mexican background: A community intervention for culturally relevant instruction. *Journal of Latinos and Education*, 2(3), 141–157.

Godinez, F. (2006). Braiding cultural knowledge into educational practices and policies. *Chicana/Latina Education in Everyday Life*, 25–38.

Gómez, L. E. (2007). *Manifest destinies: The making of the Mexican American race.* New York, NY: NYU Press.

González, C., & Gándara, P. (2005). Why we like to call ourselves Latinas. *Journal of Hispanic Higher Education*, 4(4), 392–398.

Gonzales, R. G. (2010). On the wrong side of the tracks: Understanding the effects of school structure and social capital in the educational pursuits of undocumented immigrant students. *Peabody Journal of Education*, 85, 469–485.

Greenfield, P. M., & Quiroz, B. (2013). Context and culture in the socialization and development of personal achievement values: Comparing Latino immigrant families, European American families, and elementary school teachers. *Journal of Applied Developmental Psychology, 34*(2), 108–118.

Hee Lee, M. Y. (2015, July 8). Donald Trump's false comments connecting Mexican immigrants and crime. *The Washington Post.* Retrieved from https://www.washingtonpost.com/news/fact-checker/wp/2015/07/08/Donald-trumps-false-comments-connecting-mexican-immigrants-and-crime/

Iglesias, E. M., & Valdes, F. (1998). Religion, gender, sexuality, race and class in coalitional theory: A critical and self-critical analysis of LatCrit social justice agendas. *Chicano-Latino Law Rev*iew, 19, 503.

Instituto Nacional de Estadística, Geografía e Informática (INEGI). (2004). *La población indigena de Mexico.* Aguascalientes, Aguascalientes: INEGI.

Kiyama, J. M. (2010). College aspirations and limitations: The role of educational ideologies and funds of knowledge in Mexican American families. *American Educational Research Journal, 47*(2), 330–356.

Mackenzie, I. (2013). *The linguistics of Spanish.* Retrieved from http://www.staff.ncl.ac.uk/i.e.mackenzie/index.html

Michael, M., Meyer, C., & Beezley, W. H. (Eds.). (2000). *The Oxford history of Mexico.* Oxford, UK: Oxford UP.

Moll, L. C., & González, N. (2004). Engaging life: A funds of knowledge approach to multicultural education. *Handbook of Research on Multicultural Education, 2*, 699–715.

Morales, M. I. (2016). There is space to play! Mexican American children of immigrants learning with(in) cherry orchards. *Journal for Critical Education Policy Studies, 14*(2), 41–66.

Navarrete Linares, F. (2010). *Pueblos indígenas de México.* México, D.F.: Ediciones Castillo.

Office of Head Start. U.S. Department of Health and Human Services. (2015). The benefits of being bilingual. Retrieved from http://eclkc.ohs.acf.hhs.gov/hslc/tta-system/cultural-linguistic/fcp/docs/benefits-of-being-bilingual.pdf

Passel, J. S., & Cohn, D. (2012). Unauthorized immigrants: 11.1 million in 2011. *Pew Research Center Hispanic Trends.* Retrieved from http://www.pewhispanic.org/2012/12/06/unauthorized-immigrants-11-1-million-in-2011/

Pew Research Center. (2015). *Unauthorized immigrants: Who they are and what the public thinks.* Retrieved from http://www.pewresearch.org/key-data-points/immigration/

Rumbaut, R. G. (2004). Ages, life stages, and generational cohorts: Decomposing the immigrant first and second generations in the United States1. *International Migration Review, 38*(3), 1160–1205.

Rumbaut, R. G., & Ima, K. (1988). *The adaptation of Southeast* Asian refugee youth: A *comparative* study. Washington, DC: U.S. Office of Refugee Resettlement.

Ryal Miller, R. (2006). *La guerra entre Estados Unidos y México.* PBS. Retrieved from http://www.pbs.org/kera/usmexicanwar/aftermath/war_esp.html

Secretaria de Education Pública (SEP). (2014). *Sistema educativo de los Estados Unidos Mexicanos principales cifras 2013-2014.* México, D.F.: Secretaría de Educación Pública. Retrieved from http://fs.planeacion.sep.gob.mx/estadistica_e_indicadores/principales_cifras/principales_cifras_2013_2014.pdf

Suárez-Orozco, C., & Suárez-Orozco, M. (2001). *Children of immigrants.* Cambridge, MA: Harvard University Press.

Valencia, R. R. (1997). Genetic pathology model of deficit thinking. In R. R. Valencia (Ed.), *The evolution of deficit thinking: Educational thought and practice* (pp. 41–112). Stanford Series on Education and Public Policy. London, UK: Falmer Press.

Valencia, R. R. (2010). *Dismantling contemporary deficit thinking: Educational thought and practice.* New York, NY: Routledge.

Valencia, R. R., & Black, M. S. (2002). "Mexican Americans don't value education!" On the basis of the myth, mythmaking, and debunking. *Journal of Latinos and Education, 1*(2), 81–103.

Valenzuela, A. (1996). *Subtractive schooling: U.S.-Mexican youth and the politics of caring.* New York, NY: SUNY Press.

Varsanyi, M. W. (2008). Rescaling the "alien," rescaling personhood: Neoliberalism, immigration, and the state. *Annals of the Association of American Geographers, 98*(4), 877–896.

Wortham, S., Mortimer, K., & Allard, E. (2009). Mexicans as model minorities in the new Latino diaspora. *Anthropology & Education Quarterly, 40,* 388–404.

CHAPTER 6

PUERTO RICO

Gladys R. Capella Noya and Elsie Candelaria Sosa
University of Puerto Rico

Yajaira is a nine-year old girl who migrated from Aguadilla, Puerto Rico to Providence, Rhode Island three years ago. Her fourth-grade social studies class is exploring family histories through group inquiry. It's Tuesday morning and children are working in small groups, thinking about issues they would like to address and structuring their work plan. Ms. Carver, the teacher, is walking around the room, gently approaching the groups to listen, answer questions, and offer suggestions. She hears Yajaira sharing with her peers that the first time she flew on a plane was to move to Rhode Island in the summer after finishing first grade. "I was excited to be in a plane, but a little scared at the beginning," Yajaira confessed. Ms. Carver mentioned that family migrations are very important dimensions of family histories and that it seemed very appropriate for their project. She suggested including in the research the challenges that Yajaira's family might have faced to receive permission to enter the U.S. Although Yajaira didn't remember any family conversations regarding "permission to enter the U.S.," she agreed.

Kevin is a 15-year old, very light-skinned Puerto Rican. His maternal and paternal grandparents were born in the central part of PR and moved to Chicago between the late 1960s and early 1970s. His parents were born in Chicago. Kevin began his schooling in a local parish school when he was five years old. Although his first language was Spanish, soon after entering kindergarten he began to speak English, even at home. His parents would speak to him in Spanish, and he would respond in English. By the time Kevin was in elementary school, his dominant lan-

Views From Inside: Languages, Cultures, and Schooling for K–12 Educators
pp. 99–116
Copyright © 2018 by Information Age Publishing
All rights of reproduction in any form reserved.

guage was English. He developed a passion for English class, especially spelling and literature. By eighth grade, Kevin was competing in the state spelling bee championship. One of the first assignments that Mr. Jones, his then English teacher, gave the class was to write a short autobiography. Mr. Jones was very impressed with the quality of Kevin's work. However, besides pointing out to Kevin the outstanding literary and grammatical merits of his text, he gently indicated that, since it should be an autobiography, he must write about himself. Somewhat perplexed and very respectfully, Kevin responded, "That's me, Mr. Jones." "Oh, you don't look Puerto Rican," explained Mr. Jones, somehow suggesting that his mistake should have been a compliment for Kevin. "That's okay, Mr. Jones," said Kevin. But deep inside, it hurt.

Yajaira and Kevin's experiences reflect various misconceptions that people in the United States, including classroom teachers, often have about Puerto Ricans. These misconceptions are closely related to issues of identity. When Ms. Carver suggested that Yajaira include in her project the challenges confronted by her family to enter the U.S., she was assuming that Puerto Ricans are not U.S. citizens, ignoring the fact that Puerto Rico (PR) is a U.S. territory and that Puerto Ricans received U.S. citizenship through the Jones Act in 1917.

Regarding Mr. Jones, two issues in particular led him to assume that Kevin was not Puerto Rican: his light skin and his mastery of the English language. Puerto Ricans are racially diverse, and the racial history of PR is complex. It is not uncommon to find the richness of that diversity within the same family, even among siblings with the same biological parents. The linguistic history of Puerto Ricans is also very complex. Various factors have contributed to this complexity. Among these factors are the U.S. government's systematic attempts to impose English upon the people of PR, particularly during the first half of the 20th century, and the constant back-and-forth movement of Puerto Ricans between the Puerto Rican archipelago and the U.S. mainland. There are many Puerto Ricans, who proudly identify themselves as such, whose dominant or only language is English. Finally, it is important to examine Mr. Jones' assumption that telling Kevin that he did not look Puerto Rican would be received as a compliment. This assumption reflects longtime negative structural prejudices against Puerto Ricans, which can engender microaggressions (Yosso, Smith, Ceja, & Solórzano, 2009). For Kevin, as it would have been for many Puerto Ricans, the misguided assumption was not a compliment.

BACKGROUND

Puerto Rico is an archipelago in the Caribbean. Seventy-six of the seventy-eight municipalities that comprise the country are located on the main island (approximately 100×35 miles), while the other two municipalities, Vieques and Culebra, are smaller islands located off the eastern shore of the mainland. It is the smallest of the Greater Antilles, a group of islands that includes Cuba, La Hispaniola (containing Haiti and the Dominican Republic), and Jamaica. Despite its small size, PR displays a rich combination of habitats. With a dry southern region, a cooler mountainous section that crosses the center of the main island, and valleys near its coasts, it serves as home to a diverse array of wildlife and flora. The trade winds blow from east to west (with slight directional differences depending on the season) throughout the year. These winds also bring hurricanes and tropical moisture to the region, particularly between the months of June and November.

The Gulf Stream has direct impact insofar as reaching PR by sea is concerned, since it makes travel "easier south to north, east to west—the directions by which various waves of explorers and invaders have been coming to the island for 4,000 years, ever since there has been human habitation on the island" (Flores, 2010, p. 2). Before having contact with Europe, PR was inhabited by several groups who left no written record. Therefore, archeologists have taken their clues from the artifacts left behind by the diverse waves of immigration that consisted of people who traveled from the Yucatan Peninsula and from the Orinoco River basin of South America. These immigrant groups arrived in PR, often interacting with those who came before them, adopting their ways and introducing others, until the arrival of Europeans in the Greater Antilles drastically altered the course of Puerto Rican history (Flores, 2010).

When Columbus reached PR during his second trip to America in 1493, he found the *Taíno,* the dominant cultural group throughout the Greater Antilles at the time. After Columbus's visit, PR was annexed to the Spanish Empire and became one of its colonies, yet it was not settled by the Spaniards until 1508. By 1898, when the U.S. invaded PR during the Spanish-American War, an educational system had been established by Spain that had Spanish as the language of instruction and consisted of "380 public schools for males, 138 public schools for women, and 26 private primary schools" (Torres González et al., 2016, p. 77). The Treaty of Paris, which marked the end of the Spanish-American War, gave the U.S. full control over PR, and a military government that was to be in charge of both military and civilian affairs was established. This historical event marked a dramatic change in the history of education in PR, since the teaching of English became an important part of Puerto Rican education. Moreover, the political relationship between PR and the U.S. became a controversial issue that to this day (as reflected in party politics) has remained a divisive force among Puerto Ricans.

The 1900 Foraker Act (also known as the Organic Act of 1900) established a civilian government in PR. From 1900 to 1949, the language policy in PR, through the Commissioners of Education, changed six times. Policies ranged from all Spanish to all English instruction, with different proportions of these two languages used depending on grade level (i.e., elementary, middle, and high school). The 1949 language policy has remained in place, and English has been taught as a second language since then.

In spite of the fact that the language policy has remained stable since 1949 and that English and Spanish have been in contact in PR for over 100 years, the initial intent to impose English through the educational system, along with political shifts that have occurred from 1968 up to the present, have paved the way for a rather complex linguistic situation among Puerto Ricans growing up in PR. Data from the U.S. Census Bureau (2014) related to language use showed that there were 3,364,109 persons living in PR who were over five years old. These residents have been taught English as a subject through the public school system since 1949. Yet this source also reported that 2,634,326 residents of the island older than five years old speak English less than very well. At the same time, it is important to consider that respondents reported that there were 539,958 people (among the same age group) who could speak English very well.

Also contributing to the complex linguistic situation, the 1917 Jones Act gave all Puerto Ricans U.S. citizenship and opened the door to Puerto Rican migration to the U.S. The Puerto Rican Diaspora reached a peak between 1950 and 1970, a period during which approximately 700,000 Puerto Ricans migrated north. It is important to note that migration is still occurring and it is a phenomenon that goes in both directions since Puerto Ricans tend to move back and forth between PR and the U.S. mainland. The 2010 U.S. Census shows that there were 4,623,716 individuals who identified themselves as Puerto Rican living in the U.S. These latest data also show that there are now more Puerto Ricans and Puerto Rican descendants living in the U.S. than in PR. The majority of these, according to U.S. Census Bureau (2010) data, live in New York (1,070,558) and Florida (847,550). As a response to a long-term social and economic crisis, the number of Puerto Ricans migrating to the U.S. has increased. Recent data (Krogstad, 2015) suggest that the number of Puerto Ricans moving to Florida has increased 110% since 2000, making this region the recipient of a large number of Puerto Ricans. These facts serve as a backdrop to the emergence of two groups of Puerto Rican English language learners (ELLs): *ELLs in PR* and *ELLs in the U.S.*

Salient aspects of schooling in PR include the following: The Constitution of the Commonwealth of PR establishes the universal right to an education and mandates the public educational system to be free of cost and nonsectarian. Schooling is currently compulsory for youth until they are 18 years old. The public system of education in PR was established by the U.S. soon after it occupied PR, and as in the 50 states, it must abide by the policies established by the U.S. Department of Education in order to receive federal funding. As of 2014, the public system includes an office for Montessori education (*Secretaría Auxiliar de Educación Montessori*), and a growing number of public schools in PR include classrooms guided by this philosophy. Parallel to the public system of education, there is a private system that is very diverse in its offerings. The private system includes religious as well as nonsectarian schools. A few elite and expensive schools serve upper-class families. Most private schools, however, serve middle-class families, many of whom afford school costs only with much difficulty. English is offered in all public schools, in most as a second language. In some private schools, the language of instruction is English.

   La política partidista (party politics) in PR is sometimes called *el deporte nacional* (the national sport). For many individuals, and sometimes families as a whole, political party affiliation is a major part of their identity. The three major political parties in PR correspond to three distinct visions of what the political status of PR in relation to the U.S. should be. The *Partido Popular Democrático* (PPD; Popular Democratic Party) favors the current status as it was ratified in 1952, called the *Estado Libre Asociado* (ELA), officially known as the Commonwealth of PR but literally translated as "Free Associated State." There are major criticisms regarding this status, both from local and international sources. For many it is a colonial status, in violation of international law. Within the PPD party's affiliates, there are debates regarding the direction in which the relationship with the U.S. should evolve. The *Partido Nuevo Progresista* (PNP; New Progressive Party) favors statehood for PR—that is, the annexation of PR into the federal union. A major issue within the PNP party is to what extent PR can be fully incorporated into the U.S. as a state and still retain elements that are treasured by many Puerto Ricans, such as the Spanish language and representation as an independent country in international events including the Olympic Games. Even for many pro-statehood individuals, listening to La *Borinqueña* (the Puerto Rican national anthem) at international sports competitions is a major source of pride, as experienced during Rio 2016 when tennis star Mónica Puig won the first gold Olympic medal for PR. Renouncing that possibility is thus perceived by many as a major loss. The third major political party, *Partido Independentista Puertorriqueño* (PIP; Puerto Rican Independence Party), favors independence from the U.S. Although representatives from the party often get elected as legislators, in recent elections the party has received less than 5% of the general vote. Since 1968, the other two major political parties have alternately won the general elections, often by very slim margins. Several minor parties have emerged throughout the years and have influenced the topics that are discussed in the political arena. Political campaigns in PR are lengthy and tend to be extremely passionate.

All of the aforementioned geographical, historical, political, and linguistic factors contribute to Puerto Rican culture, with all its complexity, diversity, and richness; they constitute a significant contextual dimension of its people's challenges and aspirations.

CULTURE

Traditionally, Puerto Rican culture is described as having been influenced by three major groups: the *Taíno*, who inhabited the island that they called *Borinquén* prior to the Spanish conquest; the Spaniards, who began the island's colonization in 1508; and the Africans (particularly from Western Africa), most of whom were brutally transported to the island as part of the Atlantic slave trade. The Arab influence also needs to be acknowledged, since the Spanish colonization of the Americas followed eight hundred years of Muslim rule in what became Spanish territory (Caraballo, 2013). PR has been a U.S. territory since 1898; therefore, U.S. cultural values have been a major influence during the 20th century.

In spite of the longstanding presence of the U.S. in PR and of the aggressive efforts of the U.S. government, particularly during the first three decades of the 20th century, to "Americanize" the Puerto Rican people, PR is still a predominantly Spanish-speaking country (Montilla, 1977). There is a significant segment of the population fully bilingual in English and Spanish, or with varying degrees of fluency in English as a second language (as noted previously). Besides substituting English for the Spanish language, the plan to "Americanize" the people of PR at the beginning of the 20th century also included promoting U.S. patriotism and loyalty through military exercises in schools. The U.S. military has had a strong presence in the life of the Puerto Rican people. Puerto Ricans have had a substantial representation across all branches of the U.S. Armed Forces and have served in all major U.S. military conflicts since Puerto Ricans received U.S. citizenship in 1917. This military presence has often been controversial, as reflected in individual and collective protests throughout the decades, including, for example, those of the pacifist organization *Madres Contra la Guerra* (Mothers Against War; Madres Contra la Guerra, 2016).

People and Interests

When people visit PR, they are sometimes surprised at how *Latin* or *Hispanic* it seems, others at how *American*. These contrasting perceptions are most likely related to the visitors' expectations. Everyday life in PR is in many ways similar to what it may be in parts of the U.S. We have many of the same big chain stores and restaurants, watch the same movies, and wear similar clothing. On the other hand, significant aspects of Hispanic heritage, besides the language, have been preserved. For example, the sense of what it means to be on time tends to be more fluid than that of the U.S. When making plans, it is not uncommon to ask whether it is going to be *hora americana o puertorriqueña* (American or Puerto Rican time), meaning that if it is *hora americana* it will be sharp, if it is *hora puertorriqueña*, less so (sometimes notably less!). Local celebrations include not only U.S. holidays, but also others like the *Día de los Reyes Magos* (Day of the Epiphany), a Spanish tradition celebrated on January 6th that commemorates the visit of the Magi to the infant Jesus (and which extends the Christmas season an additional week). All *municipios* (municipalities) have a patron saint who is honored in the annual *fiestas patronales*. These are major festivities traditionally celebrated in the *plaza pública* (town square), with activities for children and adults, music, and lots of food.

Following the Spanish tradition, Puerto Ricans tend to use two *apellidos,* or surnames, as opposed to only one. Usually, the first *apellido* corresponds to the father's first surname and the second *apellido* corresponds to the mother's first surname. If Manuel *Ortiz* Rivera has a child with María *Pérez* Román, their child's *apellidos* will be Ortiz Pérez. Puerto Rican culture has also been enriched by other Latino people including, among others, our Cuban and Dominican neighbors.

Family life is very much valued by most Puerto Ricans, and oftentimes family needs are privileged over individual interests. Interdependence and intergenerational continuity tend to be embraced among Puerto Rican families and can be a source of strength and stability for children (Hidalgo, 2000). Family composition is diverse and includes the traditional nuclear family of parents raising their biological children, single parents, adoptive parents, and homoparental and extended families, among others. Although with many exceptions, Puerto Ricans display affection rather openly among family, friends, and colleagues, particularly through physical gestures that might include *besos y abrazos* (kisses and hugs).

Puerto Ricans tend to appreciate collective celebrations. *"Celebramos hasta los bautizos de muñecas"* ("We even celebrate dolls' baptisms") is a common expression that captures this disposition. Celebrations among Puerto Ricans usually include food, alcoholic beverages (regrettably, often consumed in excess), music, and dance. Typical foods include *arroz y habichuelas* (rice and beans), *lechón* (pork), and *tostones* (fried plantains). Puerto Ricans listen and dance to a wide variety of musical genres, including Latin and Afro-Caribbean music like salsa and merengue. PR has a very rich and diverse tradition in the arts, including the visual and performing arts, music, and literature.

Sports are also an important dimension for many Puerto Ricans' recreational and professional lives. For a long time, baseball was the most popular sport in PR. Although it still enjoys a respectable level of popularity, as reflected in the extraordinary players that keep making it to the Major Leagues, locally it has lost popularity to other sports such as basketball and volleyball. Nevertheless, there are baseball fields all over the island, and baseball star Roberto Clemente remains a national hero. Boxing is also very popular, and PR has a long tradition of world champions in this sport.

Gender Roles

Traditionally, PR has been characterized as a society with clearly ascribed gender roles. These roles are reflected, for example, in language, social expectations, and mass media. Traits such as *sacrificada* (sacrificing), *abnegada* (selflessness), and *dulce* (sweetness) still tend to be exalted during Mothers' Day. Young boys are still admonished for crying with *"Pareces una nena"* ("You look like a girl") or *"Los nenes no lloran"* ("Boys don't cry"). Alarming rates of domestic violence against women that cross social class and educational levels attest to the power and control that many males expect to exercise over women. Domestic violence is the primary cause of violent deaths among women in PR (Noticel, 2014). However, major cultural shifts have gradually taken place over time. As of 1989, PR has a very progressive law regarding the prevention of and intervention with domestic violence (LexJuris Puerto Rico, 1989). In 2015, the state Department of Education instituted a public policy that mandates the transversal incorporation of gender perspectives in school curricula, educational practices, and extracurricular activities as an instrument to promote human dignity and equity (Departamento de Educación, 2015). Later that year, once the U.S. Supreme Court decided that the fundamental right to marry is guaranteed to same-sex couples by the U.S. Constitution, the Puerto Rican government recognized same-sex marriage (Departamento de Justicia, 2015) and adoptions for same-sex couples (Microjuris, 2015). It is important to highlight that, in spite of the sexism that still prevails, women actively participate and contribute across all spheres of Puerto Rican society.

Diversity and Racism

Overall, Puerto Ricans constitute a very mixed racial group. It is quite frequent to encounter this racial diversity even within siblings of the same biological parents. Although manifested in somewhat different ways as compared to the U.S., racism still prevails in PR. Light skin, straight hair, and blue eyes are still perceived by many as preferable. It is not uncommon to hear someone remark to a dark-skinned person who is marrying a light-skinned one, "*¡Para mejorar la raza!*" ("To improve the race!"). Hair that is dark, thick, and with naturally tight and small curls is often referred to as *pelo malo* (bad hair). Unconsciously racist remarks, such as "he is '*negro pero inteligente*'" ("black *but* intelligent," as if blackness and intelligence were mutually exclusive) can still be heard in too many social contexts. In this realm, however, major changes and initiatives have emerged that forcefully denounce systematic racism and that celebrate and affirm the enormous contributions of people of African ancestry to Puerto Rican culture and society. The text *Arrancando Mitos de Raíz—Guía para una Enseñanza Antirracista de la Herencia Africana en* Puerto Rico (Uprooting Myths—A Guide for Antiracist Teaching of the African Heritage in PR) is a valuable example (Godreau, Franco-Ortiz, Lloréns, Reinat, Canabal-Torres, & Gaspar-Concepción, 2013).

Socioeconomic differences permeate Puerto Rican society. As Colón Reyes (2005) affirms, "There was not an equitable distribution of wealth and economic growth" (p. 331). Some cultural differences that can be identified among Puerto Ricans tend to be associated with social class and formal educational level. Those differences might include issues related to gender roles, aesthetics, and recreational preferences, among others.

Religion

Regarding religious affiliation, most Puerto Ricans identify themselves as Christians, particularly as Catholics, which can be traced to the Spanish colonization and the political presence of a Catholic regime in PR for almost four centuries. However, the proportion of Catholics to other Christian denominations has decreased over the years (EFE News Service, 2010). Spiritual beliefs in PR have also been influenced by African religions and belief systems. As in other Caribbean nations, religious syncretism has traditionally been a part of Puerto Rican culture and is reflected, for example, in the ubiquity of *botánicas* (botanical spirit shops), especially in small neighborhood shopping areas. *Brujería* and *santería*, two distinct sets of belief systems and practices that can be traced to their African heritage, are sometimes observed or practiced covertly as they still carry a social stigma, at least partially related to racist perspectives. Although in much smaller proportions, but nevertheless socially and culturally significant, there are other religious groups present in PR, including, among others, Muslims, Jews, and Hindus. As everywhere else, there are also

Puerto Rican nonbelievers. Religious freedom is guaranteed by the Commonwealth's Constitution.

Pedagogy

Given PR's political relationship with the U.S., its public schools are subject to U.S. policies and are strongly influenced by U.S. pedagogical trends. What happens in Puerto Rican classrooms (see Figure 6.1)—including the existing variance among them—is very similar to what happens in U.S. classrooms, taking into account the diversity of that context. Walls are used to display didactic materials related to content knowledge, students' work, and classroom rules. Honoring Puerto Ricans' appreciation for collective celebrations, it is common to celebrate in classrooms all kinds of occasions, from students' birthdays and teachers' baby showers to school teams' performances in academic and sports competitions. Salient among academic competitions are Spanish and English forensics and science fairs. Although efforts have been made to promote more learner-centered, as opposed to teacher-centered, instruction, in most classrooms the latter tends to prevail. Many students appreciate working in groups but, within the existing diversity, the tendency is still to foster individual work, as reflected in many classrooms where desks are arranged in single rows. Field trips are among the students' favorite activities, although teachers often indicate that existing regulations can turn their implementation into quite a challenge.

Figure 6.1.   Yeraisy Cruz Peña and Sherlyn Coco Matos working in an art project in a school in Puerto Rico.

Politics

As previously stated, for many Puerto Rican individuals, and sometimes for families as a whole, political party affiliation is a major part of their identity. Consequently, it tends to be very difficult for Puerto Ricans to cross party lines regarding political issues. Nevertheless, two major collective struggles have managed to move a critical mass of people to transcend party affiliation or political preference and unite with a common purpose: the struggle to remove the U.S. Navy from Vieques (accomplished in 2003, although the effort continues to demand that federal agencies comply with the mandate to remove the toxic materials left behind), and the struggle to release from prison Oscar López Rivera, a Puerto Rican political prisoner for over three decades in the U.S. Both of these struggles unite considerable sectors of the Puerto Rican community in the archipelago and in the U.S., as well as human rights advocates worldwide.

LANGUAGES AND LITERACIES

Puerto Rican English language learners (ELLs) have commonalities that can be related to political and identity issues and are also related to a perception of bilingualism that is common in both PR and the U.S. In the case of both groups of Puerto Rican ELLs (ELLs in PR and ELLs in the U.S.), "the second language is prestigious and powerful, used in mainstream education and in the jobs market" (Baker, 2011, p. 72).

Baker (2011) makes a distinction "between bilingualism (and multilingualism) as an individual possession and as a group possession ... usually termed *individual bilingualism* and *societal bilingualism*" (emphasis in original, p. 2). Since PR as a society has English and Spanish as official languages thanks to its language policy, the government advocates a bilingual society and has used the PR's Department of Education (PRDE) English Program to comply with this linguistic aspiration. The English Program's vision statement states that its goal is "to develop students who can communicate creatively, reflectively, and critically in the English language in order for them to be college and career ready" (Departamento de Educación Puerto Rico, 2014). Consequently, PR's public school population takes English as a subject from kindergarten to 12th grade.

However, most Puerto Ricans do not see themselves as bilinguals (U.S. Census Bureau, 2010). Baker (2011) attributes this circumstance to the fact that

In PR, the government introduced English into schools to attempt bilingualization of the island. Over two-thirds of the population remain functionally monolingual in Spanish. Resnick (1993) has shown that nationalism, political uncertainty and the relationship between language and identity have made some groups of Puerto Ricans resistant to language change and the use of English. (p. 77)

A Puerto Rican variety of English, commonly referred to in PR as *inglés goleta*, that has specific phonological and syntactical characteristics, has been proposed to explain this situation (Cole, 2005; Walsh, 1994).

The aforementioned circumstances notwithstanding, English teachers in PR have to deal with the fact that they will find students at all school levels who walk into their English class and promptly state: "*Maestra, yo no sé inglés*" ("Teacher, I don't know English"). Morales and Blau (2009) provide examples of strategies teachers can use in the classroom to deal with this situation:

> Strive to create a comfort zone for building a sense of community that includes both teacher and students. We do this on day one by having students interview each other and share what they learn with classmates and the teacher, who communicates to the students that they are genuinely important to her and cares about what they say.... Another way is to occasionally use Spanish, which has been shown to facilitate second language acquisition (Cummins, 2000). Particularly if the teacher is a nonnative speaker of Spanish, students see their teacher using their language imperfectly, thus motivating them to dare to use English, their second language, albeit imperfectly. (p. 52)

Several authors (Coe, 2001; Hawthorne, n.d.; Moore & Marzano, 1979) have identified common difficulties in ELLs whose native language is Spanish. Puerto Rican students share many of these, including challenges such as:

- English and Spanish have substantial differences in the use of vowels. Distinguishing vowel sounds that Spanish does not have can be difficult for PR ELLs.
- Several consonant sounds (particularly h, j, r, y) and the distinction English makes between sh /ʃ/ and ch /tʃ/ are hard for PR ELLs to grasp, and the most common, yet different sounds, for th (/ð/ and /θ/) can be troublesome.
- Vowel sound length is not significant in distinguishing words in Spanish, as is the case in English (sheep vs. ship).
- Using the article "the" can be difficult to a Puerto Rican student since it is viewed as equal to *el/la* in all instances.
- The use of irregular past tense forms and the pronunciation of the -d and -ed past tense ending present a challenge to learners

because irregular past tense forms have to be memorized, and silent vowels do not exist in Spanish.

* Elements of syntax such as the proper placement of adjectives and adverbs can confuse an ELL learner because their placement is different in Spanish.

Our experience as Puerto Rican ELLs allows us to add two difficulties to the aforementioned list:

* Confusion with the use of capitals letters since the rules that apply in Spanish are slightly different in English (particular emphasis can be placed on months and days of the week).
* Dates in Spanish place the day first and the month later; English placement is just the opposite.

The situation faced by English language learners in the U.S. and the circumstances faced by Puerto Ricans and their descendants when they decide to return to PR are often similar because "most Puerto Ricans in the U.S. and on the island have somehow experienced discrimination based on Spanish language use, whether for using it as a first language or for the common practice of 'code-switching' or alternating between English and Spanish" (Vidal-Ortiz, 2004, p. 254). Therefore, one of the major challenges faced by these two groups, inside and outside classrooms, has to do with the labeling of their language as *broken* or *mixed*, thus diminishing its value and making the speaker feel unworthy. Furthermore, according to Nine Curt (1984), body language and personal space are employed differently by Puerto Ricans. Hand gestures, eye winks and rolls, and other bodily movements are common and have unique meaning. Private space is another challenge, since kissing and hugging are not only acceptable but also very significant and quite different from the North American view of private space.

According to Scheffner-Hammer, Rodriguez, Lawrence, and Miccio (2007), the roughly 4.6 million Puerto Ricans in the U.S. have a perception of education that is culturally embedded and view schools as having the primary responsibility for educating children. However, their study found that Puerto Ricans also display beliefs that align with U.S. mainstream views. "For example, parents believed that they [Puerto Rican mothers] should teach their children new skills, and that children should be allowed to have their own views" (Scheffner-Hammer et al., 2007, p. 221). These findings suggest that teachers and school administrators need to embrace diversity and multicultural approaches within the classroom, even within language and cultural groups.

IDEAS FOR EDUCATORS

Puerto Rican students and their families often face challenges in the U.S. school system related to culture and language. As previously discussed, Puerto Ricans are a culturally, racially, and linguistically diverse group. To varying degrees, *Taíno*, African, Spanish, Arab, and U.S. influences are present in the different manifestations of Puerto Rican culture. The sense of what it means to be on time, celebrating PR local holidays (such as the Day of the Epiphany), and the use of two surnames are examples that reflect the Spanish influence and that distinguish many Puerto Ricans from mainstream U.S. culture. Puerto Ricans are racially diverse. This diversity is often reflected within the same family. The level of fluency in Spanish and English is also very varied among Puerto Ricans, both for those living in the Puerto Rican archipelago and those on the U.S. mainland. Many Puerto Ricans tend to be physically affectionate and value family life, including interdependence and intergenerational continuity. Classroom teachers who work with Puerto Rican children and their families should be aware of the political relationship between the U.S. and PR and its implications in terms of, for example, citizenship and migration patterns. Being sensitive to all these issues can support a better understanding of Puerto Rican children and respectful home/school relations. This sensitivity can be manifested in multiple ways, including everyday social and academic interactions with children and their families where cultural and language identities are recognized, included, and affirmed.

Affirming the rich and diverse tradition that Puerto Ricans embody in the arts, including the visual and performing arts, music, and literature, and the recognition of sports as an important dimension of many Puerto Ricans' recreational and professional lives, is a possible source of curriculum enrichment approaches for Puerto Rican children and youth. For example, curricula might include the study of music and dance traditions in PR, such as *bomba* and *plena*, as celebration of Puerto Rican African cultural heritage and as an acknowledgement of political resistance. Including in the curriculum life stories of Puerto Ricans and literature by distinguished Puerto Ricans is also a valuable means of enriching the school experience of Puerto Ricans and other children and youth.

CONCLUSIONS

Describing Puerto Rican culture is a risky endeavor. Any such description will certainly exclude important elements and many may feel misrepresented. We thus hope that the information provided in this chapter will be understood as a partial portrait of the richness and complexity of Puerto

Rican culture, and that it may serve as an invitation to further explore and problematize the issues. Moreover, we hope that this background also serves to strengthen the commitment to embrace each child and young person as a unique and distinct individual whose cultural context is part of his or her multifaceted identity.

ADDITIONAL RESOURCES

Centro de Investigaciones Educativas. (2015). Professional development for teachers of English to secondary school diverse learners: Strategies for integrating art and technology for effective communication. Retrieved from http://cie.uprrp.edu

> The Center for Educational Research offers opportunities to access and disseminate educational resources, events, and research. Most information is in Spanish.

Fundación Puertorriqueña de las Humanidades. (2016). Encyclopedia of Puerto Rico. Retrieved from http://www.enciclopediapr.org/ing/

> Bilingual site with a wide variety of themes related to cultural, historical, scientific, and political aspects of Puerto Rico.

Nieto, S. (2013). *Finding joy in teaching students of diverse backgrounds: Culturally responsive and socially just practices in U.S. classrooms.* Portsmouth, NH: Heinemann.

> An outstanding work on the challenges teachers face and the joys they encounter when working with diverse students.

Nieto, S. (2015). Multicultural resources. Retrieved from http://www.sonianieto.com/educational-resources/multicultural-resources/

> This personal page for Dr. Nieto is packed with information about her books and other useful resources for educators.

Pousada, A. (2015). Dr. Alicia Pousada. Retrieved from http://aliciapousada.weebly.com

> This personal webpage for Dr. Pousada is filled with videos, presentations, and resources for teachers of ELLs.

TASKS FOR EDUCATORS

1. After reading this chapter, what did you learn about Puerto Rican history and culture that might have surprised you? How will that inform your practice? What new questions do you have and how can you explore them?

2. How can you honor within your classroom the Puerto Rican family values of interdependency and intergenerational continuity?

3. Read one of these recommended texts and create a task or activity for your peers or students:

- Urciuoli, B. (2013). *Exposing prejudice: Puerto Rican experiences of language, race, and class*. New York, NY: Waveland Press.

  Bonnie Urciuoli uses ethnographic and linguistic fieldwork to present an insightful study of discrimination as experienced by New York working-class Puerto Ricans.
- Nieto, S. (2000). *Puerto Rican students in U.S. schools*. Mahwah, NJ: Erlbaum.

  Edited by Sonia Nieto, this volume compiles a diverse collection of works that shed light on the history and experiences of Puerto Rican children and their families in the United States.
- Nieto, S. (2015). *Brooklyn dreams: My life in public education*. Cambridge, MA: Harvard Education Press.

  This autobiographical book by Sonia Nieto echoes the schooling experience of other Puerto Ricans and migrants. It tells the compelling story of a teacher, scholar, and activist who has dedicated her life to issues of diversity, equity, and social justice within the field of education.

REFERENCES

Baker, C. (2011). *Foundations of bilingual education and bilingualism* (5th ed.). Clevedon, UK: Multilingual Matters.

Caraballo, J. (2013, November 9). Dejan su huella en la cultura. *Elnuevodia*. Retrieved from http://www.elnuevodia.com/noticias/locales/nota/dejansuhuel-laenlacultura-1639340/

Coe, N. (2001). Speakers of Spanish and Catalan. In M. Swan & B. Smith (Eds.), *Learner English: A teacher's guide to interference and other problems* (pp. 90–112). Cambridge, UK: Cambridge University Press.

Cole, S. L. (2005). *Models of world Englishes: The case for Puerto Rican English* (Unpublished master's thesis). University of Puerto Rico, Río Piedras.

Colón Reyes, L. (2005). *Pobreza en Puerto Rico: Radiografía del Proyecto Americano*. Río Piedras, PR: Editorial Luna Nueva.

Departamento de Educación de Puerto Rico. (2014). *English program. Puerto Rico Core standards*. Retrieved from http://www.de.gobierno.pr/files/estandares/Estandares_de_ingles_2014.pdf

Departamento de Educación de Puerto Rico. (2015). *Carta circular 19—Política pública sobre la equidad de género y su integración al currículo del Departamento de Educación de Puerto Rico como instrumento para promover la dignidad del ser humano y la igualdad de todos y todas ante la Ley* (2014–2015). Retrieved from http://intraedu.dde.pr/Cartas%20Circulares/19-2014-2015.pdf

Departamento de Justicia. (2015). A raíz de la decisión del Tribunal Supremo federal, Puerto Rico se encamina a reconocer el derecho al matrimonio igualitario. Retrieved from http://www.justicia.pr.gov/a-raiz-de-la-decision-del-tribunal-supremo-federal-puerto-rico-se-encamina-a-reconocer-el-derecho-al-matrimonio-igualitario/

EFE News Service. (2010). Puerto Rico sees increase in Protestants. Retrieved from http://search.proquest.com/docview/734776445?accountid=44825

Flores, L. P. (2010). *The history of Puerto Rico*. Santa Barbara, CA: Greenwood Press.

Godreau, I., Franco-Ortiz, M., Lloréns, H., Reinat, M., Canabal-Torres, I., & Gaspar-Concepción, J. (2013). *Arrancando mitos de raíz: Guía para una enseñanza antirracista de la herencia africana en* Puerto Rico (2nd ed.). Cabo Rojo, PR: Editora Educación Emergente.

Hawthorne, J. (n.d.). *Common English difficulties for ESL Spanish students*. Retrieved from http://education.seattlepi.com/common-english-difficulties-esl-spanish-students-1552.html

Hidalgo, N. M. (2000). Puerto Rican mothering strategies: The roles of mothers and grandmothers in promoting school success. In S. Nieto (Ed.), *Puerto Rican students in U.S. schools* (pp. 167–196). Mahwah, NJ: Lawrence Erlbaum Associates.

Krogstad, J. M. (2015, October 30). In a shift away from New York, more Puerto Ricans head to Florida. Retrieved from http://www.pewresearch.org/fact-tank/2015/10/30/in-a-shift-away-from-new-york-more-puerto-ricans-head-to-florida/

LexJuris Puerto Rico. (1989). Ley 54—Ley de Prevención e Intervención con la Violencia Doméstica. Retrieved from http://www.lexjuris.com/lexlex/lex89054.htm

Madres Contra la Guerra. (2016). Retrieved from http://madrescontralaguerra.blogspot.com/

Microjuris. (2015). Celebran primer caso de adopción gay en Puerto Rico. Retrieved from http://aldia.microjuris.com/tag/adopcion-gay/

Montilla, A. N. (1977). *La americanización de Puerto Rico y el sistema de instrucción pública, 1900-1930*. Río Piedras, PR: Editorial de la Universidad de Puerto Rico.

Moore, F. B., & Marzano, R. J. (1979). Common errors of Spanish speakers learning English. *Research in the Teaching of English, 13*(2), 161–167.

Morales, B., & Blau, E. K. (2009). Identity issues in building an ESL community: The Puerto Rican experience. *New Directions for Adult and Continuing Education, 121*, 45–53.

Nine Curt, J. (1984). *Non-verbal communication in Puerto Rico*. Retrieved from http://files.eric.ed.gov/fulltext/ED258468.pdf

Noticel. (2014). Violencia doméstica: Principal causa de muerte violenta de mujeres. Retrieved from http://www.noticel.com/noticia/164608/violencia-domestica-principal-causa-de-muerte-violenta-de-mujeres.html

Scheffner-Hammer, C., Rodriguez, B. L., Lawrence, F. R., & Miccio, A. W. (2007) Puerto Rican mothers' beliefs and home literacy practices. Language, Speech & Hearing Services in Schools, 38(3), 216–224.

Torres González, R., Martínez Ramos, L.M., Moscoso Álvarez, M., Zambrana Ortiz, N., Sagardía Ruíz, M., & Scharrón del Río, M. A. (2016). *Educación básica en* PR *del 1980 al 2012: Política pública y trasfondo histórico, legal y curricular*. San Juan, PR: Consejo de Educación de Puerto Rico. Manuscript in preparation.

U.S. Census Bureau. (2010). Profile of general population and housing characteristics: 2010. Retrieved from http://www.census.gov/2010census/data/

U.S. Census Bureau. (2014). Age by language spoken at home by ability to speak
English for the population 5 years and over: Puerto Rico. Retrieved from
https://factfinder.census.gov/faces/tableservices/jsf/pages/
productview.xhtml?pid=ACS_14_1YR_C16004&prodType=table

Vidal-Ortiz, S. (2004). Puerto Ricans and the politics of speaking Spanish. *Latino Studies, 2*, 254–258.

Walsh, M. (1994). *Towards a Puerto Rican variety of English: An ethnographic study with implications for the English curriculum in Puerto Rico* (Unpublished doctoral dissertation). University of Puerto Rico, Río Piedras.

Yosso, T. J., Smith, W. A., Ceja, M., & Solórzano, D. G. (2009). Critical race theory, racial microaggressions, and campus racial climate for Latina/o undergraduates. *Harvard Educational Review, 79*(4), 659–690.

CHAPTER 7

NICARAGUA

Desirée Pallais
University of Texas–Austin

Ilana Umansky
University of Oregon

Tunina is eight years old; she was born in the United States into a Nicaraguan family. Her mother Maritza, a former administrative assistant, decided to emigrate in 2007 in order to give her family a better life. In her third-grade class, Tunina is one of five students whose native language is not English. Her teacher reports that Tunina reads very monotonously, avoids answering questions in front of the class, and provides unexpected responses to homework prompts. She gets particularly nervous when given open-ended tasks and when having to make presentations. In addition, according to a recent reading assessment, Tunina was identified as 'at-risk' for reading difficulties. Consequently, her teacher is very concerned. The assistant principal suspects that Tunina may have a learning or a reading disability and is urging Tunina's teacher to seek special education evaluation. At the same time, Tunina's mother, Maritza, reports that her daughter is very active and responsive at home and helps her in several ways. For example, Tunina translates and explains conversations when Maritza is doing errands or filling out forms. Maritza reports that Tunina enjoys reading Bible songs and singing during religious services at the Baptist church the family attends. Maritza has two jobs at nearby stores, but she spends all her free time dedicated to her daughter and family.

Views From Inside: Languages, Cultures, and Schooling for K–12 Educators
pp. 117–134

She wants to support her daughter in any way possible, but she has not been able to establish effective communication with her teacher.

BACKGROUND

Nicaragua is one of seven countries in Central America. It has a population of approximately 6.1 million people and has been strongly influenced by indigenous cultures, Spanish and British colonization, and U.S. intervention. The primary language in Nicaragua is Spanish, although portions of the country speak English creole and several indigenous languages. Despite economic growth in recent years, Nicaragua remains the second poorest country in Latin America after Haiti, with more than 60% of its population living in poverty, including 17.2% in extreme poverty (United Nations, 2015). Nicaragua is characterized by strong social class divisions that separate the large population of poor families from much smaller lower middle and middle classes and separate both of these from a very small wealthy business and political elite. The country's social policies have been unable to effectively serve the very large impoverished segments of the population throughout the country.

Demographics

Seventy percent of the Nicaraguan population is made up of *mestizos*, individuals of mixed indigenous and Spanish ancestry. Indigenous groups, people of African descent, and people of European descent comprise the remainder of the population. There is a strong economic, political, and cultural divide between Nicaragua's more densely populated and relatively more affluent Pacific and central areas, and eastern Nicaragua (a region called the Caribbean coast). Mestizos and Whites are concentrated on the Pacific coast and in the central and northern regions of the country.

The Caribbean coast, made up of two large autonomous regions, represents about 56% of the country's territory and has large populations of indigenous and African descent. The largest indigenous group is the Miskito, a people who live mainly in the northern autonomous region of the Caribbean coast. Other indigenous groups include the Sumus, who were dominant before the Spanish conquest and have been reduced to very few in number, and the Ramas, who live mainly in the southern region. The population of African descent is the legacy of enslaved people who were brought to the Caribbean coast by both Spaniards and English colonizers in the 16th and 17th centuries. A final group, the Garífonas, arrived from the Caribbean islands more recently, in the 19th century.

History

A region with rich and multiple indigenous communities, Nicaragua was colonized by the Spanish in the 16th century. Traditional colonization, however, was localized to the western and central regions as indigenous groups on the Caribbean coast successfully fought off Spanish influence. Rather than political and military domination, the Caribbean coast was influenced by British missionary efforts. More recently, in the 20th century, Nicaragua has been strongly impacted economically, socially, and politically by the United States, including a military presence in the country between 1912 and 1933.

Nicaraguan history is also marked by a historic rivalry between the country's two dominant political parties, the conservative party and the liberal party. Somewhat similar to the U.S.'s Democratic and Republican parties, Nicaragua's conservative and liberal parties have alternated power since the country won independence from Spain in 1821.

Nicaragua was ruled by a dynastic military dictatorship from 1927–1979. In the 1970s, widespread discontent with the Somoza dictatorship erupted in a revolutionary movement that grew in popularity inside and outside of Nicaragua. In July of 1979, the socialist Sandinistas successfully overthrew the dictatorship. One of the first initiatives of the new government was to carry out massive agrarian reform. Land redistribution, full employment, and the low cost of food and transportation, among other social policies, generated strong internal support during the first few years of the new government. At the same time, economic shortages quickly became a reality, international tensions began to emerge, and previous support for the revolutionary government eroded externally and internally. In 1984, facing growing resistance in the mountains, the Sandinistas imposed a military draft, which prompted a wave of migration of young men to other countries, including the United States. Political unrest and civil war appeared again, resulting in the election of a more conservative government in 1990.

The new government, a coalition of the historic liberal and conservative political parties, was determined to reverse what it considered to be the critical economic and political mistakes of the previous decade. Responding to demands from international lending institutions like the International Monetary Fund, austerity measures were introduced into the economy. Additionally, private business was reactivated, and the country opened up to new political organizations. In 2006, however, the Sandinistas were elected back into office with a new framing of "Christian socialism." Contrary to the anti-capitalist orientation of the 1980s, the contemporary iteration of the Sandinistas gives strong support to the private sector. Many Nicaraguan families have been torn apart and are only beginning to recover from the traumas of civil war, political tensions, and economic instability. Each wave of political change has also prompted emigration, with many Nicaraguans fleeing poverty or political instability and immigrating to other countries, including the U.S.

Geography

Nicaragua has very fertile soils and abundant water. Volcanoes are spread along its Pacific region, and the country is home to *Cocibolca*, the largest lake in Central America. Nicaragua also has the biggest forest reserve in the region, and it is home to a few gold, silver, and copper deposits. Yet because of its geographical location, Nicaragua is prone to natural disasters. Earthquakes are unpredictable but expected occurrences on the country's Pacific coast. A 1972 earthquake destroyed Managua, the capital, and killed more than 50,000 people. In October of 1998, more than 11,000 people on Nicaragua's Caribbean coast died from one of the deadliest hurricanes in the Western hemisphere.

Emigration to the U.S.

In recent years, about 3,000 Nicaraguans have come to the U.S. annually (U.S. Census Bureau, 2015). The largest wave of immigration took place between 1980 and 1989, driven by economic scarcity and civil war. In 2014, there were 427,233 Nicaraguans in the U.S. Sixteen percent—or about 70,000—of these Nicaraguans were school age (5–17 years old). The highest concentration of Nicaraguans is in Florida, followed by California and Texas. There are particularly high populations of Nicaraguans in Miami-Dade, Florida (123,912 people) and in Los Angeles, California (42,368 people). The majority of Nicaraguans who come to the U.S. have a higher education level than the Central American average, and they tend to come from urban areas (Acuña, 2013). Their children have a higher likelihood of having attended private schools in Nicaragua. Many foreign Nicaraguans in the U.S. work in the service sector and generally send money to their relatives in Nicaragua, making a valuable contribution to the Nicaraguan economy. According to data from the United Nations, in 2011, Nicaraguan immigrants contributed $900 million to the national economy, representing 10% of the country's wealth that year.

The Nicaraguan population in the U.S. is much smaller than that from Guatemala, El Salvador, Honduras, and other countries in Central America.

Education

Education in Nicaragua has been highly political, with policy swings that mirror the swings in political power. Prior to the Sandinista revolution, roughly three-quarters of Nicaraguans could not read or write. The Sandinista revolutionary government organized a National Literacy Crusade in 1980, reducing the illiteracy rate from 50.3% to 12.9%. They also gave indigenous and ethnic communities official recognition and started the Bilingual Intercultural Education Program on the Caribbean coast in 1985. Since 1990, the Nicaraguan government has promoted educational decentralization, school autonomy, and accountability. As part of this, the country now administers standardized achievement tests every four years in order to inform policy improvement efforts.

The education system faces major challenges related to systemic inequities, inefficient services, and inadequate curricula. Nicaraguans on average attend 4.6 years of schooling, but only 2.1 years in rural areas. The illiteracy rate of people 15 years or older is four times higher in rural areas than it is in urban regions (PREAL, 2014). Spanish illiteracy on the Caribbean coast is more than double that of the Pacific coast. There are persistent problems with grade retention, dropout, and enrollment in some areas of the country. Only about 40% of students who start first grade finish primary schooling (i.e., sixth grade). At least 50% of adolescents are not enrolled in secondary schools, a situation particularly salient in rural areas. Due to widespread poverty, many parents, especially in rural areas, are unable to pay for even the minimum transportation and clothing expenses associated with attending school, and they end up withdrawing their children. With all of these challenges, the literacy rate in Nicaragua has declined, from its high after the Literacy Crusade to 78% (UNICEF, 2015).

Presently, Nicaragua's spending per student is the lowest in Central America (PREAL, 2014). On both the Pacific and the Caribbean coasts, most public schools face critical shortages in infrastructure. Only 48% of schools have running water, and 60% of schools lack electricity. In rural areas, there are inadequate bathrooms and sewage systems; generally there are no sports facilities or meeting rooms. There is a critical deficit of libraries and science and computer labs in public schools in both urban and rural areas (Duarte, Gargiulo, & Moreno, 2011).

Additionally, Nicaraguan school pedagogy has been focused on passive learning, dictation, memorization, and repetition. Efforts to provide more active, practical and contextualized learning have been relatively unsuccessful. Teachers are capable and dedicated, but they are inadequately prepared (Elvir, 2009). Preservice training faces many economic, social, and curricular challenges. Inservice training, although innovative, represents less than 2% of the budget of the Ministry of Education (Guzmán, Castillo, Lavarreda & Mejía, 2013).

The above situation paints a grim picture for most Nicaraguans who enroll in public schools. However, a small but significant portion (10%) of the population attends private schools. Private schools, often Catholic, serve primarily lower-middle-class and middle-class families. Wealthy families attend very elite, expensive, and often internationally focused private schools. Private schools—mainly located in urban areas—are typically equipped with sufficient materials, enjoy basic infrastructure, and have teachers and principals who implement effective pedagogical techniques. Unsurprisingly, average standardized reading and math scores are higher in private schools, and retention rates are almost 100% (Flores, 2012). Some Nicaraguans who immigrate to the U.S. come from middle and elite social classes and have attended private schools. It is very important for U.S. educators to understand the specific educational backgrounds of their recently arrived Nicaraguan students. Some may have relatively strong academic skills, although they may need support to develop English proficiency, knowledge of academic terms, and familiarity with U.S. school routines and protocols. Others will come with weak academic preparation and will need support both linguistically and academically.

CULTURE

A Land of Poets and Writers

Nicaragua is well-known as a land of poets and writers who have made extensive contributions to Spanish literature. For example, Rubén Darío (1867–1916) was a Nicaraguan journalist, essayist, and poet who introduced the style of modernism to Spanish literature. He is well known in Spain and all over Latin America. Famous works are *Azul* and *Prosas Profanas*. Salomón de la Selva (1893–1959) was a poet, translator, soldier, novelist, and researcher who wrote against foreign occupation in Nicaragua. Famous works are *Tropical Town and Other Poems*, *The Unknown Soldier*, and *The Illustrious Family*. He became a professor at Williams College in the U.S. Other important Nicaraguan writers include Alfonso Cortés (*Ven-*

tana), Carlos Martínez Rivas (*Solitary Insurrection*), Ernesto Cardenal (*Psalms of Struggle and Liberation*), Gioconda Belli (*The Country Under My Skin*), Daisy Zamora (*Urgent Message to My Mother*), and Erick Blandón (*Rubén Darío, Un Cisne Entre Gavilanes*). The Caribbean coast has also had a rich literary tradition with poets including Carlos Rigby, David McField, Avelino Cox Molina, Brigitte Zacarías Watson, writer Marcel Jaentschke, and filmmaker Maria José Alvarez.

The written literary tradition in Nicaragua has been primarily concentrated in the middle and upper classes. However, there is a strong popular oral tradition, the most famous of which is the *Güegüense*. The *Güegüense* is a theatrical piece anonymously written in the 16th century. It represents Nicaraguans' ambivalent attitude towards colonialism and subjugation. Thought to have been written in both *Nahuatl* (the indigenous language of the Aztec people) and Spanish, it describes the interactions of an indigenous merchant who mocks the Spanish colonial ruler with dances, dialogues, and masquerades. Recognized throughout Latin America as a groundbreaking work of culture and resistance, the *Güegüense* is performed as a street dance every January. U.S. educators can stimulate student engagement with classroom tasks by having students share their knowledge and experiences with Nicaraguan popular tales and literature.

Reading

Due to poverty, most Nicaraguan children have little access to books, and reading materials are scarce in many homes, except in the middle and upper classes. In school, children's books are rare and cannot be brought home. Most Nicaraguan families cannot afford to buy books, and the presence of children's books in public libraries is a recent phenomenon. In addition, reading in school is disconnected from daily life and is associated with uninteresting tasks, like making summaries and filling out charts. Both economic limitations and school practices have contributed to low reading levels in general in the country, except for the intellectual elite, which enjoys privileged access to books and to a better education.

Music and Dance

A typical musical instrument on the Pacific coast of Nicaragua is the marimba, which was introduced by enslaved Africans. It is an instrument typically made of wooden bars and played with a mallet, producing melodious music that is usually accompanied by guitars and *maracas* in many festivities. One common festivity across social classes is *La Gigantona*, which consists of a giant puppet on a wooden frame who walks down the street usually accompanied by *el Enano Cabezón* (the big-headed dwarf), who represents a short and intelligent indigenous man. These two characters are part of a street dance that is usually accompanied by a drummer and poetic couplets. *La Gigantona* represents Nicaraguan mockery of Spanish colonization. On the Caribbean coast, the *Palo de Mayo* dance festival is celebrated in May. It is a rite of fertility that originated from the English occupation of the region in the 18th century. Music and dance are an integral part of life for most Nicaraguans, and these experiences and resources can be a source of classroom tasks and discussions that may enhance learning.

Family Life

It is very common in Nicaragua for women to be the head of the family. Cultural values give mothers the main responsibility for childcare and for primary emotional attachments with children. While women are at the center of family life due to these responsibilities, the mentality of male dominance, or *machismo,* is very salient, with men often being only tangentially involved with child-raising. Unmarried couples and single mothers are common in Nicaragua. Many poor Nicaraguan women from rural areas must leave their children to work as maids in urban households. Consequently, it is common for children in rural areas to be raised by older siblings, a grandmother, or another relative. Immigration of women to the U.S., a relatively recent phenomenon, is creating new experiences for their children in Nicaragua as part of newly created "transnational families" (Yarris, 2014). Nicaraguan children living in the U.S. may have a broader conception of family as a result of cultural traditions, but also from possible separation from their mothers for several years. They may also be grieving their separation from close family members.

Cultural Traits

The Nicaraguan tendency towards approximation, rather than exactness, when using distances or units of measure, may be relevant in classroom situations in the U.S. For example, when indicating that a place is very near, Nicaraguans will say *aynomasito* or alli no masito (very near). Similarly, area is measured by *varas cuadradas*. A *vara* is a rod or pole; it is a Spanish unit of measure more or less equivalent to one yard, or three feet. Height is measured by *cuartas*; a *cuarta* is approximately 9 inches, informally measured in Nicaragua as the distance between the pinky and the thumb of a hand. During science or math lessons, U.S. educators may want to explore Nicaraguans' everyday applications of measurement before introducing more formal concepts.

Elite literary traditions have promoted a *mestizo* (mixed race) identity with proud connections to Spain and to Spanish colonial rulers, with a tendency to erase the contributions of indigenous and Black populations in and outside of the Caribbean coast (Hooker, 2005). Notions of a civilized nation where *mestizos* have more value than indigenous or people of African descent still dominate the mentality of many Nicaraguans. Consequently, especially in the Pacific, central, and northern regions of the country, indigenous identity is only surreptitiously present. For example, in the popular *Tio Coyote and Tio Conejo* folktale, an able farmworker outsmarts a thief, with a suggestive message that can be linked to how a native personality can survive when having to confront powerful masters who take advantage of ethnic inequalities. Outsmarting as an effective strategy is also present in *El Güegüense* and is part of Nicaraguan identity. Another tendency of popular Nicaraguan culture, presumably emerging during colonial times, is to find comedy and heroism from self-mockery.

Cultural values from colonization are very different on the Caribbean coast. Compared to the Spanish, the British were more cooperative with indigenous groups and acknowledged the authority of self-determination of the Miskitos from the beginning of the 17th century until the end of the 19th century. That legacy results in strong indigenous pride in the northern region of the Nicaraguan Caribbean coast. Two salient traits of Miskito culture are the importance given to the land as a place of sharing and the commitment to passing traditions across generations.

Religion

Catholicism has historically been the dominant religion in the country. In 1950, 95.8% of the population was Catholic. However, the proportion of Catholics has been drastically reduced in the last few decades; the 2005 census reported the percentage of Catholics to be 58.5%. Official sources indicate that there are now more than 100 evangelical groups, who attend more than 10,000 churches. Nondenominational believers have also experienced a significant increase, reaching 20.3%, according to a recent poll (Grigsby Vergara, 2008).

Holidays

Nicaraguans are well known for celebrating, dancing, and enjoying vacations. Many holidays derive from Catholic traditions. The biggest holiday in Nicaragua is *Semana Santa* (Holy Week), culminating in Easter. *Semana Santa* is typically celebrated during a full week of vacation for Nicaraguan students. Nicaraguan Catholics also celebrate the *Purísima*, which is a 9-day devotion to the Virgin Mary taking place between November 28 and December 6. People gather to pray and sing to the Virgin, after which candies are distributed to those who attended the celebration around the altar. At the end of the singing, people ask *"Quién causa tanta alegría?"* ("Who causes so much joy?") and answer *"La concepción de María!"* ("Mary Immaculate!").

Like in other Latin American countries, Nicaraguans celebrate the Day of the Dead on November 2nd, gathering in graveyards and going to mass in memory of loved ones. There are other Catholic religious festivals that Nicaraguans celebrate—even in the U.S. For example, *San Sebastián* and *San Jerónimo*, street processions in honor of these two saints, involve songs and dances and sometimes elaborately decorated floats, in a unique blend of indigenous rituals and Catholicism. U.S. educators can provide spaces for acknowledging, sharing, and expressing these important cultural celebrations.

Food

Popular places to eat Nicaraguan food are the *fritangas*, street stands that serve homemade food. Typical dishes are the *vigorón*, which consists of pork, *yucca* (cassava), shredded cabbage, and tomato; *gallopinto*, rice and beans with onion and cilantro; *vaho*, a meat dish prepared in a large pan and served on plantain leaves with onion and yucca; *nacatamal*, large tamales filled with meat, onion, garlic, tomato, and potato prepared in banana leaves; and *quesillos*, white corn tortillas covered with a special Mozzarella-type cheese, pickled onions, sour cream, and salt.

LANGUAGES AND LITERACIES

Characteristics of Nicaraguan Spanish

Nearly all Nicaraguans speak Spanish (although some as their second language), the country's official language. In Spanish, consonants are pronounced more softly than in English, and generally with no aspiration. In Nicaraguan Spanish, consonants are pronounced even more softly. For example, the sound of the /s/ is commonly substituted by the sound /h/, especially at the end of syllables or words. This makes *escuela* (school) sound like "ehcuela"; *vamos* (we go) like "vamoh," and *nosotros* (we) like "nohotroh." Linguists consider this phonological characteristic an inheritance from Nahuatl. In addition, the /s/ sound is used for the majority of words that have an s and a z, and with the syllables "ce" and "ci." For example, *zopilote* (vulture), *cena* (dinner) and *cigueña* (stork) would all be pronounced with an /s/ sound.

When the Spanish arrived in 1522, many Nicaraguans in the Pacific and central territories spoke Nahuatl, the language brought by migrating Aztec tribes who left their native Mexico after confronting food shortages. With the Spanish conquest, Nahuatl acquired a written form and started influencing the Spanish used in Nicaragua, even though its culture and ethnic group eventually disappeared. Table 7.1 is a small sample of the many Nahuatl words that have been incorporated into current Nicaraguan Spanish. Since the colonial period, many new words have been formed by adding Spanish suffixes to Nahuatl words, as in the case of *jocotear* (bother), or vice versa, as in *zacate* (grass).

There are other peculiarities of the Spanish spoken in Nicaragua, as a legacy from the Nahuatl. It is very rare for Spanish words to have sounds at the end that involve a sudden interruption of air, as in the English word *cat*. Stop sounds involving two consonants, as in the words *bank* and *jump*, are even less common. Consequently, when speaking English, many Spanish speakers tend to ignore these sounds at the end of words. Additionally, in Nicaraguan Spanish, which is softer that other variations of Spanish in Latin America, stop sounds, when in the middle of words, are generally pronounced with a /c/ sound. Thus, it is common to say: *acectar* instead of *aceptar* (accept); *lactop* instead of laptop, and *roboc* instead of robot.

In social situations, Nicaraguans, like Argentinians, will generally use *vos* and *usted*, instead of *tú*, to refer to the second personal singular (you). Not commonly taught in the U.S., Spanish-speaking U.S. teachers may be

**Table 7.1. Influence of Nahuatl
in Common Nicaraguan Words From Mántica (2007)**

Nicaraguan Word	Nahuatl Origin	Meaning
Atol	Atolli	Corn-based drink
Cumiche	Cumitl	Small
Guapote	Cuapoztic	A type of fresh water fish
Nacatamal	Nacatltamalli	Typical dish made from corn meal and meat
Pinolillo	Pinolli(nah)	Typical drink made from toasted corn, cacao, cinnamon, and *achiote*
Sacuanjoche	Tsakushuchittl	Nicaraguan lily (the national flower)

relatively unfamiliar with the use of *vos* and its conjugation. *Usted* is used to show respect when referring to older adults, or to mark hierarchy in social relations. *Vos*, rather than *tú*, is used in close relationships and friendships. *Vos* is conjugated differently than *tú*, resulting, for example, in *tenés* (have) instead of *tienes*, *querés* (want) instead of *quieres*, *decís* (say) instead of *dices*, *pedís* (ask) instead of *pides*, *venís* (come) instead of *vienes*, and *sentís* (sit) instead of *sientes*. *Vos* appeared during colonial times, and it is found in folktale pieces of indigenous origin, like *Tío Coyote and Tío Conejo*: "*¡Conque vos sos, conejo bandido, el que me has hecho tantas carajadas!*" ("So it is you, naughty rabbit, who has hassled me so!"). While universally used in spoken Spanish in the country, Nicaraguans are ambivalent toward *vos*. In 2001, the *vos* form was recognized by the Spanish Royal Academy. However, the *vos* form is almost absent in official and curricular documents, and *tú* is taught formally in schools. There are several words and phrases with a very characteristic Nicaraguan interpretation. For example, "*un poco*" literally means "a little" in many Spanish-speaking countries. However, a Nicaraguan child would commonly say, "*Recogí un poco de confites en la piñata.*" While the literal meaning of the phrase is "I collected a *few* sweets in the piñata," the intended interpretation of "*un poco*" in the sentence above is quite the opposite: "a lot" (Mántica, 2007). Table 7.2 shows some common Nicaraguan sayings, also popular in other Latin American nations.

English Creole and Miskito

English Creole, a nonstandard variety of English, is active and considered part of regional identity in the southern part of the Caribbean coast (Salamanca, 2014). Many Nicaraguans of African descent speak English Creole, and different forms or English Creole are spoken all along the

Table 7.2. Common Nicaraguan Idioms From Mántica (2007)

Common Nicaraguan Idioms	English Meaning
Dime con quién andas y te diré quien eres.	Tell me who you hang out with and I'll tell you who you are.
No hay mal que por bien no venga.	Every bad happening will bring something good.
Ojos que no ven, corazón que no siente.	What you don't know won't hurt you.
Perro que ladra no muerde.	A dog that barks doesn't bite.
A caballo regalado no se le mira el diente.	Don't look a gift horse in the mouth.

Caribbean coast of Central America. Also called Nicaraguan English, English Creole—unlike "standard" English—faces a certain degree of social stigmatization and is considered less socially valued than Spanish in Nicaragua. This stigma emerges, in part, due to relatively widespread discrimination and bias against African-descent Nicaraguans by mestizo Nicaraguans.

Less frequently spoken is Miskito. Miskito, an Amerindian language, was the *lingua franca* on the Caribbean coast during English domination in the 18th century. The Moravian church stimulated this language by translating the Bible into Miskito and by training Miskito ministers. Miskito has several varieties. An interesting feature of Miskito is that it has short and long vowels for *a*, *i*, and *u*, but there are no *e* or *o* vowels. Miskito has borrowed many words from English. In the phrase: "*yan laika sna*" which means "I like it," the word "*laika*" comes from the English word "like." In this language, English words are used when constructing phrases that involve high numbers in order to avoid long phrases that would result from native words. English words that have the /f/ sound—nonexistent in Miskito—will be pronounced with the /p/ sound, so *fine* will sound like *pine*. Another feature of Miskito is that two verbs can work together in a phrase to produce a different meaning, as in *have* and *go*, creating bring (*brih waia*) (Salamanca, 2014). Efforts are being made to protect the Miskito language through use in schools, radio, and television in some regions of the Caribbean coast (Mitchell, 2012). Other indigenous languages, including Sumu, Rama, and Garífona, are rarely spoken and are now on the verge of extinction.

IDEAS FOR EDUCATORS

In this section we provide concrete examples for how teachers and other educators can support their Nicaraguan students academically, linguistically, and socially.

1. Provide Instruction in School Norms

Nicaraguan students in U.S. schools are likely to need explicit instruction about school norms, rules, and expectations. Seemingly obvious to teachers and many U.S.-born students, they are likely to be strange and new to Nicaraguan students. For example, most early elementary classrooms in the U.S. will have storybooks, activity centers, art supplies, and other activities that are not a part of education in Nicaragua. Nicaraguan children will not necessarily intuitively understand why these are present in the classroom or what to do with them.

2. Develop Student Participation

Because of traditional educational practices in place in Nicaraguan schools, Nicaraguan students may not be familiar with teaching and learning situations where they are expected to take initiative in the classroom. This lack of practice—rather than a neurologically based learning problem—may explain the shyness of Tunina in the scenario above when asked to present in front of the class. Teachers can provide students with opportunities to develop these skills in a safe and supportive environment. For example, small group work, supervised by teachers, may help students develop a stronger voice in the classroom setting.

3. Explore Home Literacies

Classroom tasks can investigate the different literacies of their students. Tunina clearly has Bible literacy and language-brokering skills that can be acknowledged, celebrated, and developed in school. Whenever possible, support students' oral and written Spanish use and development. Developing skills in students' primary languages will help them transfer knowledge and skills to English.

4. Involve Families

Nicaraguans' educational backgrounds, their literacy practices, and their family's orientations towards schooling do not follow a single pattern or the stereotype of "uninvolved" Latino parents (Warwick, 2007). Many parents of Nicaraguan children may demonstrate ambition and resourcefulness in the home that may not be immediately obvious to teachers because of a lack of adequate communication with families. One way to tackle the scenario at the beginning of this chapter is to engage in personal interactions with the family, where Tunina's literacies would emerge, pointing to a different explanation for her reading behaviors in class. Home visits, phone calls, daily greetings, and special events (in Spanish) for parents are great ways to build trust and relationships with families.

5. Explore Potential Family Assets That May Support School Expectations

Tunina's mom moved to the U.S. in large part to give her daughter a better future. Nicaraguan values that prioritize the family and highly value education should be understood and tapped. Every family will have specific assets that can support their children's learning and adaptation to U.S. schools. Getting to know families, demonstrating high expectations for their children, and valuing their culture, history, and language will allow teachers to understand and tap into family assets.

6. Compensate for the Possible Scarcity of Books at Home

Many Nicaraguan families do not have a tradition of keeping books at home. Family engagement programs that promote reading between parents and children in Spanish may be very helpful. When possible, send Spanish books home for parents and English and Spanish books home for children.

7. Identify Possible Weak or Interrupted Schooling

As described earlier, some Nicaraguan schools offer weak instruction and curricula. Children who arrive from these schools may be academically behind. Other children, due to economic hardship, violence, or the long voyage north, will have missed one or more years of schooling. Efforts should be made to catch these students up without stigmatizing them for their lack of opportunity. For example, summer school or after school programs and explicit and targeted instruction may help students catch up. Keep in mind that pulling students out of academic instruction, either for language or compensatory support, can lead to students falling farther behind. Try to make sure that students are only pulled out of class at times when they will not miss academic instruction.

CONCLUSIONS

In this chapter we have attempted to highlight the rich history and traditions, as well as some of the complex social inequalities, of the Nicaraguan peoples and cultures. We do so to help you, as educators, learn about and support your Nicaraguan students. As emerging bilingual and transnational individuals, Nicaraguan students will come to your class with vast linguistic, social, and intellectual skills and knowledge. Some may also come having experienced familial separation, violence, or acute poverty. All will come equipped to learn. We hope this chapter has inspired you to help them reach their full, immense potential.

ADDITIONAL RESOURCES

Caistor, N., & Plunkett, H. (2002). *Nicaragua In focus: A guide to the people, politics and culture* (In Focus Guides). New York, NY: Interlink books.

> This guide provides travelers and students a broad picture of Nicaragua, including information about its history, geography, economy, cultures, and traditions.

Jamison, L. (2012). Nicaraguan Spanish: Speak like a native! Retrieved from http://www.gringoguide200.com/category/nicaraguan-spanish/

> A compilation of idioms, sayings, words, and phrases used by the locals in Nicaragua.

Rushdie, S. (1987). *The jaguar smile: A Nicaraguan journey.* London, UK: Pan Books.

> Salman Rushdie's first full-length nonfiction book relates his travel adventures, his experiences meeting people, and his understanding of the political situation in Nicaragua in the mid-1980s.

Foro Nicaragüense de Cultura. (n.d.). Retrieved from foronicaragüensedecultura.org.

> Information about current cultural events and projects in Nicaragua.

Remington, F. (2012, October 19). A Margarita Debayle [video file]. Retrieved from https://www.youtube.com/watch?v=DfdphvfNseo

> An animated video of Rubén Darío's famous poem to his muse, Margarita Debayle, about a little princess and a star.

TASKS FOR EDUCATORS

1. Consider your answers to these questions:

   o Many Nicaraguan families have few or no books at home. In what ways could you support your students' literacy development by connecting with their families and providing family literacy opportunities?

   o How can you learn about the linguistic strengths and skills of your Nicaraguan students, the languages they speak or understand, and the languages that are spoken in their wider family?

2. Make a list of assumptions you had before reading this chapter that have been challenged with your reading. Explain what specific information contributed to change your thinking.

3. What aspects of Nicaraguan Spanish and of Miskito seem relevant for learning to read and write? How might the linguistic features of these languages impact learning in English?

4. What features of Nicaraguan culture did you find interesting and why?

5. What aspects of Nicaraguan life and history might explain some classroom behaviors for children who immigrate to the U.S.?

6. Based on the information in this chapter, identify three aspects of the life of a Nicaraguan child who lives in Managua. Then, do the same for a child born in the north Caribbean coast. In each case, compare those characteristics with (a) U.S.-born children you know and (b) other Latino children you know. What are the implications for your work in the classroom?

7. What are some changes to your instruction that you are thinking of implementing as a result of reading this chapter?

REFERENCES

Acuña, R. (2013). *Flujos migratorios laborales intrarregionales: Situación actual, retos y oportunidades en Centroamérica y República Dominicana. Informe de Nicaragua.* San José, Costa Rica: Organización Internacional para las Migraciones.

Duarte, J., Gargiulo, C., & Moreno, M. (2011). *Infraestructura escolar y aprendizajes en la educación básica latinoamericana: un análisis a partir del SERCE.* Washington, DC: Banco Interamericano de Desarrollo (Notas Técnicas, #IDB-TN-277). Retrieved from http://idbdocs.iadb.org/wsdocs/getdocument .aspx?docnum=36201660

Elvir, P. (2009). *Classroom pedagogy in Spanish language arts: What and how students are taught in the Nicaraguan public school context or the paradoxes of realistic pedagogical models* (Unpublished dissertation). Harvard University, Cambridge, MA. Retrieved from http://las.sinica.edu.tw:1085/search~S0?/aElvir%2C +Ana+Patricia/aelvir+ana+patricia/-3%2C-1%2C0%2CB/frameset&FF =aelvir+ana+patricia&1%2C1%2C

Flores, C. F. (2012). *La educación primaria en Nicaragua. Condiciones que favorecen u obstaculizan el aumento de la matrícula, la retención y la promoción escolar.* Managua, Nicaragua: Instituto de Estudios Estratégicos y Políticas Públicas.

Grigsby Vergara, W. (2008). *Leer o no leer: Ésa es la cuestión. Universidad Centroamericana (UCA).* Revista Envío, # 317. Managua, Nicaragua. Retrieved from http://www.envio.org.ni/articulo/3844

Guzmán J. L., Castillo, M. A., Lavarreda, J., & Mejía, R. (2013). *Effective teacher training policies to ensure effective schools: A perspective from Central America and the Dominican Republic.* Retrieved from http://www.politicasdocentesalc.cl/images/ stories/Biblioteca/Primera_Fase/TendenciasRegionalesCentroAmericaENG .pdf

Hooker, J. (2005). Beloved enemies: Race and official mestizo nationalism in Nicaragua. *Latin American Research Review, 40*(3), 14–39.

Mántica, C. (2007). *El habla nicaragüense y otros ensayos.* Managua, Nicaragua: Hispamer.

Mitchell, S. (2012). *Unheard voices: Miskito poetry and the Nicaraguan poetic tradition* (Unpublished Master Thesis). University of Vermont.

PREAL. (2014). *Calidad y equidad para el desarrollo humano. Informe de progreso educativo Nicaragua*. Managua, Nicaragua: Programa de promoción de la reforma educativa en América Latina y el caribe.

Salamanca, D. (2014). El idioma miskito: Estado de la lengua y características tipolo?gicas. *Temas Nicaragüenses, 70,* 108–128.

UNICEF. (2015). *State of the world's children 2105*. Retrieved from http://www.unicef.org/infobycountry/nicaragua_statistics.html

United Nations. (2015). *América Latina y el Caribe. Revisión regional al 2015 de educación para todos (EPT) en América Latina y el Caribe* (Draft). Oficina regional de educación de la UNESCO para América Latina y el Caribe.

U. S. Census Bureau. (2015). Selected demographics. Retrieved from http://factfinder.census.gov/

Warwick, J. M. (2007). Biliteracy and schooling in an extended-family Nicaraguan immigrant household: The sociohistorical construction of parental involvement. *Anthropology & Education Quarterly, 38*(12), 19–137.

Yarris, K. E. (2014). "Quiero ir y no quiero ir" (I want to go and I don't want to go): Nicaraguan children's ambivalent experiences of transnational family life. *Journal of Latin American and Caribbean Anthropology, 19*(2), 284–309.

SECTION 4

SOUTH AMERICAN REGION

CHAPTER 8

ARGENTINA

Sandra Mercuri
Educational Consultant

Sandra I. Musanti
University of Texas–Rio Grande Valley

Hi! My name is Estefanía.
I am 7 years old.
I am from Argentina.

This is all that Estefanía, a young girl from Argentina, knew of English when she arrived in the central valley of California with her parents and her older sister in the winter of 1997. She had worked hard to learn those phrases to be able to communicate and make friends. Upon arrival in December, Estefanía was placed in second grade, even though she had completed second grade in Argentina and was literate in her first language. She was immersed in an all-English classroom with teachers who knew very little about Argentinian students, since valley schools mostly received students from Mexico and Central America. Consequently, Estefanía did not fit the mold of the second language learners that the school served. Because the school was located in a rural area, most of the second language learners who attended this elementary school were children of farmworkers and many of them were also migrants. Estefanía's parents, on the other hand, were educated professionals who came to this country to continue their education and to expand

Views From Inside: Languages, Cultures, and Schooling for K–12 Educators
pp. 137–152

their opportunities. In addition, Estefanía's parents and sister spoke English and academic Spanish and were able to support her to navigate the educational context as she was learning English, while many of her classmates did not have this advantage.

The first encounter with the realities English language learners (ELLs) face in monolingual English classrooms was the issue of her name. Since the teacher could not pronounce her Spanish name, she started to call her "Stephanie." In a few months, Estefanía had become "Stephanie" for all her classmates and her teacher, and she began to question the way her family called her at home. She wanted to belong, and one way for her to feel part of the new school community was to be called using the Americanized version of her name.

At that time, Stephanie's mother was pursuing a master's degree in bilingual education. The new understandings about American schooling and the approaches and techniques she was learning in her program were not reflected in the way her 7-year-old daughter was taught at school. It was important for her mother to visit with the teacher and discuss her concerns. After the meeting, while well-intentioned, the teacher explained that Stephanie was only the ELL in her classroom and that it was hard for her to individualize her instruction. She believed the young girl would do well with time.

After this meeting, Estefanía's mother began to implement at home what Krashen (1996) called "de facto bilingual education." Every day after Estefanía returned home, concepts taught in English at school were retaught, explained, or clarified in Spanish. Within a few months, language transfer began to occur.

BACKGROUND

Argentina is located at the southern tip of South America. It is bounded by Bolivia and Paraguay to the north, by Chile and the Atlantic Ocean to the south, by Brazil, Uruguay and the Atlantic Ocean to the east, and by Chile to the west. The country is very diverse in terms of geographical regions, landscapes, and cultures. The biodiversity and land variety can be found from the Arctic region in the south to the jungle in the north, and from the Andes Mountains in the west to the Pampas plains in the east. With approximately 43 million inhabitants, Argentina has been defined as an important economic and cultural connection for all of South America (Presidencia de la Nación, n.d.)

By the year 1500, many different indigenous communities lived in the territory, congregated in tribes. They had different languages, social organizations, and customs, and they inhabited different geographical areas. The Spanish colonization started in 1512. Argentina was originally part of the *"Virreinato* del Rio de la Plata," the governance structure created by Spain in 1776. The arrival of the Spanish conquerors, with their own customs and values, generated a process of "cultural convergence of everlasting dimensions, not without pain in some cases and cooperation in others" (Presidencia de la Nación, n,d). This process of convergence generated a mix of races, including White and indigenous peoples. Later on, men and women from Africa and Brazil were brought as slaves, mixing with the local (*criolla*) population.

British attempts to conquer the territory in the early 1800s failed due to resistance by the local people. Over the years, local indigenous tribes were conquered by the Spaniards and outnumbered by waves of immigration. Spaniards did not value indigenous groups and therefore kept few records of those indigenous groups. The existence of 35 Argentine Amerindians or native Argentines has been recently documented by a national census (INDEC, 2005).

Argentina has been traditionally defined as a country with a large middle class formed mainly by descendants of European immigrants. Unlikemost countries in Latin America, Argentina's income distribution has been fairly equitable throughout most of the 20th century. This changed in the 1980s when levels of poverty increased significantly. Neoliberal policies implemented since the last dictatorship in 1976–1982 resulted in the impoverishment of a huge part of the population due to higher rates of unemployment (Pini, Musanti, Feldfeber, & Bravo, in press).

Ethnicity and Immigration

Historically, indigenous people in Argentina were systematically assimilated into the mainstream culture, not always in peaceful ways. Bartolomé (2003) explains how during the colonization era, indigenous peoples living in the Argentine territory were almost exterminated due to violence, epidemics, and the "ethnic disappearance" product of evangelization, relocation, and other processes that diluted the cultural identity of the people. Few indigenous communities have been able to maintain their language and customs. Some still live in conditions of extreme poverty, like the Wichis in Salta province or the Tobas in Chaco province. The exclusion and marginalization that indigenous peoples endured was not a topic of wide discussion until very recently. In 1994, the Argentinean Constitution was reformed to recognize the ethnic and cultural pre-existence of Argentine indigenous peoples and to ensure respect for their identity and their right to bilingual and intercultural education.

Millions of Europeans, mainly from Spain and Italy, immigrated to Argentina through the port of Buenos Aires during the last part of the 19th century and the first half of the 20th century. The immigration influx changed the cultural, social, and linguistic landscape of the country in many ways. This produced the Europeanization of Argentina and is one of the factors in the transition from a traditional Argentina to a modern nation. This process resulted in the transformation of the national character and generated an open immigration policy.

However, economic crisis and political instability, represented by successive periods of both democratic governments and dictatorships, have slowly transformed Argentina into a country of immigration, emigration, and transit. Emigration flows increased at moments of economic crisis. Jachimowicz (2006) notes, "Since the 1990s, dismal employment prospects coupled with strong foreign labor demand and, at times, favorable visa policies in countries including the United States, Spain, Italy, and Israel have given rise to a new wave of emigration" (n.p.). For instance, Argentina's economic collapse in 2001–2002 saw significant emigration flows of Argentine nationals to Europe and the United States. However, Argentina's strong demand for predominantly unskilled, low-wage labor ensures its role as a regional immigration hub, consistently attracting new economic migrants from its neighbors in the southern cone of Latin America. Argentina continues to receive immigrants from neighboring countries such as Bolivia, Peru, and Paraguay. This trend increased during the last 20 years when Argentina experienced economic growth and political stability.

Approximately 242,000 Argentinean people were reported living in the United States in 2011, constituting the 14th largest population of Hispanic origin in the country (0.5%) (Brown & Patten, 2013). Important to notice is the immigration status of the Argentinean population in the United States. Brown and Patten (2013) explain that "About six-in-ten Argentineans (62%) in the United States are foreign born compared with 36% of Hispanics and 13% of the U.S. population overall. About six-in-ten immigrants from Argentina (60%) arrived in the U.S. in 1990 or later. About half of Argentinean immigrants (49%) are U.S. citizens" (n.p.). In addition, Argentinean immigrants tend to have higher levels of education than the overall Hispanic population and the U.S. population overall. The Pew Research Center indicates that 40% of Argentineans ages 25 and older have obtained at least a bachelor's degree. This is compared with 13% of all U.S. Hispanics and 29% of the U.S. population (Brown & Patten, 2013). According to the 2010 census, the states with largest numbers of Argentineans are Florida, California, New York, New Jersey, and Texas.

CULTURE

Argentina has a diverse population that challenges any attempt to identify them ethnically (Rodríguez, n.d.). Argentinean culture is diverse and integrates traits of the local "*criolla*" culture and different immigration waves, especially Spanish and Italian. Immigrant groups have significantly contributed to Argentinean cuisine and other traditions. For instance, along with traditional Latin American dishes such as *tamales*, a South American variation of *tamales* called *humitas*, *locro* (a beef, potato, bean, and corn stew of Quechua origin), and *empanadas* (turnovers), there are Italian pasta dishes and pizza, and Spanish dishes such as *chorizo* (sausage). Another Argentinean specialty is *dulce* de *leche*, a thick caramel syrup made with highly condensed milk.

A traditional Argentinean beverage is *mate*, a type of green tea drunk with a metal straw (*bombilla*) in a small pot-like container, usually made from a carved, dried gourd or wood. *Mate*, pronounced *ma-té*, is usually drunk and shared in social gatherings with friends or families. Over time, it has developed into a unique symbol of Argentinean identity and expresses the value of social interaction and interconnectedness.

Another important symbol of Argentinean tradition and culture is the *gaucho*, a local version of a cowboy. The attire of the *gaucho* has evolved with time. Originally, it consisted of a simple garment known as the *chiripá*, a diaper-like cloth pulled over lacy leggings, which was usually worn with a *poncho*.

The Argentinean family is characterized by close relationships. Family gatherings are a tradition, especially on national holidays and on Sundays at lunch time for *asado* (Argentinean barbecue) or pasta. The family often extends to cousins, aunts, uncles, in-laws, and sometimes even the families of the in-laws. Grandparents play an important role within the family in child rearing, providing needed support for working parents. In Argentina, family reunions are usually carried out on a weekly basis. Children usually spend a longer time living with their parents than they do in the United States. Sometimes they stay with them until they get married.

The Argentinean communication style is direct and affectionate, and it includes human contact. It is not uncommon to see a teacher hugging a student or kissing students' parents when they arrive for a parent–teacher conference. It is customary for people to meet and greet with a kiss on the cheek. When meeting formally, people use a strong handshake to greet each other and when leaving, people say goodbye to each other individually.

Traditions and Religion

There is not an official religion in Argentina, but the population is largely Catholic. The National Constitution establishes freedom of religion or creed. However, the Argentine Constitution clearly supports the Catholic religion, as expressed in its second article. Apart from Catholicism, there are over 2,500 officially recognized religions that co-exist harmoniously, such as Judaism, Protestantism, Pentecostalism, and Islam, among others.

Religion and cultural traditions of immigrant groups have influenced Argentina's traditions and customs. Christmas celebrations are a very important holiday time in Argentina, even though today this celebration has more of a secular connotation than a religious one, with an important emphasis on family gathering. Most homes will have an artificial Christmas tree, shaped as a pine or similar, white or green covered by cotton snow. Children wait for the arrival of *Papa Noel* instead of Santa Claus at midnight on Christmas Eve, when families gather for late dinner. Clearly, these are examples of cultural syncretism, where the beliefs and practices of two unique cultures mix and create new cultural characteristics. The pagan origin of the Christmas tree and its symbolism in different cultures could be an interesting topic to explore at school.

THE ROLE OF PUBLIC EDUCATION

The Argentine education system was established by the Constitution of 1853, which legislates the right to teach and learn, and extends this right also to foreigners (Bravo, 1983). The Argentine public education system was developed with the goal to support the consolidation of a national culture and to assimilate immigrant populations, especially by expanding primary education to the entire population in the early 1900s (Novaro, 2012). Historically, secondary and higher education were intended to create the ruling elite. Argentina was one of the first countries in Latin America to achieve full coverage in elementary education, although with an uneven distribution of secondary schools and higher education (Auguste, Echart, & Franchetti, 2008).

Presently, the national education system presents a unified structure of 13 years of compulsory education that spans from 5 to 17 years old. The system includes four levels of education:

- Initial (pre-K) education includes children from 45 days old to 5 years old. The last year is mandatory.
- Primary education is mandatory and begins at 6 years of age. It consists of 6 or 7 years as decided by each state.
- Secondary education involves 6 or 5 years of schooling as determined by each state.
- Higher education (duration varies) includes the following offerings:

o   Universities and university institutes, public or private, and

o   Nonuniversity institutions such as teacher education institutions and technical education centers, among others.

Each province determines its curricular organization following national guidelines that identify common curricular content and goals for each educational level. For instance, the city of Buenos Aires lists the following as the general formation disciplines for secondary education: biology, economy, physics, sex education, chemistry, philosophy, ethics and citizenship, geography, history, entrepreneurship, mathematics, language arts and literature, information technology, arts, and music (Ciudad Autónoma de Buenos Aires, 2014). Foreign language, specifically English language, in Argentinean education has a long history. English is part of the public school curriculum and is taught as a foreign language. Private schools have embraced bilingual programs that reflect many of the characteristics of dual language programs in the United States. Education in Argentina has undergone extensive changes in the last decade (Tocalli-Beller, 2007).

School Culture

Schools are complex and integrate written and unwritten rules, rituals, and traditions (see Chapter 1 for an explanation). In Argentina, like in many schools around the world, students line up in the morning to salute the flag, and at the elementary level students line up to go to recess or to enter the classroom. Most schools in Argentina are double-shift; this means that a school day is a half-day (typically 4 hours), giving schools the possibility to serve two groups of students with the detrimental impact of fewer hours of schooling. Recently, following an international trend and to respond to the need for more schooling time, there has been an initiative to extend the school day and to transform public schools into single-shift schools, providing all students with an extended school day (IIPE-UNESCO, 2010). However, the initiative has proven challenging to implement, and very few schools have an extended school day.

Teachers are called *maestras/os* during elementary school. The word "*maestra*" comes from the Latin "magister," which alludes to someone with a high level of expertise. Typically, from 1st to 3rd grade, one teacher teaches all content areas, except for physical education and arts or music. From 4th to 6th grade, one teacher teaches language arts and social students and another teacher teaches mathematics and science. This practice is supposed to help students transition to secondary education. In secondary schools, teachers are designated as *profesor/a*. One *profesor* is assigned to teach each discipline. Typically, each day students receive instruction in several different core disciplines, and school time is organized in 45- to 90-minute blocks.

Public school classroom walls are usually bare, as they are shared by more than one teacher and different groups of students. The traditional blackboard and chalk are the main instruments for instruction. However, this is changing. Today computers are part of school life, and most students have access to a computer lab or digital notebooks. Recently, two national programs distributed notebooks to secondary and primary school students and teachers across the country to promote equity through digital inclusion (Ministerio de Educación, 2011).

Students bring their backpacks to school and they complete their school work in *cuadernos*, or notebooks that are organized by *materias*, or content area. White smocks (*guardapolvos o delantales*) are the school uniforms of public schools (K–12) in Argentina. Every morning students can be seen walking or getting out of buses or family cars dressed in their white smocks. The tradition of the white smocks started at the beginning of the 20th century. Dussel (n.d.) explains that the origin is unclear; several school supervisors and teachers have credited themselves with the creation of the idea. They also claimed that the goal was to identify a piece of clothing that was inexpensive, clean, and democratic to accompany public school expansion. Although the reason for choosing white as its color is unclear, the use of the white smock developed in an endearing way that had people referring to students for a long time as "*palomitas blancas*," or little white doves. In 1915, a decree recommended the use of the white smocks in all public schools. Teachers and students were expected and later mandated to use the uniform. Ultimately, the smocks were seen as a way of covering the differences in clothing of children and a way to homogenize society. Children wear their own clothes under their smocks (Dussel, n.d.). Private schools have formal school uniforms too; most of them have adopted English-style school uniforms, which clearly distinguish the students who attend public schools from those who attend private schools.

LANGUAGES AND LITERACIES

The official language in Argentina is Spanish, spoken with regional variations in terms of vocabulary, intonation, and in the pronunciation of certain sounds. Most of the original languages of Argentina have been lost, although some indigenous languages, such as *Quechua, Guaraní, Wichí, Toba Qom, Mapuche,* and Aymara are spoken by different communities throughout the country. *Guaraní* is probably the most widespread native language; it is spoken mainly in the north and northeast of Argentina. Argentines refer to the variety of Spanish spoken in their country as "*castellano*"—that is, Castilian Spanish.

Castilian Spanish presents some variations with respect to other language varieties spoken in Latin America. One of the salient differences is in phonology (pronunciation). These differences can usually be associated with the geographic location of the speaker. For example, in the metropolitan area of Buenos Aires the letters "y" and "ll" in Spanish are pronounced similarly to the English "j" in "John," and it is called "*yeísmo*." Elsewhere in the Americas or Spain those letters tend to be pronounced as the English "y" in "yawn," and it is called "*lleísmo*."

From a pedagogical perspective, understanding language differences between speakers of different varieties of Spanish could be used to help students analyze the nuances of the language varieties and their relationships with the target language or the language of schooling when appropriate. Beeman and Urow (2013) explain the importance of having linguistic conversations with students who are developing a second language, especially in classrooms that have students from different Spanish-speaking countries. When students engage in conversations about language, they begin to understand their own language better and are able to differentiate and apply that understanding to each language as they speak, read, and write for different purposes. This approach to language teaching is called "metalanguage" or "metalinguistic awareness" (Beeman & Urow, 2013; Escamilla et al., 2015)

Providing opportunities for language development and extension of students' linguistic repertoires within their own language (and across languages, in the case of bilingual classrooms) can be very beneficial. For example, a few of Estefanía's (in the opening scenario) classmates of Mexican descent, who spoke English and had receptive knowledge of Spanish, always made fun of her for pronouncing the "ll" sound in Spanish like the "j" sound in English in words such as *amarillo* or *caballo*. They made comments such as, "I do not understand what she said. She does not speak Spanish or English." In today's schools, teachers could capitalize on these opportunities and have a discussion about language differences and language varieties. An effective approach could be to design a mini-lesson in which the phonological aspects of the Spanish language are discussed side-by-side, as in Table 8.1, with examples provided by the students to solidify their own linguistic understandings of the language(s) of instruction.

Another aspect that could be discussed with students is that the use of *yeísmo* produces homophony in a number of cases, which could a cause confusion among native speakers and nonnative speakers alike. For exam-

Table 8.1. Sample Dialect Differences in Spanish

Argentina (How it Sounds)	Examples	Sound in English	Mexico and Other Countries (How it Sounds)	Examples	Sound in English
/y/	yegua	/j/	/y/	cayó	/y/
/y/	Caballo	/j/	/ll/	amarillo	/y/

ple, the following word pairs sound the same to speakers of dialects with *yeísmo*, but would not have the same sound in regions with *lleísmo*:

- *haya* ("beech tree" / "that there be") ~ *halla* ("s/he finds")
- *cayó* ("s/he fell") ~ *calló* ("s/he became silent")
- *hoya* ("pit, hole") ~ *olla* ("pot")
- *baya* ("berry") / *vaya* ("he goes") ~ *valla* ("fence")

Activities like the one discussed above also bring value to the language varieties of the students we teach and expand their own language practices beyond their country of origin.

Another important aspect of the Spanish from Argentina that could be discussed with students is the use of *el voseo* (Gassó, 2009). Among grammatical features, the most prominent variation among dialects is in the use of second-person pronouns. In Spanish-speaking America, the only second-person plural pronoun, both formal and informal, is *ustedes*, while in most of Spain the informal second-person plural pronoun is *vosotros*, with *ustedes* used only in formal speech. A similar difference can be found in the second-person singular familiar pronoun (e.g., *tú* and *vos*). Teachers of older bilingual students could extend their understandings about language as they discuss how to use it in sentences with different registers. Teachers can then note that, both as a subject and as an object, in English we only use the form "you." When teachers make these similarities or differences between the two languages of instruction explicit to second language learners, they facilitate language transfer and second language acquisition.

IDEAS FOR EDUCATORS

The teacher in the opening scenario of this chapter did not understand (or take the time to find out) that Estefanía was already a reader and a writer in her own language. She had the foundational knowledge about literacy to enhance second language literacy development. Teachers with Argentine students can capitalize on the linguistic and literacy abilities and experiences students already bring with them about reading and writing. Because Argentina's educational system places great importance on the teaching of reading, students commonly read and write fairly well by the time they finish second grade. Estefanía did not need to learn to read again; she needed her teacher to provide opportunities for Spanish literacy to transfer through engaging and differentiated reading and writing lessons.

Teachers might receive in their classrooms students from South America, from Spanish-speaking countries such as Argentina, Peru, Chile, Uruguay, Ecuador—among others—or from non-Spanish-speaking countries such as Brazil and Guyana. These countries might have some similar cultural and linguistic traits but also many differences. It is important to avoid overgeneralizing characteristics from one culture to another one and to be open to learn about students' specific cultural identities and to capitalize on the "funds of knowledge" that every child and family has to offer. As explained in Chapter 1, culture is complex and dynamic even within the same national boundaries. Argentina is a diverse country, with different linguistic and cultural regional variations.

Further, teachers might encounter two types of Argentine students in their classrooms: (a) newcomers who recently arrived to the United States and who have had previous schooling experiences in Argentina, such as Estefanía, and (b) children who were born in the United States and who speak Spanish at home. The latter group of students does not have schooling experiences in Argentina, but their parents might have expectations associated with their own schooling experiences. Most Argentine families migrating to the United States are middle-class families whose households are professionals or have at least completed high school; among the strategies teachers could use when working with students from Argentina are:

- Focus on metalinguistic awareness for the analysis of Spanish varieties as described previously in this chapter. In addition, add a comparison to English so students not only expand their understanding about their own language variety but also transfer some of those concepts to the target language they are learning in school.
- Engage students with popular Argentinean children's literature. For example, books and songs by Maria Elena Walsh are very popular not only at the educational level but also at the family level. She combines original music, humor, games, and theater with the intention to entertain and amuse. All her rebelliousness, her disappointment, and her love of nature and children are reflected in her

poems, stories, and songs. Students from Argentina from different generations have been exposed to this author and songwriter's work. This could validate the students' cultural experiences and enhance their class participation as experts by presenting a story, reading their favorite Walsh book, or singing a song they want to share with the rest of the class.

- Similarly, Argentinian humor could be one way to bring culture into class discussion. Braslavsky (2000) explains that a shift has happened from a more traditional and decontextualized teaching of reading to focus more on comprehension of authentic literature. *Mafalda*, a cartoon by Quino and one of Argentina's cultural icons of all time, shows this educational change through humor. Teachers could engage students in comparing and contrasting the way they learned to read in their countries of origin as well as the similarities and differences with the American educational system in regards to reading and writing instruction. Mafalda cartoons can be found all over the internet.

- Teachers can consider using culturally relevant books and bilingual books when possible to help students make connections between the readings, topics of study, and their personal experiences and current events. For example, students can make connections with places they know and with experiences they or their relatives have had. This makes students interested in the reading and in sharing what they know, especially if they see themselves mirrored in the story. Cultural relevancy is determined by a series of categories such as ethnicity, age, gender, and the characters' ways of talking. Examples of culturally relevant books are *Abuela* and My Soccer Book (Ebe, 2015). In addition, the use of bilingual books, when appropriate, shows respect for the students' first languages and allows for primary language use through the teaching event, validating students' identities and raising self-esteem.

- Teachers could extend cultural discussions by using cultural artifacts to facilitate language development and to strengthen students' pride in their heritage. For example, Estefanía, for show and tell day, brought a *mate* from home (as shown in Figure 8.1) and explained its uses for friendly socialization.

CONCLUSIONS

This chapter provides an articulated summary of central characteristics of the Argentinean culture, Spanish language, and traditions that can help teachers to better support Argentinean newcomer students. Our English

Source: Photograph taken by Sandra Mercuri.

Figure 8.1.   Vintage yerba mate gourd and bombilla (slotted straw).

language learners may not come from homes where parents can facilitate the type of opportunities for their children to become truly bilingual that Estefanía's parents offered; however, teachers of Argentinean students can use the ideas provided in this chapter to facilitate their students' social integration into the classroom community and school as well as their engagement in classroom discourse and active participation in language instruction.

ADDITIONAL RESOURCES

Latin American Network Information Center (LAINC). (2015). *Argentina.* Retrieved from http://lanic.utexas.edu/la/argentina/
> This is a site with reliable resources to learn about Argentina, its culture, traditions, literature, arts, indigenous people, immigration, government, human rights, and so on.

Explora. Pedagogía. (2016). Retrieved from http://www.encuentro.gov.ar
> A series of curricular materials and videos produced by the National Department of Education in collaboration with *Canal Encuentro*, an educative television broadcast produced and supported by the national government. In this site, teachers can find videos describing and explaining curricular and pedagogical approaches to Argentinean education.

Videos available from http://www.encuentro.gov.ar/sitios/encuentro/programas/ver?rec_id=101779
> Curricular materials available from http://explora.educ.ar/noticias/fasciculos-para-el-modulo-i-de-cs-sociales-y-cs-naturales/

Banfi, C., & Day, R. (2005). The evolution of bilingual schools in Argentina. In A. M. de Mejia (Ed.), *Bilingual education in South America* (pp. 65–78). Bristol, UK: Multilingual Matters. Retrieved from https://www.academia.edu/4977709/The_Evolution_of_Bilingual_Schools_in_Argentina
> This article provides a descriptive account of an important sector of the Argentine education system, specifically known as "Escuelas bilingües" (bilingual schools). Most of these schools are private schools that tend to middle and upper-middle-class students.

TASKS FOR EDUCATORS

1. What are some similarities and differences between what you read in this chapter and what you knew about Spanish-speaking students from other Latin American countries? Create a table with the information you gathered through the comparison.

2. Have you ever experienced or observed a situation at school similar to Estefanía's experiences discussed in the chapter? Describe the scenario and how you responded to the situation.

3. Based on the information in the chapter, make a list of what you would like to know more about students from Argentina. List different sources you could explore to find out more about these students.

REFERENCES

Auguste, S., Echart, M., & Franchetti, F. (2008). *The quality of education in Argentina*. Buenos Aires, Argentina: Inter-American Development Bank (IDB).

Bartolomé, M. A. (2003). Los pobladores del "Desierto" genocidio, etnocidio y etnogénesis en la Argentina. *Cuadernos de Antropología Social, 17*, 162–189

Beeman, K., & Urow, C. (2013). *Teaching for biliteracy: Strengthening bridges between languages*. Philadelphia, PA: Caslon.

Braslavsky, B. (2000). Las nuevas perspectivas de la alfabetización temprana. *Lectura y Vida*, *21*(4), 32–43.

Bravo, H. F. (1983). *Educación popular.* Buenos Aires, Argentina: Centro Editor de América Latina.

Brown, A., & Patten, E. (2013). Hispanics of Argentinean origin in the United States, 2011. *Pew Research Center, Hispanic Trends.* Retrieved from http://www.pewhispanic.org/2013/06/19/hispanics-of-argentinean-origin-in-the-united-states-2011/

Ciudad Autónoma de Buenos Aires. Ministerio de Educación. (2014). *Diseño curricular nueva escuela secundaria* de la ciudad de *buenos aires. Ciclo básico: 2014–2020.* Buenos Aires: Ministerio de Educación del Gobierno de la Ciudad Autónoma de Buenos Aires. Dirección General de Planeamiento Educativo.

Dussel, I. (n.d.). El guardapolvo blanco. *Revista El Monitor,* 12. Retrieved from http://www.me.gov.ar/monitor/nro12/museo.htm

Ebe, A. (2015). The power of culturally relevant texts: What teachers learn about their emergent bilingual students. In Y. S. Freeman & D. E. Freeman (Eds.), *Research on preparing inservice teachers to work effectively with emergent bilinguals* (pp. 33–53). Bingley, UK: Emerald.

Escamilla, K., Hopewell, S., Butvilofsky, S., Sparrow, W., Soltero-González, L., Ruíz-Figueroa., & Escamilla, M. (2014). *Biliteracy from the start: Literacy squared in action.* Philadelphia, PA: Caslon.

Gassó, M. J. (2009). El voseo rioplatense en la clase de español. V Encuentro Brasileño de Profesores de Español. Instituto cervantes de belo horizonte. *Suplementos* de Marco *ELE, 9,* 1–26.

IIPE-UNESCO. (2010). *Estado del arte: Escolaridad primaria y jornada escolar en el context internacional. Estudio de casos en Europa y América Latina.* Buenos Aires, Argentina: Author. Retrieved from http://www.buenosaires.iipe.unesco.org/sites/default/files/SEP%2520Mx%2520Estado_arte%2520jornada%2520escolar.pdf

INDEC. (2005). *Encuesta complementaria* de pueblos *indígenas* 2004–*2005* (ECPI). Retrieved from http://www.indec.gov.ar/micro_sitios/webcenso/ECPI/index_ecpi.asp

Jachimowicz, M. (2006). *Argentina: A new era of migration and migration policy.* Migration Policy Institute. Retrieved from http://www.migrationpolicy.org/article/argentina-new-era-migration-and-migration-policy

Krashen, S. (1996). *Under attack: The case against bilingual education* (3rd ed.). Culver City, CA: Language Education Associates.

Ministerio de Educación. (2011). *Nuevas voces, nuevos escenarios: Estudios evaluativos sobre el program Conectar Igualdad.* Buenos Aires, Argentina: Author. Retrieved from http://observatoriotic.gobiernoabierto.gob.ar/multimedia/files/Conectar%2520Igualdad%2520-%2520Nuevas%2520voces%2520nuevos%2520escenarios.pdf

Novaro, G. (2012). Niños inmigrantes en Argentina: Nacionalismo escolar, derechos educativos y experiencias de alteridad. *Revista mexicana de investigación educativa*, *17*(53), 459–483. Retrieved from http://www.scielo.org.mx/scielo.php?script=sci_arttext&pid=S1405-66662012000200007&lng=es&tlng=es

Pini, M. E., Musanti, S. I., Feldfeber, M., & Bravo, M. (in press). Teacher education and professional development in the context of Argentinean educational policies: Current trends and challenges. In K. Karras & C. C. Wolhuter (Eds.), *International handbook of teacher education world wide: Issues and challenges* (Vol. II). Athens, Greece: Athens-Atrapos Editions.

Presidencia de la Nación. (n.d). *About Argentina*. Retrieved from https://www.scribd.com/document/207970107/About-Argentina

Rodríguez, J. (n.d). Argentinean Americans. *Countries and their cultures. Forum.* Retrieved from http://www.everyculture.com/multi/A-Br/Argentinean-Americans.html#ixzz3xw157mrw

Tocalli-Beller, A. (2007). ELT and bilingual education in Argentina. *International Handbook of English Language Teaching, 15,* 107–121.

CHAPTER 9

BRAZIL AND BRAZILIAN STUDENTS IN THE U.S.

Eliane Rubinstein-Ávila and Adriana Picoral
University of Arizona

Juliana, a 5th grader from Brazil, is stressing over her upcoming science project. Her English has been improving; however, this is only her second year in the U.S., and understandably, Juliana still finds most of the science homework very challenging. Her parents recently moved the family to an apartment in the suburbs so that Juliana and her brother could attend their current, "better" school. Juliana soon realized that most of her classmates in her new school were getting assistance from their parents to complete their science projects. She found that baffling. Even if her parents were able to help her, they both worked several jobs and put in long hours to pay the bills and send money to help her grandparents in Brazil. Moreover, Juliana's parents were unaware that they were expected to help their children with their school homework or collaborate on their science projects. In Brazil, parents are expected to provide their children with a moral education at home; the school in Brazil is responsible for providing students with a formal education. Although Juliana wanted to reach out to her teacher, she did not want her teacher to assume that her parents didn't care about her education. This situation only aggravated Juliana's anxiety about her science project.

Views From Inside: Languages, Cultures, and Schooling for K–12 Educators
pp. 153–165

153

BACKGROUND

Brazil is the largest country in South America and the fifth largest country in the world (Otieno, 2015). It is the only South American country where Portuguese is the official language. Unfortunately, some Americans, many of whom are college graduates, believe that Spanish is the main language spoken in Brazil or that Buenos Aires (in Argentina) is Brazil's capital. Also, the fact that Brazil is an extremely racially and ethnically diverse nation may surprise many. Much like the U.S., Brazil is a nation of immigrants, with a long history of slavery and of genocide of indigenous people. Regardless of peoples' ethnic or racial backgrounds, Brazilians typically identify and refer to themselves by their nationality—Brazilian. We do not tend to use hyphenated identities to describe ourselves (e.g., Brazilian-Lebanese, Brazilian-Italian, Brazilian-Japanese). That said, Brazilians who are unable to claim indigenous roots descend from those who came to Brazil, willingly or not, at some point in Brazil's history.

Geography and Diversity

The equator crosses Brazil through the northern states. While the north enjoys a tropical climate, the weather in the southern states is temperate (Otieno, 2015). The north and northeastern states are inhabited by a large and diverse population of multiracial people of color, meaning Brazilians who are of African and Amerindian backgrounds. Although African cultures have shaped much of the country's mainstream culture, music, and food, those influences are more prevalent in the state of Rio de Janeiro and the states to the north.

The southern states of Brazil, on the other hand, are populated mostly by early immigrants from Europe (e.g., Portugal, Spain, Italy, Germany, and Poland). Although Brazilians of different racial/ethnic backgrounds live in relative peace, Brazilians who are descendants of White European settlers have always held positions of greater power—not unlike in other colonized nations.

As noted above, Brazilian immigrants come from many parts of the globe (Velho, 2007). Even though the official language is Portuguese, Brazil is highly multiracial and multicultural. After World War II, Brazil granted access, and eventually citizenship, to a large number of Eastern European Jews who survived Nazi concentration camps. Paradoxically, Brazil also granted access to many Nazis fleeing a defeated Germany (Fausto, 2014). In addition to European immigrants, Brazil has been home to Japanese, Chinese, Syrians, and immigrants from many other nations.

Complex and Tumultuous History

Brazil's history is a marred one. Before the arrival of the Portuguese, many indigenous groups inhabited the vast and fruitful lands (Fausto, 2014). Although most indigenous people were decimated by the colonizers, indigenous languages, foods, and rituals have in part shaped Brazilian culture (Otieno, 2015). Brazil's history of slavery lasted over 350 years. In fact, Brazil was one of the last countries to legally abolish slavery, in 1888 (Fausto, 2014). Today Brazil is a democracy. However, it endured a violent military dictatorship that lasted several decades, from 1964 to 1985. The effects of that are still being felt today.

Within the past couple of decades, Brazil has become one of world's rising economic powers, although it has more recently experienced political and economic challenges. Despite its lingering gross social inequities, the country has made major strides in lifting millions of families out of poverty in the past couple of decades.

Race and Race Relations

Although slavery has been legally abolished for over 100 years, Afro-Brazilians feel the heavy weight of this legacy (Fausto, 2014). The latest census showed that the income of White Brazilians is on average 50% higher than those of other groups. Racial inequality is a topic most Brazilians are uncomfortable addressing or admitting to; however, social inequality is a widely "accepted" norm. For example, historically, Brazil's federal universities, which are considered to be the most prestigious institutions of higher education in the nation and which are free of charge, have few Black or poor students. This trend has changed in recent years due to the establishment of affirmative action by the government (Telles, 2009). Brazilians who immigrated to the U.S. are typically lighter-skinned and members of the Brazilian middle to low-middle class. Coming to work and live in the U.S. provides families an opportunity to avoid Brazil's economic pitfalls and keep up their standard of living—and possibly even raise it. Brazilian immigrants have opened businesses, reviving many economically waning towns, especially in the state of Massachusetts. Language and Culture

People

Brazilians are known to be warm, welcoming, and fun-loving. We tend to smile a great deal and almost always seem agreeable. In fact, saying "no" is viewed in Brazilian culture as being impolite and can cause confrontations; thus, it is skillfully avoided through friendly interactions that smooth out disagreements.

Brazilians also do not tend to talk openly about racism. Much like in the U.S., Brazilians do not think of themselves as being racist; however, Black and indigenous people are more likely than those of European backgrounds to be the victims of structural inequalities. As a result, they tend to be less educated and among the poorest citizens (Telles, 2009).

Brazilian society is highly stratified (hierarchically) by class; even children are aware of the different economic classes and to what class their families belong. In general, children in Brazil are taught to be deferential toward all adults; children from lower socioeconomic classes are likely to be even more deferential—even shy—toward educators and adults they do not already know. That means they may look down towards the floor when speaking to educators, and they may not voice their opinions, pose questions, or initiate conversation.

Family Relationships

It is typical for adult children in Brazil to continue living in the home with parents and grandparents, even after they are married. In fact, several generations may live under one roof. Although this situation is mostly a result of the economic challenges young adults often face in living independently, it is also a consequence of tradition. Even when adult children leave the home, it is common (even expected) for extended families to get together every Sunday for a large meal that may last most of the day. For most Brazilians, family comes first, before school, work, or careers. Therefore, it is important for educators to know what is going on with a student's family. For example, if there is a family member sick in the home, their care may take precedence to taking a child to school.

Also, older children are often expected to care for younger siblings. A family who has recently immigrated to the U.S. may not realize that children under a certain age cannot legally babysit for their young siblings or accompany them to school without an adult being present.

Foods

Because Brazil covers a vast geographical area with different climate zones, food and customs vary a great deal across, and even within, states. The state of Minas Gerais, for example, is known for its abundance of dairy products. The southern states are known for excellent beef.

Churrasco (Brazilian barbecue), which consists of various cuts of meat that are salted, skewered, and cooked over charcoal, originated in southern Brazil; however, it is appreciated throughout the country and known worldwide (Bayor, 2011). In fact, there are high-priced restaurants that specialize in Brazilian *churrasco* sprinkled across several American cities. The *churrasco* is also a traditional gathering of family members, typically on Sundays and holidays, at least for those who can afford it.

Feijoada is a slow-cooked stew made of beans and several different cuts of meat; it is probably Brazil's most well-known national dish (Bayor, 2011). It is traditionally served on Saturdays accompanied by rice and *farofa* (fried manioc flour), collard greens, and a slice of orange, which is to help digest the heavy meal. The dish originated from slavery. Originally, it was made from scraps of meat that were deemed inedible by the masters. Today, *feijoada* is commonly served in practically every Brazilian home and restaurant—from the common to the most sophisticated.

Much of the country is tropical; therefore, Brazil has an abundance of tropical fruit, such as coconuts, papayas, mangos, and jackfruit (Bayor, 2011). Brazil's outdoor food markets boast five types of bananas. Of course, Brazil is also known for its coffee, and more recently for its sugar cane production, much of which has been converted to fuel vehicles.

Language

Hundreds of indigenous languages were once spoken throughout Brazil before it was colonized by Portugal in the 1500s. With the near extinction of the native populations by the colonizers, many indigenous languages have been lost (Fausto, 2014). However, there are current successful efforts by the Brazilian government and international nonprofit organizations to protect over 100 active indigenous languages. These languages, however, are spoken by a very small percentage of Brazil's overall population. Today, Brazil is the largest Portuguese-speaking country in the world. It is also the only South American country in which Portuguese is the official and administrative language. Through the centuries, Brazilian Portuguese has been influenced by native languages, especially the Tupi–Guarani language family (Fausto, 2014). Other influences came from the African languages spoken by slaves and the many other languages spoken by immigrants and refugees. Consequently, Brazilian Portuguese is rather different from the Iberian Portuguese spoken in Portugal. Although the two languages are mutually intelligible, they differ in vocabulary and grammatical structure.

The majority of Brazilians are monolingual speakers of Portuguese (Fausto, 2014). Despite the fact that a dialect of German is a heritage language to several Brazilian communities in the south and that English and Spanish (to a lesser extent) are taught as foreign languages in schools, a very small percentage of Brazilians are fluent in these languages.

Newcomers to the U.S. from Brazil can be expected to be monolingual in Portuguese (regardless of ethnic background). Second- and third-generation Brazilian students in the U.S. are likely to be bilingual or English dominant. Brazilians moved to Massachusetts mainly because (Iberian) Portuguese was already an established language in various parts of the state—a result of an earlier immigration wave of Portuguese immigrants from the Azores. Nevertheless, there were many tensions between the Portuguese and Brazilian communities around issues of language and culture during the establishment of a Portuguese/English dual-language program in the late 1990s (Rubinstein-Ávila, 2005).

Body Language, Dress, and Appearance

Brazilians tend to be very expressive and effusive. We are likely to touch the hand or arm of the person(s) with whom we are speaking. Also, as noted above, Brazilians do not tend to express disagreement outright, unless we are downright irate. Instead, we are likely to try to change other people's minds by using one of several friendly conversational strategies. A common expression in Brazil is *"dar* um *jeitinho"*; although there is no direct translation into English, it means to tweak a situation in order to make it work. So, rather than challenge a rule or policy outright, Brazilians prefer to find a flexible way to make things work smoothly, one way or another.

Even the poorest segment of Brazil's population is highly aware of the importance of one's appearance in public. Thus, Brazilians are known to attend to our appearance. Brazilians value not only cleanliness, but also being put-together in a stylish manner. Brazilians are not typically conservative about dress; this goes for women in particular. Female high school students are likely to wear tight pants or short dresses showing off their curves and tops with low necklines—all common in Brazil. In fact, such clothing does not carry the negative social stigma that is more commonly found in the U.S. If educators find this type of attire inappropriate for school, it is best to address the issue explicitly and directly with the students and their parents. Hints and indirect comments may not convey the intended message and can even lead to misunderstandings. American teachers meeting Brazilian mothers must be aware of this important cultural difference in attire. Mothers may dress indistinguishably from their teenage daughters.

Religions

Although Brazil has been typically known to be a Catholic-majority country, that is not an accurate representation of the many religions practiced across the country (Fausto, 2014). First, Brazil's Catholicism has been heavily shaped by African spiritual belief systems (Velho, 2007). Also, an increasing number of Brazilians who were born Catholics have become Evangelicals (Pew Research Center, 2013). The number of Brazilians who have converted to Jehovah's Witnesses and Latter-Day Saints has also been growing. Many Brazilians also practice the Spiritist Doctrine. Officially, the country has been secular since 1891, and in general, Brazilians have always enjoyed religious freedom. However, practitioners of Afro-Brazilian religions, such as Umbanda and Candoblé, have been victims of prejudice and even of hate crimes.

Non-Christians, including Buddhists, Muslims, Jews, and other less-known religions, are a minority in Brazil. Most Brazilian Arabs (from Middle Eastern nations such as Lebanon and Syria) are Catholics; the Muslim community is small. According to the latest census, Brazil has the 9th largest Jewish community in the world. Brazilian immigrants to the U.S. can generally, but not exclusively, be expected to be Christians or Catholics.

Immigration of Brazilians to the U.S.

The immigration of Brazilians to the U.S. has been mostly motivated by periods of economic uncertainties in Brazil. Brazilian immigrants to the U.S. tend to be lower middle class, mostly White, and literate. The poorest segment of the population is not likely to be able to afford the journey or to obtain U.S. tourist visas. Although many have been able to take advantage of family reunification granted by the Immigration Act of 1965, many have arrived as tourists and have remained in the country undocumented as "visas overstayers" (Rubinstein-Ávila, 2005). Learning English quickly and being light skinned makes it easier for Brazilians to "blend in" with White Americans.

Important Dates and Holidays

Brazil celebrates many holidays. Mirroring Brazil's traditionally Catholic composition, most holidays are based on Catholicism, celebrating particular saints, with a touch of Afro-Brazilian ritual. Although immigrant parents are not likely to keep children from going to school during these holidays, educators ought to be aware that celebrations often continue until late at night. Therefore, students are likely to appear slightly tired (or lethargic) the next day.

Carnival

Carnival is taken seriously in Brazil. It is celebrated right before Lent, either at the end of February or in early March. Celebrations start on the Friday before Ash Wednesday and end on *Carnival* Tuesday (40 days before Easter). Throughout the country, people celebrate by dancing and drinking in the streets for 4 consecutive days. Banks, stores, and even schools close for several days—even an entire week.

Although Catholic in origin, *Carnival* is celebrated by few Brazilians as a strictly religious holiday (Velho, 2007). Most Brazilians, regardless of religion, are likely to participate in the *Carnival* celebrations. Children will typically wear costumes. Even if *Carnival* is celebrated slightly differently across the country, it is a continuous party, enjoyed by children and adults of all ages.

Easter

Just like *Carnaval*, Easter is also observed for several days in Brazil. Good Friday is a public holiday; schools, banks, and government services close. Many private schools also observe Monday and Thursday. Catholics celebrate Palm Sunday as well. On Easter Sunday, it is customary for children to receive baskets of chocolates and candy, including large chocolate eggs.

Dia de Sao Joao—Festas Junina [June Festivals]

This holiday is celebrated all over the country with block parties. It marks the celebration of three Catholic saints: Saint Anthony, Saint John the Baptist, and Saint Peter. The festivities are popular, and much like during *Carnival*, folks take to the streets to partake in typical dances, food, and clothing that celebrate rural life. It varies a little throughout Brazil, according to local traditions. Participants usually dance in a *quadrilha* (square dancing) and celebrate a mock wedding. It is common for children to dress as *caipira* (a person from the countryside), and eat roasted peanuts, corn on the cob, and other traditionally rural foods. These festivities are also commonly held in schools, marking the middle of the school year.

Christmas

Because the majority of Brazilians are Christians and Catholics, Christmas is an important holiday for most Brazilian families. On Christmas Eve, families tend to gather for a special late meal and exchange presents at midnight. It is common for a member of the family to dress up as Santa Claus to distribute gifts, especially in families with small children.

Although increasingly less common these days, some Catholic families still attend *Missa* do Galo (Midnight Mass).

New Year's Eve

While Christmas is a family event, young adults usually celebrate New Year's Eve with friends. Firework displays at midnight are a widespread tradition across the country; for those who live on or by the enormous Brazilian coast, toasting the New Year at the beach is a tradition. Unbeknownst to many White Brazilians, many of the rituals practiced on New Year's Eve, such as the custom of wearing all white and throwing flowers into the ocean for Yemanja, the Goddess of the Seas, originated in Afro-Brazilian religions.

Our Lady of Aparecida/Children's Day

Our Lady of Aparecida is the principal patroness of Brazil (equivalent to Our Lady of Guadalupe in Mexico); the holiday in her honor is observed on October 12. The date is also the day the Empire of Brazil was founded in 1822. This holiday is currently celebrated culturally as Children's Day.

Other Holidays

Other public holidays include Labor Day (May 1), Independence Day (September 7), All Souls' Day (November 2), and Republic Day (November 15). Although parades are held on Independence Day and people visit cemeteries on All Souls' Day, most of these are not celebrated ostentatiously.

Nonofficial Holidays

There are also myriad special days that are observed but are not official government holidays such as *Dia* dos *Namorados* (equivalent to Valentine's Day), celebrated the day before Saint Anthony's Day on June 12, and Father's and Mother's days (second Sunday in August, second Sunday in May, respectively). Since Brazilian children are likely to grow in up in tight-knit, multiple-generational homes, they may want to make cards for their mothers, aunts, and especially grandmothers.

IDEAS FOR EDUCATORS

For the past several decades, public education (K–12) in Brazil has not been highly regarded. As a result, the private school market in Brazil is vast and diverse in both price of tuition and in the quality of instruction. In fact, there are private schools for almost every budget. However, efforts have been made to boost the K–8 public school system.

Families in Brazil do not tend to move (geographically) as much as American families; therefore, it is not uncommon for children to start pre-kindergarten at the age of 4 or 5 and graduate high school with much the same cohort. Since there are many more children than there are school buildings, many schools hold two shifts—a morning and an afternoon shift. Juliana, featured at the beginning of the chapter, was used to having a hot lunch with her family, as is customary in Brazil, and then attending school in the afternoon.

Parents in Brazil are not expected to engage directly in school activities, policies, or assignments. Parent–teacher conferences are held a couple of times a year for the very early grades. Although parents are expected to motivate their children to learn, they are not expected to participate in school activities, help with homework, or engage with their children in school projects.

Brazilian children are likely to be very physically affectionate with their classmates and teachers. In fact, hugging and kissing (on both cheeks) is common when greeting and saying goodbye in Brazil. It is not unusual for young students to call or refer to their teachers as *tia* (auntie). Especially in the early years, educators and students create and maintain close and affectionate bonds. In fact, young Brazilian students are likely to hug their teachers to express their affection. Ignoring them or not reciprocating may convey the wrong message. If U.S. educators are uncomfortable with this type of physical affection due to school policies or personal preference, it is essential to convey that to the students explicitly.

The most common *faux pas* American teachers are likely to make is to clump Brazilian students with other Hispanic/Latino children, assuming they speak the same language and can help each other. It is important to remember that Brazilian students do not speak Spanish. Although older children may refer to themselves as Latin Americans, terms such as "Hispanic" and even "Latino" will likely be unknown to those who are recent arrivals (Velho, 2007). Brazilians are more likely to share cultural and culinary characteristics with students from Puerto Rico, where African cultures have had a greater impact.

Further, Brazilian students may not seem highly analytical when compared to U.S. students. In fact, they may tend to conflate descriptions of events with evidence and assessment. It is important for educators to help students distinguish between description, analysis and assessment.

CONCLUSIONS

Brazilian immigration to the U.S. tends to mirror Brazil's economic downturns. Brazilian families are likely to move to states and towns where

Brazilian communities have already been established. However, Brazilian immigrants to the U.S. are not necessarily representative of the average Brazilian family. They are likely to be lighter-skinned and have more resources than the average. Although many families do return to Brazil eventually, or hope to do so, there is a large population of second- and even third-generation Brazilian Americans in the U.S. today. Overall, Brazilians are family-oriented and fun-loving. Brazilians tend to be social, expressive, and uninhibited. Since hints and innuendos are heavily culturally based, it is best to communicate messages to students and their parents in a direct and explicit manner. Like most immigrants, Brazilians are hard-working and expect their children to do well in school. As is common in other Latin-based cultures, multigenerational families are close-knit and commonly cohabitate under one roof. When visiting family and friends in Brazil for holidays, such as Christmas and the New Year, many U.S. resident Brazilian families extend their stay sometimes beyond school vacation. This information can help U.S. educators understand and support their Brazilian students.

ADDITIONAL RESOURCES

Brazil (n.d.). *CIA world factbook*. Retrieved from https://www.cia.gov/library/publications/the-world-factbook/geos/br.html
> Contains information about many aspects of Brazil's culture and economy.

Gorney, C. (2011). Brazil's girl power. *National Geographic*. Retrieved from http://ngm.nationalgeographic.com/2011/09/girl-power/gorney-text
> Explains the large drop in the nation's birthrate and what women have to do with it.

Brazil culture (n.d.). Retrieved from http://www.brazil.org.za/brazil-culture.html
> Presents tips about Brazilian culture for outsiders.

TASKS FOR EDUCATORS

Try this suggested activity yourself, or implement a version in your classroom, or adapt it for working with other learners.

Finding the Origins and Roots of Our Practices

Given that Brazilian students are likely to identify only with their national identity, not their ethnic background, they are not likely to be acquainted with the concept of multiculturalism or even bilingualism. In fact, they may not be aware that the various cultural practices in their daily lives originate from a multitude of cultures. Educators could help their Brazilian students and others in their classrooms understand that both Brazil and the U.S. share a multicultural and multiracial past and present. For example, students could be encouraged to become anthropologists of their own lives and inquire about the origins of certain practices that are common practices among their families and their communities.

Educators could begin with the simple concept that all the practices we engage in are cultural and social practices. What we eat (not only "typical" dishes), how we cook, how we eat, what we do repeatedly with our families, and what we value, are all cultural and social practices. Helpful questions:

1. Describe an event or practice that your family engages in often. What happens during that event? Who does what? When does it typically take place, and where?

2. Conduct research (on the Internet, interviewing family members, and so on); where did that event/practice originate? What are the racial and cultural/ social origins of that practice?

3. Did your family carry on that practice before they lived in the U.S.?

   o If so, has it changed in any way, and why?

   o How does the practice/event make you feel?

4. Look for explanations. Why do you think you felt this way? Why do you think families tend to continue to perform the practices they bring with them from their home countries?

5. If you moved to another state or even another country, what practices do you think you would want to continue to engage in, and why?

6. What have you learned from this activity? Why do people engage in events/practices that are familiar to them? And why is it important to understand the roots of our practices?

REFERENCES

Bayor, R. H. (Ed.). (2011). *Multicultural America: An encyclopedia of the newest Americans* (Vol. 1). Santa Barbara, CA: ABC-CLIO.

Fausto, B. (2014). *A concise history of Brazil* (Cambridge concise histories). Cambridge, UK: University Press.

Otieno, F. (2015). *Brazil: Insights*. Createspace Independent Publishing Platform. Retrieved from https://www.createspace.com/

Pew Research Center. (2013). Brazil's changing religious landscape. Retrieved from http://www.pewforum.org/2013/07/18/brazils-changing-religious-landscape/

Telles, E. E. (2009, June 1). Brazil in black and white: Discrimination and affirmative action in Brazil. Retrieved from http://www.pbs.org/wnet/wideangle/lessons/brazil-in-black-and-white/discrimination-and-affirmative-action-in-brazil/?p=4323

Rubinstein-Ávila, E. (2005). Brazilian Portuguese in Massachusetts' linguistic landscape: A prevalent yet understudied phenomenon. *Hispania, 88*(4), 873–880.

Velho, O. (2007). Missionization in the post-colonial world: A view from Brazil and elsewhere. *Anthropological Theory, 7*(3), 273–293.

CHAPTER 10

PERU

A Nation of Contrasts, Diversity, and Complexity

Gisela Ernst-Slavit
Washington State University Vancouver

Gabriela Moreno is a 7th grader in a U.S. school. She was born and raised in a well-kept middle-class neighborhood in Lima, Peru and has been in the United States for seven months. Gaby, as her family calls her, is a quiet teenager with an infectious smile. Although she appears attentive in all her classes, by the end of the day she seems tired and uninterested.

Earlier in the term, Ms. Ball, her science teacher, thought that since Gaby spoke so little English she probably did not understand much of the content.

"Boy, was I wrong," said Ms. Ball. "While Gaby can't put sentences together, she sure knows scientific terms and concepts. I didn't realize this until Ms. Rosales [a bilingual paraeducator] gave me a list of many cognates in English and Spanish for our unit on natural selection and adaptations and explained to me that many scientific terms have similar spellings in English and Spanish."

Ms. Ball also realized that many of these cognates, although written in a similar way, have a "totally different pronunciation." The list looked something like this:

Views From Inside: Languages, Cultures, and Schooling for K–12 Educators
pp. 167–182

Natural Selection and Adaptations—Spanish Cognates

English	Spanish
adaptation	adaptación
dominant	dominante
evolution	evolución
fossil	fósil
gene	gen
hybrid	híbrido
homozygous	homocigótico
phenotype	fenotipo

After talking with Gaby, Mrs. Rosales learned that not only does Gaby have an extensive knowledge of science vocabulary in Spanish, and therefore is able to access certain scientific terminology in English, but she is also a keen scientist. At home, she and her brother have a chemistry set and frequently conduct experiments. This passion of hers is nurtured by her mother's current job as a pharmaceutical lab assistant.

BACKGROUND

Geography

Peru, located in western South America, is an extremely biodiverse country. In fact, the United Nations Environmental Program (UNEP, 2010) has classified Peru as one of the world's 17 megadiverse nations. Although situated at a tropical latitude, the climate is modified by the Andes Mountains that traverse the country from north to south. Almost 80% of the world's recognized ecological zones are found in Peru, as well of 28 of its 32 climates. These climates range from the arid and slim coastal region to the majestic Andes to the tropical Amazon rainforest that gives birth to the Amazon River.

History

Peru's long, rich history makes it a destination for tourists, archaeologists, anthropologists, and ecologists. Peru was known as the capital of the Incan Empire in the 15th century, although it was also home to many diverse indigenous groups prior to the Incas. In fact, while Andean societies began about 2500 BC, human presence in Peru can be traced back as far as 9000 BC. With the arrival of Europeans on the continent came epidemics (including smallpox), conquest, colonization, cultural demise, and the Roman Catholic Church. The city of Lima, founded in 1535 by explorer Francisco Pizarro, became the capital of the viceroyalty of Peru, which extended throughout South America. In 1821, Peru revolted from Spain and proclaimed its independence.

The 19th and early 20th centuries were marked by central state power and oligarchic domination. Although Peru is now a democratic nation, much of the 20th century was filled with military dictatorships and revolutionary movements. However, since the 1980s, Peru has had elected presidents and officials and, beginning in the 21st century, steady economic growth.

Like several other nations in South America, Peru is a multiethnic nation formed by the combination of different groups over the centuries. Indigenous groups inhabited Peruvian lands for several millennia before the Spanish conquest in the 16th century. During the 17th and 18th centuries, Spaniards and Africans arrived in large numbers under colonial rule, mixing widely with each other and with indigenous peoples. Most Peruvians would describe themselves as *mestizos*—that is, persons of combined European and Amerindian descent. In the mid-19th century, the Chinese arrived as a replacement for slave workers. Gradual immigration from England, France, Germany, Japan, Italy, and Spain during the last two centuries has added to the cultural and ethnic diversity of Peruvian society. Although, during most of Peru's history, power was in the hands of those of European descent, the last three decades saw presidents who represented the hybrid and diverse nature of Peru's population. For example, in 1990, Peru elected Alberto Fujimori, the son of Japanese immigrants. In 2001, the nation elected the first full-blood Quechua president, Alejandro Toledo, a man of humble origins with graduate degrees from Stanford University. In 2011, Peru elected the son of an indigenous Quechua lawyer, Ollanta Humala. In 2016, Pedro Pablo Kuczynski was elected president for a five-year period. He is the son of a German father and a mother of Swiss French descent and is currently married to Nancy Lange, born and raised in the United States.

Peru's history points to tensions between hierarchical dichotomies such as Europeans versus indigenous populations, Spanish versus Quechua and Aymara, urban versus rural, and Lima versus the rest of Peru. Peru's population of about 30 million is divided between the highlands and the population centers of the coast, and that division marks a sharp cultural as well as geographical divide. About 75% of Peruvians live in urban centers, with almost 10 million Peruvians living in Lima, Peru's capital, located on the coast. Inland regions are marked by extreme poverty and subsistence agriculture, while the fertile river valleys on the coast have produced a wealthier, more cosmopolitan culture.

EDUCATION AND CULTURE

Education and Socialization

There are major differences in child-rearing practices between indigenous and urban White and *mestizo* populations in Peru. For example, indigenous mothers often carry their infants for many hours at a time in colorful slings on their backs while doing chores, selling in the market, or even when doing strenuous agricultural work (see Figure 10.1).

Source: Photograph by Rudolf Ernst Alvarado, used with permission.

Figure 10.1.   Julia carrying her 19-month son in Cupiche, 30 miles away from Lima.

Children of both genders, regardless of ethnicity, location, or social class, are strongly encouraged to attain an elementary and high school education; however, the lack of money or the need for the child's labor at home (e.g., taking care of younger siblings and relatives, helping the family business) sometimes precludes children from attending school regularly. Bromley and Mackie (2009) concluded that about 500 children worked as street traders in Cuzco, a mid-sized Andean city that attracts millions of tourists en route to Machu Picchu every year. While street trading does not involve heavy labor or unhealthy conditions, it does reduce the time these children have for playing and doing homework. Bromley and Mackie (2009) assert that most of the child traders in their study worked part-time, attended school, played for about an hour a day, and often gave all or part of their earnings to their parents. Most of the children in their study displayed a certain self-esteem and confidence in the knowledge of their street-trading skills. For example, these children often used their language abilities to convince tourists to buy their products and negotiate prices. About two-thirds of the children were able to do this in both Spanish and English! This information might be helpful in understanding some of the resourcefulness and early responsibility displayed by Peruvian children in your classroom. Education is a high priority for most Peruvians, even when there are other responsibilities to attend to.

The Peruvian Ministry of Education is in charge of formulating, implementing, and overseeing national educational policy. Education in Peru is compulsory and free in public schools at the initial, primary, and secondary levels. It is also free in public universities for students who are unable to pay tuition and have an adequate academic performance. Among these public institutions is the Universidad Nacional Mayor de San Marcos, established in 1551, making it the oldest officially recognized university in the Americas and one of the oldest universities in the world. Mario Vargas Llosa, a Nobel Prize laureate in literature, is a graduate from that university.

Teachers and college professors are given great respect in Peru. In fact, in remote areas in the highlands or the Amazon rainforest, teachers assume many leadership roles, and humble school buildings afford spaces for community gatherings. If you get to have Peruvian students in your classroom, chances are they will show a great deal of respect towards you and all the school personnel. In general terms, Peruvian children are raised to be respectful of their elders, obedient, and hard-working. Peruvian parents will also be respectful. If you invite parents to the school for curriculum night or parent–teacher conferences, make sure your invitation clearly states the purpose of the meeting. Otherwise, parents may assume that the invitation is the result of their student's poor performance or behavior.

For centuries, education in Peru was a vehicle to preserve the status quo. It gave access and control to privileged classes and taught indigenous and underrepresented groups to conform to Westernized forms of thought. Access to elementary and secondary education has also been uneven between indigenous and non-indigenous groups. For example, indigenous children were traditionally excluded from schooling until the mid-20th century, and only in recent decades has their access to school become widespread (Ames, 2012). Presently, almost all indigenous Quechua children attend primary school. The situation is different for indigenous groups in the Amazon whose enrollment rates are lower when compared to both indigenous Quechua and non-indigenous populations (Ames, 2012).

In recent decades, private education has become a growing enterprise, particularly in urban settings. Approximately one-third of the students in Peru attend private elementary and secondary schools (Calónico & Ñopo, 2007). These numbers increase slightly at the college level. Because speaking more than one language is highly valued in Peru, most elementary and secondary private schools have robust foreign language programs.

Religion

Freedom of religion is a fundamental right in Peru, although over 80% of Peruvians identify themselves as Roman Catholic (Instituto Nacional de Estadística e Informática, 2007). In fact, until recently, religion—that is, the Catholic religion—was part of most schools' curricula. In the last century, many diverse churches have appeared as a result of North American and European missionaries (e.g., Mormons, Methodists, Lutherans, and Adventists). There are also Jews, Buddhists, Muslims, Hindus, Hare Krishnas, and Baha'i temples.

Naming Practices

One reflection of Catholic influence in diverse aspects of life is apparent in the traditional practice of using religious names and terms as given names. Do not be surprised if you have students whose first names are Alma (soul), Asunción (assumption), Candelario (refers to the Catholic feast of Candlemas), Concepción (conception), Dolores (sorrows), Jesús (Jesus), Mercedes (mercies), Pastor (shepherd), Rosario (rosary), Salvador (savior), or Soledad (solitude). Of course, biblical names (e.g., Sara,

Raquel, David, Gabriel) as well as European names (e,g., Piero, Karen, Alexander, Wendy) are also not unusual.

In Peru, people use two last names. The first last name is the father's last name, while the second one is the mother's last name. Often, when students first come to the United States, they will write their complete name, including their middle name, as in "Carlos José Romero Martinez." In Peru, all legal paperwork would have this student listed as:

Last Names: Romero Martinez
First Names: Carlos José

If using only one last name, the main last name will be the first one, in this case, Romero. When students come to the U.S. and write their complete name on forms, the system uses the last name entered. In this case, the student name appears as Carlos Martinez.

Many married Peruvian women take their husband's last name. This means that if Guillermina Rosales Sanguinetti marries Carlos Morales Perez, she becomes Guillermina Rosales de Morales. The preposition "de" means "of," as if the wife belongs to the husband. Fortunately, this practice is changing in Peru as well as in Spain and in other countries in Latin America.

Food Traditions

Most Peruvian celebrations and festivities are complemented with large amounts of food and drink, a practice that resonates with both indigenous and Spanish cultures. Peruvian cuisine exemplifies the kind of national identity that embraces multiple cultures and traditions. Considered among the best in the world, Peruvian gastronomy developed its fusion of flavors, aromas, and cooking styles derived from its geographic diversity and over a long process of cultural exchanges with Europe, West Africa, and Asia. Peruvian food is remarkable for the diversity of its ingredients, from wonderful fresh seafood to an amazing variety of potatoes (over 1,000 varieties), corn, chilies, and fresh fruits and vegetables. White rice is an important component of most meals. While tortillas are used in Mexican or Central American restaurants, they are not used at all in Peruvian cuisine.

LANGUAGES, LITERACY, AND NUMERACY

Peru is a multilingual nation, dominated by Spanish (known as *castellano* or Castilian Spanish) but home to a diversity of indigenous languages. The nation's linguistic complexity is recognized and supported by Peru's

Constitution, which states: "Official languages of the State are Spanish and, wherever they are predominant, Quechua, Aymara and other native tongues in accordance with the law" (Article 48). While Spanish, Quechua, and Aymara are official languages, there are over 104 individual languages used (Paul, Simons, & Fennig, 2016). Most of these languages are spoken in the central Andes and the Amazon forests. Unfortunately, about 25 of those languages are endangered or might become extinct within the next decade.

Approximately 84% of the Peruvian population speaks Spanish. Spanish is the main language of the Peruvian government, the media, and the education system. Quechua ("Ketch-u-wa") is the most widely spoken indigenous language. It is spoken by about 13% of the population, primarily in the central and southern Andes. Although Quechua was the language of the Incan Empire, it existed long before the Incas came to power. There are many subdivisions within the Quechua language family, to the extent that Quechua speakers find it hard to communicate with those from different regions. For example, a resident of a Quechua town in Cuzco may not be able to completely understand the Quechua spoken by a person from Cajamarca, in northern Peru.

Although Aymara is an official language, currently there are only about half a million speakers in Peru. Aymara is spoken in the southeast of Peru, along the border with Bolivia. In addition to indigenous languages in the highlands, the Amazon region is home to at least 13 ethnolinguistic groups, each containing further subdivisions of native languages. The remaining indigenous languages of Peru, such as Aguaruna, Campa, and Shipibo, are spoken by less than 1% of the Peruvian population.

A classroom teacher in the United States could possibly have two students from Peru who do not speak the same language. Although this possibility is remote, there is also a chance of having two students who, while speaking Spanish, may have very different upbringings, customs, and traditions. In Florida, for example, I worked with students from urban coastal cities in Peru who related more easily with students from other countries than with students raised in rural Andean regions. In these cases, social class and cultural differences played an important role in generating this division.

Spanish speakers have a huge advantage when learning English compared to speakers of other languages that, for example, use a different alphabet (e.g., Urdu, Russian) or characters (e.g., Chinese, Japanese, Korean). Spanish and English use the same alphabet and share about 25,000 cognates. Cognates are words in different languages with a common origin and similar spelling and meaning, as depicted in the opening scenario and in Table 10.1.

Table 10.1.

English	Spanish	Portuguese	Italian	French
activity	actividad	atividade	attività	activité
cultural	cultural	cultural	culturale	culturelle
legal	legal	legal	legale	légale
politically	politicamente	politicamente	politicamente	politiquement
volcano	volcán	vulcão	vulcano	volcan

As can be gathered, many of these cognates have Latin and Greek roots and form a large portion of scientific vocabulary. Spanish, French, Italian, Portuguese, and Romanian are called Romance languages, not because they are more romantic than other languages, but because they are derived from Latin. English and these languages share many words due to common Latin and Greek roots.

Language Transfer Issues

Language transfer refers to speakers or writers applying knowledge from one language to another language. In other words, English language learners will rely on their native language experiences as they learn English. While some of those transfers may be positive (e.g., cognates), many other items and structures are not similar in Spanish and English. Table 10.2 lists selected examples of errors your Spanish-speaking students may make when learning English.

A word of caution: Knowledge of transfer issues can be beneficial for understanding students' errors. However, overt correction may raise students' anxiety, which can affect language learning. Awareness of these errors can help teachers identify patterned errors and teach specific grammatical structures or model appropriate use.

Numeracy

Although there are many similarities among number systems across the world, mathematics, particularly as taught in schools, is far from being a universal language (Ernst-Slavit & Slavit, 2013). English language learners from Peru have to learn new words (e.g., quadratic) and concepts (e.g., exponential) and, in some cases, relearn different procedures and representations. Table 10.3 depicts selected examples of those differences

**Table 10.2. Common Errors Made
by Spanish-Speaking Students Learning English**

Linguistic Aspect	Common Error in English	Explanation
Nouns: Possessive form	Not including 's to describe posses-sion *The car of my parents.* Instead of *My parents' car.*	In Spanish, a prepositional phrase structure is used to express possession. *El carro de mis padres.*
Possessive pronouns	Learners may not understand that the possessive pronoun does not need to agree with the object *The pencil is my* *These candies are mines*	In Spanish, the possessive pronoun refers to (and agrees) with both the "person" and·the "object." *El lapiz es mio* *Esas velas son mias*
Subject pronouns	Subject pronouns, e.g., *he, she, I, you* are obligatory elements *Is my uncle* *Left early*	In Spanish you can "drop" the subject pronoun. The verb carries the person and number. *Es mi tio* *Salí temprano*
Articles	Overuse of articles *In the Cuzco we saw a llama.* *The price of the gas* *He brushes the teeths*	Definite articles are used differently *En el Cuzco vimos una llama* *El precio de la gasolina* *El se lava los dientes*
Adjectives	Adjectives appear *before* the noun that is being modified *The star bright* *The actor handsome* *The dog black*	In Spanish the adjective goes *after* the noun it modifies. *La estrella brillante* *El actor buenmozo* *El perro negro*

between math in Peru (and in many other Spanish-speaking countries) and in the United States.

IDEAS FOR EDUCATORS

Additional important information for U.S. educators includes:

- Your Peruvian student may call you *maestra* or *profesora* if you are female or *maestro* or *profesor* if you are a male teacher. *Profesor/a* refers to any teacher, whether in elementary school or university. A principal in Peru is called *directora* if female and *director* if male.
- Self-discipline is strongly advocated among Peruvians, perhaps an inheritance from the rigid and hierarchical Incan cultures and Spanish colonialism.

**Table 10.3. Differences Between Mathematics
in Peru and in the United States**

	Math in Peru	Math in the U.S.
Symbols: Commas instead of periods	Periods are used to separate multiples of thousands and commas to separate decimal numbers from the integer, for example: 9.865,12	Commas are used to separate multiples of thousands and periods are used to separate decimal numbers, for example: 9,865.12
Measurement system	Metric system (centimeters, liters, grams, Celsius)	British system (inches, quarts, pounds, Fahrenheit)
Curricula	Emphasis on calculations	Emphasis on mathematical thinking
Some numbers and letters might be written differently	7 Z	7 Z
Operations: Long division	1430|11 130	130 11|1430
Reading of decimal numbers	−0.25 *menos cero punto veinticinco*	−0.25 negative one-fourth or negative point two five
Plural forms	Mostly plural *seis docenas* *doscientos* *cuatro millones* *cinco billones*	Always singular *six dozen* *two hundred* *four million* *five billion*
Date and time system	Day-Month-Year 10-3-1999	Month-Day-Year 3-10-1999

- Education in Peru begins from the age of three. Half of children between three and five years old go to preschool (also called *Kinder* or *Educación inicial* in Peru). Students then attend primary school (grades K–6) and secondary school (grades 1–5).
- Students may attend just one school throughout their lives, since most private schools house preschool, primary, and secondary education.
- The typical school year runs from March through December.
- There is a wide difference between private and public schools. Most private schools are well-equipped and have computers and small libraries. Public schools, on the other hand, may only have desks and chairs and lack basic materials.

- Your Peruvian student might feel overwhelmed with all the "stuff" in your classroom, such as materials (e.g., paper, pencils, scissors, markers), technology (e.g., computers, TVs, tablets), visuals (e.g., posters, bulletin boards, artwork), and other things available in U.S. classrooms (e.g., a bathtub for reading, furniture, a sink). Carpeting, air conditioning, and pets are not found in most Peruvian schools.

- An 80-year-old church in Peru is considered new by Peruvians but old by folks in the United States. Students in the U.S. may refer as "ancient" to something that is 200 years old. For a Peruvian student, "ancient" refers to something that is typically 1,000 to 5,000 years old.

- Peruvian girls do not play soccer, only volleyball. Boys play soccer. Surfing is a popular sport among the middle and upper classes in Lima and on the northern coast of Peru.

- Chances are that your Peruvian student has been raised in an urban environment. Don't expect your student to know about raising llamas or living in the highlands. Remember, one-third of Peru's population lives in Lima, a large city on the coast.

- An informal way to say "hello" and "good-bye" is *ola* and *chau* (derived from the Italian *ciao*). You can use both terms with your students; however, you might want to use a more formal *buenos días* (good day or good morning), *buenas tardes* (good afternoon), and *buenas noches* (good evening or good night) with parents and students.

- Peruvians stand very close to each other and touch each other. Your student might get closer to you than you expect.

- Greetings vary between genders. Men shake other men's hands and they kiss women on the cheek (one kiss only). Women will kiss each other on the cheek. Men will also pat each other on the back.

- Peruvians have a relaxed concept of time. Meetings and gatherings do not necessarily start on time.

- Peruvians use a lot of hand gestures and are animated when they talk.

- In urban settings, Peruvians wear Western-style clothing; in the highlands and provinces you will see some folks (mostly women) wearing traditional garb.

- Just as in English you end a children's story with "and they lived happily ever after," in Spanish we often say "*y colorín colorado este cuento se ha terminado.*" In this rhyme, *colorín* refers to the word "color" and *colorado* is the color red. The remainder means this story has finished.

CONCLUSIONS

Peru is a diverse nation with a multiplicity of geographical regions and a varied cultural and linguistic landscape. Although Spanish is the dominant language throughout the nation, Quechua and Aymara are also recognized official languages. Adding to the rich indigenous traditions, different waves of immigration coming from Spain, African nations, China, and other European countries have contributed to its *mestizo* tapestry.

Education in Peru is compulsory and free in public schools for the initial, primary, and secondary levels. It is also free in public universities for students based on need and merit. However, many families will make every effort to have their children attend private schools and universities. Since knowledge of a second or third language is considered a key to success, most private schools have intense foreign language programs. Having this awareness of their Peruvian students will allow U.S. educators to serve them in culturally responsive ways.

ADDITIONAL RESOURCES

Egbert, J. L., & Ernst-Slavit, G. (2010). *Access to academics: Planning instruction for K–12 classrooms with ELLs.* Boston, MA: Pearson Education.

>   This book is written specifically for K–12 teachers who work with ELLs. The book focuses on the academic language students will need to learn and use across different content areas. It also suggests strategies to plan instruction that builds on students' backgrounds and strengths.

Ernst-Slavit, G., & Mulhern, M. (2003). Bilingual books: Promoting literacy and biliteracy in the second-language and mainstream classroom. *Reading Online,* 7(2). Retrieved from http://www.readingonline.org/articles/art_index.asp?HREF=ernstslavit/index.html

>   This article discusses the benefits of and strategies for using bilingual books in mainstream classrooms and in classrooms with ELLs. The article also suggests strategies for using bilingual books to foster literacy development for second language learners.

Ernst-Slavit, G., & Mason, M.R. (2012). Making your first home visit: A guide for classroom teachers. ¡*Colorín Colorado!: A bilingual site for families and educators of English language learners.* Retrieved from http://www.colorincolorado.org/article/59138/

Interested in making a home visit? You do not know what you can do while visiting your students' homes? This article written for *Colorín Colorado* provides practical tips for home visits with English language learners (ELLs), including steps to take before, during, and after the visit.

Forrest, J. (2012). *Peru: The essential guide to culture & customs*. New York, NY: Random House.

This new edition charts the rapid changes taking place in the country. It describes how history and geography have shaped values, beliefs, traditions, and attitudes. It provides some insights into Peruvian ways of living at home, doing business, and relating to each other.

Starn, O., Degregori, I., & Kirk, R. (2005). *The Peru reader: History, culture, politics*. Durham, NC: Duke University Press.

This anthology covers Peru's history from pre-Columbian civilizations to its citizens' 21st-century struggles to achieve dignity and justice in a multicultural nation where Andean, African, Amazonian, Asian, and European traditions meet. The collection includes a vast array of essays, folklore, historical documents, poetry, songs, short stories, autobiographical accounts, and photographs.

Children's Books on Peru

Cecilia, M. (2010). *Kusikiy* a child from *Taquile, Peru*. Woodstock, NY: Keepers of Wisdom and Peace Books.

Ehlhert, L., & Prince, A, (2003). *Moon rope/Un lazo* a la *luna*. New York, NY: Houghton Mifflin Harcourt.

Giraud, H. (2005). *Children of the world—Tomasino: A child of Peru*. San Diego, CA: Blackbirch Press.

Lewin, T. (2012). *Lost city: The discovery of Machu Picchu*. New York, NY: Philomel Books.

Neuschwander, C., & Langdo, B. (2007). *Patterns in Peru: An adventure in patterning*. New York, NY: Henry Holt and Company, LLC.

Oler, C., & Oler, A, (2014). *Molly and the magic suitcase: Molly goes to Peru*. Carmel, IN: Color Marketing and Design.

Palacios, A. (1993). *The llama's secret: A Peruvian legend*. Mahwah, NJ: Troll Associates.

Roman, C. P. (2014). *If you were me in … Peru: A child's introduction to cultures around the world*. Seattle, WA: Createspace Independent Publishing Platform.

Simmons, C. (2015). *Nate and Shea's adventure in Peru*. Phoenix, AZ: Equator Creative Media.

TASKS FOR EDUCATORS

1. Watch the YouTube video *Do You Know How Much Your Children Are Learning?* (World Bank, 2010). It shows different schools and class-

rooms in both rural and urban settings. It was produced by the Education Ministry and the World Bank to support national assessments in Peru. Notice that in many schools the students are wearing uniforms. In Peru, most school children, starting in first grade, wear a uniform. In the 1970s, the government required all students, whether attending private or public schools, to wear the same uniform. This was a way for students to be equal and not worry about designer brand clothing. What do you think about school children wearing uniforms? What are the positive sides? What are the negative sides? Don't forget to consider that, in sports, every team wears a uniform.

2. Compare the schooling contexts of rural/public and urban/private schools in Peru by watching these two videos. The first video shows a group of tourists arriving at a remote rural 1–6 grade school located in Tito, a town on the road from Cuzco to Puno (*Elementary School in Peru*: https://www.youtube.com/watch?v=R40XnjgVPig). The second video focuses on the high price of private schools in Lima and showcases one private school in Lima and its facilities (*Colegios Privados en Lima Más Accesibles Para los Padres de Familia:* https://www.youtube.com/watch?v=SDqq0apN6LQ).

3. If you have a Peruvian student in your classroom, plan a home visit! For guidance about how to plan and conduct a home visit, see the article "Making Your First ELL Home Visit: A Guide for Classroom Teachers" by Ernst-Slavit and Mason (2012) in ¡*Colorín Colorado!* at http://www.colorincolorado.org/article/making-your-first-ell-home-visit-guide-classroom-teachers

4. A great strategy to gather information about your students is to ask parents to write letters about their children. These letters can be written in English or the home language (hopefully, you can find interpreters who can help you read them). In your request for this letter, you can ask parents to write about their child's personality, interests, schooling experiences, siblings, and any other aspect that can help you better understand their child.

REFERENCES

Ames, P. (2012). Language, culture and identity in the transition to primary school: Challenges to indigenous children's rights to education in Peru. *International Journal of Educational Development, 32*, 454–462.

Bromley, R. D. F., & Mackie, P. K. (2009). Child experiences as street traders in Peru: Contributing to a reappraisal for working children. *Children's Geographies, 7*(2), 141–158.

Calónico, S., & Ñopo, H. (2007). *Returns to private education in Peru*. Washington, DC: Inter-American Development Bank, Research Department Series, 603.

Ernst-Slavit, G., & Mason, M.R. (2012). Making your first home visit: A guide for classroom teachers. *¡Colorín Colorado!: A bilingual site for families and educators of English language learners*. Retrieved from http://www.colorincolorado.org/article/59138/

Ernst-Slavit, G., & Slavit, D. (2013, March). Mathematically speaking. *Language*, 32–36.

Instituto Nacional de Estadística e Informática. (2007). Censos Nacionales. XI de Población y VI de Vivienda. http://censos.inei.gob.pe/censos2007/

Paul, L. M., Simons, G. F., & Fennig, C. D. (Eds.). (2016). Peru. *Ethnologue: Languages of the world* (19th ed.). Dallas, TX: SIL International. Retrieved from http://www.ethnologue.com/country/PE

Peru's Constitution of 1993 with Amendments through 2009. (2016). Article 48. Retrieved from https://www.constituteproject.org/constitution/Peru_2009.pdf?lang=en

United Nations Environment Programme (UNEP). (2010). *State of biodiversity in Latin America and the Caribbean*. Retrieved from http://www.unep.org/delc/Portals/119/LatinAmerica_StateofBiodiv.pdf

World Bank. (2010, January 21). *Do you know how much your children are learning?* [Video file]. Retrieved from https://www.youtube.com/watch?v=tnpfbVNc-yg

SECTION 5

SOUTHEAST REGION

CHAPTER 11

VIETNAM

Eric Ambroso
Arizona State University

Nguyễn Thị Thu Điệp
Da Nang University

In her 16 years as a high school English teacher in Texas, Laurie Branham has become well acquainted with English language learners (ELLs). Laurie has taught hundreds of Spanish-speaking students over the years, and most of them do very well in her class with a little extra help. Laurie wants all of her students to feel comfortable sharing opinions and speaking out. She works hard to engage her students and takes great pride in creating a welcoming atmosphere in her classroom.

Linh's family moved to the area from Hanoi a few months ago, and she is having problems fitting in socially and academically. Laura's colleagues had told her that Vietnamese students could be shy, but she never expected to struggle so much with her first one. Unfortunately, Linh is just not responding to the strategies that usually work with Spanish-speaking ELL students. At first, Laurie tried to group her with some of the Chinese-American children, but Linh seemed reluctant to speak out, especially with the older students. When that failed, Laurie facilitated some student-centered games to show Linh how much fun the other ELLs have in her class. No matter what Laurie tries, Linh does not actively participate in the lessons. Instead, she sits in the front of the room with her head down, writing frantically in her notebook while the rest of the students engage in class activities or discussions.

Views From Inside: Languages, Cultures, and Schooling for K–12 Educators
pp. 185–199
Copyright © 2018 by Information Age Publishing

The most frustrating thing for Laurie is that she thinks Linh is cheating on written work. She does not understand how Linh can perform so well on tests and homework if she can barely speak the language. Laurie has a lot of experience teaching ELLs, and the disparity between Linh's spoken English and her written assignments is like nothing she has ever experienced before.

BACKGROUND

Vietnam is the easternmost country on the Indochinese peninsula, bordered by China to the north and Cambodia and Laos to the west. The socialist republic is approximately the same size as California and has a population of more than 90 million. In recent years, pristine beaches and a subtropical climate have increasingly lured tourists to Vietnam. However, a large part of the country is still rural farmland or dense forest with little access to modern technology or transportation. Two distinct regions dominate the country politically and economically: the Red River Delta and the city of Hanoi in the north, and the Mekong River Delta and Ho Chi Minh City in the south (Jamieson, 1995).

The devastation wrought by the Vietnam War is still evident in many parts of the country, but the war is a distant memory for most people these days. Vietnam has earned its peace and has developed significantly in the last 40 years. The Vietnamese people, especially the younger generations, are warm and open-minded. They have opened their arms wide to welcome the multitude of Americans and other Westerners who come to work, live, and travel throughout the country.

Chinese Influence

For people outside of Vietnam, the Vietnam War is often the first thing that comes to mind when they think of the country. But for the Vietnamese people, that war and the previous Indochinese War against the French came as the culmination of many centuries of occupation—first by the Chinese, then the Mongols, the Chinese (again), the French, and the Japanese (Corfield, 2008). Each invasion left an imprint on a rich Vietnamese culture that is very different from the more homogenous cultures of other countries in Asia. The result is a truly unique environment in which one can sit and watch a Chinese lion dance to celebrate Lunar New Year while enjoying a French-inspired *bánh mì* (sandwich).

According to archaeologists, patches of civilization began to develop in Vietnam around 1000 B.C., when the early Viet people began farming and irrigating the areas around the Red River, in central Vietnam, and in

**Table 11.1. Examples of Vietnamese
and Mandarin Chinese Similarities**

Vietnamese	Mandarin Transliteration	English
Cao (/kaw/)	gao	tall
Đáo (/daw/)	dao	come

the Dong Nai River Delta (Nguyen, 2006). The history of this region is infused with mythical stories of the people's origin and successive wars between Vietnamese and Chinese dynasties, or among the Vietnamese dynasties themselves (Nguyen, 2006). Vietnam has had a long, complicated relationship with China, having been invaded and colonized by its northerly neighbor during four separate periods between 111 B.C. and A.D. 1427. In the first period of *Bắc Thuộc*, or Chinese domination, the northern territory known as Nam Viet came under the control of the Han dynasty (see the chapter on China for more information on this dynasty). During this time, the people in the northern plains of Vietnam were forced to assimilate into Chinese culture in all aspects of life, which had a lasting impact on everything from religious beliefs to language (Trần, 1920). The Vietnamese language was also heavily influenced by Chinese rule during this time; several modern Vietnamese words have the same meaning and similar pronunciation to those in Mandarin (see examples in Table 11.1).

One salient example of the Chinese influence in Vietnam is the ubiquity of Confucian philosophy, which was introduced to Vietnam in the first *Bắc Thuộc* and rejuvenated under the Ly dynasty in the 11th century (Jamieson, 1995). Confucianism is deeply entrenched in almost every facet of Vietnamese life, from respect for educators to behavior towards strangers. Similar to many other groups of Asian people, Vietnamese people tend to be passive in initiating conversations with strangers. Approaching a stranger to start a conversation may be considered rude, especially with older generations. Today, life in Vietnam involves a constant juggling of varying etiquettes that center on the Confucian hierarchy of social position and age. This plays an extremely important role in education, as educators are considered to be at the top of the social ladder and deserving of the utmost respect. As described by the anecdote that started this chapter, Vietnamese children are taught from a young age not to interrupt their teachers or speak out when they disagree with a teacher's opinion. Linh was following Vietnamese tradition by remaining silent in class and taking notes on Laurie's lesson.

During the seven centuries of Chinese rule, the way of life in the Red River Delta and northern coastal plains of the Indochina peninsula was not lost to the Chinese policy of assimilation. Instead, genes and traditions intermingled to produce a local Sino-Vietnamese culture that is still distinctive to the region today (Jamieson, 1995).

Buddhism in Vietnam

Around the time of the first Chinese occupation in 218 B.C., Buddhism also arrived in Vietnam along the Silk Road. Traders from India and China brought their customs, art, and religions when they traveled through northern Vietnam, which became a flourishing center of Buddhism (Wickremeratne, 2007). The combination of cultures at the birth of Vietnamese Buddhism, along with Confucian, Christian, and Taoist influences in different time periods, has produced a modern version of Mahāyāna Buddhism that can be found nowhere else in the world (Nguyen, 2008). Many Vietnamese eat vegetarian food on the 1st, 14th, and 15th of each month to pray for inner peace, avoid bad consequences, and show love and sympathy to other species on the earth (Tâm, 2016). They also avoid eating garlic and onions, as they believe these foods used to be living things before they were punished and turned into spices by Buddha.

Vietnamese Buddhists normally reserve a special room in their homes to worship. Young members of the family, especially females, avoid the room at night because they believe that the souls of their ancestors stay in the room. Families clean the room during the day and burn incense before bed so the spirits will come back in the evening. Fruits and sweet soups or sticky rice are also dedicated on the 1st and 14th of each month of the lunar calendar. People believe that frequent worship will bring their family health and luck.

Regional Differences

Vietnam's geography is commonly divided into the two major areas previously mentioned in this chapter. The country has been split into north and south at many important points in its history (Drummond & Thomas, 2005). However, Vietnamese people most often separate their country into three geographic and cultural regions: north, central, and south (Jamieson, 1995). Although all Vietnamese share the same national language, each of these three regions has a distinct and mutually understandable dialect. Consider the word for *tofu* in all three regions: *đậu phụ* in the north, *đậu khuôn* in central Vietnam, and *đậu hũ* in the south. The food is also different in all three of the regions. Southern Vietnamese food is typically characterized by large portions and a sweet flavor, while dishes from the north are often bland. The cuisine from central Vietnam, on the other hand, is mostly spicy, with the former imperial city of Huế serving as the region's de facto capital for delicious food. People from all areas of Vietnam have immigrated to the U.S., and food from all three regions can be found in most big cities, but the majority of Vietnamese restaurants in the U.S. serve food that is typical of southern Vietnam.

EDUCATION

Vietnam is no longer the isolated country full of jungles and straw huts that is commonly depicted in movies about the Vietnam War. In 1986, the government approved broad economic reforms that opened up the country for foreign investment and dramatically improved Vietnam's business climate (Drummond & Thomas, 2005). In the 1990s, Vietnam became one of the fastest-growing economies in the world, averaging approximately 8% annual gross domestic product (GDP) growth from 1990 to 1997 (U.S. Department of State, 2012). Since 1995, Vietnam has been part of the Association of Southeast Asian Nations (ASEAN) and has actively worked to encourage international trade and tourism. In central Vietnam, in particular, backpackers, sunbathers, and 5-star resorts now line the beaches from Hue to Hoi An. Unfortunately, as the demand for skilled staff grows, the Vietnamese education system is struggling to keep pace with the new job market.

The education system in Vietnam is extremely prescriptive and controlled by the federal government. There is a specific curriculum for each subject at every grade level of Vietnamese school. Educators may not deviate from the curriculum and are expected to teach the prescribed material on the allotted day. Likewise, every Vietnamese student in the same grade is required to study the same material on an appointed day. Students throughout the country are also expected to complete the same homework each day.

Although English is one of the compulsory subjects at school, most local schools have failed to provide the second-language skills needed to work in an international environment. The typical classroom in Vietnam is very restrictive. Classrooms are jammed with lines of tables and chairs while educators rely on the "banking model" of feeding students information and discouraging them from being creative or interactive during lessons (Freire, 1970). The usual pedagogy consists of teachers lecturing in the front of the classroom for hours while the students take notes. Natural interactions in these classrooms are minimal, and students in these classes are often discouraged from speaking out. Thus, the students become very passive in participating in conversations or raising questions. As a result, the speaking, listening, and pronunciation skills of the average Vietnamese ELL are well below his or her reading and writing skills. During most English lessons at school, students are overloaded with grammar and writing exercises, while communicative interaction is very limited. As this is common practice throughout all levels of Vietnamese schooling, students like Linh may at first find it challenging to participate in communicative activities or freely interact with their teachers or peers.

According to Lantolf (2000), the communicative pedagogical approaches that have dominated English as a second language (ESL) classrooms since the 1980s represent Anglocentric goals of communication that often conflict with the cultural values of ELLs. This seems to be especially true for Vietnamese students, whose history includes a strong Confucian heritage that emphasizes dependence over independence and hierarchy rather than equality. Confronted with communicative language teaching (CLT) methods in American schools, Vietnamese students often find it difficult to engage in dialogue with their educators or speak during a lesson. Although students in Vietnam are becoming more active due to global influences, strong cultural norms still influence their behavior in school, whether they are in Vietnam or abroad.

Confucianism dictates that the teacher is considered "the master," to serve as an ethical model that teaches students appropriate behaviors associated with their role and rank (Ornstein & Levine, 2008). Open discussions between educators and students are usually avoided because it is considered disrespectful to teachers. In this tradition, students are positioned as subordinate and passive recipients of knowledge, which contradicts the American ideas of equality and participation that are generally emphasized in CLT theory. Laurie's experience with Linh exemplifies the difficulty that Vietnamese students may have working in small groups or pairs. Grouping in a classroom tends to divide up a class, which goes against the Confucian tradition of group harmony (Lantolf, 2000). Unlike most American students, who learn how to debate and work independently at a young age, Vietnamese students are usually more comfortable working together as an entire class.

CULTURE

Behaviors

There are many differences between appropriate behaviors in Vietnam and those in the U.S. For example, Vietnamese do not generally:

- hug and kiss when they meet; very little body contact is generated among friends and colleagues;

- wear shoes when entering a house; they are usually left at the door;
- talk about sexuality in public; this is considered a very private topic;
- bring an infant outside for the first three months; newborn babies and mothers usually stay inside and avoid contact with people to protect themselves from illness;
- call somebody by his/her name when they first meet, which is considered disrespectful. A prefix (*anh/chị/em/cô/bác*) should be added. The appropriate prefix to use when addressing someone is determined by the person's age (e.g., *anh* = an older male; *chị* = an older female; *em* = a younger person; *cô* = someone at an aunt's age; and *bác* = someone at an uncle's age);
- beckon somebody over using a finger with palm facing up; it is considered very rude and should be used for dogs only; and
- shake hands using only one hand with older people; two hands should be used to show respect.

Values

Although there are always exceptions, the following values are generally common among Vietnamese people:

- Vietnamese parents have high respect for their children's teachers, as they believe teachers are the most important influences on their children's lives. A teacher is not only a person who transfers knowledge, but also a moral model.
- Family is the center of life in Vietnamese culture. Taking good care of one's parents and children is very important.
- Old people are believed to be wise and experienced, and young people should listen to them at all times.
- Saving face is important, especially for men. Vietnamese tend to believe that a person is successful when he reaches a certain position or level of wealth. In other words, being perceived as a moral or successful person determines a man's character. The fact that a man appears less successful or moral than others could make people look down on him.
- Dressing properly in public with long trousers and collared top is a way to show respect to others. Dressing immodestly in public is considered rude; however, trends are changing due to an increase in international tourism.

- Vietnamese typically do not directly object while another person is speaking because it is considered aggressive.

Important Holidays

Holidays are a big part of life in Vietnam, especially towards the end of the year in the lunar calendar. Most holidays have a cultural significance. However, since a majority of the population practices some variety of Buddhism, a few holidays have some Buddhist influence. For example, people usually worship at Buddhist shrines and eat vegetarian food during mid-autumn festivals or on the first day of *Tết*.

Vietnamese also celebrate the anniversaries of family members' deaths to pay tribute to their loved ones. During these celebrations, people make offerings and burn incense to communicate with their dead family members in the other world. Below are more details about the two biggest holidays in Vietnam.

Tết

Tết, or Vietnamese New Year, falls on the first three days of the lunar calendar (the same as the Chinese New Year). This is, by far, the most important holiday of the year in Vietnam. Most schools and companies close several days before and after *Tết* to give their employees a chance to get home early and prepare to celebrate. Students are often extremely distracted for the period leading up to *Tết*, so educators in Vietnam rarely schedule assessments or important assignments during this time. It is also common for Vietnamese living abroad, especially students, to return to Vietnam during *Tết* to spend time with their families.

Before the holiday, people will decorate their houses, shop for new clothes, and prepare traditional foods such as *bánh chưng* (rice cake) and *bánh tét* (glutinous rice cake). Typically, lots of sweet dishes and alcohol are also consumed. Vietnamese believe that a house full of food and drink will bring prosperity to a family in the New Year. They often treat visitors to meals to show hospitality during *Tết*. Children and old people also receive *lì xì* (lucky money) from their family members or guests as a gesture of luck for the new year.

Tết Trung Thu (Mid-Autumn Festival)

The mid-autumn festival in Vietnam is another holiday inspired by Chinese tradition. It is celebrated during the day of the first full moon in August of the lunar calendar. Traditionally, the festival is geared towards children, but it has recently become a celebration for young adults as well. Schools and companies do not close for this holiday, but the festival is a big topic in conversations leading up to the event. *Bánh trung thu* (moon cake) is a typical dessert given to children and business clients during the festival, which is usually highlighted by lanterns and dragon dance performances.

Vietnamese Scholars

Poetry is a highly respected form of literacy in Vietnam. Some important Vietnamese scholars include:

Ho Chi Minh (1890–1969)

Known affectionately as *Bác Ho* (Uncle Ho) to the Vietnamese people, Ho Chi Minh was the founder and leader of the Vietnam Communist Independence movement and the president of the Democratic Republic of Vietnam (North Vietnam) from 1945 to 1969. In 1945, he proudly declared Vietnam independent from France in Ba Dinh Square in Hanoi, reading the Proclamation of Independence that he had written himself (Drummond & Thomas, 2005). His ideals of independence, freedom, and national democracy have been the backbone of Vietnamese political strategy for the better part of the last century.

Apart from his political achievements, his work as an author is also greatly appreciated by Vietnamese scholars. *Nhật Ký Trong Tù*, which is a compilation of poems that he wrote during the time he was imprisoned by Chinese government from 1942 to 1943, is widely read and studied in literature classes in schools throughout Vietnam.

Nguyen Du (1766–1820)

The poet Nguyen Du, also known as To Nhu, was the author of the masterpiece *Truyện Kiều*, (The Tale of Kieu), which is considered one of the finest examples of Vietnamese literature of all time (Phạm, 1963). The poem, which is familiar to every student in the country, was written in *chữ nôm*, the ancient Vietnamese writing system. Du also served as *Đông Các Học sĩ*, a highly respected scholar who taught princes and princesses as well as consulted with King Le in political matters.

LANGUAGES AND LITERACIES

Vietnamese is an Austroasiatic language that has been heavily influenced by Thai, Mandarin Chinese, and, more recently, French. Approximately 75 million people speak Vietnamese, which includes over a million people of Vietnamese origin living abroad (Baker & Jones, 1998). Education

Table 11.2.   Vietnamese Tones

Tone	English Description	Example Word	English Definition
không dấu	no tone	ma	ghost
dấu sắc	high rising	má	cheek
dấu huyền	falling	mà	but
dấu hỏi	dipping rising	mả	tomb
dấu ngã	high rising glottalized	mã	horse
dấu nặng	low glottalized	mạ	rice seedlings

Source: Adapted from Ager (2016).

is a high priority in Vietnam, and literacy rates are high, especially among younger generations. The United Nations Organization for Education, Science and Culture (2012) estimates that 93.2% of the adult population in Vietnam is literate.

The Vietnamese language makes use of the *quốc ngữ* writing system, which is based on the Latin alphabet and includes six tones, which alter the pronunciation and meaning of words. Table 11.2 below outlines the six different tones and the different meanings each tone brings to one specific word.

Avery and Ehrlich (1992) state that "as the sound systems of English and Vietnamese differ greatly, Vietnamese speakers can have quite severe pronunciation problems" (p. 153). The most notable difference is that the tones in Vietnamese change the meaning of words, whereas in English the intonation often dictates the function of the sentence. For example, a native English speaker will typically use a rising intonation at the end of a sentence to indicate a question. A falling pitch, on the other hand, usually signifies agreement. The intonation flux in English can be difficult for Vietnamese students to acquire. They often have problems understanding the function of a sentence and mimicking the sounds in their own speech. Vietnamese ELLs may speak in a monotone and have trouble expressing their intentions or emotions with English. Similarly, these learners might speak in inappropriate tones that convey inaccurate feelings or functions.

There are also considerable differences in the consonant sounds of the two languages. For example, English has more consonant phonemes and a wider variety of consonant sounds in different positions. Vietnamese, comparatively, has far more vowel phonemes and fewer consonant sounds (Avery & Ehrlich, 1992). Also, consonant sounds are often made only at the beginning of a word.

The absence of consonant phonemes in word endings may cause significant pronunciation problems for Vietnamese ELLs. For example, "in

Vietnamese, the voiceless stop consonants /p/, /t/, and /k/ occur at the end of a word, but these consonants are never released in final position and are much shorter than their English equivalents" (Avery & Ehrlich, 1992, p. 153). Following this logic, the final consonants in English words such as *bat*, *kick*, and *lap* would be inaudible or nonexistent for a Vietnamese speaker.

Vietnamese ELLs may also have difficulty using fricatives (i.e., sounds like *f*, *v*, *sh*, and *th*) in English. "As fricatives do not occur in word-final position in Vietnamese, Vietnamese speakers may omit fricatives at the ends of the words" (Avery & Ehrlich, 1992, p. 154). This may cause them to leave out consonant sounds at the end of words, which can alter the meaning of words such as present simple tense verbs and plural forms of nouns. For example, spoken by a native Vietnamese speaker, the sentence *"The boys always pass the garage on their way home"* may sound like *"The boy alway pa the gara on their way home"* (Avery & Ehrlich, 1992, p. 154).

Using intonation to express emotion while speaking English may also pose a challenge to Vietnamese-speaking students. Vietnamese is a tonal language, which means that intonation is used to change the meaning of words instead of the function or feeling of words. Vietnamese speakers with limited English proficiency often pronounce words with a flat intonation that can lead educators to misunderstand their feelings or intentions. Table 11.3 presents a few common Vietnamese words that could be useful for educators in the U.S.

IDEAS FOR EDUCATORS

Vietnamese immigrants come from a rich cultural background that can both support and hinder their transition to schools in the U.S. While their respect for teachers and good study habits might be a breath of fresh air, other Vietnamese traditions could be problematic in U.S. schools. Educators should be aware of any dietary restrictions Vietnamese students may have, especially during times that correspond to holidays in the lunar calendar. They might also take pity on any Vietnamese students that have to attend school during *Tết* (usually in late January or early February). As stated previously, Vietnamese children often find it difficult to focus on assignments and tests during this holiday.

Grouping is another issue that educators should be aware of when teaching Vietnamese students. Students like Linh might be very hesitant to participate in pairs or small groups. The Confucian tradition in Vietnamese schools makes students more comfortable working as one united class. Likewise, Vietnamese students could also seem very shy or disengaged in U.S. classrooms. Many Vietnamese students are very proficient

Table 11.3.   Common Words in Vietnamese

English	Context	Literal Meaning	Vietnamese Phrase
hello	to greet people	hello	xin chào /xin ʧaw/
you	a pronoun that represents the listener	older brother/older sister/younger person/aunt/uncle	anh/chị/em/cô/chú/bác
I	a pronoun that represents the speaker	I (older brother/older sister/younger person/aunt/uncle)	tôi (formal) /toi/ anh/chị/em/cô/chú/bác (informal)
What's your name?	introductions	What's your name?	Bạn tên gì? /bæn tɛn gi/
How are you?	introductions	How are you?	Bạn khỏe không? /bæn khoe khong/
yes		yes	vâng/dạ/có /væŋ/za/ ko/
no		no	không /kon/
	an attachment to a name to express intimacy or friendliness; to answer somebody's call	no literal meaning	ơi /oi/

in written English but lack basic communication or listening skills. This is most likely the result of a different teaching style in Vietnam, where students are taught to listen attentively to their educators and not interrupt or ask questions.

Pronunciation can also be challenging for Vietnamese students learning English. Gilbert (2008) states that teachers and students can overcome the frustrations, difficulties, and boredom often associated with pronunciation by focusing their attention on the development of pronunciation that is "listener friendly" (p. 1). This is an important distinction to make because the ultimate goal of learning and using a language is to be understood. Thus, pronunciation exercises should be practical and communicative in nature, with the goal of getting a message across to a conversation partner. One such activity involves using a nonsense word (like "banana-num") to convey different feelings and functions in English. To play the game, teachers should write down feelings and function expressions on slips of paper and hand these to the students. They may include words and expressions such as *angry, sad, impatient,* and *not sure.* Students then use only the one nonsense word (and gestures) to make other people in the class guess what is written on their slip of paper. The purpose of the game is to have the Vietnamese ELLs practice the use of appropriate intonation.

Role plays can also be adapted to work on intonation. One idea is to give students a dialogue that they practice together one time. After that, one student in each pair is given a slip of paper with an emotion or phrase written on it. The students are asked to read the dialogue again, this time using intonation to change the function of the dialogue according to the word or phrase written on their slip of paper. Words or phrases on the paper might include *in a hurry*, *romantically interested*, or *sad*. The activity will allow the students to use intonation in a practical, communicative way. This supports the understanding that "the best of contemporary language teaching incorporates attention to pronunciation in ways compatible with communicative language teaching and task-based approaches to learning language and is, therefore, sensitive to the learners' real world needs" (Murphy, 2003, p. 126).

For many Vietnamese students, pronouncing the final consonant sounds can be very difficult, especially /s/, /iz/, and /z/. Goodwin (2001) maintains that "learners will usually have difficulty with sounds that don't exist in their L1" (p. 122), which includes final consonants for students whose first language is Vietnamese. It is important to make students aware of the difference between /s/, /iz/ and /z/. One possible activity makes use of a worksheet in which the students group words according to the final sound. As Goodwin (2001) notes, "At the beginning, in more controlled activities, the learner's attention should be focused almost completely on form" (p. 125). After the completion of this activity, teachers can use a puzzle for a production activity in which students complete the puzzle by linking words with the same sound (/s/, /iz/, or /z/). By the end of the lesson, students should be aware of final word sounds, which can be reinforced in future lessons.

CONCLUSIONS

The purpose of this chapter is to present elements of Vietnamese culture that could affect students' educational opportunities in American classrooms. Steeped in a rich history of intermingled traditions and beliefs from various peoples, Vietnamese students present a unique set of challenges in an American academic environment. From Confucian ideals to Buddhist superstitions, the learning behaviors of these students can be very different. The phonology in Vietnamese and English is also very different, creating several pronunciation problems for Vietnamese ELLs. For many Vietnamese students, these are extremely difficult challenges to overcome, but knowledgeable teachers who anticipate these problems can help point them in the right direction.

ADDITIONAL RESOURCES

Hồ, C. M. (1967). *On revolution: Selected writings, 1920-66*. B. B. Fall (Ed.). New York, NY: Praeger.

Jamieson, N. L. (1995). *Understanding Vietnam*. Berkeley, CA: University of California Press.

Nguyễn, D., Huỳnh, S. T., & Thong, H. S. (1983). *The tale of Kiều: A bilingual edition of Truyện Kiều*. New Haven, CT: Yale University Press.

TASKS FOR EDUCATORS

1. Find a clip on the Web of a native Vietnamese speaker speaking in English. What do you notice about the speaker's pronunciation and intonation? What are some ways you might address these issues?

2. How might you introduce Vietnamese culture into a U.S. public school? What might be most useful or most engaging to American students?

3. Create an activity based on the suggestions above to help students pronounce the final consonant sounds in words. Share your activity with your peers or colleagues.

REFERENCES

Ager, S. (2016). Vietnamese. Online encyclopedia of writing systems and languages. Retrieved from http://www.omniglot.com/writing/vietnamese.htm

Avery, P., & Ehrlich, S. (1992). *Teaching American English pronunciation*. Oxford, UK: Oxford University Press.

Baker, C., & Jones, S. P. (1998). *Encyclopedia of bilingualism and bilingual education*. Bristol, UK: Multilingual Matters.

Corfield, J. (2008). *The history of Vietnam*. Westport, CT: Greenwood Press.

Drummond, L., & Thomas, M. (Eds.). (2005). *Consuming urban culture in contemporary Vietnam*. London, UK: Routledge.

Freire, P. (1970). *Pedagogy of the oppressed*. New York, NY: Seabury Press.

Gilbert, J. B. (2008). *Teaching pronunciation: Using the prosody pyramid*. New York, NY: Cambridge University Press.

Goodwin, J. (2001). Teaching pronunciation. In M. Celce-Murcia (Ed.), *Teaching English as a second or foreign language* (3rd ed., pp. 117–137). Boston, MA: Heinle & Heinle Publishers.

Jamieson, N. L. (1995). *Understanding Vietnam*. Berkeley, CA: University of California Press.

Lantolf, J. P. (2000). *Sociocultural theory and second language learning*. Oxford, UK: Oxford University Press.

Murphy, J. (2003). Pronunciation. In D. Nunan (Ed.), *Practical English language teaching* (pp. 111–128). New York, NY: McGraw Hill.

Nguyen, N. Q. (2006). History of Vietnam. Retrieved from http://www.mekongresponsibletourism.org/wp-content/uploads/kalins-pdf/singles/viet-nam-history.pdf

Nguyen, T. T. (Ed.). (2008). *The history of Buddhism in Vietnam*. Washington, DC: The Council for Research in Values and Philosophy.

Ornstein, A. C., & Levine, D. U. (2008). *Foundations of education* (10th ed.). Boston, MA: Houghton Mifflin.

Phạm, T. N. (1963). *Việt Nam văn học sử giản ước tân biên (Quyển 2)*. Saigon, VN: Quốc Học Tùng Thư.

Tâm, T. T. (2016). *Ý nghĩa của việc ăn chay*. Retrieved from http://www.tinhdo.net/phathoccanban/188-ynghiacuasuanchay.html

Trần, T. K. (1920). *Việt Nam sử lược*. Hà Nội, VN: Tân Bắc Trung Văn.

United States Department of State. (2012). U.S. relations with Vietnam. Retrieved from http://www.state.gov/r/pa/ei/bgn/4130.htm

United Nations Educational, Scientific and Cultural Organization. (2012). Education in 2012. Retrieved from http://unesdoc.unesco.org/images/0022/002204/220416e.pdf

Vũ, T. B. (2012). *Non nước Việt Nam*. Hà Nội, VN: Lao động Xã hội.

Wickremeratne, A. (2007). Buddhism in Vietnam. In D. Keown & C. Prebish (Eds.), *The encyclopedia of Buddhism*. London, UK: Routledge.

CHAPTER 12

INDIA

Rani Muthukrishnan and Sreejith Thankappan
Washington State University

In a kindergarten class in a small-town public school in the U.S., the kids were excited to talk about and choose parts for the upcoming Pilgrim play for Thanksgiving. Gita watched her classmates hustle around. When the teacher assigned her the part of a non-speaking Pilgrim, she remained seated. That afternoon, when the class went to the kitchen and stuffed the turkey, Gita threw up right outside the kitchen. When her mother learned that Gita had been in the kitchen touching turkey, she approached the teacher to understand the situation. The teacher said that this was a part of the class activity for Thanksgiving. Gita's mother explained to the teacher that theirs was a vegetarian family and that Gita had never seen a bird dead, stuffed, or cooked. The teacher said the celebrations could not be canceled for the sake of one child.

Gita was reluctant to return to the classroom after the Thanksgiving break. In order to resolve this issue, Gita's mother requested a meeting with the teacher. The teacher said that children in her classroom were expected to speak up for themselves. Gita's mother pointed out that Gita was the only non-Caucasian child in the class and, although her daughter was fluent in English, it was inappropriate for an Indian child to speak up to adults. The teacher said that all children in the

Views From Inside: Languages, Cultures, and Schooling for K–12 Educators
pp. 201–215

classroom would be treated equally. In practice, this meant that Gita would not be treated equitably; Gita's mother noticed several cultural differences and expectations that were disadvantageous to her daughter. The year rolled by with little responsiveness from the teacher, and Gita's school experience did not improve all through the elementary school years. Gita's mother still firmly believes that teachers should be sensitive and prepared to help students from different cultural backgrounds to have the best school experience.

BACKGROUND

India is the seventh-largest country in the world in land area, with continuous habitation that can be traced back to the Stone Age (Allchin & Allchin, 1982). Being the second most populous nation in the world, there is enormous diversity in terms of language, culture, and religious practices in India, and Indians have varied genetic makeups resulting from diverse waves of migration over time (Bhasin, 1994). Although 1,652 languages were counted in the 1961 census, these were pared down to 190 languages by excluding languages that had numerically sparse populations. Today, despite having more than 1,000 languages in use, India recognizes only 22 as official languages (Sayeed, 2004). Interestingly, English is recognized as one of the official languages of the country (Const. of India. art. CCCXLIV, § 1; Const. of India. art. CCCLI).

The political map of India is drawn on the lines of linguistic similarities (Const. of India. Amend. VII). One of the major languages used in India is Hindi. Although it is not widely accepted as the national language, Hindi is the official language per the constitution ("Hindi, Not a National Language," 2010). Hindi is an Indo-Aryan language with about 545 million speakers, of which 425 million are native speakers (A Guide to Hindi, 2014). Hindi was first used in written form in the 4th century AD (Hindi, 2012). Hindi is written with the Devanagari script, used from around the 1st century AD, and its vocabulary is drawn from Sanskrit (Bhatia, 2008).

Geography

India is called a subcontinent because its geographic boundaries include snowy mountain peaks, mangrove forests, mountain forests, evergreen forests, thorn forests, and deserts. Its boundaries include the Himalayan mountain range in the north, and it has a coastline of 7,517 kilometers (4,671 miles). India is a peninsula in the south, surrounded by the Bay of Bengal, the Arabian Sea, and the Indian Ocean.

History

Evidence from the Narmada Valley shows that India could have been inhabited with hominoids since the middle Pleistocene era, about two million years ago (de Lumley & Sonakia, 1985). The Indus Valley civilization was one of the largest civilizations of the time, with more than 5 million inhabitants (Kahn & Osborne, 2005). After the collapse of this civilization, the Magadha kingdom allowed the establishment of new philosophies by Mahavira (Jainism) and Gautama Buddha (Buddhism) during the 5th and 6th centuries AD. By the 3rd century BC, the Mauryan Empire extended from present-day Afghanistan into southern India. Trade contacts with the Roman Empire were established by 77 AD, and Indian cultural influence was evident in Southeast Asia (Tarling, 2000). India has been a part of the historical Silk Road and the Spice Route, and it hosted a steady stream of traders from the Middle East even before Islam was established there ("Trade History," n.d.).

Muslim rule started in the 13th century in northern India, but it waned in a century due to other powerful kingdoms and dynasties. This was followed by expansion of the Sikh empire and the establishment of the Moghuls in the 16th century. By the 18th century, European nations such as Britain, France, and Portugal had established trading posts and gradually expanded to create colonies. After the revolt of 1857, the British Crown directly began to administer the subcontinent, extending from modern-day Afghanistan in the north to Bangladesh in the east and Sri Lanka in the south. This 300-year colonial rule ended when India was partitioned into the domains of India and Pakistan. This was preceded by pre-partition of two major territories, Bengal and Punjab. Afghanistan, Burma, and other regions were also separated from India. All these events led to unprecedented mass migration and death (Dalrymple, 2015). Thus, millions of people living in India are refugees. India has followed the path of democracy since 1947. People of all socioeconomic strata and castes above the age of 18 have the right to vote and participate in the democratic process.

Historically, and due to colonialism, Indian people settled all around the world. The Indian diaspora is the second largest diaspora in the world (Ministry of External Affairs, 2004). Diaspora communities help Indian students to stay connected with their traditions, language, and culture as they explore their new environments.

CULTURE

The West has often promoted India as a poor, savage nation. However, since ancient times India has been a leader in the fields of chemistry, mathematics, astronomy, medicine, and allied sciences. The number zero, the Hindu number system (called Hindu-Arabic numerals), precision medicine, advanced aeronautics, and quantum physics have been developed from ancient times (Narasimhan, 2016). In addition, India is home to 32 World Heritage Sites (for example, the seashore temple complex at Mahabalipuram and the heritage railways at Darjeeling), with 46 pending the status ("India," 2016). Nalanda, founded in 5 AD, was the first university in the world, attracting scholars from Tibet, China, Korea, and Central Asia. This was a seat of learning for Buddhist philosophies and it also formalized the learning of linguistics, reasoning, medicine, law, astronomy, and city planning (Sharma, 2013).

Religion

The 2011 census of India reports that followers of all major religions can be found in India. Additionally, Indian philosophy also recognizes atheism as a spiritual practice. Children from India are exposed to many religions besides their own and are aware of their holidays and practices. The majority of Indians follow Sanatana Dharma, known in the west as Hinduism; other Indians are Muslims, Christians, Sikhs, Buddhists, Jains, and others (Office of the Registrar General & Census Commissioner, India, 2011).

Vacations and holy days are spread throughout the calendar year and change every year. A student may seek vacation to celebrate sacred days and festivals with her friends and family. Due to the history of colonial rule, the Gregorian calendar and 12-hour day/ night clock is followed by the government, business establishments, and schools (Klostermaier, 2007).

People

To date, 11 Indians (5 Indian citizens and 6 of Indian origin or residency) have received Nobel Prizes in literature, economics, and other areas. There are numerous film personalities and artists who bring honor to India. Several authors have also been shortlisted or received the acclaimed Booker Prize.

Some famous people you might know from India include:

- Gandhi (full name Mohan Das Karamchand Gandhi) was a famous civil rights leader who was born in India, educated in England, and lived in South Africa before returning to India. He led a nonviolent freedom struggle based on civil disobedience and economic boycott when India was a colony of the British Empire.
- Tagore (full name Rabindranath Tagore) was awarded the Nobel Prize in literature in 1913 for his collection of poems with spiritual underpinnings called *Gitanjali*. He composed the national anthems of India and Bangladesh.
- Indira Gandhi, daughter of the first Prime Minister of independent India, Jawaharlal Nehru, was the first and only woman Prime Minister of India to date. She was assassinated in 1984. (She is not related to Gandhi).

Ethnicity and Tribes

There are more than 500 indigenous tribes or ethnic groups recognized in India (Ministry of Tribal Affairs, 2015). Tribes with significant population also have leaders of regional and national stature. The language, culture, and food is distinct between the tribes. People often have a surname indicating their affiliation to their tribe. Some tribe members learn Indian languages to find employment locally. Several tribes are wanderers with no claim to a fixed location except for the seasonal rite of passage through private or forest lands. Many tribes face missionary pressure to convert to Islam or Christianity.

Caste System

Known as *varnashrama* dharma in Sanskrit, the caste system was established based on functional roles in society centuries ago when people contributed in certain ways. There are four "Scheduled Castes." Scholars and keepers of knowledge were called *Brahmanas* [Braam-ha-naas]. The tradesmen were called *Vaishyas* [vhy-sh-yaas], the warriors were called *Kshatriyas* and people with no specialization were called *Shudras*. *Jati*, not the caste system as it was called by colonists, was prevalent in India (Flood, 2009). Western society has a missionary view of the caste system in India and often focuses on the "untouchable" or political *Dalit* caste. Colonialism created economic disparities by training and providing employment to some sections of the society and marginalizing certain populations like the Dalits. Although the government has enacted laws to protect against caste prejudices, the caste system is practiced by many sections of the society even today. In cities, the caste system is porous. Interestingly, the caste system is practiced even among people who are not Hindu.

Traditional Clothes

Traditional male and female clothing is often a long piece of cloth that is worn in different regional styles. *Sari* is the female way of tying the 5- or 9-yard piece of cloth. There are 80 ways to wear a *sari* (Kashi, 2007). The male way of wearing the cloth is called *dhoti*. There are as many ways of wearing a *dhoti* as a *sari*. Traditional clothes such as *ghagra-choli* (a long skirt and blouse, usually elaborately embroidered and decorated) and *salwar-kurta* (pajama bottom and a top) are also worn by women. The pajama-kurta is also worn by men in the western part of India. Most Hindu women wear a saffron dot between their brows as a part of their daily ritual; men, women, and children of all ages can wear the saffron dot. Women may wear many ornaments, including bangles and anklets. *Purdah* is followed in parts of northern and western India, where women cover their faces with a *sari*.

Unacceptable Behaviors to Indian People

In general, taboos include:

- eating from the same plate (unless you are parent of a very young child),
- sharing food that has been eaten by someone else,
- holding someone's neck,
- putting your feet up on a chair when someone else is talking to you,
- refusing to share or give water (but don't share if you have already tasted it),
- using the left hand to eat or hand things to people,
- wearing shoes into homes,
- entering someone's kitchen or worship room without invitation,
- spitting in front of a person,
- sitting down when an older person approaches or talks to you,
- passing judgment without understanding the context or history, and
- ignoring or insulting the hosts' feelings or sentiments.

Values

In general, Indian people have the following values:

- People respect and honor personnel who sacrifice for the sake of the greater good. Spiritual leaders and monks are thus more respected than politicians and businessmen.
- Guests are given a high place of honor and respect. They receive the best of everything the host has.
- Indians, in general, have a very relaxed relationship with time. Often, you will hear comments like "I will do it in my next birth." Across all religions, people in India believe in rebirth.
- If you are an older teacher, you will feel much valued and respected by parents.
- If you get close to Indian people, they casually ask deeply personal questions about family, age, and marital status. Usually, they ask these questions to feel that they have some similarities with you and to make a personal connection.
- Several generations of the same family live under the same roof. Your student might not be closest with the children of their same age. Some of them have strong relationships with their grandparents or cousins. Learning about the family will help you assist the child in participating.

Important Holidays

Indian people celebrate New Year and other festivals throughout the year. Christians, Muslims, and Parsee people follow their own calendars. The traditional New Year calendar begins in March or April for most Hindus. Most parents are willing to help host classroom celebrations. Holidays include:

- The Harvest Festival is celebrated over 5 days in January in various parts of the country.
- The goddess of learning, *Sarasvati*, is worshiped in Bengal and the eastern parts of India and the Himalayas in February.
- *Holi*, or playing with colors, is celebrated in February or March every year.
- June to December is a season of festivals. There are car festivals all over the country where millions of people congregate, pull chariots, and participate in fairs.

- August–September is the season for celebrating the special relationship or bond that brothers and sisters share during *Raksha Bandhan*.
- *Ganesh Chaturthi*, the birthday of the elephant-faced god, is celebrated with great pomp during September–October.
- October–November is also the time for mother worship, called *Navaratri*, when feminine energy is celebrated for 10 days.
- *Diwali*, the most important festival for Hindus, is celebrated in November–December. People light lamps, buy new clothes, make sweets, invite friends and families, and share gifts.

The dates for these events change every year depending upon the calendar.

In addition, devout Hindus fast once every 15 days following their calendar. During religious festivities, a strict vegetarian diet is observed by most of the population until the end of the rituals, when some groups offer meat and consume it. Several generations of families could have been raised as total vegetarians, which excludes eggs or meat from the diet.

SCHOOLING

Oral learning has deep cultural significance in India (Bajpai, 2014). For most Hindu children, learning begins at home well before the child goes to school, with formal initiation into traditional learning at the age of 3. The Indian constitution provides the right for free and compulsory education for all children 6–14 years of age (Department of School Education and Literacy, 2016b). Most children in India enter school at the age of 5 and graduate from high school at grade 10, after 12 years of education. In order to increase enrollment and improve nutrition, elementary students have been provided with midday meals since 1995 (Department of School Education and Literacy, 2016a). For the first time in the history of independent India, in 2015, 96% of children of eligible age were enrolled in schools, and the enrollment of girls went up significantly (Sahni, 2015).

India has a large private school system, with about 29% of students enrolled there (Joshua, 2014). The syllabus and standards are complementary to those in schools run by the government. *Gurukuls* and *madrassas* are traditional schools that blend modern education with a religious-based curriculum. Enrollment is restricted to members of the religion or sect. In most schools, memorization, writing, and homework are accepted as a part of learning, and textbooks are an essential part of primary education. Unlike in the U.S., children often carry a heavy burden of books to school and back daily.

The school calendar year starts in August, with annual examinations completed in April. Students have a brief break after exams and resume their academic year until mid-May. Schools take a break during the peak summer season between May and July. Students from India are used to testing as they have weekly, monthly, quarterly, and semiannual testing. Although there are no board examinations in the primary or elementary levels, students may be held back to repeat a grade. The testing system, unfortunately, adds to extreme pressure on students at later stages (Dhankar, 2016). There is little support for special education students in the school system (Singal, 2010).

English is a popular medium of instruction in urban schools, while rural schools continue to instruct students in regional languages. Indian students may be proficient in more than one language, as most children study three languages at school—the medium of instruction, a second language, and a third language. Students can choose to study their mother language as the second or third language. For example, a child studying in Bengaluru in an English-medium school would have English as the language of instruction, learn Sanskrit as the second language, and study Kannada (the local language) as the third language.

Many students continue education in pre-university (known as +2), equivalent to the last two years of U.S. secondary school. After pre-university, students can compete via examinations for placement in professional degree programs such as medicine or engineering, which last 3 to 4 years. This is followed by a master's program (2 years) and doctoral program (5–7 years). All placements in professional degrees and graduate degrees require placement via competitive examinations, as there are limited seats. In elite engineering schools such as the Indian Institute of Technology, only 10,000 in 500,000 applicants are admitted (TNN, 2012).

LANGUAGE AND LITERACY

Challenges for Indian English Language Learners

Not all students learn the English language in India. Students can complete their entire education in a regional language. The regional language influences the pronunciation of words and use of phrases (Sindkhedkar, 2012). One of the main problems associated with learning the English language is with the phonetics (sounds of the letters). Most Indian languages use the actual names of the letters rather than the sounds of the letters. When students learn the English language, they may try to make the same connection and pronounce the word with the name of the letters. For example, "spoon" could be pronounced as "espoon." Many Indians cannot pronounce the sound "shh"; they may say it as "ss." Thus, "share" would be pronounced "sare."

There are other possible challenges for Indian English language learners (ELLs). These include:

- There is no concept of silent letters in Hindi or other Indian languages.
- Many Indian languages have their own unique structure and do not necessarily have the same articles (i.e., *a, an*, and *the*) as English.
- The placement of the verb in an English sentence is different in Indian languages.
- Due to language interference, Indian speakers may mix up gender, with "he" and "she" becoming misattributed.
- Verbs tenses are more complicated in Indian languages, and ELLs may try to simplify communication by keeping to one tense (usually past).
- Indian English is recognized as having separate grammar and phonetics from other variants of English, and most Indians can speak Indian English (Pingali, 2012). This makes their pronunciation of words and concepts unique.

Common Greeting Words in Hindi

If an Indian student is not fluent in English, a few phrases in Hindi might help the student understand what is required (see Table 12.1 for examples).

IDEAS FOR EDUCATORS

Many students from Indian homes experience drastic differences between their school and home environments in the U.S. Students can experience severe separation anxiety because of these differences, and they may also feel isolated from their peers because they dress, look, or speak differently. Introducing students to different cultures right from the beginning is important for Indian children so that their U.S. peers can learn to accept students who cannot speak English well or do not yet understand U.S. cultural norms.

Table 12.1.   Greeting Words in Hindi

Hindi	Pronunciation	English Translation
नमस्ते	NA-muss-thae	Hi/Greetings
आप कैसे हैं ?	AAP-kae-say-hein?	How are you?
मैं ठीक हूँ।	Mein-THEEK-hoon	I'm fine, thanks
शुक्रीया	SHOO-CREE-YAH	Thank you
शुभ रात्री	SHUBHA-RAATHRI	Good night
फिरफमलंगा	FIR-mill-ENN-gay	See you later
क्षमा कीफिए	SHAH-mah-kee-jee-AYE	Excuse me
आपका नाम क्या है?	AAAP-kah- naam- kyah- hein?	What's your name?
शुभ कामनाएँ	SHUBHA- KAAM-naa-yein	Good wishes
बधाई हो	BADDHA-YEE-HOH	Congratulations
इ पढ़ें	IS-aye-pad-YEN	Read this
यहाँ	YA-han	Here

Working With Families

In order to work with Indian students and their families, educators can consider that:

- For Indian children younger than 10 years of age, personal boundaries are not enforced in most homes.
- Many parents from India will have trouble with the American accent. Therefore, communicating expectations in writing will help both parties.
- Some Indian parents speak quickly and may have a strong regional accent. Asking them to repeat themselves or speak slowly is advisable.
- If a parent–teacher meeting involves discussing the details of rule infractions, having a neutral party present and establishing ground rules in a cordial atmosphere will be beneficial.
- As immigrants, many parents are under severe emotional and psychological stresses themselves. Although the culture is changing in urban India, Indian parents might make severe objections to suggestions of counseling for the children.
- If your student does not speak English yet, using a higher pitch may scare the student. In India, a raised pitch in speech is an indication of fault that is punishable.

- Easing language learners into the language using songs and activities will be popular with the child and family.
- Students can come from a variety of socioeconomic and religious backgrounds.
- Same-sex marriages or couples are recognized traditionally but are banned by colonial law.
- Mothers are expected to manage the finances, cook meals, and take care of the needs of the family, even if they are working. The female parent may not be proficient in English but will strive to communicate with the teacher.
- Educators can use the assistance of extended family members to communicate with parents, especially if the parents are not fluent in English. Extended families are quickly formed with people who speak a similar native language or are from a similar region back in India.
- Most Indian parents consider careers in science or law as important and acceptable careers. Many children feel obligated to follow their parents' wishes in this respect.
- Parents spend money to provide education in music and art and access to opportunities in sports outside of school in India, and they may seek similar opportunities for their children in the U.S. Understanding these interests could help educators support students' connections with their peers and provide topics for lessons.
- Indian students often travel to and from India and are likely to be familiar with the nuances of international travel. An educator can leverage and extend such practical life situations to explain unfamiliar nuances of American culture. For example, one teacher explained the writing process in her classroom in terms of travel—check in your idea, state your purpose, show your evidence, and let us know what you learned from the experience.
- Learning disabilities are not well diagnosed in the Indian school system. Although many parents support the child, many others simply refuse to acknowledge the disability. It is important for educators to take Indian parents into their confidence right away and seek their cooperation during diagnosis and problem solving.

CONCLUSIONS

India is a vast country with enormous diversity in language, culture, and customs. Students from India deal well with testing and homework and have an awareness of the expectations their family has for them. Student learning is probably supported in their homes. When American traditions are observed in the classroom, it is beneficial to detail the sequence of events, include any expectations, and send a note to parents. Educators can keep in mind that the usual stereotype of Indians as portrayed in movies—having a heavy accent, wearing a certain type of clothing, having certain mannerisms, and excelling in math—is not true for every student.

ADDITIONAL RESOURCES

Binu, V. (2016). Learn Indian languages. Retrieved from http://www.languageshome.in/
> Learn how to converse in Indian languages and become familiar with scripts in Indian languages by exploring this website.

Indian History. (2015). *Gateway for India*. Retrieved from http://www.gatewayforindia.com/history.htm
> This website provides a backdrop of ancient history, from 6500 BCE to current India.

National Portal of India. (2016). Retrieved from https://india.gov.in/
> Unified portal giving information about everything Indian. The website has information and statistics regarding education, languages, and socioeconomic profile.

TASKS FOR EDUCATORS

1. Read children's books that involve Indian characters. How are the characters portrayed? How does the portrayal fit with the information given in this chapter?

2. Sometimes what is not said is as important as what is. Read the chapters on Pakistan and Bangladesh, and then come back to this chapter. What might be missing in these chapters that would help teachers better understand the relationships among students from these three countries?

3. What do children in India like to do in their free time? How can you find out?

REFERENCES

A guide to Hindi—10 facts about the Hindi language. (2014). *BBC News*. Retrieved from http://www.bbc.co.uk/languages/other/hindi/guide/facts.shtml

Allchin, B., & Allchin, R. (1982). *The rise of civilization in India and Pakistan*. New Delhi, India: Oxford University Press.

Bajpai, L. M. (2014). Complementary disciplines and their significance in India— Oral traditions, folklore and archeology. *International Journal of English Language, Literature* and Humanities, 2(1), 125–143.

Bhasin, M. K. (1994). *People of India: An investigation of biological variability in ecological, ethno-economic, and linguistic groups*. New Delhi, India: Kamla-Raj Enterprises.

Bhatia, T. (2008). *Colloquial Hindi: A complete course for beginners* (2nd ed.). New York, NY: Routledge.

Const. of India. art. CCCXLIV, § 1. Government of India. (2003). Eighth schedule articles 344 (1) and 351 constitution of the nation of India. Retrieved from http://lawmin.nic.in/coi/coiason29july08.pdf

Const. of India. art. CCCLI. Government of India. (2003). Eighth schedule articles 344 (1) and 351 constitution of the nation of India. Retrieved from http://lawmin.nic.in/coi/coiason29july08.pdf

Const. of India. amend. VII. (n.d.). The constitution (Seventh Amendment) Act, 1956. Retrieved from http://indiacode.nic.in/coiweb/amend/amend7.htm

Dalrymple, W. (2015, June 29). The great divide: The violent legacy of Indian partition. *The New Yorker*. Retrieved from http://www.newyorker.com/magazine/2015/06/29/the-great-divide-books-dalrymple

de Lumley, M. A., & Sonakia, A. (1985). Première découverte d'un Homo erectus sur le continent indien à Hathnora, dans la moyenne vallée de la Narmada. *Anthropologie (L')(Paris)*, 89(1), 13–61.

Department of School Education and Literacy. (2016a). *Mid-day meal scheme*. Retrieved from http://mhrd.gov.in/mid-day-meal

Department of School Education and Literacy. (2016b). *Right to education*. Retrieved from http://mhrd.gov.in/rte

Dhankar, R. (2016, June 17). Staying power of the pass fail system. *The Hindu*. Retrieved from http://www.thehindu.com/opinion/lead/staying-power-of-the-passfail-system/article8737707.ece

Flood, G. (2009, August 24). Hindu concepts. *BBC*. Retrieved from http://www.bbc.co.uk/religion/religions/hinduism/concepts/concepts_1.shtml

Hindi, not a national language: Court. (2010, January 25). *The Hindu*. Retrieved from http://www.thehindu.com/news/national/hindi-not-a-national-language-court/article94695.ece

Hindi. (2012). *Interpreters and Translators, Inc*. Retrieved from http://www.ititranslates.com/language/hindi/

India: World heritage sites. (2016). *World heritage site*. Retrieved from http://www.worldheritagesite.org/countries/country.php?id=50

Joshua, A. (2014, January 16). Over a quarter of enrolments in rural India are in private schools. *The Hindu*. Retrieved from http://www.thehindu.com/features/education/school/over-a-quarter-of-enrolments-in-rural-india-are-in-private-schools/article5580441.ece

Kahn, C., & Osborne, K. (2005). *World history: Societies of the past*. Winnipeg, Canada: Portage & Main Press.

Kashi, A. R. (2007, October 25). How to wear a Sari in India. *World Hum*. Retrieved from http://www.worldhum.com/features/how-to/wear_a_sari_20071025/

Klostermaier, K. (2007). *A survey of Hinduism* (3rd ed.). New York, NY: State University of New York Press.

Ministry of External Affairs. (2004). *The Indian diaspora*. Retrieved from http://indiandiaspora.nic.in/

Ministry of Tribal Affairs. (2015). *State/Union territory-wise list of scheduled tribes in India*. Retrieved from http://tribal.nic.in/content/list%20of%20scheduled%20tribes%20in%20India.aspx

Narasimhan, R. (2016). Math, science, and technology in India: From the ancient to the recent past. *Asia Society*. Retrieved from http://asiasociety.org/math-science-and-technology-india-ancient-recent

Office of the Registrar General and Census Commissioner, India. (2011). *Census of India: Religion*. Retrieved from http://censusindia.gov.in/Census_And_You/religion.aspx

Pingali, S. (2012). Indian English: Features and sociolinguistic aspects. *Language and Linguistic Compass*, *6*(6), 359–370.

Sahni, U. (2015, January 20). Primary education in India: Progress and challenges. *Brookings*. Retrieved from https://www.brookings.edu/opinions/primary-education-in-india-progress-and-challenges/

Sayeed, A. (2004). *Know your India: Turn a new page to write Nationalism*. New Delhi, India: Vij Publications.

Sharma, Y. (2013, May 29). India's ancient university returns to life. *BBC News*. Retrieved from http://www.bbc.com/news/business-22160989

Sindkhedkar, S. D. (2012). Objectives of teaching and learning English in India. *Journal of Arts, Science & Commerce*, *3*(1), 191–194.

Singal, N. (2010). *Education of children with disabilities in India*. Retrieved from http://unesdoc.unesco.org/images/0018/001866/186611e.pdf

Tarling, N. (2000). *The Cambridge history of Southeast Asia: Volume one, part one, from early times to C. 1500*. New York, NY: Cambridge University Press.

TNN. (2012, April 7). 5 lakh aspirants to sit for IIT-JEE in 2012. *The Times of India*. Retrieved from http://timesofindia.indiatimes.com/home/education/entrance-exams/5-lakh-aspirants-to-sit-for-IIT-JEE-in-2012/articleshow/12564776.cms?referral=PM

Trade history of Silk Road, spice & incense routes. (n.d.). *Silk Routes.net*. Retrieved from http://www.ipekyollari.net/SilkSpiceIncenseRoutes.htm

CHAPTER 13

BANGLADESH

Shampa Biswas
Washington State University

Sayeeda Rahman
American International University Bangladesh

Raihan Sharif
Washington State University

Rina is part of a Muslim family from Bangladesh. Although her two boys were born in the U.S., she and her husband tried to bring them up in the Bangladeshi Bengali culture with Islamic beliefs. One day around 3:00 p.m., the phone rang in Rina's apartment. She ran to answer the call. Surprisingly, the phone call was from the principal of her boys' school. The principal politely greeted her and then informed her that an incident had taken place with one of her sons that day. Toward the end of rehearsal for a school concert, in the middle of a song that the students were practicing, one of her boys had refused to sing two sentences of the song where he had to utter repetitively, "Jesus is our God and He is our Lord." He stopped singing and told the teacher, "As a Muslim, I believe Jesus is one of our prophets, but not our God!" The principal told Rina, "The school has organized many events with the participation of immigrant children from different ethnic groups and religious beliefs. Students have been performing this song for the past couple of years. Nobody has ever had any objection to this verse before, so we never thought of changing the song." Rina felt very thankful to the school as they con-

Views From Inside: Languages, Cultures, and Schooling for K–12 Educators
pp. 217–227

sciously informed her about the incident and apologized for creating discomfort for her son. After completing the conversation with the principal, she had to sit down and rest for a minute as her heart sank. She felt helpless and wondered how she could help her kids to learn how to negotiate diverse American cultural identities, perspectives, and situations.

Adapting to American culture, language, and school for immigrant children from Bangladesh can be challenging due to the difference between the U.S. and their home cultures. Most families in the U.S. maintain traditional Bengali culture, including speaking Bengali at home, which limits the children's exposure to American English and culture. Most Bengali mothers desire their children to speak Bengali at home, although children may not feel comfortable speaking it. Even though parents are aware of the need to develop the English language skills of their children, their native use of English (i.e., stress, tone, pronunciation, and intonation) is different from the use of English in the U.S. These differences could interfere with the process of language development.

United States schools play a big role for Bengali children and parents in creating a bridge between the two cultures and languages. The children's interactions with teachers and peers can interest them in learning more about U.S. culture and language. Most important, education materials, activities, and resources from school, in addition to social media, can help them to explore different cultural, linguistic, and educational ideas. This chapter provides suggestions for U.S. educators to gain a better understanding about Bengali culture and implement culturally competent teaching strategies in their classrooms.

BACKGROUND

Bangladesh is a low-lying South Asian country under the Hindu Kush Himalayan (HKH) region, which is geographically connected with other seven countries: Afghanistan, Bhutan, China, India, Myanmar, Nepal, and Pakistan. Bangladesh hosts ten large Asian river systems that are the water source for 1.3 billion people across the region. Bangladesh was known as the Bengal region, a part of the Indian subcontinent, during the British colonization of India from 1757 to 1947. In 1947, India was divided and the land area of Bangladesh was named East Pakistan, a province of Pakistan. In 1971 it became independent through a 9-month liberation war and came to be known as Bangladesh. In other words, Bangladesh was a part of the British Empire for 200 years, and then the British rulers were replaced by Pakistani rulers for 24 more years. In response, citizens and leaders of Bangladesh played an immense role in raising awareness among people locally, nationally, and globally about the inherent disparities and injustices in the colonial system. Their promise to end colonial rule and reshape the systems of governance led to the establishment of the constitution of Bangladesh according to the will of the people; it is now the supreme law of the republic. However, Bangladesh is still not free from the effects of colonial rule due to remaining confusion, distrust, and immature attitudes.

The constitution of Bangladesh reflects the ideals of liberation with democratic and progressive principles; however, the administrative culture of Bangladesh has stayed under the shadow of the colonial system. Freedom of thought and mass participation of the people are not considered in decision making. Bangladesh's governance is still influenced by native cultures, traditional cultures, modern culture, and diverse languages (Rahman & Alauddin, 2016). In addition, religion and nationalism play decisive roles in defining the relationships between Bangladesh and its neighboring countries (which can be at times hostile). For example, although Bengali is the national language of Bangladesh, it is also an official language in several Indian states: West Bengal, Tripura, Assam, and the Andaman and Nicobar Islands.

In 2015, Bangladesh had a total population of 161 million people, with a gross domestic product (GDP) growth of 6.6% (World Bank, 2016). The economy of Bangladesh mainly depends on agriculture, garment factories, and the remittance sent by migrant workers; it is a very poor country but continues to grow economically. In addition, most people in Bangladesh are proud of their mother language, ethnicity, social bonds, and natural environment. The Language Movement of 1952 remains as evidence of a strong love for the mother tongue. It was the movement where the people of every profession fought the government of Pakistan, of which Bangladesh was then a part, to establish the right to speak Bengali. Their enthusiasm for their mother tongue is part of their extraordinary history and they love to relate their victory to be allowed to speak it in everyday life. This triumph helped the people of Bangladesh to become citizens of an independent country through the independence war of 1971. These successes still provide inspiration to overcome any national or international challenges. Although it is familiar worldwide as one of the poorest countries in the world, in reality, Bangladesh is one of the most overpopulated yet happiest countries in the world (Hamadani & Tofail, 2014; Rahman, 2014).

Jones (2014) discussed Bengali identities in South Asia in terms of nationality and ethnicity. Considering nationality, Bengali people living in Bangladesh are Bangladeshi, and Bengali people living in West Bengal are Indian. In view of ethnicity, the Bengali people of Bangladesh and

India are all Bengali and have a similar language, social beliefs, customs, and appearance. Most important, religion does not divide the Bengali people of India and Bangladesh; many people do not realize that Bangladesh has a 90% Muslim population.

U.S. educators will be amazed to know about two Bangladeshi physicists, Dipongkar Talukder and Shahariar Selim, LIGO (Laser Interferometer Gravitational Observatory) professionals, who contributed to the biggest discovery in the 21st century: gravitational wave detection (Hoque, 2016a, 2016b). Both scientists studied in public primary and secondary schools in Bangladesh, but strong determination and great effort helped them to overcome language and cultural barriers over time and establish their identity as physicists and members of LIGO Scientific Collaboration. Furthermore, Salman Khan, the founder of Khan Academy (https:// www.khanacademy.org/), is the son of a Bangladeshi pediatrician. Khan grew up in the U.S. in a Bengali immigrant family, a close and extended one, and this has impacted his vision as a global educator (Ferster, 2014).

CULTURE

Bangladesh has a very rich cultural heritage (Hossain, 2010). Bengali people are very communal, emotional, loving, and hospitable. Kinship is very important to them (Inden & Nicholas, 2005). They are very open to learning others' education systems, languages, and cultures. Moreover, Bangladesh is a country of mainly four religions: Islam, Hinduism, Buddhism, and Christianity. Nationally, however, the people of Bangladesh celebrate diverse traditional festivals as one Bengali nation. As Jones (2014) reports, "One of the slogans of the Bangladeshi Independence Movement was 'Hindus of Bengal, Christians of Bengal, Bhuddists of Bengal, Muslims of Bengali, we are all Bengali'" (p. 296). These days, religious festivals are becoming more like cultural celebrations to young adults, and they are considered as Bengali community gatherings.

Nonetheless, Bangladeshi culture remains influenced by historically constructed religious sentiments and class affiliations. This influence can still be felt in distinctive costumes, food habits, and socio-religious ceremonies and festivals. For example, most Bengali Hindus would avoid beef at a party; similarly, most Bengali Muslims would avoid pork. Both Hindu and Muslim women wear *tip* (different colored dots on the forehead) to decorate themselves, but married Hindu women use red *tip* on their foreheads. Other religious groups—Christians (mainly Catholics), Buddhists, and indigenous people (e.g., Chakmas, Marmas, Santals, Garos, Manipuris, Khaseas, and Moorangs)—also contribute to shaping cultural patterns. For example, sometimes children and women in big cities wear costumes of indigenous people during different cultural celebrations. However, Bengali culture is not a monolith, and there are, for example, both conservatives and liberals.

In families, Bengali mothers mostly devote themselves to parenting; in Bengali culture, strong family bonds between parents and children are common (Hamadani & Tofail, 2014). Bangladeshi-American parents generally encourage their American children to follow a Bangladeshi cultural orientation and try to foster a sense of community by forming locally based social, cultural, and religious associations (Khondaker, 2007). Second-generation immigrant children in the U.S. are influenced to support intergenerational cultural continuity (Alam, 2013). However, the lack of knowledge of Bangladeshi-American parents about U.S. culture could create intergenerational gaps between immigrant adults and their children (Begum & Khondaker, 2008). The children experience different modes of socialization; with parents they learn the native culture (i.e., primary socialization) and with multicultural friends from U.S. public schools or neighborhoods, they learn U.S. culture (i.e., secondary socialization; Alam, 2013).

LANGUAGES AND LITERACIES

Cheap internet communication in Bangladesh has influenced the rate of literacy in Bangladesh. The Bangladesh adult literacy rate from 1990–2015 increased from 35.3% (male literacy 44.3%; female literacy 25.8%) to 61.4% (male literacy 64.8%; female literacy, 58.0%). Despite these successes, there is a great deal of progress yet to be made. The number of illiterate youth is approximately 7 million. In 2015, Bangladesh was one of the countries where both males and females notably lacked basic literacy skills. Approximately 44 million adults were reported as illiterate in Bangladesh in 2010 (Huebler & Lu, 2012).

The expansion of social media and satellite TV channels has influenced the use, expression, and overall development of the Bengali language. In particular, there are tremendous variations in using Bengali (e.g., in word and verb use) due to access to mobile phones and Facebook. Linguistic similarities and differences between Bengali and English include:

- Words borrowed from English:
  - Okay, bye, chair, school, university, road, apartment, mobile, noodles, TV, Facebook, call, problem, department, Skype, e-mail, account, ID, temperature, ringtone, laptop, online, cam-

era, video, accident, confuse, justify, revenge, slow, complain (Bhattacharja, 2011)

- Sentence structure:
  - o Bengali = subject + object + verb (I school go);
  - o English = subject + verb + preposition + object (I go to school)
- Sentence differences:
  - o Bengali: *Tomar* (Your) *nam* (name) + *ki* (what) (verb use is invisible here)
  - o English: What is your name?
  - o Bengali: *Tumi* (You) + *kemon* (how) + *accho* (are) (verb use is visible)
  - o English: How are you?
- Sentence similarities:
  - o Bengali: *Ha* (yes), *ami kori* (I do).
  - o English: Yes, I do
- Persons in grammar (sense of hierarchy in language):
  - o Bengali: *Apni korun* (you [older in age] do), *tumi koro* (you [younger in age] do), *tui kor* (you [subordinates or close friends] do)
  - o English: You do (same for all ages)
- Third person:
  - o Bengali: *Shey/uni/tumi* (same for all genders as objective pronoun),
  - o English: "She" for feminine gender; "he" for masculine gender

In Bangladesh, English is in media, law, and educational institutions. Bengali professionals (e.g., bankers, engineers, financial analysts) use English as a convenient professional language. Most social interactions and conversation with friends, relatives, and professionals occur through social media and mobile phones. Noticeably, code switching (mixing different languages, sometimes with local dialects) has become common in daily Bengali conversation due to the influence of foreign satellite TV channels. This is in part because people in Bangladesh have easy access to Hindi and English cartoons, serials, and movies. These popular satellite TV channels are introducing not only the Hindi and English languages, but also Hindi and English cultures to people (Islam, 2013). Since both Hindi and Bengali have similar sentence structures (i.e., subject + object + verb) and the same borrowed vocabulary from English, Urdu, Arabic, Sanskrit, Persian and French, it is easy for Bengali people to understand Hindi conversations. As a result of all these language influences and different media uses, the expression and development of the Bengali language, along with English and Hindi, reflects different language use, behaviors, culture, and overall lifestyle for different age groups in Bangladesh (Islam, 2013).

Furthermore, there are different uses of language between Bengali Hindus and Bengali Muslims. For instance, Hindus prefer to use the word "*jol*" for "water," whereas Muslims prefer the word differently "*pani*." These different word uses for similar meaning might confuse not only Bengali children, but also educators.

U.S. educators might notice that Bengali children face challenges in perceiving some sounds in English. Due to the phonological differences between the expression of English and Bengali, they may not understand classroom instructions and questions. Hence, they may not participate in class discussion. In addition, Bengali is a syllable-timed language, where all syllables are spoken with equal intervals of time in the speech rhythm. On the other hand, English is a stress-timed language, where the stressed syllables recur at equal intervals of time whether they are separated or not separated by an unstressed syllable (Roach, 2000). These differences can be addressed by teaching speech rhythms through games and chants.

In addition, Roach (2000) noted three levels of stress while describing the English stress system: primary stress (the strongest type of stress), secondary stress (weaker than the primary stress, but stronger than unstressed syllables) and absence of any stress. On the contrary, there is no stress in Bengali. Placement of stress on the right syllable may be very difficult for Bengali English learners (Maniruzzaman, n.d.). Bengali children who speak Bengali may need a longer time to adapt to the stress patterns of English. As a result, understanding rapid conversation in school can be challenging for them.

IDEAS FOR EDUCATORS

United States educators might work with Bangladeshi parents to provide culturally responsive teaching. As noted above, Bengali parents want their children to hold onto their first language and culture. The Avro Bengali keyboard with Bengali language phonetic features is a familiar tool to communicate in Bengali. Bengali students in the U.S., who usually do not have institutional instruction in Bengali, could use this tool to learn to write in Bengali while teaching their teacher or peers important aspects of the language or useful words.

Further, U.S. educators might hold an International Mother-Language Day celebration on February 21st to help their students and themselves become familiar with Bengali culture. This day could focus on traditional clothes, foods, houses, festivals, cultural events, female and male indicators in names, historical events, famous poets and leaders and their contributions, and a New Year celebration. This experience could be a jumping-off point for lessons integrating events from Bengali history and culture such as the Bengali New Year (*Pohela Boishakh*), the Spring Celebration (*Pohela Fagun*), or the Autumn Festival during harvest season (*Pousher mela/fair*). Including other nations and cultures that celebrate in similar ways might help learners to associate ideas across different cultures.

United States educators might also encourage students to explore their parents' Bengali culture by assigning a classroom project. For instance, an essay on a mother's or a father's childhood can help teachers and student not only to learn about different traditions in Bengali culture but also realize the extent of cultural similarities and differences between U.S. and Bengali cultures. U.S. educators might also explore parents' perspectives about their children's challenges during the transitional phase of adjusting to a new culture, language, and school context.

United States educators can organize extracurricular activities for immigrant Bangladeshi Bengali students who do not have experience with different recreational activities (i.e., hiking, biking, swimming, different types of camping). During vacations, Bengali children usually visit grandparents, their native towns, and relatives, but due to their immigrant status and economic condition in the U.S., they may not have these options. Therefore, they are often forced to confine themselves within their yards and play with other kids in the neighborhood. This situation also may cause parents to ask for more homework and activities from the school so that they can keep their children involved.

Pedagogy in Bangladesh and the U.S. is different. In Bangladesh, the teaching style is completely lecture-based and exam-oriented, compared with more experiential learning in many classrooms in the U.S. Bangladesh schools do not support individual creativity or focus on students' learning interests, and they do not provide students opportunities to identify their mistakes and redo a test. In Bangladesh, schools also do not address health education in the same way as U.S. schools, and culturally shocking words may include *sex, pregnant, love,* and *hugs.* Further, Bangladeshi students celebrate different holidays from children in the U.S.—for example, there is no Halloween culture in Bangladesh—and parents need to be informed about this and other holidays before their children are asked to participate. In addition, because Bengali students may be shy to respond compared to many U.S. students, teachers can consider explicit explanations of U.S. school customs and expectations and provide students from Bangladesh time to become accustomed to them.

As the majority of people in Bangladesh are Muslim, U.S. educators might have misconceptions about Bangladeshi people based on their religion; however, the foundation of the Bangladeshi people's identities is

based on the concepts of Bengali ethnicity, language, culture, and secular-
ism, and they traditionally maintain multicultural social practices. This
means that, although the Muslim people of Bangladesh value Islamic culture and traditions, they do not come from or want an Islamic theocratic
state (Hossain, 2010). However, teachers can be aware that Bengali Muslim children may not eat pork and Bengali Hindu children may not eat
beef and support these choices.

United States educators might take the responsibility to introduce U.S.
culture to Bangladeshi parents. In particular, cultural gaps between Bengali parents and their children in the U.S. could be reduced though educators' conscious efforts to dialog, reflect, and question. Educators and
parents could connect diverse intellectual values with experiential activities in the classroom. These ideas will help educators to understand Bengali students deeply and create a negotiated space for sharing differences
(Hardee, Thompson, Jennings, Aragon, & Brantmeier, 2012).

CONCLUSIONS

United States educators can help their students by taking the initiative to
learn and integrate different cultural values into their classrooms. Learning about Bengali culture could be an interesting experience for both U.S.
educators and students in American schools. Experiential activities
involving traditional foods, clothing, and music from Bangladesh could
help all students develop cultural insights. Teachers can also work with
Bengali parents to reduce the cultural gaps they experience between the
U.S. and Bangladesh.

ADDITIONAL RESOURCES

Belt, D. (2011). Bangladesh: The coming storm. *National Geographic*. Retrieved
from http://ngm.nationalgeographic.com/2011/05/bangladesh/belt-text
This link to an article called "The Coming Storm" shows how climate
change is affecting Bangladesh and how they are dealing with it.
Virtual Bangladesh. (2015). Welcome to Bangladesh! Available from http://
www.virtualbangladesh.com/
This website contains comprehensive information about the nation.

TASKS FOR EDUCATORS

1. Compare and contrast the culture of Bangladesh to that of other
   Muslim countries. What does each culture emphasize, and why
   might that be?

2. Read up on Bangladesh's history. How might historical events color the attitudes of Bangladeshi/Bengali families toward people from neighboring countries? How could you address these attitudes in your classroom?

3. Create a task for your students that helps them understand how stereotypes might get started and persist. Ask them to list stereotypes that they find about Bangladeshis and to find information that dispels these misconceptions.

REFERENCES

Alam, M. F. (2013). Bracing for and embracing difference in America's majority minority metropolis: Bangladeshi immigrant children coming of age in New York City. *British Journal of Social Work*, *43*(4), 631–650.

Begum, N., & Khondaker, M. I. (2008). Immigrant Bangladeshi communities and intergenerational conflict: The need for multicultural education. *PAACE Journal of Lifelong Learning*, *17*, 19–36.

Bhattacharja, S. (2011). Benglish verbs: A case of code-mixing in Bengali. In R. Singh & G. Sharma (Eds.), Annual review of South Asian languages and linguistics (pp. 17–33). Berlin, Germany: De Gruyter.

Ferster, B. (2014). *Teaching machines*. Baltimore, MD: John Hopkins University Press.

Hardee, S. C., Thompson, C. M., Jennings, L. B., Aragon, A., & Brantmeier, E. J. (2012). Teaching in the borderland: Critical practices in foundations courses. *Teaching Education*, *23*(2), 215–234.

Hamadani, J. D., & Tofail, F. (2014). Childrearing, motherhood and fatherhood in Bangladeshi culture. In H. Selin (Ed.), *Parenting across cultures* (pp. 123–144). Netherlands: Springer.

Hoque, A. (2016a, February 14). Bangladeshi among discoverers of gravitational waves. *Prothom Alo*. Retrieved from http://en.prothom-alo.com/bangladesh/news/95093/Bangladeshi-among-discoverers-of-gravitational

Hoque, A. (2016b, February 16). Another Bangladeshi at forefront of gravitational waves discovery. *Prothom Alo*. Retrieved from http://en.prothom-alo.com/bangladesh/news/95299/Bangladeshi-at-forefront-of-gravitational-waves

Hossain, M. (2010). The Emerging consumer culture in Bangladesh: Everyday life and festivals in rural areas. *Journal of Social Sciences 3*, 488.

Huebler, F., & Lu, W. (2012). *Adult and youth literacy, 1990-2015: Analysis of data for 41 selected countries*. Montreal, Quebec: UNESCO Institute for Statistics.

Inden, R. B., & Nicholas, R. W. (2005). *Kinship in Bengali culture*. New Delhi, India: DC Publishers.

Islam, A. (2013). Hindigenization of Bangladeshi culture through the penetration of satellite TV: Paradigm of modernization vs. dependency theory. *New Media and Mass Communication*, *18*, 15–23.

Jones, R. (2014). The false premise of partition. *Space and polity*, *18*(3), 285–300.

Khondaker, M. I. (2007). Juvenile deviant behavior in an immigrant Bangladeshi community: Exploring the nature and contributing factors. *International Journal of Criminal Justice Sciences*, 2(1), 27–43.

Maniruzzaman, M. (n.d.). Language problems of Bengali EFL learners. Retrieved from http://www.streetdirectory.com/travel_guide/106632/

Rahman, R. B. (2014). *Strengths, cultural differences, and coping strategies among Bangladeshi immigrant families in the United States* (Doctoral dissertation). California State University, Northridge, CA.

Rahman, M. D. M., & Alauddin, M. D. (2016). Good governance and colonial entanglement in Bangladesh. *Indian Journal of Society and Politics, 3*(1), 1–6.

Roach, P. (2000). *English phonetics and phonology: A self-contained, comprehensive pronunciation course*. Cambridge, UK: Cambridge University Press.

The World Bank. (2016). Bangladesh: Country at glance. Retrieved from http://www.worldbank.org/en/country/bangladesh

CHAPTER 14

PAKISTAN

Tariq Akmal
Washington State University

Romella Husain
Poolesville High School, Maryland

Ayesha and Farooq are parents of two boys and a girl. All three children attended a suburban public elementary school, but middle school presented problems. Middle school years coincide with the onset of puberty and adolescence. At and after this time, male-female intermingling becomes a major concern. To address this concern in the public-school setting, the parents asked their children to observe purdah (veiling). Although this caused some level of discomfort for the boys (shorts were not allowed, even for sports); the practice was more invasive for their daughter; who had to wear a head scarf, long tunics over pants and long-sleeve blouses. Their daughter expressed displeasure at having to dress differently from everybody else and objected to being separated from friends of the opposite sex. Ayesha and Farooq also wanted their children to observe the practice of daily prayers. As the timings of the prayers coincided with the school day, Ayesha had arranged with the school principal to have a room set up in school for their children to use. However, the children resisted leaving their classrooms to use this facility. Eventually, Ayesha and Farooq made the difficult decision of placing their children in a private Muslim school where a school uniform, segregation of sexes, and communal prayers resolved all religious and cultural requirements. Unfortunately, private school was expensive and provided only limited curricular opportunities as compared to local

Views From Inside: Languages, Cultures, and Schooling for K–12 Educators
pp. 229–248

public schools. Further, as their boys approached their high school years, the parents begin to worry about the academic and professional future of their sons: how would the boys successfully compete with others in the world job market without access to a more rigorous curriculum? To address this issue, they placed their boys back into public school, but kept their daughter in the private school.

BACKGROUND

As is clearly evident in the opening scenario, religion and culture have a powerful influence on the lives of Pakistanis. Pakistan is situated in the Indus Valley of the Asian subcontinent and lays claim to being the world's first Islamic Republic. Its northern boundary is defined by the Himalayas and its southern boundary by the Arabian Sea. It shares a border with India to the east, China to the north, and Afghanistan and Iran to the west. During its 5,000-year history, it survived and absorbed invasions from the Indo-Aryans, Persians, Greeks, Scythians, Arabs, Afghans, Turks, and, finally, the British. Each left its own legacy, from architecture and art to religion, language, culture, and governance. For example, the Arabs brought Islam to the region and the Mughal Dynasty, of Mongol-Turkish origin, made Islam the state religion and Persian the state language. Although the British were present through the East India Company in the 1700s and during the gradual decline of the Mughal Empire, the *British Raj* (Crown Rule) did not officially begin until 1858 and lasted until 1947, when the Indian subcontinent was carved into West and East Pakistan and India by the departing British.

History

Pakistan means "land of the pure," and it was created to serve as a haven for Muslims in India prior to the end of British rule after World War II. Its official name is the Islamic Republic of Pakistan. The British divided the subcontinent into two nations according to majority vote, an act referred to as Partition. The state of Kashmir was disputed at the time of Partition, as it had a Muslim majority but a Hindu ruler. In 1948, Kashmir was recognized as a disputed territory by the United Nations Security Council, and its fate was to be decided by local plebiscite. No such referendum has been held, and Kashmir continues to be an area of contention between India and Pakistan. The decision to divide India into two nations has left a deep imprint on the psyche and behaviors of both nations. Two wars (1965, 1971) have been fought based on that division, and tensions continue to simmer.

Another area of tension between the two nuclear-armed nations is terrorism. Terrorist attacks on India's Parliament in 2001 and in Mumbai in 2008 were blamed on Pakistan, which denied responsibility. Each event increased tensions and army activity at the border between the two countries; however, the international community stepped in to ameliorate the situation. Despite the tension and conflict, cross-border trade and diplomatic relations continue. At the time of this writing, India's Prime Minister Modi was visiting Pakistan on an impromptu invitation from Pakistan's Prime Minister Sharif, with the goal of easing tensions around Kashmir and issues related to terrorism.

Pakistan and the United States have been allies since Pakistan's creation in 1947. Pakistan has been a supporter of U.S. foreign policy and the United States has reciprocated with financial and military aid and support in its regional disputes with India. The last decade since the September 11 attacks, however, has been particularly tumultuous for U.S.–Pakistan relations. Events have included the Afghan War and drone attacks in 2011 to root out Osama bin Laden. Both sides have worked to repair relations. Nonetheless, Pakistan has received much negative media coverage and disreputable Hollywood mention; for example, Pakistan's name and linkage to terrorism and militancy has been mentioned in two recent blockbuster Hollywood movies: *Iron Man* and *Captain America: The Winter Soldier*. Recent terrorist activity within the United States in San Bernardino, California, brought further direct negative attention to Pakistanis within the United States. The reverse is also true—Pakistanis do not view the U.S. favorably due to its involvement in Afghanistan and Pakistan.

Politically, and for just over half its history, Pakistan has vacillated between military rule and democracy. Pakistan's politicians have experienced forced resignations, execution by the state, assassinations, and corruption charges. In addition, Pakistan continues to suffer from power outages, a struggling education system, and multiple natural disasters (floods and earthquakes). Despite the problems and criticisms, however, Pakistan endeavors towards establishing democracy and addressing its critical issues. In May 2013, Nawaz Sharif, of the Muslim League Party, was elected and Pakistan witnessed its first peaceful transition from one democratically elected government to another. This tumultuous history has had an effect on the people of Pakistan, as the rule of law has not been consistently followed and people's faith in government and law has been severely tested.

CULTURE

Pakistan does not have a monolithic culture. As noted earlier, numerous ethnic groups have invaded this region over the last 2,500 years and left their legacy. Although some cultural traits are common throughout Pakistan, including religion, conservatism, and language, each of the provinces has its own unique heritage and ethnicity, which also explains why two students from different parts of Pakistan may seem to have little in common at first.

Regardless of the differences among the peoples of the different regions, there are some general behaviors that can be called Pakistani. One major trend is the Westernization of the upper-class, educated Pakistani family. The more education and the higher socioeconomic status of an individual or family, the more access they have to Western culture and the more influence Western culture tends to have on them, including speaking English in the home. Finding cultural balance between East and West is strongly sought among Pakistanis who live outside Pakistan while they move between two or more cultures—though not always easily or comfortably—and they do so by trying to maintain their culture at home and school. The following guidelines may help educators understand the influence of their culture on their behavior and to successfully interact with Pakistani students.

People

Pakistanis are polite and formal people—especially when they first meet you—and are extremely hospitable, as Islamic values require (Al-Sheha, 2000). In fact, they go out of their way to please guests and to make sure that guests are comfortable. Among the educated elite, who are more Westernized, this is less the case, but generally speaking, guests or elders in the home are given the highest level of hospitality. This may include but is not limited to the best, most comfortable seat, the choicest (and most) food or drink, or any item that might provide comfort (such as a blanket if there is a chill in the air).

Religion

Islam is the official religion of Pakistan, with 97% of Pakistanis professing to be Muslim. The observance of the religion has a pronounced effect on Pakistanis' personal and professional lives. For example:

- Among observant Muslims, prayer five times a day is obligatory. Prayers only take a few minutes and occur with the daily cycle of the sun that correspond roughly to dawn, noon, afternoon, sunset, and evening. Friday is the Sabbath, or day of religious observance and rest. Friday noon prayers are a little more special and take a little longer. Practicing adults will take time off work to go the mosque to pray. Older students who are religious may wish to have a place in school and excused time off from class to observe these prayers.

- Like other Muslims (see, for example, Chapter 3), Pakistanis commit to the Five Pillars of the Islamic religion that are mandatory for believers: (a) the testimony of faith (*kalma*), (b) praying five times daily, (c) giving *zakat* (charity or support for the needy), (d) fasting during Ramadan to self-purify and practice self-sacrifice, and (e) making the pilgrimage, or *haj*, to Mecca (the most holy center of the Islamic world and the birthplace of the Prophet Muhammad, its founder).

- Pakistanis observe the holy month of Ramadan, when Muslims fast from sunrise to sunset. Fasting for adults includes no consumption of food or drink (or even chewing gum), no sexual relations, and no smoking. Fasting may affect students in school. One major area of concern is that older students who play sports will not drink water, and this is a health hazard. It would be prudent to discuss the dangers of dehydration and come up with some solution for fasting athletes (for example, fasting students can run laps after the breaking of the fast and may be excused from practice on extremely hot days). The second major consideration is determining a place that fasting students in middle or high school can go during lunchtime, as being in the cafeteria may be uncomfortable for them since they cannot eat. Not eating may also raise questions among peers (which could be positive or negative). Finally, lack of food and water all day will definitely have an effect on fasting students' focus and concentration.

- Because most Pakistanis are Muslim, they follow the dietary guidelines for consuming food or drink that are *halal* (permitted) or *haram* (not permitted). Pork products or byproducts are not permitted (these exist in many Western products, including some chewing gums), nor are alcohol or other intoxicants. Pakistani families tend to cite food as one of their main school concerns, especially for their younger children, who may not recognize pork products or may not know to ask whether a food has pork in it.

Greetings

- Verbal greetings may be accompanied with a handshake, hug, or kiss, but strict gender guidelines are observed. Men and women who are strangers to each other will not touch and often may avoid eye contact. If a female extends her hand to a male first, then it is acceptable to shake it.

- Men shake hands and, once a relationship is developed, they often hug as well. Both adults and teens will often shake with one hand and hug with the other.
- Women generally hug when greeting someone they know well and sometimes kiss on the cheek; they shake hands if they do not know someone well.
- During greetings, it is appropriate to inquire as to the person's health, family, and work. This small talk is highly appropriate and often takes several minutes.
- Personal space during greetings or during any conversation is considerably closer than in the U.S. and often makes some Westerners uncomfortable.

Family and Family Names

- The family is the basis of the social structure as well as a person's identity. This includes the nuclear family, immediate and distant relatives, tribal members, close friends, and neighbors. Divorce is not common among Pakistanis, and Pakistani children are often confused by the split families they encounter in the U.S.
- Loyalty to the family comes before other social relationships and thus, family information is extremely private and not to be shared until someone is known well.
- Female relatives are typically to be shielded from influences outside the family, particularly if they are observant of *purdah*. It is inappropriate to ask questions about a female member of the family if you do not know the family well.
- Adults in the family make decisions and children are not asked to do so.
- Boys and girls who are not family members may grow up together, but they are separated close to puberty.
- Relationships among extended family members, between friends, and with neighbors are given great importance. They are built based on trust and, therefore, whom you can trust matters a great deal. Family relationships hold primacy because that is where trust bonds begin.
- Pakistan is a hierarchical and male-dominated society. The elder males of the family typically hold the positions of highest status.

This is not to say that women have no say in what goes on in a given household—as Islam emphasizes women's rights to control their lives—but that these rights are interpreted in many different ways (Halliday, 1990).

- Within the family, it should also be noted that children are sometimes raised very permissively until a certain age (perhaps even seen as being spoiled) and then both cultural and disciplinary expectations are applied as they become young adults. Sons (and boys in general) are privileged within the family.

- After a certain age, children do not question their elders, nor do they refuse a request from someone within the family who is their elder. During disciplinary situations, children are expected to look at the floor rather than make eye contact with the adult. Eye contact is a delicate matter because looking away from elders demonstrates respect and deference and affirms the hierarchical relationship that exists.

- Although Western naming conventions have made their way into how families name their children or how names change during marriage, Pakistanis may also choose to follow older naming conventions that often include a name that denotes a person's religion (e.g., *Mohammad* Iqbal, named after the Prophet Mohammad), class (e.g., *Syed* Abdullah, meaning *Lord* Abdullah), tribe (e.g., Ali Akhtar *Durrani,* the last name being the tribe), or other status indicator (e.g., *Chaudhry* = landowner). If this is the case, it is difficult to sometimes decipher familial relationships. For example, one author's name is *Tariq Akmal*, his father was named *Mohammad Akmal*, his grandfather was *Chaudhry Mahbub Alam*, and his grandmother was named *Ahmad Noor.*

- Names may also include two names that have a specific meaning when used together, and the meaning is lost if the names are separated. Thus, Ali Akhtar Javaid, in which the first name Ali means *high, exalted one* and Akhtar means *star* or *good luck*, would always be called Ali Akhtar instead of just Ali because the name is doubly fortunate, indicating a great future. A good rule of thumb is to ask "How would you like to be addressed?"

Orientation to Time

While expectations for timeliness abound in the West, time is viewed more fluidly in Pakistani culture. To be on time to a social event means to arrive anywhere from 15 minutes to an hour later than the invitation listed (Halliday, 1990). To be on time for a meeting means to be there when expected, but the host may keep you waiting. Deadlines are also considerably more flexible than fixed and one can expect some revisions to a deadline while a task is in process. Any kind of negotiation will almost always take more time than expected. The Urdu language itself invites fluidity, for example, as the word for yesterday and tomorrow (*kal*) is the same and is only discerned by use in context by the verbs which accompany it—was it done already or is it still to be done? Students are less likely to be tardy because parents expect children to respect teachers, but they may not always be timely with work with a partner. Parents and children may be late to school social events (school carnivals or fun nights) but on time to meetings (parent–teacher conferences).

Because Pakistanis are a very polite people and their orientation to time is much more relaxed, directness is not valued in interactions outside the home. Direct questions are often sidestepped or given an oblique answer. When asking a student, "Why isn't your homework done?" one might receive some kind of story in response. This is not a lie, but merely a redirection of a direct and perhaps uncomfortable question. Educators may listen to the story then ask, "Ah, so this is why the homework was not done?" and move toward a plan to get the homework completed.

Relationships and Communication

As noted earlier, relationships are built around trust, and trust begins with family. Thus, Pakistanis prefer to work with people they know (and trust), and it may take time to warm up when among strangers, such as new classmates. The following tips may be helpful for educators when meeting or working with parents or students:

- While Pakistanis may not wish to answer direct questions, they will almost always ask personal questions about you and your family in order to get to know you as a person. These questions are also asked in order to establish a relationship with you through mutual friends, relatives, or some past acquaintance.

- Pakistanis do not like conflict when talking with people they are not close to. Thus, what is stated may not necessarily directly answer the question, and the listener is expected to interpret. Hyperbole and praise are also liberally applied to conversation. Sometimes very flattering statements are made—in some cases with the goal of attaining something and in others just to compliment. For example, "You are the very best friend a person could ever have, so I wondered if you would be interested in going to ...?" or "You are the best teacher of all the teachers here. What can I buy you that you would like?" Direct and unfiltered statements are only shared after a relationship is established and perhaps even long-standing.

- During indirect communication, Pakistanis may also tell you what they think you want to hear rather than provide a direct answer, thus "saving face" in an uncomfortable situation (such as conflict with others) or when a difficult question is asked. Saving face is very important, and a student may choose to remain silent rather than asking an adult at school to re-explain something. Also, to ask for re-explanation means "I didn't understand it and that means you didn't explain it well." Asking, therefore, would be disrespectful.

- In terms of friendships and romantic relationships, parental concerns are high in relation to interactions of boys and girls—especially after puberty—so chaperoning is highly likely. Concerns over co-ed mingling tend to place limitations on the extracurricular activities of Pakistanis. Parents are reluctant to allow their children to go to dances and will also discourage parties, other social events, overnight trips, and trips abroad. Marriage by arrangement is still a widespread practice in Pakistan, and most parents are not eager to see the type of dating that is common in countries like the U.S. Thus, open demonstrations of physical affection (e.g., holding hands, hugging) at school may cause concern among Pakistani students.

- Relatedly, few formal systems of learning about relationships, development, and sex are available—and are generally need- or event-based (i.e., puberty or marriage). As a fairly conservative culture, quality information in this area is limited, leading to stress and confusion about sexual development (Hennink, Rana, & Iqbal, 2005).

Dress

The traditional dress of Pakistan is the *shalwar kameez*, a loose-fitting pair of pants and tunic length (or longer) shirt. This is worn across all regions of Pakistan with variations for weather. Clothing is typically conservative and covers as much skin as possible. Brighter colors are worn during festivals or weddings, but a variety of colors on both females and males is now accepted. When girls approach puberty, Islam prescribes veiling and segregation from boys and men in public spheres. In Pakistan, the veil can take the form of a *burqa* (a head to toe garb that covers the whole body where only the eyes are uncovered), a *chadur* (a shawl wrapped around the upper body), a *dupatta* (a long scarf wrapped around the chest and head), or a *hijab* (a coat with a headdress that covers the hair but leaves the face open). Depending on whether a family is educated, from a higher socioeconomic class, Westernized, Western-educated, visiting from abroad, or in an urban setting, women may not wear the traditional veils or may mix and match Pakistani and Western clothing. Veiling can be an individual decision or it may be imposed by the girl's family. Individual girls may choose to veil themselves in the U.S. This may cause an issue when the girl is an athlete, as she may insist on covering herself in the manner she has chosen as a veil. In these cases, whenever possible, allowances help the girl continue participating in the sport.

LITERACY AND EDUCATION

Percentages and data regarding literacy rates in Pakistan show a nation with roughly half its population as literate in Urdu (the national language). The CIA World Factbook (2013) reported national literacy at 57.9%, with 69.5% for males and 45.8% for females. UNESCO (2012) data was lower: it reported 54.9% of the total population as literate, with 68% of males and 40.3% of females as literate. The government of Pakistan's (2013) data for 2011–2012 was higher: 58% for the total population, 70% for men, and 47% for women. Regardless of the source, it is clear that literacy percentages for the overall population are distressingly low and the gender parity index is cause for concern. As illustrated in the opening scenario, parental concerns were much more focused on the sons and their future than on the daughter and her future.

In Pakistan, education and literacy are impacted, as they are elsewhere, by poverty and rural living. An added concern in Pakistan is terrorism, which affects women and girls in particular, as militants have targeted girls and schools due to their misguided idea that Islam dissuades the education of girls. This is untrue. The first word the Prophet Muhammad recited as the word of *Allah* (God) was "*Iqra*." This word has "read and recite" as its meaning—thus Islam supports education. It is unfortunate that women and children face terror in schools. The shooting of Malala Yousafzai in 2012 and the terror attack on the school in Peshawar in 2014 are horrific and extreme examples of anti-female-education behavior. Both galvanized Pakistani opinion against the Taliban, the group that carried out the attack.

LANGUAGES

English, along with Urdu, is an official language of Pakistan and is used by the elite and by the government. English was an integral part of the modernization of Pakistan, but Pakistan plans to drop English as its official language and switch to Urdu (although no timetable has been set). English will continue to be taught in schools, and official documents will be bilingual to increase accessibility to the population that does not speak English (Agrawal, 2015). Therefore, students coming to U.S. schools from elite families, and those who have had the benefit of education, are likely to have some background in written and spoken English.

Urdu is not a native language of any of the provinces of Pakistan but it is the official language. Forty-eight percent of Pakistanis are native Punjabi speakers, 12% speak Sindhi, 10% speak Saraiki, and 8% each speak Urdu, Pashto, and English. Therefore, students coming from Pakistan will most likely have a background in their provincial language, at least in its spoken form. Many Pakistani families in the U.S. speak multiple languages in their homes, including Urdu, English, and their provincial tongue.

The choice of Urdu as the official state language remains controversial because it was a minority, non-native language in Pakistan. Its choice as the sole state language—excluding Bengali as a possibility in East Pakistan—was a major cause of the secession of Bangladesh (East Pakistan) from West Pakistan in 1971 (see the previous section for more information about this issue). Urdu was chosen as the national language for Pakistan specifically to serve as a unifier because it was spoken by a majority of people in the Indian subcontinent historically and at the time of Partition. Currently, it is spoken by more than 100 million people, predominantly in Pakistan and India.

Characteristics of the Urdu Language

- All the languages of Pakistan are members of the Indo-European family of languages.
- Each of the languages has an extensive literary history and rich oral folk tradition.
- Urdu and Hindi are mutually intelligible.
- After Pakistan's creation, all of the languages of Pakistan were pushed to adopt Perso-Arabic scripts. As a result, the languages all use an Urdu-like script with special letters and diacritical marks for tonal accents and sounds specific to the particular language.
- The Urdu alphabet has 39 basic letters and 13 extra characters, 52 total.
- Urdu is written from right to left and is closely related to the Arabic and Persian alphabets (but Arab or Persian students will not be able to translate to or from Urdu or vice-versa).

**Table 14.1.   The Basic Urdu Alphabet
With English Sounds (Written Right to Left Here)**

ا [a] alif like **ask**	ب [b] bay like **ball**	پ [p] pay like **pen**	ت [t] tay like **tea**	ٹ [t] Tay like **top**
ٹ [s] say like **summer**	ج [j] jeem like **joy**	چ [ch] chay like **charm**	ح [h] hay like **hot**	خ [kh] khay like **Ba<u>ch</u>**
د [d] dal like **dove**	ڈ [ḍ] Dal like **drink**	ذ [z] zal like **zoo**	ر [r] ray like **rice**	ڑ [r] Ray like **rabbit**
ز [z] zay like **zoo**	ژ [zh] zhay like **vi<u>s</u>ion**	س [s] seen like **small**	ش [sh] sheen like **shrine**	ص [ṣ] swad like **salt**
ض [ẓ] zwad like **those**	ط [t] toy like **tower**	ظ [z] zoy like **this**	ع ['] aeen like **none**	غ [gh] ghaeen like **none**
ف [f] fay like **food**	ق [q] quaf like **queue**	ک [k] kaf like **kilo**	گ [g] gaf like **guest**	ل [l] laam like **life**
م [m] meem like **moon**	ن [n] noon like **nice**	و [v, o] wow like **wet, cool**	ہ [h] he like **house**	ھ [h] hay like **house**
ء ['] humza like **art**	ی [y, i] yay like **yes**	ے [aiore] yay like **way**		

- Table 14.1 shows the sounds and letters of Urdu. Urdu has three short vowel sounds. In writing, short vowels are represented by special symbols above or below the word, known as *diacritics*. However, these diacritics are often left off written Urdu, so a reader cannot always tell how a word should be pronounced unless it is in context. Short vowels sound like the *a* in the English word *about*; the *i* in *bin*; the *u* in *put*.

- Urdu has seven long vowel sounds. Long vowels are written using the letters ا [*alif*], و [*wao*], ی [*choti* ye], and ے [*bari* ye] combined with diacritics, but the diacritics are often left out. Advanced readers of Urdu are used to looking at a string of consonants and determining the sound based on context and reading fluency. The seven long vowels in Urdu sound similar to these English sounds: *a* in *father*; *ee* in *seed*; *oo* in *boot*; *o* in *order*; *au* in *Australia*; *e* in *help*; *a* in *apple*.

- Two of the letters that represent vowels can also represent consonants; و [*wao*] can also represent a *v* sound or a *w* sound; ی [*choti* ye] can also represent a "y" sound (Urdu Language, 2016).

Urdu-speaking students may experience difficulty with the following:

- The English /v/ sound does not have an equivalent in Urdu; Urdu speakers will tend to pronounce this sound as /w/. "Valentine" will sound like "walintine."
- The /p/ sound in English is aspirated, but not in Urdu. Therefore, "Pakistan" pronounced in Urdu sounds like "Bakistan" to native English speakers.
- Urdu speakers often read the long /ā/ sound as a short /ĕ/ sound; therefore, *bake* sounds like *bek*; *there* sounds like *ther*.
- The /r/ sound in Urdu is trilled (dental); Urdu speakers may trill the guttural /r/ of English.
- The sentence order of English is subject-verb-object, whereas the sentence order of Urdu is subject-object-verb. When translating Urdu into English, Urdu-speakers may reverse the verb-object order: *boy flies kite* may become *boy kite flies*.
- In English, prepositions come before nouns to form prepositional phrases. In Urdu, *post* positions are placed after nouns to show location. In English: *in the park*; in Urdu: *the park in*.

Table 14.2 presents some common phrases in Urdu for educators to use with Pakistani students.

IDEAS FOR EDUCATORS

Many of the ideas already shared in this book related to Islamic cultures are adaptable for educating children of Pakistani heritage. Because most Pakistanis you are likely to encounter in U.S. schools come from educated, middle-class or above families, they are likely to have strong support (and expectations) from home that say, "Do not waste the opportunity we have created for you by the many sacrifices we have made," or "Do well in

**Table 14.2.   Common Phrases
in Urdu That Educators Can Learn and Use**

English	Transliteration	Urdu
Hello	AssalAM-alEIkum	السـلام علــی م
Good-bye	XhuDA-HAfiz	خدا حـافظ
What is your name?	AApkaNAamKYAhai?	آپ کـا نـام کیـا ہے؟
My name is ___.	MEraNAam___hai.	مـیرا نـام ... ہــے
Thank you	SHUkria	شـــکریہ
You are welcome.	KOyiBAatnahin	؟ وی بـات نہـی؟
Pleased to meet you!	AApseMILkerXHUshiHUee!	آپ سَــے ملـر خوشـی ہـوّی!
How are you?	AApkaaSIhain? (formal female) AApkaasEHhain? (formal male)	آپ ؟ یسـی ہــی؟ آپ ؟ یســے ہــی؟

school and beyond—the family name is at stake." This does not mean that it will be easy for them to succeed, nor does it mean it will be easy to teach them due to differences between school in Pakistan and the U.S.

Misconceptions and Stereotypes

Given the current perceptions of Pakistan being a "terrorist state" and media perpetuation of these views, Pakistani students in U.S. schools are likely to be stereotyped and experience prejudice. Students are likely to hear negative comments about dress or cultural or religious heritage. They may be called names, asked to react to some news story from their home or other Muslim country, told to go back where they belong, and experience general antagonism. As always, educators need to be aware of how students talk to each other both in and outside of class. Developing a positive relationship with students will help in seeing changes in behavior among peers. Despite cultural differences, parents are still partners and allies in the education of students, and educators should collaborate with parents to optimize the learning of the students. In all situations, issues of discrimination or prejudice need to be dealt with according to school policy.

Gender

In some cases, gender plays a role in problems that may develop. Although males have been taught to respect educators, having lived in a country and a family where they are privileged because of their gender, they may not be willing to acknowledge either a female educator or female group members who are in positions of leadership in the classroom or school. Where gender-role stereotyping is reinforced in the home, boys may exhibit generalized chauvinism that may manifest as recalcitrance, defiance, and disrespect towards women and girls. Female Pakistani students may present a different kind of problem: discomfort with a male educator or working with male peers in group situations. Their discomfort may appear as withdrawal from participation, argument, failure to complete tasks, or apathy. Further, girls who are experiencing gender-role stereotyping in their homes while being exposed to other views outside of it may either embrace the freedom offered and stand up for their rights or withdraw emotionally if they cannot do anything about it. In both cases, educators need to make contact with the family to discuss these behaviors and garner support, as well as talk to the student to explain why it is important to learn how to work with the opposite sex. Students will encounter situations both at school and in the workplace that will require comingling, cooperation, and mutual respect in order to be productive. Emphasizing success in the future workplace is an effective strategy because, among educated Pakistanis, the expectation is that their children, whether male or female, will go on to college and work. Educators should not expect a quick solution to this situation but continue to work on this over time.

Personal Space and Physical Contact

The perception of personal space among Pakistani students may create awkward situations in school. In general, Pakistanis have a smaller sphere of personal space and feel comfortable with close proximity. Pakistanis are also comfortable with same-sex proximity, including boys and men, and do not exhibit the same discomfort with same-sex closeness as their American counterparts. The exception to personal proximity occurs between males and females who have reached sexual maturity. In this case, men and women experience great discomfort with physical proximity involving the opposite sex. Educators who prefer personal space around them will need to make that very explicit and realize that Pakistani children of all ages are likely to enter that space at some point. Expect discomfort and misunderstanding, particularly from boys who are not Pakistani, if a Pakistani boy, while in play or work, gets too close (Western girls worry less about personal space, but this might also be an issue). In situations like this, explaining the difference in cultural expectations for space may work toward both students' understanding this difference.

When children are younger, gender awareness is not as much of a concern in Pakistani families or culture. Therefore, younger students will not experience anxiety with mixed-gender interaction, closeness, or groupings, or with teachers of the opposite sex. As the children grow older, however, educators should be aware that physical closeness will affect students when opposite genders are involved. As educators, we often employ various physical and nonverbal forms of relationship-building such as high-fives, pats on the shoulder, or hugs. Students of some Western cultures respond positively to these gestures of affection. In the case of Pakistanis, however, one must establish a relationship before physical gestures of affection become accepted and effective. Relationships with Pakistanis tend to be based on the length of time an educator or coach has known the student, as well as the nature of the relationship (e.g., multiyear relationship, an educator with whom the student has bonded, a coach, an activity instructor) and whether the parents know and trust the educator. Again, it is most respectful of the culture to avoid any physical contact with students who have reached sexual maturity. Students who are more acclimatized to American culture may recognize the gesture as a form of affection, but it may still produce anxiety and withdrawal. One exception may be the pat on the head. This is a form of affection, encouragement and approval that elders use in Pakistan towards those who are younger. This is a relatively safe physical gesture that boys and girls will accept—once a relationship has been established.

Eye Contact

In Pakistan, children do not make direct eye contact for extended periods of time with adults or a member of the opposite sex outside the family. It is likely that when they are in U.S. classrooms and schools, they will look at the educator and briefly make eye contact then look away. Making direct eye contact with adults, particularly in disciplinary situations, is seen as defiance or disrespect. Educators should not expect students to look up and make eye contact with them in this case but can still have meaningful conversation that helps the student understand expectations. Forcing a child to make eye contact ("Look at me when I'm talking to you!") is likely to result in the student hearing very little else that is said. Gender will also figure prominently in this as students become older. Looking into the eyes of an educator of the opposite sex may be very uncomfortable for the student. Therefore, when working with students in these situations, be aware that fleeting or no eye contact does not signal dishonesty or disrespect but is a cultural behavior.

Curricular Adaptations

Group interaction and collaboration are highly valued in U.S. schools. Being aware of the historical and cultural influences on Pakistani students will be beneficial in the design and organization of student groups. Grouping students is fine, but be careful with whom Pakistani students are grouped both by gender and ethnicity. If you have Pakistani students present in your classroom or school, you will likely also have Indian or Bangladeshi students. While there may be no tension or enmity between them at first, there may be some later as they get to know each other's origins, especially if there is pressure from the home not to associate. Pairing them up as support for each other, either culturally or linguistically, is unlikely to result in positive outcomes. Placing them in small, mixed-gender groups should also probably be avoided until later in the year when the classroom culture has been well established and students understand the expectation that they must all learn to work together.

Schools in Pakistan tend not to emphasize individualized thinking, critical thinking, or creative thinking—even in modern schools that resemble schools in developed countries. This may be due to the hierarchical and group-oriented culture. This may mean that memorization of information is valued over interpretation, analysis, or individual innovation. Also, Pakistanis tend to be group-oriented and wish to provide educators with the answer they think educators or adults want to hear. This may create a conundrum. How can they act and think as creative individuals when they may have no experience—especially in this context of education and with adults—with the process of generating new and individual ideas, synthesizing information for innovative thoughts, or elevating the importance of the self over the group or the elder? Teachers must provide a great deal of structure and very explicit instruction on the desired outcome of a lesson. Questions such as: "What do you think the character's motivation was for taking this action?" or "What would you do in this situation?" or "What are alternative ways to solve this problem?" may provide difficulty to Pakistani students since the questions require independent thought, especially when neither the context nor the teacher is providing clues as to the "right" answer. Explicit instruction in creative and critical thinking skills with practice and encouragement are instrumental in teaching all students new ways of approaching knowledge and the synthesis of information.

A further problem presented with an emphasis on memorization and a focus on convergent questions by traditional Pakistani education means that new students may not be prepared to produce original or creative work and may *reproduce* someone else's work as their own without proper acknowledgment of original sources. In Pakistani schools, providing the "book" answer is considered correct and no citation or reference is deemed necessary. Thus, Pakistani students may not understand or may not be schooled in rules regarding plagiarism. They will, therefore, not understand why plagiarizing is a problem. Should an educator notice critical issues with plagiarism or a lack of proper citations in student work, it may be fruitful to explain and teach why plagiarism is not acceptable and provide the opportunity for practice and the correction of mistakes rather than immediately grading students down.

CONCLUSIONS

This chapter provides information that is important for educators to know that focuses specifically on Pakistani students. The general information about Muslims, Islam, and Islamic holidays and customs found in other chapters may also apply to Pakistani students, as the majority are Muslim. Our aim is to provide a clearer understanding of Pakistani culture and the Urdu language, as awareness of the implications of culture on learning is the first step within the broader context of teaching. This awareness becomes most effective when implemented with engaging and relevant curricular approaches and strategies for supporting language development at the level of the students' abilities so that children like those of Ayesha and Farooq can be supported and successful regardless of which schools they attend.

ADDITIONAL RESOURCES

Amin, M., Willets, D., & Hancock, G. (1997). *Journey through Pakistan*. Karachi, Pakistan: Paramount Books.

> This book provides an excellent understanding of Pakistan's rich history and diverse culture, geography, and people.

Jalal, A. (2014). *The struggle for Pakistan: A Muslim homeland and global politics*. Cambridge, MA: Belknap Press.

> A U.S.-published book that examines global politics related to U.S. and Pakistan.

Haqqani, H. (2013). *Magnificent delusions: Pakistan, the United States, and an epic history of misunderstanding*. New York, NY: Public Affairs Press.

> This is another helpful U.S.-published book that examines the tumultuous and quirky relationship between the U.S. and Pakistan.

Customs and Traditions. (2016). Retrieved from http://nationalheritage.gov.pk/customtraditions.html

> The government of Pakistan's official site for information on Pakistani heritage including customs, traditions, and holidays.

TASKS FOR EDUCATORS

1. Reflect on these questions:
    *   What might the history and education of Pakistan mean for students coming into U.S. schools? How might current media attention on Pakistan affect Pakistani students and families? What should teachers consider?
    *   Which of the cultural traits and practices provided above are in direct contrast to the cultural traits and practices of U.S. schools? What kinds of issues might arise? How might these differences need accommodating during classroom activities and within the confines of the school?
    *   What might you need to do to help ELLs from Pakistan to learn to use English in your classroom?
2. Consider your own perceptions of Pakistan prior to reading this short chapter. How has this chapter changed your thinking and perhaps how you might work with Pakistani students?
3. Ask your Pakistani student(s) to teach you a few words that might be useful for you to use with them (like a secret code for the two of you). Also ask the student to teach you how to write your name in Urdu (if they know how). This will help you see firsthand how language might provide challenges to her/his writing and comprehension.
4. As part of the first week or two of school, consider how you might have students (with their families) share their funds of knowledge. Students might, for example, share who makes decisions in their household, how their family and friends spend time together, what the family values are, what language(s) is (are) spoken in the home, the holidays the family celebrates, their most enjoyable traditions, or any other details so that students can build community through understanding.

REFERENCES

Agrawal, A. (2015, July 28). Why Pakistan is replacing English with Urdu. *Time.* Retrieved from http://time.com/3975587/pakistan-english-urdu/

Al-Sheha, A. R. (2000). *The message of Islam.* Herndon, VA: International Institute of Islamic Thought.

Government of Pakistan. Bureau of Statistics. (2013) *Pakistan Social and Living Standards Measurement Survey.* Retrieved from http://www.pbs.gov.pk/content/pakistan-social-and-living-standards-measurement

Halliday, T. (Ed.). (1990). *Insight guide: Pakistan.* Singapore: APA Publishers.

Hennink, M., Rana, I., & Iqbal, R. (2005, July–August). Knowledge of personal and sexual development amongst young people in Pakistan. *Culture, Health, and Sexuality Journal, 7*(4), 319–332.

UNESCO. (2012). Adult and Youth Literacy, 1990–*2015: Analysis of data for 41 selected countries.* Retrieved from http://www.uis.unesco.org/literacy/Documents/UIS-literacy-statistics-1990-2015-en.pdf

United States Central Intelligence Agency. (2013). *World Factbook* 2012–*2013: Japan.* Retrieved from https://www.cia.gov/library/publications/the-world-factbook/goes/print_ja.html

Urdu Language. (2016). *Encyclopedia Britannica Online.* Retrieved from http://www.britannica.com/topic/UrRudu-language

CHAPTER 15

PHILIPPINES

Being Filipino

Jeom Ja Yeo
University of Washington

Sandy came to the United States when she was 12. She was born in Pangasinan, the third most populated province, a gateway to northern Luzon, and a major producer of salt in the Philippines. When she was two years old, her parents left for the United States, leaving Sandy behind under the care of her godmother, whom she calls "Auntie." Her parents sent remittances from the U.S. to provide her with a quality education, healthcare, and other living expenses. She attended a private school, which she recalls had a rigorous curriculum and supportive instruction. All the subjects were taught in English, and she performed well academically. English was one of the most comfortable languages for Sandy, along with her mother tongue, Pangasinan, and Filipino. During the ten years of prolonged separation from her parents, Sandy came to build strong social and emotional bonds with her godmother and other extended family members in the Philippines. When she eventually left the Philippines to join her parents, Sandy felt torn apart from her family in the Philippines and her parents in the United States. Soon after her arrival, Sandy passed the Washington English Language Proficiency Assessment (WELPA) test; she seemingly had a good enough command of English to be put in mainstream classes without any ESL transitional support.

Views From Inside: Languages, Cultures, and Schooling for K–12 Educators
pp. 249–263

Sandy's first year in the U.S. went fine, but she began to fall behind when she entered middle school. School work became difficult to understand and complete on her own. She suffered emotional detachment from her parents while coping with the new rules and responsibilities in her home in a new land. She felt alone. No one seemed to understand her feeling of "homesickness-at-home," longing for the care given by her Auntie (her surrogate parent) in the Philippines. No schools appeared to pay attention to her struggle for academic English development. She became disinterested in school work and disengaged from learning. She dropped out of school when she was in 9th grade. A year later, she was enrolled in a charter school and shortly transferred to a local high school and was placed in the ESL program. When I met her, she was a high school senior in the advanced ESL class, trying to balance school and the care of her 2-year-old son.

BACKGROUND

The Philippines is an archipelago of 7,107 islands in Southeast Asia spanning more than 300,000 square kilometers of territory. Its population was estimated at approximately 99 million in 2014, marking it as the 12th most densely populated country in the world (The Philippines-National Government Portal, 2016). Taiwan lies to the north across the Luzon Strait, while to the south sit the islands of Indonesia. Its closest neighbor to the west across the South China Sea is Vietnam, and to the east across the Pacific Ocean is the U.S. island territory of Guam. The Philippines is composed of three major island groups. The largest is Luzon to the north, the western side on which the capital Manila is located. To the south lies the second biggest island, Mindanao, home to most of the country's Muslim population. In between are the smaller island groups called the Visayas. The archipelago is volcanic in origin, mostly mountainous, with narrow coastal plains and abundant swift-running streams. Its tropical climate features a mix of a hot, rainy season (May to November) and a dry, cool season (December to April); the islands abound in natural resources such as fertile lands, diverse flora and fauna, and rich mineral deposits.

Due to its geographical location, the Malayo-Polynesian Philippines has been under a constant influx of different cultures and languages throughout its history, forging a unique cultural and racial blend. Indonesia and China were the dominant influences during its early history, while Islam was brought to Mindanao in the 14th century, spreading to part of Manila and Tondo from the 16th century onward when the Spaniards occupied the country (Bautista, 2002). Three centuries of Spanish colonization (1565–1898) left traces of Hispanic/Latin culture in the language, religion, traditions, and customs of the archipelago. Spanish surnames are an example of this, originated by the colonists' implementation of the

Spanish Naming Decree in 1849. This decree required all colonial subjects "to choose from a catalog of Spanish names prepared by the government, forbidding the adoption of names that belonged to the hereditary elite or nobility of precolonial times" (Blanco 2009, p. 3), and thus often masking the Malayo-Polynesian ancestry of the majority Filipinos.

Roman Catholicism is another legacy of Hispanic tradition. All major Roman Catholic holy days are official national holidays in the Philippines. During these holidays, celebrants hold "*fiestas*" (festivals) to honor their patron saints, to celebrate local history and culture, and to promote local products and businesses. The *fiesta* embodies the geographical, historical, and cultural diversity of the Philippines with indigenous rituals and a variety of performances and activities such as bamboo dances (e.g., *Tinikling* and *Sinkil*), street dances, parades, boat processions, music, and contests.

Toward the end of the 19th century, Filipinos started an independence movement against Spanish rule, allying with the United States. The alliance resulted in the American occupation of the Philippines in 1898. American colonizers intervened in the archipelago's social, cultural, economic, and political ecology until 1946, when the country was granted independence. The new government adopted the form of a republic. Religious freedom was introduced, along with the de-Catholicization of the country. The American education system and curriculum were adopted, with basic education becoming public and free. Democratic governance was promoted along with American value systems, pop culture, and English language. During this time, Filipinos were American nationals, often patronized as "little brown brothers" (Takaki, 1989), whose status was believed to be almost analogous to Americans and granted access to the "American Dream." Massive labor out-migration in search of monetary rewards and success ensued, for the most part to Hawaii, Washington, Oregon, and California. These early Filipino migrant workers, called "Manongs," were typically uneducated, single, male migratory workers, occupying agriculture, fisheries, and menial service jobs on U.S. soil. They encountered and fought against harsh living conditions and deep racism by White Americans, planting the roots of today's Filipino America. During the late 1940s and 1950s, another massive migration to America occurred. This time, the majority of Filipino immigrants were war brides, plantation contract workers, and military recruits.

After the 1965 U.S. Immigration Reform Act, which abolished the quota system based on national origins, the massive Filipino migration resumed. These Filipino immigrants were much more diverse in their places of origin, educational and socioeconomic statuses, and settlement patterns. They ranged from highly educated professionals to semiskilled workers to unskilled immigrants. Some were relatively easily incorporated into the professional sectors of mainstream society, albeit often into the low ranks of the profession, while others came to the United States under the provision of family reunification to join their family.

CULTURE

Filipinos have a rich, multiethnic, multilingual heritage. While Malayo-Polynesians with some mixture of foreign blood—such as Chinese, Spanish, American, or Indian—are the most dominant racial group, the colorful, vibrant, hybrid Filipino cultures and languages are represented by eight major ethnolinguistic groups. These are Tagalog, Ilocano, Pampango, Pangasinan, and Bicolano in Luzon, and Waray, Hiligaynon, and Sugboanon in the Visayan Islands. Tagalog, Cebuano, and Ilocano are the most spoken among more than 100 local languages, while English is the de facto national language of government, business, law, education, mass media, and popular entertainment (Kachru & Nelson, 2006).

Despite their diversity in ethnicity and language, Filipinos as a whole embrace the rich Roman Catholic, democratic, and spiritual values that tie them together. They emphasize *pakikisama* (good public relations), *utang-na-loob* (a sense of gratitude), and *hiya* (a sense of harmony). Filipinos are affectionate, humble, industrious, proud, respectful, and spiritual, being devoted to family, religion, and education. Home, church, and school are the major institutions for them to build strong social relationships with their family members, religious affiliations, and peer groups and to construct daily activities and practices that define their values, customs, and lifestyles. Multigeneration and extended families are common in a single household, which may be composed of the core family plus aunts, uncles, grandparents, cousins, or other relatives from the maternal or paternal side of the family. Like Sandy in the vignette at the beginning of the chapter, fictive kin, including godparents, are also regarded as being part of the family, sharing affection, concern, duties, and responsibilities.

Filipino culture is in a transitional stage. Traditionally, it has favored collectivism over individualism but nowadays, as diverse views and identities emerge, Filipinos are encountering a new, more complex culture. For example, family's shared interests and goals are negotiated with those of individual members, rather than taking priority (Puyat, 2010). Self-sacrifice, harmony, and conformity, previously focused by patriarchal structures and power, are now balanced with respect for and focus on the centrality of women (Root, 2005). Watkins and Gerong (1997) also observed strong ties to global identity among youth as an emerging self-concept. Filipinos value personal wishes and goals as well as others' expectations and wishes, looking for opportunities to maximize their strengths and resources as competent members of society.

For decades, the Philippines has been among the top countries of origin in the traditional emigration to countries such as the United States, Canada, and Australia. *The Philippine Overseas Employment Administration* (www.poea.gov.ph/) reports that during the year 2011, more than 50,000 Filipinos migrated to the United States, 34,991 to Canada, and 12,933 to Australia, which more than doubled the numbers from the early 2000s. Consistent growth in labor migration and family reunification are major components of this outflow. As noted above, many Filipino migrants are educated and skilled professionals, for example, doctors, nurses, engineers, physicists, chemists, and computing professionals. Overseas employment is by and large regarded as the main vehicle for success, aspired to by many adult and young Filipinos. Acknowledged are the benefits not only from monetary gain but social remittances such as the acquisition of skills; career development in certain professions such as seafaring, nursing, or information technology; family reunification; the experience of other cultures and societies; and living in a more developed country, to name a few. As a result, the Philippines contends with the issues of brain drain/brain waste, family disruption, and social injustice toward migrant workers overseas. As more skilled and educated workers opt for foreign jobs, the country is left with less qualified and undereducated laborers. In the overseas workplace, Filipino migrants are often unprotected from long working hours, few rest days, and inadequate health coverage and safety measures, and they are more vulnerable to risky behaviors such as poor dietary habits, smoking, drinking, and unhealthy lifestyles (Battistella & Asis, 2013).

As Filipino outmigration continues, transnational family arrangements become an inevitable option, particularly when mothers leave their children behind (Root, 2005). Extended family members and fictive kin become surrogate parents who provide immediate care and take on the day-to-day responsibility for raising the children. Migrant parents, on the other hand, provide financial funds for the economic sustainability of the family left in the Philippines. A new family ideology that redefines the parent–child separation as a viable option for their children has emerged. Expected are financial gain and the consequent social benefits such as access to higher education and professional career pathways and exposure to advanced knowledge, information, and opportunities to enjoy commodities from developed countries. A virtual presence, regular and real-time, through communication technology, is employed as a way to maintain familial ties. Although children long for the care and attention of their parents, they perceive themselves as more independent compared to their peers from nontransnational households and develop moral obligations to pay back and return the benefits of their parents' sacrifices.

A recent study by Orbeta and Abrigo (2009) reports that Filipino transnational households with at least one or two overseas migrants earn four to five times more than their nonmigrant counterparts. The remittances secure family stability by funding various expenses such as debt repayment, daily household operations, acquisition of consumer durables, children's education, business capital, home purchases, and savings. The children in such households are much healthier and academically more successful than their counterparts. Many of them aspire to become future migrants like their parents; they tend to dream of working abroad.

When the children left behind in the Philippines finally immigrate to the United States for family reunification, they take part in the process of transnationalism—the social process "by which immigrants build social fields that link together their country of origin and their country of settlement" (Schiller, Basch, & Blanc-Szanton, 1992, p.1). The process, however, as shown in the case of Sandy, is intertwined with complex, multifaceted transformation: facing acculturation stress, enduring homesickness, reconciling intergenerational conflicts, and creating a new position and identity as transnationals. Yeo (2013) observed the active participation among Filipino immigrant students in transnational space. The students, using international phone calls and internet communication systems, frequently shared their American lives and experiences with their families in the Philippines, sought emotional support, and even looked for future opportunities both in the Philippines and the United States.

Contrary to the significance of transnational space among Filipino immigrant students, Yeo (2013) notes that U.S. schools largely failed to acknowledge the significance of the transnational relations and engagements among these Filipino students by forcing them to assimilate into the mainstream culture that defends Eurocentric, monolingual, White privilege while attempting to impose a "model minority" identity on them. In response, the Filipino students resisted this culturally unresponsive schooling. Instead, they developed a new Filipino identity as transnational agents to seek opportunities in both countries. They viewed the Philippines as their home, where they can have their ideas, actions, and beliefs more understood and welcome. At the same time, they acknowledged the U.S. as the place where they can benefit from a good education and good employment opportunities.

Educators who might consider the transnational family and its pertinent transnational engagement as lack of adaptation and detrimental to students' learning may need to reconsider their view and accept it as an integral part of the Filipino culture. Filipino transnational students encounter varying degrees of social and emotional challenges when they readjust to their parents, from whom they may have been living apart for a long time (Parreñas, 2000). Family rituals, duties and responsibilities, parental care and supervision, and even living under the same roof with their parents can be new experiences. While readapting to their family in the U.S., Filipino students also seek care, love, and social and emotional support from their surrogate family in the Philippines. Thus, schools and educators should acknowledge the complexity of these students' adaptation processes and further develop curricular and programmatic accommodations that can utilize these transnational ties as a support system for the Filipino students' academic achievement and social integration.

LANGUAGES AND LITERACIES

As stated earlier, the Philippines is a multilingual country speaking more than 100 languages, with Filipino and English being the official languages. The typical Filipino is thus trilingual – they use the mother tongue in home/private domains and Filipino and English at school and in other public institutions (Dayag, 2012). According to the Philippine FLEMMS (Functional Literacy, Education, and Mass Media Survey) (Bersales, 2013), around 96% of Filipinos aged 10 to 64 years old responded that they have basic literacy skills in reading, writing, and understanding a simple message in any of these languages.

The term "Filipino," in fact, evolved from "*Pilipino*"—that is, Tagalog, the language of central Luzon Island. It does include some syntactic structures and lexicons from other Philippine languages, but it mainly prescribes the features of Tagalog. The proclamation of Filipino as the national language in 1987, thus, may be the most practical and political choice, considering its widespread use across the country; however, it creates unequal economic, educational, and cultural relations between Tagalog and non-Tagalog speakers. A recent study sheds light on the wide regional gaps in the basic education completion rate: Tagalog-speaking regions including Manila consistently shows high levels of completion rate while non-Tagalog speaking regions remain below the national average rates (UNESCO Internal Bureau of Education, 2015).

That the primary mediums of instruction are Filipino and English has remained a source of controversy. As the Filipino language is essentially Tagalog-based, despite the attempt to invent a more inclusive national language, non-Tagalog-speaking educators raise concerns about the effectiveness of Filipino/English bilingual education for language minority students (Tupas, 2009). Math and science are taught in English, while all other subjects are in Filipino. This Filipino/English medium of instruction has been challenged as flawed, especially among speakers who do not speak either language. Its validity and effectiveness remain unproven; research maintains that mother tongue instruction has a significant positive influence on children's cognitive and literacy development (Walter & Dekker, 2008). Children who do not speak Filipino and English are much disadvantaged compared to those who do.

Amid the persisting tension between Filipino and local languages, English maintains its practical and symbolic power over other local languages, controlling the domains of government bureaucracy, legislation, judiciary, mass media, science, technology, and higher education. Recent research suggests that the English literacy rate is well above 90%— although there is a rising concern that English fluency is declining (Bernardo, Salanga, & Aguas, 2008). Since the U.S. occupation, the English language has undergone acculturation and nativization. It has become a hybrid featuring the integration of local Philippine languages and deviations from American English. Codeswitching between Tagalog and English is also common. Presented below are some linguistic features of Philippine English:

- Vowels. Philippine English consists of five vowels, [a], [ɛ], [ɪ], [ɔ], and [ʊ]. There is no distinction between tense and lax vowels in that [æ], [e], [i], [o], [u] are pronounced as [a], [ɛ], [ɪ], [ɔ], and [ʊ], respectively. Unstressed vowels that are typically reduced in American English are fully articulated—for example, the American English [ə] sound in the initial position in words like *above, alone,* and *around* is pronounced as [a] (Kachru & Nelson, 2006).

- Consonants. There are 18 consonants, [p], [t], [tʃ], [k], [b], [d], [dʒ], [g], [s], [ʃ], [h], [l], [m], [n], [ŋ], [r], [w], and [j]. Stops are neither aspirated in the initial position nor released at the end. The fricative [f] does not exist, even though the national language is called "Filipino." The fricatives [s] and [z] are allophonic in that *sink* and *zinc* are pronounced as [sɪŋk]. The interdental fricatives [θ] and [ð] are replaced by the stops [t] and [d] respectively (Kachru & Nelson, 2006).

- Suprasegmentals. Unlike stress-timed American English, Philippine English is syllable-timed, in that every sound is articulated for the same length. Word stress and intonation patterns change in some cases. For example, words like *category* and *affluent* have their primary stress on the second syllables –te-, and –lu-, not the first syllables, ca- and aff-, which is the typical case for English speakers in North America. In addition, rising intonation is common for statements and why-questions; falling intonation is, for the most part, for yes-no questions (Gonzalez, as cited in Bautista, 2002).

Table 15.1. Semantic Changes in Philippine English

Word	Meaning
American time	Being punctual
Amorpripio	Self-esteem
Arbulario	Quack doctor
Asalto	Party on the eve of one's birthday
Balikbayan box	Box in which Filipinos returning from abroad put all the things they bought
Barangay	Village
Batchmate	A member of the same batch
Bibingka	Rice cake
Buko juice	Juice from young coconut
Colgate	Toothpaste
Comfort room	Restroom
Concienticize	Conscience +ticize
Folk	Provincial, barrio, tribal
Green joke	Vulgar or crude joke
Hacienda	Tracts of land
Imeldific	Extravagant, derived from former First Lady Imelda Marcos
Inihaw	Broiled pork or chicken
Kwan	Referring to something at the tip of the tongue
Osterize	Process of using a food blender
Pampers	Disposable diapers
Pentel pen	Color marker
Saying!	What a pity, what a waste, how unfortunate
Solon	Lawmaker

Source: Adapted from Bautista (1996).

- Lexical features. Original English words have undergone many changes in their meaning and use in Philippine English. Some words expanded in their meanings and others were added, removed, or altered, often to the degree that cognates have become unrelated. Table 15.1 provides a list of examples of semantic change.
- Grammatical features. Philippine English exhibits innovative grammatical features that are quite different from American English. Bautista and Gonzalez (2006) highlight several features of Philippine English grammar as follows:

o Articles are often missed when required and are added when not required:

Examples:

- Ø majority of teachers want a pay increase.
- In that task, the medium of *the* television offers advertiser a powerful tool.

o Mass nouns are often pluralized and non-count nouns pluralized:

Examples:

- *Equipments* were purchased using the previous year's budget.
- *Feedbacks* were given on the proposal.
- Agreement is not required in tense, number, and person.

Examples:

- I *had not gone* to class yesterday.
- The secretary *had not reported* for work last week.
- She *would* give you the correct answer if you ask her for it.
- The students *could* not understand why they will have to come to school on Sunday.
- *The teacher*, along with her students, *were* in the library yesterday.
- *The work* is so heavy that *they* are taking *their* toll on the health of people.

o "One of the" can be followed by singular noun.

Example:

- The principal reprimanded *one of the student*.

o Adverbials can be placed at the end of the sentence.

Example:

- The walk-in participants will join the post-conference tour *also* (p. 136).

The deviations in Philippine English may cause unique challenge among Filipinos, particularly those who come to the United States. Like other speakers of English varieties around the world, Filipinos wrestle with the validation of their English when it comes to the term "native speaker" (Kachru & Nelson, 2006). Teachers' acknowledgment of the value of Philippine English as a resource can motivate Filipino students to learn American English as an additional language. Teachers can adopt cross-linguistic investigation between Philippine English and American English, particularly academic English, so that all students can become aware of the differences between the two languages. In doing so, teachers can help Filipino students develop fuller competence as English speakers in the multilingual U.S. society.

IDEAS FOR EDUCATORS

The following are some ways to support Filipino immigrant students in our schools.

First, classroom teachers are encouraged to address the linguistic differences between Philippine English and American English. This approach helps Filipino students develop cross-linguistic competence in both Englishes. Like Sandy, many Filipino students come to U.S. schools with a good command of English, as English is the official language in the Philippines. Due to this proficiency, many Filipino students are excluded from receiving sustained support in their American English development, particularly in academic English. As discussed earlier, Philippine English has lexical, phonological, and grammatical innovations different from American English. Filipino students with the Philippine English accent, without teachers' intervention, might be unfairly treated by their peers and others, which might cause them to suffer from low self-esteem and lack of academic English competence. Thus, teachers may consider the integration of content and language teaching when they teach Filipino students, particularly those like Sandy who speak good English but are still in need of academic English support.

Second, teachers can provide more attention to identifying Filipino students' individual differences in learning and respond to their diverse needs, interests, and experiences. As discussed earlier, Filipino students are a multiethnic group with a multilingual background. Differentiating instruction and assessment with careful design and implementation can be effective. For example, self-assessments would be useful to assess student learning preferences and content understanding while small group presentations may work well with a project that focuses on Filipino history or culture. Visual presentation using PowerPoint slides or other visual art forms can be useful to assess how Filipino students process complex ideas and concepts.

Third, teachers and educators might strongly consider rejecting the model minority stereotype of Asian Americans by refusing to accept negative attitudes and biases toward those who do not fit into the stereotype. The model minority stereotype in itself is a false representation based simply on high test scores among certain groups of Asian students. Not all Asian ethnic groups are performing well in schools. Hune and Takeuchi (2008) shed light on academic disparities among students of Asian heritage in the Seattle Public School District, reporting that Chinese, Japanese, and East Indians are doing relatively well while Filipino and other Southeast Asians are struggling academically. Those who do not meet the model minority image suffer from teachers' biases that view them "as being less intelligent, not as hard working, and culturally deficient ... being tracked into less academically demanding courses, and being denied information that could better prepare them for college admission" (Hune & Takeuchi, 2008, p. 33). Learning and knowing Filipino American history and culture could help teachers develop better ways to support positive learning experiences for students.

CONCLUSIONS

Despite the long history of immigration and a large number of resettlements, Filipinos in the United States remain marginalized at the political and economic edges of American society (Okamura, 1995). Filipino students may be struggling at school, facing bullying, racial violence, peer group pressure, mental health problems, and model minority stereotypes (Hune & Takeuchi, 2008). The transnational relations between the Filipino American community and their home country are largely unspoken and unattended to. Monetary remittances, home visits, consumer goods sent in a *balikbayan* box, charitable contributions, and other sociocultural transfers are regular and circular through familial, economic, political, religious, organizational and other social ties between the two countries. Transnational engagement is an integral part of the Filipino students' identity construction and adaptation to American society. When schools and educators understand, acknowledge, and use as educational resources the Filipino diasporic transnational engagement, it validates the culture of Filipino immigrant children and thus contributes to their learning.

ADDITIONAL RESOURCES

Below is a list of resources that can help teachers better understand the Filipino culture and community and incorporate them into their teaching.

Aroy, M., & Devlin, D. (2009). *Little Manila: Filipinos in California's heartland*. Sacramento, CA: KVIE Public Television.
> This video captures the history and the immigrant story of Filipinos in Stockton during the 1930s.

Bender, P. (Producer & Director), Brown, J. (Producer & Director), Vasquez, A. A. (Producer & Director), & Brier, S. (Producer). (2006). *Savage acts* [Motion picture]. New York, NY: American Social History Project.
> This documentary depicts U.S. colonization of the Philippines at the turn of the century.

De Guia, K. (2005). *Kapwa: The self in the other: Worldviews and lifestyles of Filipino culture-bearers*. Pasig City, Philippines: Anvil Pub.

This book contains a collection of Filipino worldviews and lifestyles.

Dunn, G. (Producer), Schwartz, M. E. (Director), & Golez, T. C. (Narrator). (2005). *Dollar a day, ten cents a dance: A historic portrait of Filipino farmworkers in America* [Motion picture]. San Francisco, CA: Center for Asian American Media.

This video presents a portrait of Filipino farm laborers who came to the United States in the 1920s and 1930s expecting a more prosperous lifestyle but facing the reality of poverty and multiple forms of discrimination.

Onodera, L. (Producer), & Cajayon, G. (Director). (2003). *The debut* [Motion picture]. Culver City, CA: Columbia TriStar Home Entertainment.

This coming-of-age story portrays the journey of a talented Filipino high school student looking for his place in the family, friendships, and American society.

Ostrander, L., Corpuz, G., Rapada, D., & Berry, A. (2007). *Island roots*. Bainbridge Island, WA: IslandWood.

This video contains the narratives of Bainbridge Island residents Gina Corpuz, Doreen Rapada, Angela Berry, and others about the history of the Filipino-American community on the island.

Smithsonian Asian Pacific American Association. (2016). *A century of challenge and change: The Filipino American story*. Retrieved from http://sites.si.edu/exhibitions/exhibits/singgalot_filipinos_in_america/main.htm

This is an interactive, multimedia curriculum featuring four lessons exploring the waves and experiences of Filipinos who immigrated to the U.S., contributions Filipino Americans have made to American society, and the history and culture of the Philippines.

TASKS FOR EDUCATORS

1. Compare the immigrant experience of Filipinos with those of other groups from the region. What are the differences and similarities? How might you create lessons that address the needs of all of these students?

2. Create a lesson that plays to the multilingual strengths of Filipino students. What would the lesson include?

3. Based on the information in this chapter, make a list of strategies that you could use to help Filipino students share their stories.

REFERENCES

Battistella, G., & Asis, M. M. B. (2013). *Country migration report: The Philippines 2013*. International Organization for Migration. Makati City: International Organization for Migration.

Bautista, M. L. S. (1996). An outline: The national language and the language of instruction. In M. L. S. Bautista (Ed.), *Readings in Philippine Sociolinguistics* (pp. 223–227). Manila, The Philippines: De La Salle University Press.

Bautista, M. L. S., & Gonzalez, A. B. (2006). Southeast Asian Englishes. In B. Kachru, Y. Kachru, & C. Nelson (Eds.), *The Handbook of World Englishes* (pp. 130–144). Oxford, UK: Blackwell Publishing,

Bautista, V. (2002). *The Filipino Americans (From 1763 to the Present): Their History, Culture, and Traditions* (2nd ed.). London, UK: Bookhaus.

Bernardo, A. B. I., Salanga, G. C., & Aguas, K. M. (2008). Filipino adolescent students' conceptions of learning goals. In O. Tan, D. M. McInerney, G. A. D. Liem, & A. G. Tan (Eds.), *What the West can learn from the East: Asian perspectives on the psychology of learning and motivation* (pp. 169–190). Charlotte, NC: Information Age.

Bersales, L. G. S. (2013). *2013 FLEMMS: Functional literacy, education, and mass media survey.* Quezon City, The Philippines: Philippine Statistics Authority.

Blanco, J. D. (2009). *Frontier constitutions: Christianity and colonial empire in the nineteenth-century Philippines* (Vol. 4). Berkley, CA: University of California Press.

Dayag, D. T. (2012). Philippine English. In E. Low (Ed.), *English in Southeast Asia: Features, policy and language in use* (pp. 91–99). Amsterdam, NLD: John Benjamins Publishing Company. Retrieved from http://www.ebrary.com

Hune, S., & Takeuchi, D. (2008). *Asian Americans in Washington State: Closing their hidden achievement gaps.* Report prepared for Washington State Commission on Asian Pacific American Affairs. Seattle, WA: University of Washington.

Kachru, Y., & Nelson, C. L. (2006). *World Englishes* in Asian context. Asian English Today. Hong Kong: Hong Kong University Press.

Okamura, J. Y. (1995). The Filipino American Diaspora: Sites of space, time, and ethnicity. In G. Y. Okihiro (Ed), *Privileging positions: The sites of Asian American studies* (pp. 387–400). Pullman, WA: Washington State University Press.

Orbeta, A., & Abrigo, M. (2009). *Philippine international labor migration in the past 30 years: Trends and prospects.* Discussion Paper 2009-33. Manila: Philippine Institute for Development Studies.

Parreñas, R. S. (2000). New household forms, old family values: The formation and reproduction of the Filipino transnational family in Los Angeles. In M. Zhou & J. V. Gatewood (Eds.), *Contemporary Asian America: A multidisciplinary reader* (pp. 157–174). New York, NY: New York University Press.

The Philippines-National Government Portal. (2016). The Philippines. Retrieved from https://www.gov.ph/about-the-philippines

Puyat, J. H. (2010). The Filipino youth today: Their strengths and the challenges they face. In F. Gale & S. Fahey (Eds.), *Youth in transition* (pp. 191–205). Bangkok, Thailand: Regional Unit for Social and Human Sciences in Asia and the Pacific, UNESCO.

Root, M. P. P. (2005). Filipino families. In M. McGoldrick, J. Giordano, & N. Garcia-Preto (Eds.), *Ethnicity and family therapy* (pp. 319–331). New York, NY: Guilford Press.

Schiller, N. G., Basch, L., & Blanc-Szanton, C. (1992). Transnationalism: A new analytic framework for understanding migration. *Annals of the New York Academy of Sciences, 645,* 1–24.

Takaki, R. T. (1998). *Strangers from a different shore: A history of Asian Americans*. Boston, MA: Little Brown.

Tupas, T. R. (2009). Language as a problem development: Ideological debates and comprehensive education in the Philippines. *AILA Review, 22,* 23–35.

Walter, S. L., & Dekker, D. (2008). *The Lubuagan* mother tongue education experiment (FLC)—A report of comparative test results. Report prepared for Committee on Basic Education and Culture, Committee on Higher and Technical Education, House of Representatives. Quezon City, Philippines: SIL International.

Watkins, D., & Gerong, A. (1997). Culture and spontaneous self-concept among Filipino college students. *Journal of Social Psychology, 137*(4), 480–488.

UNESCO Internal Bureau of Education. (2015). *Philippine Education for All 2015: Implementation and challenges*. World Data on Education. Retrieved from http://unesdoc.unesco.org/images/0023/002303/230331e.pdf

Yeo, J. (2013). "I want dual": Transnational identity formation among Filipino ELL immigrant youth. In E. L. Brown & A. Krasteva (Eds.), *Migrants and refugees: Equitable education for displaced populations* (pp. 237–258). Charlotte, NC: Information Age.

SECTION 6

ASIAN REGION

CHAPTER 16

CHINA

Congcong Wang
University of Northern Iowa

Tingting Wang
Princeton University

Before Zhang Xiaohua's family moved to the U.S., Xiaohua finished 4 years of elementary school education in China. Due to differences between the education systems of China and the U.S., since coming to the U.S., Xiaohua has experienced many challenges. For example, Xiaohua prefers numeric test scores, but her U.S. teacher always gives her letter grades. Although her grade is always an "A," she is annoyed by not having proof of her top position in the class. In addition, the teacher always calls her by her surname, "Zhang," instead of by her given name, "Xiaohua," or full name, "Zhang Xiaohua." Therefore, she often fails to respond when being called on.

The teacher has noticed that Xiaohua never hugs her parents or verbally expresses her love to them like most of the other kids do, and the teacher has therefore inferred that there is some problem at home. In the teacher's mind, Xiaohua is a very quiet student; in Xiaohua's, the teacher often fails to meet her needs. To Xiaohua and her parents, the teacher needs to learn about Chinese immigrant/heritage students' home language, culture, and schooling history in order to better implement instruction as well as improve cross-cultural communication with these students and their parents.

Views From Inside: Languages, Cultures, and Schooling for K–12 Educators
pp. 267–288

BACKGROUND

The People's Republic of China (PRC) is located in eastern Asia. Occupying 9.6 million square kilometers (about 5,965,163 square miles) and extending 5,500 kilometers (about 3,418 miles) from north to south and 5,200 kilometers (about 3,231 miles) from west to east, China is the third largest sovereign country in the world by land area. However, even though China is of a similar size to the continental United States, it currently has only one time zone, Beijing Standard Time, and it does not utilize daylight savings time. Since such a vast land crosses different latitudes, its climate and temperatures vary from cold-temperate zones (e.g., Harbin, the capital city of a northeast province, is known for its annual Ice and Snow Sculpture Festival) to tropical and subtropical zones (e.g., Hainan, an island province, is known for its tropical climate, beaches, rainforests, and waterfalls).

As the most populous country in the world, with a population of over 1.35 billion, China is a multiethnic and multilingual country of 56 officially recognized ethnic groups. These include the Han Chinese majority, who constitute 91.51% of the total population, and 55 ethnic minority groups, who account for 8.49% of the total population (National Bureau of Statistics, 2010). China's administrative divisions consist of 22 provinces, 5 autonomous regions, 4 direct-controlled regions, and 2 special administrative regions. Excluding special administrative regions, all other administrative divisions in the PRC can be referred to as "mainland China." Although the PRC claims sovereignty over Taiwan as its 23rd province, for historical reasons Taiwan is not currently under the governance of the central government in the PRC but instead has been ruled as the Republic of China (ROC) since the end of World War II (more details of this issue are discussed in the Taiwan chapter). China is the only country in the world that has adopted two political systems: A socialist system in mainland China and a capitalist system in its two special administrative regions of Hong Kong (a previous colony of Great Britain) and Macau (a previous colony of Portugal).

History

Chinese people appreciate a great deal about their history and it is a part of their daily lives. In fact, some students' families have a very long history and keep good records of their family trees. For example, the family name of Kong is known for Confucius (in the Zhou dynasty) who has many descendants (e.g., 73–75 generations) in the U.S due to persecution in China. They often still go back to Qufu, China, for ancestor worship.

This is a practice unique to the Kong clan and shows the importance of history to Chinese people. For Chinese, history is not only a storybook of the past but also connects to their linguistic and cultural heritage (Wang & Winstead, 2016). History can help to explain our students' language and behavior as well as their pride and sorrows at a deeper level where teacher–student verbal expression may fall short. Through understanding Chinese history, educators can gain insights into students' thinking patterns and social norms as well as learn to appreciate who they are and thus better support their learning.

With over 5,000 years of continuous history, China is one of the oldest civilizations in the world. Human habitation dates back to Paleolithic times (about 1.36 million years ago). Fossil specimens of Homo erectus discovered near Beijing dating to 125,000–80,000 BC show activities of the so-called "Peking Man," who is considered the ancestor of early Chinese people. In addition, evidence of millet agriculture, constructed buildings and villages, pottery, tools, burial of the dead, and the creation of written Chinese language during the Neolithic age indicates the beginning of Chinese civilization tracing back to 5,500 BC. According to ancient historical records (e.g., *Records of the Grand Historian* and Bamboo Annals) and archaeological evidence of an unearthed bronze smelter, the Xia dynasty (around 2100–1600 BC) was the first true dynasty in Chinese history. In the second dynasty (Shang, 1600–1046 BC), inscriptions record ancient Chinese writing on animal bones and shells.

Overrunning the Shang, the Zhou dynasty (1045–256 BC), the longest-lasting dynasty in Chinese history, began its rule with a semi-feudal system. To legitimize his rule, the Zhou king invoked the concept of the "Mandate of Heaven," which states that "the heaven gives the king a mandate to rule only as long as he rules in the interests of the people" (Ebrey, 2006, p. 18); this mandate influenced almost every succeeding dynasty. The spring and autumn period (722–479 BC) witnessed the blossom of influential Chinese philosophies known as the Hundred Schools of Thought (e.g., Confucianism, Taoism, legalism, and monism). In 221 BC, the Qin state's unification of the other six battling states marked the end of the Warring States period (476–221 BC) as well as the beginning of imperial China. Proclaiming himself the First Emperor above all previous kings, Qin Shi Huang (meaning the "First Qin Emperor") established a feudal monarchy with a centralized government that influenced China for the next 2,132 years, unifying language, currency, and measurement. During this period, the Great Wall and the underground Terracotta Army, world famous tourist sites, were constructed.

Soon after the Qin emperor's death, this strongest and largest empire in the world at the time (221–206 BC) collapsed in a peasant uprising. A commoner emperor established the Han Dynasty (202 BC–220 AD) and consolidated a unified central imperial bureaucracy by officially elevating Confucianism to orthodox status; this has had a lasting influence on traditional Chinese culture. During this time, China not only experienced prosperity in art, culture, and science (Eberhard, 2005; Ebrey, 1999), but people's ethnic identities became solidified (Dong, 2014). Dong (2014) notes that "in contrast to the non-Chinese peoples outside the Han Dynasty, the Chinese people considered themselves the Hàn people. Hence one of the names of the Chinese language is *h*ànyǔ, meaning the language of the Han people" (p. 7).

This 400-plus years of stability were broken by political division (200–580 AD) and during this time China was ruled by independent kingdoms founded by non-Han peoples. There was significant cultural exchange, assimilation, and acculturation through centuries of warfare, large-scale Han- Chinese migration, and intermarriage. Some of the non-Han Chinese rulers adopted Han Chinese culture and Confucian ideology and were acculturated over time. For this reason, some of those ancient ethnic groups no longer exist separately among today's officially recognized ethnic groups. Also during this time, Buddhism started to spread throughout China.

The Sui dynasty (589–618 A.D.) reunified China and was soon succeeded by the Tang (618–907). Along with the Han dynasty, the Tang is considered as one of the most brilliant dynasties in Chinese history (Pye & Pye, 1972). During this golden age of Chinese civilization, Chinese art, poetry, and technology reached new heights, and Buddhism became the predominant religion. As the largest city in the world of its time, the national capital Chang'an (modern city Xi'an) was connected by the "Silk Road" to Central Asia and the West for business and cultural communication (Eberhard, 2005). This openness had an influence: "Because of the presence of foreign merchants, many religions were practiced including Nestorian Christianity, Manichaeism, Zoroastrianism, Judaism, and Islam, although none of them spread into the Chinese population the way Buddhism had a few centuries earlier" (Ebrey, 2006, p.91). Through keeping the Silk Road open over land and ocean, extending the border, linking the longest man-made canal (which is still in use) to river systems from north to south, settling foreign traders and merchants (e.g., Turks), developing a civil examination system to select scholar-officials, adopting tolerant domestic policies and reshaping relations with nomadic groups and neighbor countries, and pressing neighboring states into a tributary system, the Tang established a large cosmopolitan empire stretching from the Pacific Ocean to the Aral Sea with over 50 million people. The Tang dynasty is also known for China's only female emperor, Wu Zetian.

During subsequent periods, China experienced deeper cultural exchanges between the Han Chinese and other ethnic groups. Among those dynasties, "Song China (960–1276) was the most advanced society in the world in its day, known for producing the world's first government-issued paper money," and for "the spread of printing and increases in literacy, the growth of cities, the expansion of the examination system, the decline of aristocratic attitudes, and so on" (Ebery, 2006, p. 113). However, these kingdoms were defeated by the Mongols from the north who established the Yuan dynasty (1271–1368) and a large empire across Asia and Europe. Through Western explorers (e.g., Marco Polo) and Mongol warfare, advanced Chinese technologies were introduced to the West. Intensified ethnic conflicts and brutal rule also caused drastic population decreases and greatly threatened Chinese civilization. Less than a century later, the Yuan were overthrown in peasant revolts. A peasant emperor established the Ming dynasty (1368-1644 A.D.) as the last Han Chinese-ruled dynasty. The Ming emperors relocated the capital city from Nanjing to Beijing (the capital city of China today), started constructing the Forbidden City (a famous tourist site), sailed the Indian Ocean and traded with countries in the Arab peninsula and East Africa, defeated the Dutch in Taiwan, and consolidated the Great Wall. During this time, novels started flourishing that have had a large and lasting influence on Chinese literature as well as the entertainment industry in eastern Asian countries today.

Rising from outside the Great Wall, the Manchus founded the Qing dynasty (1644–1911) which was the last imperial dynasty in Chinese history. The Manchus depended on Han Chinese officials and soldiers to help administer their empire, but they perfected ways to ensure that the Manchus would maintain their dominance. For example, they forced the Han Chinese to adopt the Manchu hairstyle and clothing. The Manchu "queue" hairstyle was later abolished during China's revolution, but modified Manchu-style clothing such as the *qipao* (often worn by Chinese female leaders and celebrities at big events), *tangzhuang* (worn by world leaders, including U.S. President Bush and Russian President Putin at the 2010 APEC summit), and *zhongshang zhuang* (often worn by Jackie Chan and Chinese leaders from the 1950s to the 1970s) still symbolize Chinese traditional clothing. Formally adding Xinjiang, Tibet, and Mongolia to its territory and seizing control of Taiwan from the Ming loyalists, the Qing dynasty established a unified multiethnic empire on which today's China is based.

In the 19th century, China faced threats from the West, including the British importation of opium to China, British colonization of Hong Kong, and invasions and treaties that made China into a semi-feudal, semi-colonial country. Peasant uprisings and rebellions (e.g., the Boxer Rebellion) sped up the decline of imperial China. During this time, thousands of years of Chinese civilization faced unprecedented ruination.

These humiliations in relatively recent Chinese history have greatly influenced Chinese people's current views on many world issues.

In 1911, China's revolution overthrew the Qing dynasty, ending over 2,000 years of monarchy. The Republic of China was established in China. Sun Yat-sen, the founder and first elected president, was considered the father of modern China in both mainland China and Taiwan today. This new nationalist government then faced a threat from warlords, imperialism, and a Japanese invasion. In the following decade, China experienced unification by the nationalists. Fighting against feudalism, imperialism, colonialism, and warlords, "intellectuals struggled with how to be strong and modern and yet China" (Ebrey, 2006, p. 244).

From the late 19th century until the end of WWII, Japan became the gravest threat to China's sovereignty and culture. After colonizing Taiwan (1895) and southern Manchuria (1905), Japan soon gained broad economic privileges (1915). After a series of foundational events, Japan launched a full-scale invasion, sweeping south in 1937. In the Nationalist capital, the Japanese army massacred 300,000 civilians and fugitive soldiers and began the Rape of Nanking, a tragedy that many Chinese still cannot speak of today. With biological warfare, Japan adopted the "Kill All, Burn All, and Loot All" policy. Rooted in this historical conflict, Chinese people are still deeply disturbed by Japanese chemical weapons left in China, controversies with how this history is portrayed in Japanese history textbooks, the legacy of comfort women, Japanese worship of war criminals, disputes over ownership of territory, and Japan's remilitarization; these issues can agitate Chinese people and cause anti-Japanese sentiments to arise.

After the Japanese surrender at the end of WWII, the Chinese Civil War (1947–1949) broke out. It resulted in the victory of the Communist Party and the establishment of the People's Republic of China on the mainland. The Nationalist Party and its leader Chiang Kai-shek fled to Taiwan and relocated the government to its new capital city of Taipei. The unification of China and Taiwan is an issue still under political debate. Because many Chinese families were split over the decades of separation and education on historical issues differs between the mainland and Taiwan, many Chinese people find this topic very sensitive and/or find themselves easily offended when this issue comes up. Since the PRC does not recognize Taiwan as a sovereign country and the Taiwan issue is widely considered to be an internal domestic issue in mainland China, embarrassment, silence, tension, or even conflict may occur when this issue arises in front of students from mainland China and Taiwan, especially among newcomers.

From 1949 until today, the PRC has experienced Soviet economic support and split/threat, economic sanctions by the West, the Cold War, normalization of China–U.S. relations (1972), the Cultural Revolution (1966–1976), Deng Xiaoping's economic reforms (1978–1992), the Tiananmen Square incident (1989), joining the World Trade Organization (2001), and hosting the 2008 Beijing Summer Olympics. Under the "One China, Two Systems" policy and due to years of diplomatic effort, the PRC also reclaimed sovereignty over Hong Kong (1997) and Macau (1999).

The success of economic reforms has largely eliminated dire poverty in China, but development between the coastal cities and remote rural areas is very unbalanced. For example, the 9-year compulsory education (6 years of elementary education and 3 years of middle school) has greatly reduced the illiterate population. From 1950 to 2010, the literacy rate among the population over the age of 15 increased from 20% to 94%. However, a big gap in educational quality between rural and urban areas still exists. This difference can be reflected in Chinese immigrant students' varying literacy levels. Although Chinese immigrant students are often stereotyped as "model students" (Derderian-Aghajanian & Wang, 2012; Li, 2001), they are raised in all kinds of different families (e.g., farmers, blue-collar workers at restaurants or factories, intellectuals at universities or research institutions, business investors and managers, etc.), and not all Chinese children have the same educational resources.

In addition, education in ethnic minority areas falls behind the developed eastern areas of the country (Wang & Winstead, 2016). Chinese ethnic minority students may enter bilingual schools or regional schools in which subjects are taught in languages other than Chinese; ethnic minority students enjoy enrollment priority (e.g., lower required admission scores). However, English education in special economic zones and major cities such as Shanghai is far better than inland remote agricultural areas or ethnic minority areas.

Regardless of self-identification, religious background, skin color, or socioeconomic status, Chinese students may enter the U.S. as Chinese citizens or immigrants with Chinese backgrounds. Thus, American teachers should not simply judge students' literacy skills and financial status based on their nationality but learn about and respect their home languages and cultures.

Schooling in China

Despite a common U.S. stereotype of Chinese immigrant/heritage students as model minorities, these students often face linguistic, cultural, and academic challenges in the U.S. (Derderian-Aghajanian & Wang, 2012). This may be, in part, due to differences in schooling contexts.

In China, compulsory education (discussed previously) is applicable to all school-aged children. However, while rich families may afford the higher expense of private schools or good public schools, poor children are more likely to attend public schools funded by the government or "hope schools" that are established to educate rural populations and eliminate illiteracy. Children with disabilities may attend special schools to learn to read and write as well as life skills. Although elementary to middle school education is mandatory, some rural parents prefer to send their sons to school while keeping their daughters home to do farm work. This discriminatory action is illegal.

In China's school system, teachers are recognized as the authority. Since Confucius' time, this tradition has been practiced at all levels. From kindergarten to university, students are educated to respect teachers. Challenging teachers is not accepted. Most commonly, students are expected to fold their arms while seated at their desk. If a student violates classroom order for any reason, the teacher may report that student to the principal and/or the student's parents directly. Often, parents are called to the school and blamed along with the child. Sometimes, the student receives physical punishment from the teacher and/or parents.

High school education is not mandatory; students need to pay for their tuition. Public school education costs significantly less than private school. Usually, the top high schools in each major city are public schools. Competition for entering these schools is very fierce. In a city of 10 million residents, the top few high schools may only admit 2,000 students annually. Sometimes, extra entrance credits may be given to ethnic minority students. Because the one-child policy has just replaced by two-child policy and schools stopped offering extra credits. Ethnic minority students still enjoy varied extra credits.

Scholarships and assistantships are available for top students, and poor children from rural areas may enter top high schools through excellent scores on the standardized high school entrance exam. A small percentage of underqualified students may also enter top schools through their parents' *guanxi* (network, often related to bribing). Rural teenagers or poor children who have less satisfactory test scores may attend technical schools instead, where they will master a skill to become a blue-collar worker such as a welder or a carpenter; some others may enter the labor market and start working as a factory worker, taxi driver, cashier, and so on. Rich urban teenagers who are not admitted to high schools may enroll in private high schools and/or study abroad. Today, with budget issues facing many American schools and the advent of broader U.S.–China economic and cultural exchanges, American schools are more welcoming to urban Chinese teenagers. Misconceptions such as thinking that study abroad should start as early as possible leads many Chinese parents to send young children overseas. These students face many challenges, as do their American teachers.

In cities, high school starts with student self-study time at 7 a.m., followed by four morning classes from 8 a.m. to 12 p.m., a lunch break, four afternoon classes from 1 p.m. to 5 p.m., a dinner break, and finally a 3–4-hour evening self-study time. Students go back home around 9:30 p.m. or 10:00 p.m. and then do homework or have extra study time before bed. It is common that high schools offer courses 6 days a week and students only have Sunday off. Often, parents hire private tutors/teachers to help the children on Sundays. Not entering a top high school often means a student has little hope of entering a good university, so students and their parents work very hard for high exam scores.

In rural areas, boarding schools are common. Some high schoolers gather for morning exercises at 4 a.m., followed by self-study time at 5 a.m. and first classes at 7 a.m. School ends at 10 p.m., and then students and teachers go back to their dorms. It is not uncommon that teachers and students both live on campus and are only allowed to go back home once a month. Further teachers' salaries are often directly linked to students' test scores. To ensure fairness and eliminate cheating, exams are highly monitored by teachers as well as cameras installed in each classroom.

U.S. high schools are considered easier than those in China, but academic rigor is much more valued in U.S. universities. In China, to enter a university through diligent study and intensive exams is much more difficult than to earn a college degree, which only requires completing required courses with a passing grade. Unlike the last generation who studied hard and strived to earn a degree, many of the younger generation do not cherish the opportunities for higher education.

CULTURE

China is surrounded by mountains in the northeast, the Gobi and Qinhai-Tibet plateaus in the west, and the Pacific Ocean in the east. The monsoon (May to October) brings heavy rainfall and seasonal flooding, which often reshapes the landscape. Such seasonal climate changes contributed to the early agricultural civilization of the Yellow River Valley and the Yangtze River Valley. This agricultural civilization played a crucial role in the formation of Chinese culture (Yong, Wang, & Wang, 2006). For example, agricultural production required concentrated settlement, which influenced the Chinese language. The modern Chinese character "年" depicts an image of a man carrying crops on his back. This symbol represents a good harvest, which in ancient times contained an auspicious meaning for the new year. Differences in climates across the country are the basis for many other aspects of Chinese culture presented in this section.

People

The words for Chinese peoples (中国人, or *zhong guo ren*) literally refers to "people of the Middle Kingdom" rather than the narrower English translation "Han Chinese." Likewise, the term "Chinese people" refers to a very diverse population of descendants of all of the peoples of China (Wang & Winstead, 2016).

In history, many well-known Chinese people have made notable contributions to the world. For example, Confucius (551–479 B.C.) was an educator, thinker and the founder of Confucianism. According to Ebrey (2006), "Confucius's ideas are known to us primarily through the sayings recorded by his disciples in the *Analects*. The thrust of his thought was ethical rather than theoretical or metaphysical" (p. 30). He adds, "Confucius talked mostly about the social and political realms rather than the world of gods, ghosts, or ancestral spirits" (p. 31). Among many Confucian virtues, *ren* (indicating humanity, perfect goodness, benevolence, human-heartedness, and nobility) is the ultimate virtue, because, as Ebrey notes, "A person of humanity cares about others and acts accordingly" (p. 31). Other virtues include *li* (propriety, ritual decorum), *xiao* (filial piety), *yi* (integrity, righteousness), *zhong* (loyalty, constancy), *xin* (honesty), and *jing* (reverence, respect). In *The Analects of Confucius*, Confucius said to all Chinese people,

> When you go out, treat everyone as if you were welcoming a great guest. Employ people as though you were conducting a great sacrifice. Do not do unto others what you would not have them do unto you. Then neither in your country nor in your family will there be complaints against you. (Ebrey, 2006, p. 30)

Over 2,000 years, Confucianism has had a profound impact on the nature of Chinese government, education, and personal behavior within Chinese society (Ostrowski & Penner, 2009). It has also influenced many other eastern Asian countries (e.g., Korea and Japan). Confucian thought on "a hierarchical approach to social organization, a heavy emphasis on scholarship, and a focus as the primary unit of social organization" continues to exert influence in Chinese society (Ostrowski & Penner, 2009, p. 24).

Tang Taizong (598–649 A.D.), also known as Li Shimin, was one of the greatest emperors in Chinese history. Li Shimin's "Reign of Zhenghuan" set an exemplary model for other emperors in many aspects. Tang China was the largest and the strongest nation in the world and his rule brought lasting peace and prosperity. He was known for appreciating knowledge, selecting wise advisers, and achieving greatness through enduring criticism. Tang China, by its culture, legal code, language, religion, architecture, and so on has had a lasting impact on neighboring countries, including Vietnam, Korea, and Japan.

Lu Xun (1881–1936) was the greatest writer in modern Chinese literature and a leading writer in the New Culture Movement. After witnessing a Chinese person being executed by the Japanese, he "concluded that it was more important to change the spirit of the Chinese than protect their bodies" (Ebrey, 2016, p. 240). He quit medical study in Japan and returned to China to devote his life to awakening Chinese people through writing. His major works are the vernacular short stories *Diary of a Madman* (1918), *The True Story of Ah Q*, and two short story collections, *Nahan* (*A Call to Arms* or *Outcry*) and *Panghuang* (*Wandering*).

Sun Yat-sen (1866–1925) was the founder of the Republic of China. He studied Western medicine overseas, but he devoted his life to China's revolution. The 1911 revolution overthrew the Qing dynasty, ending over 2,000 years of monarchy. Sun worked out the theory of the Three People's Principles: nationalism, democracy, and the people's livelihood.

Chinese Traditional Values

Although there are always exceptions, in general Chinese people have the following traditional values:

- Harmony: Chinese people value the harmonious relationship between human and nature, which is also an essential part of traditional Chinese ideology. To reach a harmonious relationship, Chinese people are supposed to emphasize moral cultivation, temper refinement, and spiritual enlightenment. The Master said, "The gentleman agrees with others without being an echo. The small man echoes without being in agreement" (*The Analects of Confucius*, Ebrey, 2006, p. 31).

- Filial virtue: Chinese people consider respecting and taking care of aged people as a social obligation. They believe that good people are filial to their parents.

- To respect the aged and love the young: Respecting the aged and loving the young are Chinese traditional virtues, and people who ignore these tenets will be criticized by the public.

- Integrity and credit. Although not all students appreciate it today, traditionally Chinese people value the quality of keeping one's word and never cheating others. "When you know a thing, to hold that you know it; and when you do not know a thing, to allow that you do not know it" (*The Analects of Confucius* (知之为知之，不知为不知，是知也).
- To respect teachers and value education. Chinese people pay much attention to education, and respecting the teacher is a traditional Chinese value. The position of education is very high in Chinese people's minds; there is an old saying that to be a scholar is to be the top of society. Therefore, the status of teachers is high in China, and there is another old saying that "a teacher for a day is a father for a lifetime." In Chinese history, the position of the teacher was honored by both the masses and the emperor.

Chinese Foods

In China's vast landscapes and varied climates, diverse cultures began to gestate, exchange, merge, and develop over history. From the southeastern coast to inland northwestern parts of the country, the yearly amount of rainfall gradually decreases. Such differences make for different types of agriculture and thereby support different regional cuisines. Eight distinctive regional cuisines (Shandong, Guangdong, Sichuan, Hunan, Jiangsu, Zhejiang, Fujian, and Anhui cuisines) originated within Han Chinese populated areas, as well as several ethnic minority cuisines such as Hui cuisine, representing Chinese Muslim food without pork, and Tibetan cuisine, known for *zanba* (barley dough with yak butter) and milk products. Due to different agricultural products, in northern China wheat is the main ingredient in staple foods such as noodles, dumplings, and *baozi* (a filled bun); however, rice is widely used in southern cuisines. Seafood is common in coastal areas, while river fish are favored in the areas along the Yangtze River. In the nomad groups populating areas where lands are less suitable for agriculture, daily foods are milk and meat. Some Chinese people who rely on rice may suffer a stomach ache after drinking milk due to the lack of an enzyme needed for digestion, while descendants of nomadic groups might be more used to dairy products.

Unacceptable Behaviors in China

According to Ostrowski and Penner (2009), Chinese people may find it uncomfortable or rude to:

- Kiss and hug someone in public as a greeting. Chinese usually feel uncomfortable showing emotion (e.g., hugging) in front of others. Chinese tend to express their emotions in an indirect way, even between parents and children. For example, the Chinese way of expressing love is often through specific actions such as studying hard, fixing dinner, cleaning the dishes, or taking care of someone when they are sick. It is very unusual to see Chinese children hug or kiss their parents in public or say "I love you" in front of others.

- Address someone directly by their first name, especially in a formal setting or when it is a respected person of higher status (e.g., teacher, boss, senior citizen). For example, an American professor (e.g., Dr. John Smith) may prefer to be called "John," while some Chinese students and their parents may feel hesitant to address him so and are more likely to address him as "Smith Teacher." In China, the polite way to refer to others is to address people by their last name and "Mr."/"Ms." or last name and a professional title (e.g., professor, teacher, doctor, director). Modern Chinese names consist of a surname followed by a given name. For example, following Zhang Xiaohua's last name, "Zhang," is her given name, "Xiaohua."

- Pointing at others in a conversation. It is politer to use the person's name to get their attention during the conversation or use your hand with your fingers closed instead of pointing at someone with one finger.

- Complain.

- Eat or drink while the teacher is lecturing.

- Leave the classroom without requesting permission from the teacher.

- Express opinions by speaking out loudly in class without raising a hand.

- Use one hand to give a gift or business card. Especially in formal occasions or at a first meeting, Chinese use both hands to deliver and receive a business card. It is appropriate to bow slightly or lower your head while saying "Thank you," as well.

- Make direct eye contact in a conversation or stare at someone's eyes while talking. Often, direct eye contact means questioning, suspecting, or expressing anger. This can make the Chinese speaker uncomfortable and even nervous during a conversation.

- Accept a compliment with "Thank you" instead of denying it; it is the Chinese way to show humbleness.

- Pour your own drinks when being treated in a restaurant or someone's home. Unless the host invites you to "help yourself," as a guest you should wait for the host to pour drinks and put food on your plate. In China, having guests treat themselves means that the host failed to treat the guest properly and thus the host loses face. Chinese hosts feel most honored when they treat each guest with more food than the guest needs and takes care of each guest. Thus, a potluck in which guests bring food, joining and leaving at any time and serving themselves, is not common in China.
- Embarrass the teacher by challenging his/her authority in class. This includes asking questions or making a statement that contradicts the teacher.
- Decline a student and/or a parent's request to know the student's test score. In the U.S., especially in college, test scores are often considered as private information that may not be disclosed to a student's parents without the student's consent. In China, it is common that students' exact test scores and rankings are announced in class after an exam or disclosed at parent meetings. To many Chinese parents, a strict teacher who regularly reports the student's performance to his/her parents is considered to be responsible. U.S. teachers may need to specifically address this difference with the parents and student, explaining the reasoning and the legal repercussions.

Important Days and Holidays

Teachers should be aware of Chinese holidays in case they need to support their Chinese students in meeting the requirements of these celebrations and in order to share them with the class.

The Chinese New Year, also known as the Spring Festival, is the most important holiday in China (equivalent to Christmas in the U.S.). The beginning date of this holiday on the solar calendar varies each year; it is usually in January or February. During this holiday, Chinese people put money into red envelopes and give them to children. People wear red clothes representing happiness, eat New Year cakes made of glutinous rice flour, set off fireworks, and visit friends and relatives. In the northern part of China, the whole family gets together and makes dumplings. The Spring Festival is a national vacation and thus schools and universities have their winter break. Other holidays include Mid-Autumn Day, the Dragon Boat Festival, Qing Ming, and National Day. Information on these important days can be found throughout the Internet.

Religion

In contemporary China, major religions include Buddhism, Christianity, Islam, Daoism, and Catholicism. Except for Daoism, these religions were introduced to China during different historical periods and influenced China to various degrees. Daoism, "one of the foremost religions in Chinese society, was originally a philosophy with its roots in nature worship" (Ostrowski & Penner, 2009, p. 21). According to China's constitution (1982), Chinese citizens enjoy religious freedom, but foreign citizens are currently not allowed to recruit Chinese citizens to practice a foreign religion in mainland China (although conversion between people of the same nationality is possible). Due to the influence of traditional philosophies and later the spread of Marxism during the Chinese revolution, most Chinese people are nonreligious or identify themselves as atheists.

Chinese Inventions

Chinese people are proud of the Four Great Inventions that symbolize the scientific and technological advances of ancient China: papermaking, invented by Cai Lun in 105 AD in the Han Dynasty; the magnetic compass, invented in the Han Dynasty around 206 BC and adapted for navigation in the Song Dynasty, 1040–1044 AD; gunpowder, discovered by Chinese alchemists in the 9th century; and printing (the Tang Dynasty).

In addition to many other feats, the Chinese developed techniques for casting iron and making steel during the Shang dynasty. In engineering, the Chinese developed flood control and irrigation systems along the Yellow River as early as 2000 BC, and by the 6th century had constructed the 1,200-mile Grand Canal, computed the ancient world's most accurate value for *pi*, used negative numbers 1,000 years before the Europeans, and discovered the algebraic triangular pattern for coefficients about 500 years before it was named by Pascal in Europe.

Chinese medicine is well known around the world. In addition to advances in acupuncture and natural cures, "anesthetics in surgery and acupuncture have been practiced in China for two millennia. China's first medical college was established 1,000 years ago, and over the centuries the empire's medical practitioners developed many useful drugs for various maladies" (Grasso, Corrin, & Kort, 2009, pp. 4–5).

There are many other inventions and achievements (e.g., *cuju*—ancient football, and noodles and pizza, which were introduced to Italy) that reflect the glory of Chinese civilization and were developed centuries before they were known in Europe. The advances of ancient Chinese technology can be a source of cultural pride for Chinese students.

LANGUAGES AND LITERACIES

Unlike other early Western Eurasian writing systems that were gradually replaced by phonetic scripts, China retains a logographic writing system. Such a writing system enables Chinese readers "to communicate with a wider range of people than those who read scripts based on speech" (Ebrey, 2006, p. 14). This system also benefits educated Chinese who want to read texts written centuries ago without translation.

Chinese is very different from English, and Chinese language speakers may face a number of challenges in learning English. Simplified Chinese characters and Mandarin are used as the official written and spoken language across almost all administrative divisions in mainland China (however, traditional characters are still used in Hong Kong and Taiwan) (Wang & Winstead, 2016). People in different areas speak their own languages and dialects, too (e.g., the Tibetan language in Tibet and the Cantonese dialect in Guangdong). Often, people a 30-minute drive in geographic distance from each other may experience communication barriers due to distinctive dialects; for example, when traveling to each other's homes, a Mandarin speaker and Cantonese speaker may find themselves unable to communicate.

To overcome this communication challenge, the central government promotes Modern Standard Chinese (based on the Mandarin dialect spoken in Beijing) as an official, common spoken language in mainland China (Dong, 2014). It shares the same origin with the national language in Taiwan, but is very different from the Cantonese or Taiwanese dialects. A common misconception Westerners have is that all Chinese people speak Chinese. Teachers need to be aware that a student from China may not always speak fluent Mandarin Chinese despite Mandarin's status as China's official language.

Written Chinese

The written form of Chinese consists of characters known as "*han zi*," which is one of the oldest continuously used writing systems in the world (William & Li, 1999). Although there are tens of thousands of different characters, to be considered as functionally literate, people only need to master three to four thousand (Ye, 2011).

The Koreans and Japanese also adopted the written form of the Chinese language beginning in the 6th century (Okimori, 2014); some ancient Chinese characters actively used in Japan are no longer in use in mainland China. American teachers should be careful when asking a Chinese-born student, "Do you know this Chinese character?" It could embarrass the student if it is a foreign or unfamiliar form.

Spoken Chinese

Mandarin Chinese is a tonal language in which each character is pronounced with one of the following tones: a rising tone, a falling tone, a high flat tone, a rising-falling tone, and a silent tone (Everson, 1994). It is important that teachers become aware of Pinyin (the Chinese phonemic alphabet), which is used to spell out the sound of Chinese characters, input Chinese characters through an English keyboard, and transcribe Chinese names. Since in pronunciation each Chinese character consists of at most one initial sound (which can be understood as a consonant) and one single or compound sound (which can be interpreted as a vowel), each character is equally and clearly pronounced. Comparatively, spoken English sentences may sound very blurry to Chinese speakers. Therefore, Chinese speakers may find it difficult learning to speak multisyllabic English words as well as stress and the uneven flow from one word to another.

Mandarin Chinese also has a moderately high ratio of morphemes per word (Ye, 2011). Many words in Chinese are comprised of two or more characters (compound words). For example, the word *yī yuè* is a compound word made up of two characters: *yī* (one) + *yuè* (month), which together make the compound word that means January. Since much of the Chinese language follows that same logic, speakers can predict the spelling of February by following the same pattern: number + month. Likewise, counting from 1 to 100 in Chinese is based on the characters 1 to 10. Comparatively, the months and numbers 1 to 100 in English are much more complicated than in Chinese.

Uninflected Language

Chinese has almost no inflectional affixes (plurals, "ed" for past tense, and so on) at all to convey grammatical relationships. For example, *sān tian*, or "three days," can be translated literally as "three day." Rather, Chinese conveys meaning through word order, adverbials, or shared understanding of the context (Wen, 1997). In other words, the concept of time in Chinese is not expressed through the use of different tenses and verb forms but through the use of adverbials and context. Some common mistakes Chinese students make in learning English include misuse of singular/plural forms and tenses such as past tense; a native Chinese speaker might say in English. "Yesterday, I have three class," because this sentence translated word by word in Chinese would be correct.

Cultural Connotations in Chinese

Besides being familiar with its linguistic characteristics, to better understand Chinese language speakers, teachers can become aware of the cultural connotations that are reflected in this language. In other words, like in other languages, some words and phrases have idiomatic meanings based on national customs and other cultural norms. For example, in explaining the term 白事 (white affairs), speakers must know that white is commonly used as the background in funerals according to Chinese culture: the dead were dressed in white clothes, and funerals were decorated with white as the central color. Therefore, the term "white affairs" is another expression for "funeral affairs." However, in other cultures white may symbolize purity and charity and be in line with wedding customs. In this case, if such differences were not conveyed to Chinese speakers, they may wrongly associate white with death instead of weddings.

Because of linguistic and cultural differences, Chinese-speaking English-language students may experience difficulty with the following:

- Multisyllabic words while listening to English.
- English clauses, tenses, and plural and singular forms, since Chinese grammar is simpler than English in these aspects.
- Vocabulary and spelling, such as irregular spellings and borrowed words, Latin roots, and slang and abbreviations.
- In reading, the uneven length of English words. Each Chinese character takes the same amount of space without space between the characters; due to this difference, Chinese students may take longer to read English texts and take longer to adjust to the difference.
- In Mandarin Chinese, each character is associated with a standard pronunciation. In English, a borrowed word (e.g., French words and German words) may reflect its pronunciation in the original language.
- Functional words (e.g., in, at, of) and the usage of "the" in English can be very challenging to Mandarin speakers because they do not exist in Mandarin.

IDEAS FOR TEACHERS

Based on the discussion above, to teach and help Chinese students, American teachers might want to pay attention to:

- The interpretation of Chinese names. To avoid unnecessary confusion and problems in helping Chinese students register for classes and in addressing a Chinese person appropriately in conversation, American teachers can study the correct formation and use of Chinese names, as described earlier. Another solution is to ask specifically about the child's name, including the pronunciation.

- Being quiet. For Chinese students, asking a teacher questions that the teacher is unable to answer makes the teacher lose face (Ostrowski & Penner, 2009). A Chinese student hesitating to speak up or to take risks expressing opinions during a class discussion probably implies obedience and respect for a teacher. To help this student adjust to the new classroom environment, American teachers may introduce American school culture to the student and his/her parents directly and openly. Given that a Chinese student may feel uncomfortable interrupting the teacher by asking for what he/she needs, the teacher may ask this student about his/her needs in a positive way.

- Strict classroom order. In mainland China, classroom management is stricter than that in the U.S. Because of this, sometimes an accident may happen, for example, if a child feels embarrassed to tell the teacher that he/she needs to use the restroom during class time; he/she may also not understand that is it permissible to use the restroom. It is especially difficult for newcomers who are used to China's classroom environment but are unfamiliar with the new environment or know too little about the language to ask for help. Therefore, it is crucial for American teachers to teach how to say "I need to use the restroom" or to provide photos or other pictures to point to on the first day of class, show the children where the restroom is, and inform the children and their parents the procedure for the children to use the restroom in the middle of class.

- Eating habits. Many Chinese children will not be used to the cold water from the water fountain or uncooked foods, such as vegetable salads, served in the school cafeteria; Chinese children may have grown up with very different styles of home cooking. In China, water is often boiled to disinfect it and then it is cooled down before being served. It is also very common to serve warm water in public or at home in China instead of ice water. Uncooked vegetables are not usually treated as a main dish, but as appetizers instead. In addition, not all Chinese children are able to digest milk and may suffer a stomach ache after drinking it. In America, Asian stores are often favored by Chinese immigrants because they can find ingredients they need for cooking Chinese dishes. Therefore, after noticing a Chinese child who does not eat the food served in the lunchroom, the teacher may ask the child about what kind of food might be better. The teacher may also contact the student's parents about what he/she eats at home.

CONCLUSIONS

This chapter provides a global picture of major aspects of Chinese schooling, culture, and language. Starting with a historical review of Chinese civilization, it shares insights of how China's past shaped what it is today and gives teachers advice on improving communication with students of Chinese backgrounds. However, China is such an ancient and expansive country that it cannot be fully captured in any one text; this presents an excellent opportunity, then, for teachers and students to explore further this complex and ever-changing society.

ADDITIONAL RESOURCES

BBC Languages Chinese. (2016, October 31). Retrieved from http://www.bbc.co.uk/languages/chinese/
    Videos for Chinese beginning learners.
CCTV Learn Chinese. (2016, October 31). Retrieved from http://english.cntv.cn/learnchinese/
    Videos addressing a variety of themes for different learning levels.
China.org. (2016, October 31). Retrieved from http://www.china.org.cn/learning
    Chinese pictures and videos for Chinese culture and language.
Confucius Institute Online. (2016, October 31). Retrieved from http://www.chinesecio.com/
    Resources for both Chinese teaching and learning. Users can also join in discussions and make language friends.
CRI English. (2016, October 31). Retrieved from http://english.cri.cn/08chinese/
    Introductions for Chinese popular culture.
Digital Dialects. (2016, October 31). Retrieved from http://www.digitaldialects.com/Chinese.htm
    Games for Chinese vocabulary learning.
Sapore di China. (2016, October 31). Retrieved from http://www.sapore-dicina.com/english/learn-chinese-online-25-excellent-free-resources/
    A summary of websites and software for Chinese learning.
Study More Chinese. (2016, October 31). Retrieved from http://studymorechinese.com/
    A Chinese learning community, people can participate in discussion and upload videos and pictures.
Yellow Bridge. (2016, October 31). Retrieved from http://www.yellowbridge.com/
    A resource to learn Chinese.

TASKS FOR EDUCATORS

1. Answer the following questions:
   o What might Chinese history, linguistic and cultural diversity, and education mean for Chinese students coming into U.S. schools? How might the complex and rich Chinese culture shape students' identities, views, behaviors, language, and school performance? What should teachers consider?
   o How do the educators', philosophers', and revolutionaries' sayings in this chapter compare with your understanding of traditional and modern Chinese values? Why might your understandings be different from those of the Chinese authors of this chapter? How do they compare to U.S. values?
   o Some of the values listed above conflict with U.S. school values. What might this mean for Chinese students in your classroom? How might you address differences in accepted behaviors in your classroom?

2. Based on the information in the chapter, about what do you need more information concerning Chinese students from different areas in China? List three places you might find this information.

3. What are your perceptions of Chinese language and culture before and after reading this chapter?

4. What similarities between China and your country have you found in terms of diversity? How might you design an activity to engage not only Chinese-speaking students but also all of your students?

REFERENCES

Derderian-Aghajanian, A., & Wang, C. C. (2012). How culture affects on English language learners' (ELL's) outcomes, with Chinese and Middle Eastern immigrant students. *International Journal of Business and Social Science, 3*(5), 172–180.

Dong, H. (2014). *A history of the Chinese language.* New York, NY: Routledge.

Eberhard, W. (2005). *A history of China.* New York, NY: Routledge.

Ebrey, P. B. (1999). *The Cambridge illustrated history of China.* Cambridge, UK: Cambridge University Press.

Ebrey, P. B. (2006). *China: A cultural, social, and political history.* Boston, MA: Wadsworth Cengage Learning.

Everson, M. E. (1994). Toward a process view of teaching reading in the second language Chinese curriculum. *Theory into Practice, 33*(1), 4–9.

Grasso, J., Corrin, J., & Kort, M. (2009). *Modernization and revolution in China.* New York, NY: M.E. Sharpe.

Li, G. (2001). Literacy as situated practice. *Canadian Journal of Education, 26*(1), 57–75. doi:0100104009004

National Bureau of Statistics. (2010). *Population census of the People's Republic of China*. Beijing, China: China Statistics Press.

Okimori, T. (2014). Korean and Japanese as Chinese-characters cultural spheres. *Acta Linguistica Asiatica, 4*(3), 43–70.

Ostrowski, P., & Penner, G. (2009). *It's all Chinese to me: An overview of culture & etiquette in China*. Hong Kong: Tuttle Publishing.

Pye, L. W., & Pye, M. W. (1972). *China: An introduction*. Boston, MA: Little, Brown.

Wang, C. & Wintead, L. (2016). *Handbook of research on foreign language education in the digital age*. Hershey. PA: IGI Global.

Wen, X. (1997). Motivation and language learning with students of Chinese. *Foreign Language Annals, 30*(2), 235–251.

William, M. & Li, Y. (1999). *Reading and writing Chinese*. North Clarendon, VT: Tuttle Publishing.

Ye, L. (2011). *Teaching and learning Chinese as a foreign language in the United States: To delay or not to delay the character introduction*. Manuscript submitted for publication.

Yong, M., Wang, K., & Wang, H. (2006). *Chinese culture: An introduction*. Beijing, China: Higher Education Press.

CHAPTER 17

TAIWAN FOR TEACHERS

David Herman and Aichia Chang
Washington State University

Kai-Wei Chang arrived in Ms. Johnson's sixth-grade class at the beginning of the school year, six months ago. Kai-Wei moved to the U.S. from Taiwan over the summer with his mother, who is enrolled in a master's degree program at the local university. Kai-Wei's father has remained in Taiwan and is supporting the two during their time in the U.S. Kai-Wei and his mother plan to stay in the U.S. through the completion of her master's degree program and likely through the completion of a doctoral program as well. It is Kai-Wei's mother's hope that Kai-Wei will eventually enter a university program in the U.S.

In Taiwan, English classes are a mandated part of the curriculum starting in the third year of public school. However, Kai-Wei's parents began introducing him to the language at a much earlier age through CDs, DVDs, and a preschool with English-speaking teachers. Despite this background in the language, however, Kai-Wei is not very confident in his English abilities. He remains quiet for most of the day in Ms. Johnson's class and tends to prefer activities that require reading and writing to those that require speaking and listening.

Despite his shyness during class, Ms. Johnson has found Kai-Wei to be quite grade-driven and competitive. She has noticed that he gets visibly frustrated when he receives low scores on assessments and tends to look for the scores on the papers of his peers in order to compare. Kai-Wei performs well on tasks that require rote memorization and direct answers but struggles with abstract and critical thinking as well as problem solving. He also struggles with peer collaboration. When put in

Views From Inside: Languages, Cultures, and Schooling for K–12 Educators
pp. 289–304

a collaborative group, Kai-Wei tends to sit quietly or do the work himself. He rarely shares his thoughts or opinions with the class during whole-class discussion and never volunteers to participate. If he has a question, he will ask the teacher individually after class. All of this, paired with his unwillingness to speak up during class, has created some challenges for him in developing friendships in the class. Kai-Wei recently got into an argument with another Chinese speaker at school, Xuan Xuan, who insisted that Kai-Wei is Chinese, not Taiwanese. Ms. Johnson did not know what this meant so she simply told Kai-Wei that he could identify however he pleased.

Kai-Wei's parents, both of whom are professionals with a fairly good command of English, are very invested in their child's education; his mother has even hired a student from the university to tutor Kai-Wei after school and on weekends. Kai-Wei's mother has expressed how important it is for her son to receive good grades and to be competitive with his American peers. Unfortunately, Kai-Wei's mother and Ms. Johnson have had some disagreements with regard to Kai-Wei's schooling. Ms. Johnson and the district's ELL specialist feel that Kai-Wei would benefit from the school's special pullout instruction program for English language learners, a program in which students are removed from the classroom three times a week to receive specialized English language instruction. Kai-Wei's mother, however, believes that total sink-or-swim immersion with American peers is the best method for the linguistic and cultural development of her son and does not want him separated from his native-English-speaking peers. His mother has also said that she feels her son is not being challenged enough at school. She regularly requests Ms. Johnson to send home extra homework that Kai-Wei can work on with his tutor. She also requests to see all of Kai-Wei's test scores, often inquiring about how well the rest of the class has scored in comparison. She maintains regular communication with Ms. Johnson.

This year is the first year Ms. Johnson has ever worked with a child from Taiwan. She has worked to make Kai-Wei feel welcome but is unsure how to accommodate his needs. She is still embarrassed by the realization that she had been telling people he was from Thailand. She was also confused by an incident where the parent of a Chinese student at her school informed her that Taiwan is a province of China, but when she referred to Taiwan as being Chinese to Kai-Wei's mother, she seemed to be offended and quickly corrected her, telling her that Taiwan is an independent nation. She is now not sure what to think. Ms. Johnson also struggles when addressing Kai-Wei. He does not have an English name and does not seem interested in being given one. Ms. Johnson struggles to correctly pronounce the name "Kai-Wei" and worries that she is calling on him less than others partially to avoid mispronouncing his name. She also faces challenges in helping him with his English pronunciation and syntax.

Overall, Ms. Johnson is struggling to connect with Kai-Wei. She prides herself on building positive relationships with her students, but she is having trouble understanding this student. She is wondering how many of these struggles are a direct result of cultural differences and how many are due simply to personality differences.

BACKGROUND

Kai-Wei was born on the subtropical island of Taiwan. This sweet-potato-shaped island is roughly the size of the U.S. state of Maryland, nearly 14,000 square miles, and is located off the eastern coast of China. Despite Taiwan's small size, it is densely populated, housing roughly 23 million residents. Taiwan is home to a highly developed economy, thanks in part to a thriving technology industry. As a result, Taiwan has been designated as one of the "Four Asian Tigers," alongside Hong Kong, Singapore, and South Korea; this term is used to refer to the highly free-market and developed economies in the region (Bruno, 2014). Taiwan is also the ancestral home of more than 500,000 Taiwanese Americans living in the U.S. (Lowther, 2016).

Taiwan has a history of political unrest, which continues today. Previously under the rule of China's Qing Dynasty and viewed as part of the mainland's Fujian province, Taiwan was overtaken by the Japanese military in 1895 during their strategic expansion across Asia and the Pacific. The Occupation lasted 50 years, during which time the Japanese developed and modernized the island by building schools, hospitals, railway systems, roads, tunnels, and other infrastructure (Zhang, 2003). This period had a sizable impact on the culture of the island, and Japanese influence can still be observed today.

At the end of World War II in 1945, the Japanese were forced to relinquish all seized lands outside of their territory. Taiwan was given to the then-ruling government of China led by Chiang Kai-Shek. This rule was short-lived, however, as a civil war led by Mao Ze-Dong and the Communist Party ended with Chiang and his supporters fleeing the mainland into exile in Taiwan. Chiang's group had originally planned to fight to retake control of the mainland, but these plans were later abandoned in favor of establishing Taiwan as an independent and democratic island nation, the Republic of China (ROC).

Taiwan's wish for independence has yet to be granted, however, as mainland China, also known as the People's Republic of China (PRC), views Taiwan as a "renegade province" destined for reunification with the mainland (Roberge & Lee, 2009). The Chinese government has threatened to wage war with Taiwan if its government declares official independence. The United Nations also does not recognize the ROC as being a legitimate government, instead recognizing the PRC as the government of China including Hong Kong, Macau, and Taiwan. As a result, there remains some animosity between the people of mainland China, many of whom seek reunification, and the people of Taiwan, many of whom seek independence. In 2016, the people of Taiwan democratically elected their first female president, Tsai Ying Wen, a politician interested in maintaining the status quo—avoiding reunification with China but without seeking formal independence (Taiwan Today, 2016).

Taiwan's political climate is important for American teachers to be aware of when teaching about or referring to China or Taiwan. Many young Taiwanese have been raised to believe that Taiwan is, or at least should be, an independent nation, free from Chinese rule. This has become a large part of Taiwanese youth's identities. Likewise, mainland Chinese have been raised to view Taiwan as being a part of China, with Taiwan's unofficial status being seen as a national embarrassment. These differences in perspective can lead to uncomfortable and sometimes heated confrontations when discussing the region. Although Taiwan is not officially a country, students from Taiwan tend to prefer to be called Taiwanese rather than Chinese. This can sometimes result in correction from Chinese classmates with responses such as, "She is Chinese. Taiwan is part of China." This tends to be more of an issue with older students or with the parents of younger students than of young children themselves.

There is currently no solution to the question of Taiwan's independence, and it may be best if teachers do not take sides. Teachers should respect that the side of the Taiwan Strait (the strait dividing Taiwan and China) one was born on likely determines how one was educated to view Taiwan's independence, and although a student or parent may look for Americans to support their cause, taking a stance may only cause problems. However, calling Taiwan by its name is no problem as it does not speak directly to governmental allegiance.

SCHOOLING

Despite many Taiwanese political views of mainland China, China holds the basis of Taiwanese culture. Taiwan's dominant traditions, religions, languages, and philosophical influences all originated in mainland China. In school, Taiwanese students learn Chinese history, philosophy, literature, and arts, and many cultural practices stem from Confucianism, Buddhism, Taoism, and the lunar calendar, all of which were brought over or adopted from China.

Taiwan's school system is a mix of Chinese, Japanese, and American educational practices. Taiwan's current educational system is made up of six years of elementary school, three years of junior high school, three years of high school, and four years of university. Currently, the first nine years of schooling are compulsory.

Taiwan's students rank as some of the highest performing in the world in terms of international test scores, particularly in reading and math (Coughlan, 2015). Taiwan also boasts a literacy rate of 98% (Kuo, 2011). The education system does receive criticism, however, for the amount of pressure put on students and an emphasis on high-stakes exams that often test rote memorization skills rather than problem-solving and critical-thinking skills. Many classrooms are teacher-centered and driven by the textbook, and many Taiwanese teachers are unwilling to stray or supplement textbook lessons. Classwork is typically done by students individually, and the learning environment can be quite competitive.

Much of the competition in Taiwanese education comes from the expectations of Taiwanese parents. Taiwanese parents tend to place strong emphasis on their children's educational success, especially the success of their sons. Parents often invest a great deal of time and energy into helping their children receive advantages in and outside of the classroom and helping them stand out among their peers.

One advantage many students participate in is *buxiban*, or cram school. Cram schools are attended by students in the evenings and on weekends and provide an opportunity for students to support and continue their learning outside the classroom. Cram schools are offered to all levels of students and typically focus on math, science, English, and the performing arts, skills needed to test into good high schools and universities. Cram schools differ in their level of support, and this difference is often determined by cost. Students may spend their time at cram school working on homework assigned by their school teacher, being introduced to next week's math lesson using their school textbook, preparing for an upcoming midterm exam, or working on a specific skill in music or art. Many students attend cram school immediately after regular school hours, studying anywhere from 6 p.m. to as late as 9 or 10 p.m. The more students attend cram schools, however, the more pressure is put on their classmates to attend cram schools as well to avoid being left behind. This especially puts low-income households at a real disadvantage, as they may not be able to afford the additional tuition costs. Cram schools have also strengthened the focus on academic performance and test scores over extracurricular activities and personal interests.

In the past, class sizes in Taiwanese public schools were large, upwards of 60 students per class. Due to a steeply declining population, however, most classrooms today do not exceed 30 students. The decline in student numbers is so dramatic that each year more and more schools are forced to close due to low student enrollment. Many schools, especially in rural areas, have annual enrollments of fewer than 100 students. Statistically,

Taiwanese women are choosing to have children later in life, to not have children at all, or to have children abroad. Many claim the reason for this phenomenon to be a combination of a steep rise in the cost of living, avoidance of bringing children into a society that puts such high social pressure on student success, and an increase in education and career aspirations among Taiwanese women. As a result of this trend, more and more Taiwanese men, particularly in more rural parts of Taiwan, are seeking wives from mainland China and southeastern Asian countries such as Vietnam, Thailand, and Indonesia.

Having an understanding of traditional educational practices in Taiwan can be beneficial for American teachers, as the transition from Taiwanese schools to American schools can sometimes be challenging for both students and teachers. Because of the strong reputation of many American universities and the economic strength of the United States, many Taiwanese parents hold great respect for American education. However, many of them actually understand very little about common American educational practices. This can lead to cultural conflicts during the schooling transition, such as feeling that the American teacher is not pushing students hard enough or that the learning environment is too relaxed. Taiwanese parents often remain very involved in their child's schooling and may wish to be in regular contact with their child's teacher. Some may also make suggestions as to how the teacher may best help their child, such as only pairing them with the highest achievers in the class and assigning them additional homework. They may also inquire about private tutoring. Many parents also believe in the "sink or swim" method of language learning and cultural immersion and may opt out of opportunities for specialized support for English language learners, believing that their child will learn best when surrounded by American peers.

CULTURE

Values

Although Taiwan is becoming more and more Westernized, traditional Taiwanese values still remain today and can influence how students interact at school. Based on Confucianism, social hierarchy is an important part of Taiwanese society. Students are likely to value the wishes of their teacher over those of their classmates and the wishes of their parents over those of their teacher. Taiwanese parents often plan the futures of their children, sometimes with little concern for their children's own dreams or desires. This can often seem overbearing by American standards, but this is an area in which teachers have little control. Teachers' wishes may likely trump those of classmates, and this can sometimes lead to a sense of Taiwanese students being viewed as "teacher's pets," doing anything to support the teacher with less regard to the feelings of their classmates. Some Taiwanese students may need support socializing with their peers, and a teacher can support this by providing opportunities to collaborate and work cooperatively with others, especially in a semistructured learning environment. Again, as these types of learning environments are not common in traditional Taiwanese classrooms (although this is changing), students may need the support of modeling and direction.

Another traditional value is that of social status, specifically with the concept of "face," or a person's public persona. It is important for Taiwanese to maintain a positive public persona and work hard to avoid public embarrassment of themselves and others. This value can lead to students avoiding taking risks such as answering questions in front of the class when they are not completely sure of the answer; they may also avoid asking a question or for help in front of others. Many Taiwanese students choose to handle these issues privately with the teacher after class rather than risking "losing face" in front of their classmates. A fear of public failure can be a big deterrent regarding a student's participation in class. Working to create a safe learning environment that supports risk-taking is very important, and it may take Taiwanese students a while to adjust. They may need to be directly taught not only to take risks themselves but also to respect others who take risks.

Food

Food is an important element of Taiwanese society and often a source of pride. Traditional meals are often made up of a meat dish, two vegetable dishes, a soup, and rice or noodles as the staple. These same types of meals are served at public schools for lunch. Chains such as McDonald's and Pizza Hut are popular in Taiwan, but they may be seen more as a special treat than part of a regular diet. Parents may opt to send children to school with a home-cooked lunch. Because of the differences in Taiwanese food and American food, however, Taiwanese students sometimes feel insecure about standing out from their peers. Teachers can address this by asking their Taiwanese students to introduce Taiwanese food to their class and possibly even bring some in to share with the class.

LANGUAGES AND LITERACIES

Mandarin is the official language of Taiwan and is the language of instruction in schools, but this has not always been the case. Taiwanese was the language spoken by the majority of Taiwanese people until the occupation of Japan, when Japanese became the official language and the language of instruction in schools. After the Japanese relinquished power over Taiwan and the ROC was established, Mandarin was made the official language. During this period, the use of any language other than Mandarin in schools and in government buildings was prohibited, and students were often subjected to scolding and public shaming, such as being forced to wear a sign around one's neck that says "please speak Mandarin to me," for breaking these rules.

Today, Mandarin remains the language of the schools and dominant culture, but the government has begun making an effort to preserve Taiwan's minority languages, which include Hakkanese and 14 aboriginal languages in addition to Taiwanese. Public schools now offer courses in these languages as a way to avoid language extinction and as a way to strengthen Taiwan's multicultural identity. In addition, on the train system, all stops are announced in Mandarin, Taiwanese, Hakkanese, and English, and on the eastern side of Taiwan, where the aboriginal populations are more highly concentrated, stops are also announced using aboriginal languages.

English is taught as a foreign language in public schools beginning in 3rd grade, but for many families, English education begins earlier at cram schools, English-language daycares, and with the help of English-language children's programs and books. English classes in public schools are typically held two or three times per week with each class lasting around 40 minutes. The number of courses may increase in middle and high school, but it often depends on the school and county. English education is still primarily focused on the written exam, with little emphasis put on speaking. The primary motivation for learning English in Taiwan is the university entrance exam taken during the junior year of high school, which contains an English section.

Because of an emphasis on written testing in language classes, Taiwanese students may need additional practice building speaking and listening skills in the U.S. Teachers may offer additional opportunities for students to engage in speaking practice during class time with activities such as think-pair-share, small group discussions, and collaborative projects. Some teachers take for granted that their students know how to and appreciate the opportunity to collaborate with peers, but as was demonstrated in the opening vignette, students not used to this type of learning environment may initially feel uncomfortable with these types of activities or may not be clear on what is expected of them during these activities. Teachers can consider assigning clear roles and expectations for collaborative tasks, even those that may seem informal such as "talk to your neighbor." Making sure that expected behaviors are modeled by the teacher and/or pointed out when demonstrated by classmates can support the understanding of all students in the class.

Chinese Language System

Mandarin Chinese is a tonal language. In order to convey meaning, speakers and listeners must pay attention to tone and word order. As noted in the chapter on China, spoken Mandarin is made up of five tones—high-flat, rising, rising and falling, falling, and neutral. The tone accompanying a word is used to help differentiate that word from the many homonyms in the language. For example, the word "ma" spoken in isolation can mean many things. If it is spoken with a high, flat tone (mā), it means "mother." When spoken with a rising then falling tone (mǎ), however, the meaning is "horse." Attention to tones can be important for American teachers when speaking a child's Chinese name. It is possible that by using the wrong tone, a teacher may inadvertently be calling a child something other than their name. For example, when the tones are spoken Kǎi Wéi's name means "gentle, deep water." However, if a teacher were to correctly pronounce (note the tone markers) his name "Kāi Wèi," she would be referring to him as 'Appetizer.' Fear of mispronouncing a student's name should not be strong enough to deter a teacher from using a student's name at all. Chinese speakers tend to be aware that non-Chinese speakers find the Chinese language difficult to pronounce. Nonetheless, as a way of respecting children's languages and cultures, it is worth making the effort to learn to pronounce their names as they wish them to be pronounced.

In addition to tones, word order is important in Mandarin Chinese. Fortunately, Mandarin syntax is similar to English syntax: subject + verb + object (SVO). For example, "She goes to the park" follows the same SVO word order in English and Chinese. A notable difference, however, is the lack of many of the grammatical markers found in English. For example, "She goes to the park" would be directly translated as "She go park." These absent markers can often lead to negative transfer both in speaking and writing English, and teachers should be aware of the issue. With awareness of this negative transfer, teachers can help students understand English grammar through its similarities and differences to Mandarin. For example, a teacher might share with a student, "I know that in Mandarin there is no word like 'the,' but in English, when we refer to a general place, we put a 'the' in front of the place, for example 'She goes to the park, the bank, the store'."

Another difference in language systems relates to formality and addressing individuals. As opposed to English, where we might respectfully address an adult female using an honorific such as "Ms." followed by her last name, Mandarin speakers respectfully address people using their surname followed by their job title. For example, Ms. Johnson, the teacher, would be referred to as "Teacher Johnson" ("Johnson Teacher"

Table 17.1. Common Phrases in Mandarin

Characters	Pronunciation	Meaning in English	Direct Translation
你好 .	nǐhǎo	Hello.	You good.
你好嗎？	nǐhǎoma	How are you?	You good?
我是強生老師 .	wǒshìqiángshēnglǎoshī	I am Teacher Johnson.	I am Johnson teacher.

using Chinese syntax). In many cases, it is also common to simply refer to a person by their job title, such as Teacher, Principal, or Doctor. Therefore, if your student calls you "Teacher" rather than "Ms. Johnson," it does not necessarily mean that she does not know your name; this is likely just cultural transfer.

Table 17.1 provides some examples of common phrases American teachers can use with their Taiwanese students. Included are pronunciation markers (the curve above a vowel indicates the rise or fall of the tone) and direct translations.

The writing system used in Taiwan varies dramatically from English and is made of a system of tens of thousands of Chinese characters. The character system used in Taiwan is known as "traditional characters," the written form of the Chinese language used for the last several thousand years. This system varies slightly from the system used in mainland China, which is called "simplified characters" and is a shorthand version of the traditional characters that China adopted in the 1950s.

Because the use of Chinese requires the memorization of thousands of characters, as Taiwanese children are developing their literacy skills they are introduced to a system of phonetization of oral Mandarin called *zhuyin* (pronounced joo-een), or "*bopomofo*" colloquially, a system unique to Taiwan. *Zhuyin* is essentially an alphabet made up of 37 characters and four tone markers. Each character is associated with a sound found in the spoken language. For example, the sounds bo, po, mo, and fo (hence the colloquial name) are written as ㄅ , ㄆ , ㄇ , and ㄈ respectively. Taiwanese children learn this alphabet in kindergarten and use it to express themselves in writing as they slowly learn to write characters. In elementary textbooks and in children's books, text is written only in *zhuyin* in the earliest stages. Then as children learn to recognize Chinese characters, text is written in characters paired with *zhuyin*. Eventually text is written only using characters (see Table 17.2).

Because of the existence of an alphabet-like writing system (*zhuyin*), Taiwanese students should not struggle too much with the concept of the English alphabet and how letters are put together to form words. One of the challenges Taiwanese learners of English face, however, is negative

Table 17.2.   Text Teaching Process in Taiwan

Writing Level	Writing	English Meaning
Level 1: Zhuyin only	ㄋ ㄧ ˇ ㄏ ㄠ ˇ	Hello
Level 2: Zhuyin + characters	ㄋ ㄧ ˇ ㄏ ㄠ ˇ 你 好	Hello
Level 3: Characters only	你好	Hello

transfer between *zhuyin* and the English alphabet. Because Taiwanese students are more familiar with the Mandarin alphabet, many students tend to use it as a reference for making unfamiliar sounds in English. For example, the "rl" sound in "girl" does not exist in Mandarin, so many Taiwanese learners of English will use the closest equivalent in the *zhuyin* alphabet to say the word. In this case, the closest equivalent would be the sound "er" and the sound "lo," leading to many Taiwanese learners of English pronouncing the word "girl" as "ger-lo." Many Taiwanese learners of English also struggle to end words with a consonant when no words end in a similar consonant in Mandarin. One example can be seen above with "lo" as opposed to "l." Other examples include "do-guh" instead of "dog" or "fi-shee" instead of fish. Having a basic understanding of *zhuyin* can help teachers of Taiwanese students gain a better understanding of common pronunciation problems, help students notice these issues, and find ways to address them.

Mandarin Chinese is a language quite different from English, but having a general understanding of the language can be an asset for American teachers working with Taiwanese students. Having a working knowledge of the oral and written forms of Mandarin can help teachers understand the source of many of their Taiwanese students' English errors and pronunciation issues, which they can then use to build students' understanding of the English language.

IDEAS FOR EDUCATORS

National Identity

As noted previously, Taiwanese national identity can be a hot-button topic for both Taiwanese and mainland Chinese, particularly for older students and parents. Due to differing perspectives on either side of the Taiwan Strait regarding the sovereignty of Taiwan, teachers should be mindful when discussing Taiwan in relation to China. Taiwan is an island in a state of political limbo; it is not recognized as an independent nation but is self-ruled and maintains its own unique identity, free from the Chinese government.

High Expectations and Competition

Test scores and class rank can be very important to Taiwanese students and parents, who may view school as a competition with the goal of becoming the highest-ranking student in the class. This competitive spirit can sometimes detract from the student's personal growth and can also isolate them socially from their peers. Teachers can address this issue by helping students focus on their own improvement over time rather than their performance in comparison to others. This can be done, for example, through the maintenance of a portfolio that students can look through to compare their current work to work they completed earlier in the year. Teachers can also help students focus on their own improvement by not publicly sharing or posting test scores and by teaching students that it is okay not to reveal their test scores to their classmates even when asked. Teachers can also show support of accomplishments not directly related to test scores, such as teamwork, helping others, and hard work.

Educational Expectations

Taiwanese students may be used to a more traditional, teacher-centered learning environment than is provided in many American classrooms. New arrivals may struggle to adapt to an environment they may initially view as too relaxed and unstructured. Parents, who typically have high expectations for their child's education, may initially disagree with American teaching and learning practices. Parents may ask for additional homework for their child, for the teacher to push their child harder, for them to be stricter toward their child, or even for them to be better organized during class. It can be important for teachers to be patient with children and parents who are still adapting to the new educational environment. Teachers should be as transparent as possible regarding their teaching practices and expectations and assure newcomers that these practices are done in the best interest of the children's education and socialization. Teachers can pay attention to their students' reactions during class and help them ease into situations they may initially feel uncomfortable with, such as volunteering answers in front of the class, group work, and peer discussions. Initial expectations can be relaxed, and students can be provided with modeling and plenty of opportunities to practice engaging in what to them may be new educational opportunities.

Names

Many Mandarin speakers in the U.S. opt to choose an English name. It is worth noting, however, that many Mandarin speakers choose their English names by translating their Mandarin name or nickname directly into English, and these names may not always conform to traditional English name standards. For example, a Taiwanese mother once told me her son's English name was "Bear Stone" because that was the direct translation of his Mandarin name. Another example comes from a Taiwanese friend named "Dragon Nine," a direct translation of her Mandarin nickname. Not all Mandarin speakers choose an English name, however, and students should be encouraged to decide for themselves by what name they wish to be addressed.

Negative Transfer

Teachers can also understand that tones in Mandarin and phonemes that differ from English can cause pronunciation issues, in the form of negative transfer, for some English learners. Teachers can teach about English word syllable stress in comparison to tones in Mandarin verbs to help their learners gain a better understanding of the differences and similarities in tone use between English and Mandarin. Teachers can also use a basic understanding of the phonemes found in Mandarin to gain an understanding of why their Taiwanese English learners struggle with certain English phonemes. Letter blends such as "th," "st," and "rl" are examples of challenges for native Mandarin speakers, as these sounds do not exist in Mandarin. Helping students recognize that different languages use different sounds and helping them develop phonemic awareness can be beneficial to these learners.

Language differences such as the lack of many grammatical markers can also become causes of negative transfer for Taiwanese learners of English. To help combat these issues, teachers can also introduce their Taiwanese students to language activities such as Syntax Surgery (Herrell & Jordan, 2016) to help them pay attention to English syntax and parts of speech used in English sentence building. Syntax Surgery is an activity where students are presented with English sentences written using the sentence structure of their native language. The students are asked to cut up and reassemble (i.e., perform "surgery" on) the sentences so that they accurately follow English sentence structure. This activity helps students recognize the differences and similarities between their native language and English and teaches them how to self-correct when writing in English.

The "model minority" myth contends that Asians come from affluent backgrounds, are good at math and sciences, and are likely to succeed in American society. Taiwanese students are often placed under this umbrella, and as a result, expectations for them to succeed academically are often set high. It is important for teachers to recognize that students are individuals and for them to assess the needs that all of their students should have met in order to succeed. Because of the model minority myth that asserts that they already have a strong support network, Asian students may not be provided with the services they need. Any Taiwanese student may struggle in math and have no one who is able to help. It is important for teachers to recognize that Taiwanese people come from all socioeconomic backgrounds with all different kinds of support systems, skill sets, and future aspirations.

CONCLUSIONS

Taiwan is a unique, multicultural island with a complicated history and political status. Immigrants from Taiwan embody many traits similar to those coming from mainland China such as language and traditional culture, but they often identify as independent and different from those from mainland China. Taiwanese students often work hard academically and are strongly supported by their parents. Traditional Taiwanese perspectives of education, with a focus on test scores and rank, may differ from more progressive perspectives that may be found in American classrooms. Taiwanese students may struggle initially to adjust to their new academic learning environments, but anecdotally, it appears that most parents and students find the transition a positive one. To help during this transition, teachers can be patient and open-minded, gauge the reactions and responses of their students to different activities and situations, and be as transparent as possible about why they do things the way they do them.

ADDITIONAL RESOURCES

Taiwan Today. (2016). Taiwan today: A multilingual website tracking the nation's latest developments. Retrieved from http://www.taiwantoday.tw/mp.asp?mp=9

> This multilanguage news site provides information and updates about all aspects of Taiwan.

Wu, F.-M., Madden, C., & Gerock, J. (2016). Republic of China at a glance. *Ministry of Foreign Affairs, Republic of China (Taiwan)*. Retrieved from http://multilingual.mofa.gov.tw/web/web_UTF-8/MOFA/glance2015/English.pdf

This full-color pamphlet provides information on everything from National Parks to foreign affairs and could be a great resource for research on Taiwan for teachers and students.

TASKS FOR EDUCATORS

1. Learn the four tones of spoken Mandarin with this video produced by NTDTV: https://www.youtube.com/watch?v=kYjFB-MF1KU. How did you do? Can you find these tones in spoken English? Think about ways you can use these similarities and differences to teach your students about intonation in spoken English.

2. Create a short slideshow to share with your students. Include your hobbies, favorite foods, favorite forms of entertainment, and so on. Ask your students to create their own and share with the class.

3. Read the following research brief (https://www.wida.us/ get.aspx?id=752; Wisconsin Center for Education Research, 2014) to explore strategies that may help your Taiwanese students learn to collaborate effectively with peers. Try these strategies in your own classrooms and see which ones work for you and your students.

REFERENCES

Bruno, S. M. (2014, October 14). *The Asian tigers from independence to industrialisation*. Retrieved from http://www.e-ir.info/2014/10/16/the-asian-tigers-from-independence-to-industrialisation/

Coughlan, S. (2015, May 13). Asia tops biggest global school rankings. *BBC Business*. Retrieved from http://www.bbc.com/news/business-32608772http://www.bbc.com/news/business-32608772

Herrell, A., & Jordan, M. (2016). *50 strategies for teaching English language learners* (5th ed.). Boston, MA: Pearson.

Kuo, G. (2011, February 21). Taiwan's literacy rate hits record high. *Taiwan Today*. Retrieved from http://taiwantoday.tw/ct.asp?xItem=152196&CtNode=413http://taiwantoday.tw/ct.asp?xItem=152196&CtNode=413

Lowther, W. (2016, May 5). U.S. states name a week to celebrate Taiwanese heritage. *Taipei Times*. Retrieved from http://www.taipeitimes.com/News/taiwan/archives/2016/05/05/2003645562

NTDTV. (2012, July 23). *Learn Chinese—the tones of Mandarin Chinese* [Video file]. Retrieved from https://www.youtube.com/watch?v=kYjFB-MF1KU

Roberge, M., & Lee, Y. (2009). China-Taiwan relations. *Council on Foreign Relations*. Retrieved from http://www.cfr.org/china/china-taiwan-relations/p9223http://www.cfr.org/china/china-taiwan-relations/p9223

Taiwan Today. (2016, January 17). Tsai Ing-wen wins 2016 presidential election. *Taiwan Today*. Retrieved from http://www.taiwantoday.tw/ct.asp?xItem= 241346&ctNode=2175http://www.taiwantoday.tw/ct.asp?xItem =241346&ctNode=2175

Wisconsin Center for Education Research. (2014). *Collaborative learning for English language learners* [Research brief]. Retrieved from https://www.wida.us/ get.aspx?id=752

Zhang, W. B. (2003). *Taiwan's modernization: Americanization and modernizing Confucian manifestation*. Singapore: World Scientific Printers.

CHAPTER 18

JAPAN

Saeun Lee
Washington State University

Leslie Huff

Mr. Anderson has one Japanese English language learner, Ayaka, in his science class. Ayaka has been in his class for six months. Her quiz scores and test performance are good, indicating that she understands math and science well; however, Ayaka does not participate actively in group work or class discussions. Mr. Anderson knows from talking with her one-on-one that her English proficiency is good enough to participate in class. He worries because Ayaka must participate actively in addition to scoring well on tests in order to achieve an overall final grade representative of her science knowledge. Mr. Anderson wonders if Ayaka does not get along with her classmates or whether she might have some other problems in her life that keep her from fully participating in class.

BACKGROUND

Ayaka, in the scenario above, is a product of her culture, as we all are. Japanese culture centers on the concept of harmony. This concept is expressed through language, behavior, architecture, art, and many other aspects of life in Japan. The Japanese are famously innovative and future-

Views From Inside: Languages, Cultures, and Schooling for K–12 Educators
pp. 305–323

oriented, but they maintain strong ties to their past. Their strengths come from the harmony and collective nature of their culture, a culture built from harsh geographic, political, and economic environments.

An island country located between the Pacific Ocean and the Sea of Japan, Japan has no land borders, but it has nearly 30,000 km (approximately 18,641 miles) of coastline. The overall size of Japan is comparable to the state of California (Tidmarsh, 2007). The north-south stretch reaches from cold temperate winters on the island of Hokkaido to tropical climates on the island of Okinawa. There are over 6,800 islands that make up Japan, but the vast majority of the population lives on four main islands, Honshu (the main island), Kyushu and Shikoku (south of Honshu), and Hokkaido (north of Honshu), which account for more than 98% of the total land area (Tidmarsh, 2007). Most of Japan is located on the Pacific's Ring of Fire, a series of volcanos in and around the Pacific Ocean, and it is susceptible to volcanic and seismic activity. The scarcity of exploitable natural energy resources has led Japan to be a large importer of coal, gas, and oil, as well as a leading developer of nuclear energy (Gordon, 2014). Japan has over 50 nuclear power stations and is third, behind France and the United States, in nuclear energy production (Tidmarsh, 2007).

Japan is home to approximately 127 million people, which is equal to about half the population of the United States (United States Central Intelligence Agency, 2013). Of these people, 98.5% identify as Japanese, 0.5% as Korean, and 0.4% as Chinese. The remaining 0.6% includes a sizeable Brazilian-Japanese population that immigrated to Japan for work in the 1980s (United States Central Intelligence Agency, 2013) as well as two indigenous groups, the Ainu and Okinawan, native to current day Japanese territories. Most of the land area of Japan is mountainous terrain, leading to high population density in its urban areas (Gordon, 2014; Tidmarsh, 2007). Due in part to this density of the population, social harmony has remained one of the priorities of social development for Japanese.

History

In the last two centuries, Japanese society has undergone massive transformation in societal structure and political rule. From 1600 to 1853 A.D., a series of men from the Tokogawa clan took the title "Tokugawa Shogun" and held the country in relative peace, mostly isolated from the West. The Tokugawa era resembled feudal Europe in its hierarchy, but it included a far more urban orientation due to the density of populations in Tokyo, Osaka, and Kyoto (Gordon, 2014). In 1853, American warships sailed into Tokyo Harbor (which had been closed to foreign trade for centuries) and essentially forced the government to loosen its restrictions on foreign trade and missionary work. This opening of borders began planting the seeds for revolution. From 1868 to 1905, the samurai class overthrew the Shogun and reinstated the emperor at the center of the political system (Fogel, 1984; Gordon, 2014). The Meiji emperor appeared publicly in both traditional Japanese and Western military attire and sought to include a broader Western focus in efforts to "construct a modern nation" of "civilization and enlightenment" (Gordon, 2014, p. 106).

Following the Meiji Revolution, Japan's economy grew as transportation and other aspects of infrastructure developed rapidly to support increased wealth and more modern ways of life (Fogel, 1984). Beginning in January 1930, Japan began to fall into the Great Depression with growing unemployment and social unrest. From the late 1920s through WWII, Japan sought to expand its empire and redefined its colonial philosophy from one of local profits to one that sought the exploitation of human and material resources for the benefit of the empire (Fogel, 2000; Uchida, 2011). As the military grew stronger and conquered more territory in Asia—including parts of Korea, China, Manchuria, and Taiwan—the army also gained significant power, leading to a politically destabilized system of governing and a rise in fascism (Gordon, 2014; Uchida, 2011). Japan aligned with the Axis powers during World War II, committing it to war with the Allied powers and launching its empire into an ultimately disastrous endeavor.

During WWII, Japanese people sacrificed greatly. On August 15, 1945, following the complete devastation of Hiroshima and Nagasaki as a result of atomic bombs dropped by the Allies, the emperor of Japan announced Japan's surrender to the country via radio address (Gordon, 2014). The ultimate conclusion to the war resulted in Japan's loss of colonies as well as land considered part of the homeland. WWII had launched the civilian population of Japan into desperate circumstances and, following the war, city dwellers escaped en masse to the countryside in search of food and sustenance (Avenell, 2010). In addition, American military officials occupied Japan for seven years. The occupying forces set to work immediately demilitarizing and democratizing Japan. The Emperor was downgraded from an absolute monarch to a "symbol of the State and of the unity of the people" (Gordon, 2014, p. 229), land and wealth were redistributed, and over 900 military men were tried and executed for war crimes (Avenell, 2010). The occupation also established a new constitution with sweeping human rights for the people of Japan, which was shocking for the elite but well-received by the majority.

The occupation of Japan ended in 1952, although the United States still maintains numerous controversial military bases in Japan. Despite many new social and political structures, much of the old systems continued, somewhat reorganized, to provide stability and continuity as the economy grew. Banks and big business were two areas that offered much of this continuity (Gordon, 2014). The economy grew with little political unrest through the 1980s. In fact, much of the political debate that did occur was around Article 9 of the Constitution, which restricts Japan's military efforts to defense only, eliminating any opportunity for empire expansion. With its economic growth, Japan blossomed into a financial powerhouse and became more and more influential; this trend continues to the present day (Garon, 1997). Japanese influence remains despite the "bubble economy" that resulted in more than a decade of economic stagnation in the 1990s and the beginning of the new century.

In modern Japan, the Ministry of Education, Culture, Sports, Science, and Technology controls curriculum in Japanese schools centrally. The Ministry approves all the texts, and schools are offered a choice from approved texts (Tidmarsh, 2007). Generally, history texts, in particular, are the focus of demonstrations and protests when they are released. This is due to the lack of mention in Japanese textbooks of atrocities committed by Japanese soldiers in China and Korea prior to and during WWII. There are still tensions between Japan and its neighbors around wartime atrocities (Avenell, 2010; Garon, 1997), and Japan still has disputed territory with China, Korea, Russia, and Taiwan. These tensions are generally political and do not interfere with daily life.

Modern Day

An interesting fact about Japan is its adherence to a reign-based system of timekeeping. The Japanese use the same calendar as is typically used in the United States for things such as English-medium newspapers, but official Japanese documents and many other aspects of Japanese life are recorded by the year of the current emperor's reign. In this system, 2015 was the 21st year of the Showa emperor and is written as 昭和 21 年; 1977, the 52nd year of the Heisei emperor is 平成 52 年. Official documents like school records, birth records, drivers' licenses, family registries and the like are all recorded using the year of the reigning emperor. The Japanese are meticulous record keepers. Through the use of family registries, Japanese families can typically trace their lineage back hundreds of years.

Families in Japan tend to live in apartments/condominiums or houses. In urban areas, apartment buildings may be 30 stories high and filled with hundreds of families. It is not uncommon to have multiple generations in the same residence. This is in part due to the honor and respect the Japanese have for the elderly, but also due to a lack of other options for family members who need care (Avenell, 2010). That being said, grandparents serve an essential role in the family and it is rare for children to not have close relationships with their grandparents.

CULTURE

People

The Japanese have a deep connection to history and hold historical figures, both public and familial, in high regard. Similar to American culture, politicians, athletes, and television and movie personalities hold celebrity status. In addition, art and artists are especially admired in Japanese society. In addition to traditional art forms such as *Nihon Buyou* dancing and *haiku* poetry, newer categories of art like *manga* (comic books) and *anime* (animated films) originated in Japan but have a global reach among young people in particular. A single volume of a Japanese *manga* may be 300 pages long. It is common to see people of all ages enjoying *manga* as they commute on the train.

In present day Japan gender equality is a hot issue. Every aspect of life has been questioned by journalists, activists, or government officials with regard to equality and opportunity for girls and women. The rise of national female athletes, such as the Japanese women's soccer team and Ryoko Tamura, the world judo champion, are a symbol of this fight.

The historical figures described below are from politics, business, science, sports, and the arts. They are a representation of important people in Japan but by no means comprise an exhaustive list. The people below are listed with their family names first, which is typical of Japanese names.

- Murasaki Shikibu (973 or 978–1014 or 1031). Author of *Genji Monogatari* (*The Tale of Genji*), considered to be the first novel·ever written and a classic literary piece. Lady Murasaki was a novelist, poet, and lady-in-waiting during the Heian period of Japan.
- Oda Nobunaga (1534–1583). A samurai warrior who first unified Japan through conquest. He is considered the first ruler of a unified Japan following a long period of separate warring states. His successors, including Tokugawa Ieyasu, maintained and expanded this unification until the Meiji restoration.
- Tokugawa Ieyasu (1543–1616). Tokugawa Ieyasu was the patriarch of the Tokugawa period of Japan. Tokugawa Ieyasu ruled over unified Japan, employing sometimes brutal tactics. He implemented policies that secluded Japan from Western influence. After encouraging the emperor to bestow the traditional title of "*shogun*" on

him, he "retired" after only seven years to install his son in the position. The Tokugawa period lasted from 1600 to 1868.

- Noguchi Hideyo (1876–1928), aka Noguchi Seisaku. Noguchi was a bacteriologist who made several contributions to fighting diseases such as syphilis. Although his work was wrought with scandal, including scandals involving the unethical use of human subjects, his contributions to medicine were great.
- Akiko Yosano (1878–1942). Born Sho Ho, Yosano was an author, poet, feminist, and antimilitarism activist during the Meiji, Taisho, and Showa periods in Japan. Her poem *Kimi Shinitamou koto nakara* (*Thou Shalt Not Die*) was a protest against the Russo-Japanese War. Her other literary accomplishments also expressed feminist and antimilitary viewpoints.
- Matsushita Konosuke (1894–1989). Matsushita was the founder of Panasonic, a large Japanese electronics company. He was an icon of Japanese managerial practice and industry success worldwide.
- Sugihara Chiune (1900–1986). Sugihara served as a diplomat in Lithuania during WWII. Sugihara is credited with saving the lives of 6,000 European Jews by writing travel visas that allowed them to travel to Japanese territory and escape the Nazi occupation.
- Miyazaki Hayao (1941–present). Cofounder of Studio Ghibli, Miyazaki is a world-renowned animator, storyteller, screenwriter, and producer. His films, the most famous of which is *Spirited Away*, have brought anime to audiences around the globe.
- Tajiri Satoshi (1965–present). A video game developer, Tajiri is most famous for founding the *Pokemon* franchise and has also worked on *Mario* games and The Legend of Zelda.
- Suzuki Ichiro (1973–present). A star baseball player in both Japanese and American professional leagues, Ichiro played on the Orix Blue Wave team in Japan before moving to the United States to play baseball. He has played right field for multiple teams, including the Seattle Mariners, New York Yankees, and Miami Marlins.
- Tani Ryoko (maiden name Tamura) (1975–present). Six-time Olympic medalist and world champion in judo. Tani is also active in social issues such as equity in Japan.

Religion

Nearly 80% of Japanese people follow the native *Shinto* religion (United States Central Intelligence Agency, 2013). Shintoism is "the indirect, but culturally pervasive, source of many of the attitudes and customs that distinguish the Japanese from all other people" (DeMente, 1993, p. 14). The beliefs of Shintoism are founded on the concept of *kami*. Kami is the central god in Shintoism, but it is "an elusive concept and can be found not only in shrines but also in trees, mountains, water and even people" (Rarick, 1994, p. 220). Shinto encourages the concept of harmony among people and between people and their environments. Shintoism shares compatible beliefs and values with Buddhism, a religion in which approximately 60% of Japanese people believe (Rice, 1978). These two religions are compatible and many Japanese practice both; in fact, in modern Japanese society, many Japanese people perform their wedding ceremony following the customs of Shintoism and funerals following Buddhist traditions (Makhlouf, 1988). These two religions have a strong impact on people's behavior, particularly their avoidance of conflict and desire to not stand out among their peers.

Values

One of the main characteristics of Japanese culture is a group-oriented mindset with a strong emphasis on harmony. Harmony "is a cardinal value of Japanese interpersonal relationships. To them, harmony between people is essential for living together" (Shelley, 1993, p. 142). Japanese people hesitate to behave unexpectedly because it may disrupt the harmony of a group. The group "goals override individual interests, the Japanese underemphasize self-expression and creativity" (Kubota, 1999, p. 11). The individual must be suppressed to conform to the group (De Mente, 1990) in order to preserve overall harmony. This value is becoming more challenged by the young, but it still holds as a prominent value in society. In schools, efforts to maintain harmony may be why students do not volunteer when they know an answer (to not "rock the boat" among peers) and do not ask questions when they are confused (to avoid implying that the teacher has failed at her or his job).

Since Japanese people highlight harmony, they tend to respect others more than themselves and refrain from entering conflicts and disagreements. The ability to empathize with others "is valued more than the ability to be rational and practical" (Shelley, 1993, p. 143). Japanese endeavor to empathize and find common ground rather than appealing to differences and uniqueness. This is another important aspect of Japanese culture.

In addition to harmony and empathy, ultimate loyalty is a significant cultural trait in Japan. Loyalty is rooted in the traditional imperial systems of Japan but can be found throughout its history into modern times in all areas of social, professional, and political life. From the *kamikaze* pilots of WWII to the lifelong employment of the 1980s to Olympic sporting events, loyalty is a central value to the Japanese way of life.

Holidays

Two big Japanese holidays are *Oshogatsu* and *Obon*. *Oshogatsu* (New Year break) lasts from December 31 to January 3. The schools usually have a winter break from around December 26th until January 7th. It has no fixed days, but Japanese people celebrate the New Year during this time. Japanese people send *nengajyo*, New Year's greeting postcards, to express appreciation for relationships of the previous years and wishes for continued positive friendships in the coming year. They eat traditional o*sechiryori* during the holiday and go to the local shrine or temple to pray for a good new year to come. *Osechiryori* includes various dried food, which allows those in a family who typically prepare meals to relax during *Oshogatsu* since dried foods last for a few days.

Obon is the big summer holiday in mid-August (a few days before or after August 15) every year. *Obon* was originally an annual Buddhist event that has become a major summer holiday. During *Obon*, people often travel to their ancestral homes and gather at family grave sites to honor their ancestors.

Summer festivals are also common in Japan, with nearly every community holding a festival sometime during July or August. The festivals vary greatly, but they often include a parade of sorts, traditional games that pit neighborhoods against one another in friendly competition, and fireworks. These summer festivals are similar to Culture Day and Sports Day activities at many schools, where classes compete against one another in singing or field day-type sports.

Traditional Clothes

The traditional Japanese costume for women is called *kimono*. People wear *kimono* for special occasions such as weddings, New Year celebrations, and *shichi-go-san* celebrations that honor children as they reach the ages of three, five, and seven. Those ages are considered important because child mortality was high during the Heian era. *Kimono* are also worn by women at coming-of-age celebrations that are held in January every year, celebrating those who turn 20 years old, the age of adulthood. *Kimono* are colorful and vibrant except for those worn to funerals. Japanese people wear black *kimono* to celebrate weddings, and brides often wear white *kimono* for weddings. For university graduation, many students wear *hakama*, another type of *kimono*, when they graduate. *Kimono* has many layers and is often sufficient attire even on cold winter days. In Japan's hot and humid summers, a much simpler, cotton version of *kimono* called *yukata* is worn for celebrations.

Japanese men traditionally wore *hakama*, loose pleated trousers. This is the dress of some current sports such as *kendo* as well.

Behaviors/Manners

Bowing is a traditional greeting for everyone and shaking hands is also acceptable, mostly in business and formal settings. These physical greetings are always accompanied by a verbal greeting such as "good morning" (*ohayo-gozaimasu*) or "hello" (*konichiwa*). Japanese children are taught to show respect by offering enthusiastic greetings to their elders. Close physical contact, such as hugging, is uncommon in Japanese culture, even among close friends.

The Japanese have long-established table etiquette that differs significantly from traditional Western cultures, but which suits their typical diet well. For example, the Japanese tend to have rice with every meal. In fact, Japanese people often refer to food eaten without rice as a snack, not a meal. The rice bowl at each meal is generally held in the left hand with chopsticks in the right hand (or vice versa for left-handed people), and additional food is picked up from central plates, placed on the rice, and then the two are eaten together. Miso soup is another staple, which Japanese people commonly drink from the bowl rather than using utensils. Conversely, noodle soup bowls are almost never held in the hand. When eating noodle soups, the Japanese make a slurping sound when they eat to show that the food is good. Eating while walking or making any other motion is unacceptable.

The Japanese do not blow their noses in public because it is considered bad manners. Tipping is uncommon in Japanese contexts and can be interpreted as disrespectful, implying that the business does not pay its employees a fair wage. People take off their shoes when they enter a home, in schools, and some businesses.

SCHOOLING

The Japanese compulsory education program consists of six years of elementary school and three years of junior high school. The school year starts in April, with the first term ending in July. The second term starts in September and ends in December. The final term of the year starts in January and wraps up at the beginning of March. Most Japanese young people then enter three years of high school followed by university, although both would require students to first pass an entrance exam. After graduating from high school, young people take a *senta shiken*, or college entrance exam. This is an annual standard exam that students must take and earn a good score on to matriculate to a prestigious school. In 2013, approximately 1,125,000 students were admitted to high school and approximately 1,000,000 students enrolled in colleges and universities (Ministry of Education, Culture, Sports, Science and Technology [MEXT], 2015). As these numbers show, the majority of Japanese students go to colleges or universities to obtain higher education.

The school atmosphere is more geared toward collectivism than individualism. All students act together as a group in the classroom. Approximately 30 students are grouped as one homeroom class; however, one classroom can consist of up to 40 students. Once 41 students enroll, the class is split. This is a national standard and applies from elementary through high school. Students stay in their classroom and teachers come to the classroom by schedule except for classes that require special equipment such as music, art, and P.E. classes. During lunchtime, students serve each other and then begin eating at the same time after saying "*itadakimasu*" ("thank you for the meal"). After all classes finish lunch, all students clean the school together. Some elementary schools require students to wear school uniforms, and all junior high schools require school uniforms.

Shintoism requires showing respect to those of higher status. In schools, this is shown by students' use of formal speech patterns and the students standing, bowing, and greeting the teacher before each class. One student also goes to the teacher's room before each lesson to collect any books or materials the teacher may want brought to the classroom.

The language that the Japanese school system uses is Japanese, except for a few schools that use English for specific purposes. English instruction has begun in fifth grade in Japan since 2008, but it is more emphasized in junior high and high school. The responsibility for teaching social harmony over individual desire falls to teachers and schools. Teamwork is frequently observed in both academic and nonacademic activities in school (Duke, 1986), including class sporting competitions, singing competitions, and room decorating; however, Japanese universities and colleges allow more individual practice.

The Shinto and Buddhist religions have a strong influence over the relationship between teachers and students. Japanese people have a mindset of respecting elders; therefore, teachers and students have a hierarchical relationship. Students tend to listen and follow what teachers say without questioning. This respect is often demonstrated by students in the classroom through silence. In Japanese classrooms, "most students, seemingly unconcerned with content, laboriously and uncritically write down whatever teachers say. They seldom challenge either the teacher or their readings; controversy, and debate, when they arise, usually are about grading policies, and requirements" (Gimenez, 1989, p. 184). The common American saying "if you don't know, ask" would be seen as disrespectful in many Japanese classrooms.

LANGUAGES AND LITERACIES

As with all languages, Japanese is tightly bound to the culture of those who speak it. It is hierarchical, meaning that the words one uses to express an idea depend, in part, on the speaker's relationship to the listener. Using language that is too casual or too formal for the situation can cause tension and hinder communication, upsetting harmony. Students would tend to use less formal language with their peers than they would with their teacher; however, teachers generally use informal language with students and slightly more formal language with their colleagues of equal rank. Aside from the much less hierarchical nature of English, there are many differences in the way English and Japanese are structured.

Characteristics of Japanese

- Japanese has three writing systems: two syllabaries (*hiragana* for Japanese words and *katakana* for foreign words) and traditional Chinese characters (*kanji*). All three systems are used for daily communication.
- There is no stress on Japanese syllables. The stresses on words such as "*konNIchiwa*" are added by nonnative speakers to match the expected stress pattern of their native language. Japanese speakers add inflection to sentences to show agreement, question, and so on, but not within words. Each syllable has the same length and stress as every other.
- Japanese has five vowel sounds, similar to many Pacific Island languages. These sounds include "aw," "ee," "oo," "e" (as in "get") and "oh." There are no other possible vowel sounds in the language, although these vowels can be lengthened to provide more variety in words.
- There are a total of 46 distinct phonemes (possible sounds) in the Japanese language.

- The English sounds /th/, /l/, /v/, and /r/ do not exist in Japanese, although Japanese does have a sound that falls between the English /r/ and /l/ sound.

- Japanese words follow a strict vowel-consonant pattern. Aside from "n," all consonants are always followed by a vowel. All words in Japanese end in a vowel or "n." For this reason, many Japanese English learners often struggle to learn blends such as "st," "bl," or "tr." Blends that begin with "n," such as "nd," or "nt," though, are easily acquired and could be used to help students understand more difficult blends (e.g., "Macdonalds" = マックドナルド "Ma-ku-do-na-ru-do").

- Japanese uses post-positions where English uses prepositions. For example, the English sentence "There is an apple on the table" would be "Table on apple there is" using Japanese word order. It is worth noting that verbs are found at the end of Japanese sentences.

- Japanese uses no articles. "The," "a," and "an" do not exist in Japanese and have no translation in Japanese. This makes understanding the concept quite difficult and learning when an article is appropriate a long process for Japanese-speaking English learners.

- Expressing plurals is done by using an appropriate counter in Japanese. Japanese uses a variety of counters depending on the type, shape, and size of the object being counted. For example, "*hiki*" is the counter for small, four-legged animals, so two dogs would be "*inu ni hiki*" (dogs + two + small, four-legged animal counter). Belts and pencils are counted by "*hon*." "Seven pencils" translates to "*enpitsu nana hon*" (pencil + seven + long-cylindrical counter).

- Japanese numbers, like in Chinese and other Asian languages, are counted by digits. For example, the number 273 would be said, in Japanese, "two hundreds seven tens three." Every digit is labeled in the name of the number. Anything over ten thousand is sometimes difficult for Japanese speakers to identify in English because ten thousand is its own label, unlike in English. The number 264,200 would be said in Japanese as "twenty-six ten thousands four thousands two hundreds."

- Japanese is more formulaic than many other languages. There are many phrases that "go together" in conversation, particularly in small talk. This aspect of language is also important to the preservation of harmony. For example, when a colleague must leave before others at the end of the day, she or he will say "*Osakini shitsureishimasu*" and colleagues will respond "*Gokurousama desu*." Roughly translated this means "Forgive me for leaving first" and "You've worked hard." There is no other response to the initial phrase. Similarly, greetings such as "How are you?" ("*Ogenkide-suka*") are met with "I'm well" ("*Genki desu*"). The formulaic nature of greetings, in particular, allows people to save face when doing something that is socially unacceptable, like leaving work before others. Table 18.1. includes some Japanese phrases that are used in daily conversation.

IDEAS FOR EDUCATORS

Listening Participation

Giving credit for active listening would help Japanese ELLs, especially when they first arrive in their new school. Active listening will ultimately improve their overall performance and support their social and cultural integration as well. When ELLs do not have the language proficiency or the cultural comfort to actively participate, it is better to encourage those things they *can* do successfully. In this regards, emphasizing active listening is a good way for these students to participate in the class.

Student and Teacher Roles

ELLs are often unable to articulate why they feel they should be quiet in the classroom, but culturally this stems from the idea that asking questions would be disrespectful to the teacher, implying that she or he did not teach the content well. Japanese classrooms tend to focus on rote learning, so group work and project learning may also be confusing for Japanese ELLs, and they may need help understanding what their role should be.

Dialogue Journals

Dialogue journal writing is a good activity to build rapport between teachers and Japanese ELLs (e.g., English & Gillen, 2001; Marefat, 2002). In Japan, teachers often take on multiple roles for children, including moral guide, academic coach, and trusted adult. Since writing tends to be less intimidating than speaking for these ELLs, students may take more care to express what they are thinking. Also, they often feel safer writing their thoughts for a specific audience than expressing themselves without practice in front of peers. Dialogue journals can be used for guided writ-

Table 18.1. Useful Expressions in Japanese

English	Context	Transliteration	Literal Meaning	Japanese Phrase
Good morning	Greeting prior to about 11 a.m.	Ohayo (gozaimasu) Gozaimasu added to the phrase makes it more formal.	Good morning (honorific form, most commonly used form in school)	おはよう（ございます）。
Hello	Greeting, generally between about 11 a.m. and dusk.	Konichiwa	This day (is)	こんにちは。
What's your name?	Initial meeting	Onamaewanandesuka	What's your name?	お名前はなんですか。
Departure greeting	When students/ colleagues are finishing with their day.	Otsukaresamadesu.	You've worked hard and you must be tired.	お疲れ様です。
How are you?	Used following greetings or when concerned	Ogenkidesuka *response will always be "genkidesu."	Are you healthy? I'm healthy.	お元気ですか。
Nice to meet you.	Used following initial introduction only.	Hajimemashite	First meeting	はじめまして。
Please	Used following "hajimemashite" and when asking a favor of someone	Yoroshikuonegaishimasu	Please (honorific form)	よろしくお願いします。
Thank you	Used casually to show appreciation	Domo	Thank you. (The level of formality will depend on both the level of the action being thanked and the relative honor of the people in the conversation).	どうも。
	Slightly more formal	Arigatou		ありがとう。
	More formal	Arigatougozaimasu Domoarigatougozaimasu		ありがとうございます。 どうもありがとうございます。

318

ing practice as well. To support a student's verbal language development, a teacher can also use audio dialog journals using podcast websites, voice recorders, or other simple technology. Focused feedback from the teacher can provide Japanese ELLs with specific grammar or goal-oriented guidance. However, many teachers may choose to use dialogue journals strictly for relationship development. Japanese students may get excited about how the teacher responds to their journal entries. It would be most beneficial for teachers to pay careful attention to the content and respond with encouraging comments and messages. Furthermore, teachers can provide monthly student reports to Japanese ELLs and their parents to show progress and get input.

The Choice of Questions

Asking many questions may give the impression that the teacher cares about Japanese ELLs; however, this may also seem overwhelming and culturally awkward to the ELL. Teachers should develop semistructured, thoughtful questions that lead to more open questions. For instance, "How did you like the group projects?" would be too broad for Japanese ELLs, and may cause an obligatory "I liked it" or "Good" in an effort to avoid insulting the teacher. Instead, the teacher can ask "What part of this project did you enjoy?" or "Did you learn something new from your group?" Either of these can be followed with more specific questions to understand the students' thoughts on the group project.

Classmate Assistant

Japanese ELLs should eventually become friends with all their classmates; however, assigning one fixed student who the teacher thinks appropriate as a "helper" or "buddy" would be appreciated by most Japanese ELLs. Since asking others for help is not common in Japanese society, proactive students who can provide support consistently will be necessary. This approach is not only beneficial for Japanese ELLs but also good for encouraging further social and academic development for native English speaking students.

Integrate Culture in Class

Being a minority in class is not easy for any ELL. It is particularly difficult for Japanese students whose culture focuses on group dependence. In this regard, teachers can create a classroom atmosphere of respecting differences to reduce feelings of marginalization. To create an open-minded classroom, teachers can ask questions about Japan and emphasize that the

Japanese culture is ancient, interesting, and helpful to know for the rest of the class. Learning and using Japanese greetings can also be an effective way to show respect for differences and encourage other students to try their hand at Japanese. Japanese ELLs will feel proud to be the expert on the language, and the other students may think it is fun to be different by learning another culture and language.

Focus Instruction on Common Language Difficulties

Identifying the common areas of language difficulties for Japanese ELLs will help learners understand more readily how to produce unknown sounds, such as "v" and "l," as well as identifying when and how to use aspects of language that are non-existent or different in Japanese. For example, explicitly teaching strategies for when to use and not use "the" could give ELLs tools to employ as they interact with peers, develop writing skills, and progress generally in their language proficiency. ESL websites can often provide some clear explanations of language use (e.g., http://esl.fis.edu/grammar/rules/article.htm and http://englishpage.com/articles/index.htm).

Invite Parents for Tea

Japanese people are used to having tea (or coffee) when they have meetings or are just chatting with friends. Inviting ELLs' parents to the classroom for a casual talk will give teachers an opportunity to find out more about the students, their strengths, interests, and difficulties, and provide the teachers with a means of building a relationship with the parents, who may or may not be comfortable speaking English. To help ensure success, teachers can have some goals for the discussion and prepare specific questions to help meet the goals; for example, "Can you tell me about Sayaka's interests or hobbies?" would be a good opening question to help parents relax and talk about a subject they know well. Also helpful to the parents would be to have a clear list of events that they may be interested in, with dates and brief descriptions of the events.

CONCLUSIONS

This chapter will be beneficial for teachers who have Japanese ELLs in their classrooms. However, although this chapter provided information about the history and culture of Japan, Japanese ELLs are individuals and may not follow all the characteristics of "typical" Japanese students. Ayaka, in the opening scenario, shares some typical traits with other Japanese students, but in other ways she is different. Acceptance, patience, and clarity of expectations are some of the keys to opening students' minds and supporting their willingness to take risks in the classroom.

ADDITIONAL RESOURCES

Fujiwara, K. (2006). *A study of Japanese ELL students in mainstream classrooms* (Doctoral dissertation). University of Tennessee, Knoxville, TN. Retrieved from http://trace.tennessee.edu/cgi/viewcontent.cgi?article=3395&context=utk_graddiss

> This research paper focuses on five Japanese ELL students in mainstream classrooms.

Gordon, A. (2014). *A modern history of Japan: From Tokugawa times to the present.* New York, NY: Oxford University Press.

> Reads like a history textbook and offers an overview of modern-era Japanese history.

LoCastro, V. (1996). English language education in Japan. In H. Coleman, (Ed.), *Society and the language classroom* (pp. 40–58). Cambridge, UK: Cambridge University Press.

> The book (particularly Part I: Chapter 3) provides valuable information about Japanese students' English education in Japan to understand students' background in terms of English proficiency.

Ministry of Education, Culture, Sports, Science and Technology (MEXT) (2015). *Statistics.* Retrieved from http://www.mext.go.jp/english/statistics/

> An official website (English version) of the Japanese Ministry of Education. It can be used to find various education policies and conditions that may be helpful in understanding students' behaviors and opinions toward learning/education.

United States Central Intelligence Agency. (2013). *World Factbook 2012 01502013: Japan.* Retrieved from https://www.cia.gov/library/publications/the-world-factbook/goes/print_ja.html

> A website that offers general demographic and historical facts as well as cultural information about Japan.

TASKS FOR EDUCATORS

1. Consider your answers to these questions:
    - National honor for typical Japanese citizens is strong. Some lessons in U.S. schools, especially about history, could be particularly shocking or upsetting for Japanese students because of

the differing perspectives. How might you anticipate and miti-
gate the emotional turmoil that may arise from such lessons?

- Some Japanese values contradict or are ill-aligned with typical American school culture and expectations. How might you approach these differences to best support your ELLs?
- Considering the structures of Japanese language, what could you do to facilitate the acquisition of English among your Japanese ELLs?

2. Consider what you knew about Japan before reading and what you have learned in this chapter. Then, discuss with others what you found was similar and different. Have your understanding and expectations about Japanese students or culture changed?

3. Harmony has been a foundational value in Japanese culture for centuries. This value leads to behaviors that are sometimes in conflict with traditional U.S. school behaviors that are focused on individualism. Discuss how could you help Japanese ELLs to develop behaviors you need them to in the classroom. Alternatively, how could you adjust your teaching or student expectations to accommodate for students' home cultures?

4. Confidence is one of the keys for developing language and literacy proficiencies. How could you encourage Japanese ELLs to build their confidence? This may be especially tricky considering that many common Japanese behaviors could be interpreted as a lack of confidence, when the underlying hurdle is cultural, not intrapersonal. What strategies might you use to distinguish the underlying cause of a behavior?

5. Discuss whether values of harmony and cooperation could be addressed when establishing rules for the classroom. What might these rules look like? Would they be different from rules that you and your students currently develop?

REFERENCES

Avenell, S. (2010). *Making Japanese citizens: Civil society and the mythology of the shimin in postwar Japan*. Berkeley, CA: University of California Press.

De Mente, B. (1990). *Etiquette guide to Japan*. Rutland, VT: Tuttle.

De Mente, B. (1993). *Behind the Japanese bow*. Lincolnwood, IL: Passport Books.

Duke, B. (1986). *The Japanese school*. New York, NY: Praeger.

English, L. M., & Gillen, M. A. (2001). Journal writing in practice: From vision to reality. *New Directions for Adult and Continuing Education, 90*, 87–94.

Fogel, J. (1984). *Politics and sinology: The case of the naito konan (1866–1934)*. Cambridge, MA: Harvard University Press.

Fogel, J. (2000). *The Nanjing massacre in history and historiography.* Berkeley, CA: University of California Press.

Garon, S. (1997). *Molding Japanese minds: The state in everyday life.* Princeton, NJ: Princeton University Press.

Gimenez, M. E. (1989). Silence in the classroom: Some thoughts about teaching in the 1980s. *Teaching Sociology, 17,* 184–191.

Gordon, A. (2014). *A modern history of Japan from Tokugawa times to the present* (3rd ed.). New York, NY: Oxford University Press.

Kubota, R. (1999). Japanese culture constructed by discourses: Implications for applied linguistics research and ELT. *TESOL Quarterly, 33*(1), 9–35.

Makhlouf, G. (1988). *The religions of Japan.* Englewood Cliffs, NJ: Silver Burdett Press.

Marefat, F. (2002). The impact of diary analysis on teaching/learning writing. *RELC Journal, 33*(1), 101–121.

Ministry of Education, Culture, Sports, Science and Technology (MEXT). (2015). Statistics. Retrieved from http://www.mext.go.jp/english/statistics/

Rarick, C. (1994). The philosophical impact of Shintoism, Buddhism, and Confucianism on Japanese management practices. *International Journal of Value-Based Management, 7,* 219–226.

Rice, E. (1978). *The nature religions: Bon and Shinto.* New York, NY: Four Winds Press.

Shelley, R. (1993). *Culture shock! Japan.* London, UK: Kuperard.

Tidmarsh, C. (2007). *Focus on Japan.* Milwaukee, WI: World Almanac Library.

Uchida, J. (2011). *Brokers of empire: Japanese settler colonialism in Korea, (1876–1945).* Cambridge, MA: Harvard University Press.

United States Central Intelligence Agency. (2013). *World Factbook 2012–2013: Japan.* Retrieved from https://www.cia.gov/library/publications/the-world-factbook/goes/print_ja.html

CHAPTER 19

KOREA

Hyun-Gyung Lee and Saeun Lee
Washington State University

Mr. Smith is an elementary school teacher in the U.S. He has five ELLs in his class; three Korean and two Arabic students. Since the beginning of the semester, the Korean ELLs' parents have come to school and called him often to ask about school events, homework, and so on, instead of asking their children. He wondered whether the students and parents had a lack of communication or they both did not understand what was going on in class and at school. Mr. Smith was overwhelmed from explaining the same things to all of the parents and students. He decided to research online about the Korean school system and parental involvement. During his research, he discovered that school involvement was one of the biggest responsibilities of Korean parents. After learning this, he came up with an idea to convey his messages more easily; Mr. Smith decided to create a monthly letter for his ELLs and their parents.

BACKGROUND

The scenario above shows how important it is for educators to understand students' cultures in order to communicate with students and their parents effectively. In the vignette, knowing about the Korean school system and parental involvement helped Mr. Smith to integrate Korean school culture into current school practice. This improved his communication

Views From Inside: Languages, Cultures, and Schooling for K–12 Educators
pp. 325–346
Copyright © 2018 by Information Age Publishing

with the Korean students and their parents and helped make them feel included in the learning experiences. In order to get educators acquainted with Korean culture, this section will focus on basic information about Korea and discuss geographical, historical, and demographic facts.

Geography and History

Korea is located on the Korean Peninsula and shares a border with China to the northwest and Russia to the northeast. It is divided from Japan to the east by the East Sea and the Korean Strait. Korea comprises two sovereign states, South Korea and North Korea, which are also called the Republic of Korea (South) and the Democratic People's Republic of Korea (North).

History books record Korean history back over thousands of years (Kim, 2012). When the country was the Kingdom of Goryeo (from which the current English name "Korea" derived) from 918 to 1392, it was known to the Western world through foreign merchants and Marco Polo's *The Travels of Marco Polo*. As Asia and Europe became more connected through the Silk Road and sea routes, trading among countries across the world became more frequent and Goryeo became more internationally known.

There are two fairly recent historical events that have influenced the country and people's lives significantly. First, Korea fell under Japanese influence in the late 1800s and was made a Japanese colony in 1910. Many Koreans were killed or sent to labor in foreign countries or for the Japanese military during WWII, and the use of the Korean language, including Korean names, was not allowed. Although Korea regained its independence with the surrender of Japan in 1945, this event impacted Korean demographics, language, and relationships with Japan. Certain animosities exist between the two countries to this day.

Another influential historical event was the Korean War, which resulted in a divided nation with two states, South Korea and North Korea. When Japan left Korea in 1945, according to the United Nations' plan, Korea was administered by two countries—the U.S. south of the 38th parallel and the Soviet Union in the north—with two separate governments. War broke out in 1950 when North Korea, under the Communist Soviet Union's administration, invaded South Korea. The war involved many other countries—for example, China on the North Korean side and many countries of the United Nations, including the U.S., on the South Korean side. The war ended in 1953, and since then, Korea has remained as two sovereign states, democratic South Korea and Communist North Korea.

South Korea has kept a close relationship with the U.S., and the U.S. army still has a presence in the country.

Demographic Information

Although the Korean population dropped significantly during Japanese rule and the Korean War, currently Korea has a population of approximately 75 million people, 25 million in North Korea and 50 million in South Korea. Historically, Korea has been occupied by the Koreans, a highly homogeneous ethnic group who speak the Korean language; however, since Japanese rule its foreign population has constantly increased (Kim, 2015). According to national census data, about one million foreigners reside in Korea. Most of them are Chinese (624,994) and Japanese (443,566); however, the Vietnamese and American populations are growing.

Regarding Koreans in the U.S., nearly 3% of the total U.S. population in 2013 was Korean immigrants, and about 1.1 million Korean immigrants live in the United States (Zong & Batalova, 2014). Today, South Korea is the country that sends the fourth most international students to the United States, after China, India, and Saudi Arabia (Institute of International Education, 2016). Data from the Institute of International Education indicates that in the 2015–2016 school year, approximately 61,007 South Korean students—5.8% of all international students in the U.S—were enrolled in U.S. public or private schools.

According to Zong and Batalova (2014), Korean immigration to the United States occurred in three phases. The first Korean immigration wave took place from 1903 to 1905 due to the Japanese occupation of Korea; Japan sent about 7,000 male and 1,000 female Koreans to work on sugar plantations in Hawaii. Most of them did not speak English and no schooling was offered. The second wave started in 1951 due to the Korean War and the U.S. Army in South Korea, which resulted in many war orphans and international marriages. These Korean immigrants ranged from young women and children of American servicemen to refugees, orphans, students, and professionals. The third wave began after the U.S. Immigration Act of 1965 that stressed family reunification, and the majority of Korean migrations to the U.S. took place during this period. Many South Koreans moved to the U.S. to join their family members, to have better jobs, and to pursue political freedom during the military dictatorship. Many of this third wave of South Korean immigrants were well-educated, and the majority of them settled in the U.S as lawful citizens. Zong and Batalova (2014) write that, compared to other foreign-born populations, South Korean immigrants were more likely to have a college diploma and higher incomes, and they were also less likely to experience poverty.

CULTURE

According to Fillmore and Snow (2002), educators need to be able to communicate with students and to evaluate their needs and performance in order to teach effectively. For example, many educators and researchers have misinterpreted students' cultural differences as signs of deficiency (Johnson, Christie, & Yawkey, 1999) because they did not understand who their students were and how cultural factors could influence their learning. With rapid growth in the Korean American and Korean-speaking student populations in the U.S., it is crucial for educators to know Korean culture to work with Korean students effectively. Thus, this section discusses key aspects of Korean culture that can influence Korean students' behaviors and learning in U.S. classroom contexts.

Philosophy, Religion, and Values

As discussed in Chapter 1, each culture includes shared values and behaviors that distinguish the members of a cultural group from those of another group. Philosophies and religions that influence Korean people's cultural values and ways of being are discussed below.

Confucian Philosophy and Values

Korea is often characterized as one of the world's most Confucian nations, since the country was run based on strict Confucian rule longer than any other country in the world (Paxton, 2013). Confucianism was introduced to Korea during the Goryeo dynasty when Buddhism was a national religion and the dominant ideology. With the fall of the Goryeo dynasty in 1392, the Joseon dynasty took over and made Confucianism the ruling philosophy to structure the new kingdom. To most Koreans, Confucianism is more "a system of ethics than religion" (KOCIS, n.d.b, para. 2), since it has been very closely related to their ways of thinking and behaviors for a long time. Although not many Koreans actually identify themselves as Confucians, many traditions that Korean people practice subconsciously are rooted in Confucian philosophy. Many towns still have *hyanggyo*, a Confucian school, which teaches Confucian values and ethics.

Korean Confucianism emphasizes that in order to maintain social order, all people within a society should be ranked by social parameters, know their social positions, and perform their given responsibilities diligently (Yoon & Williams, 2015). Thus, in Confucian philosophy, loyalty, obedience, dutifulness, and diligence are valued to maintain hierarchical harmony and the existing social order (Chung, 2006). The *samgang-oryun*, Confucian moral principles translated as "three bonds and five cardinal relationships" (Yoon & Williams, 2015, p. 31), are a good example that captures these Confucian values. According to these principles, there are three bonds—sovereign to subject, parents to children, and husband to wife—and two additional relationships—older to younger and friends to friends. All the relationships except for friendships are hierarchical; thus, in order to maintain hierarchical harmony, people at the lower ranks (i.e., subjects, children, wives, the younger) must obey and respect those at higher ranks (i.e., sovereign, parents, husbands, and elders) (Yoon & Williams, 2015).

Even today, Confucian philosophy can be seen in Korean beliefs and behaviors that are considered desirable or acceptable in Korea. For example, as the smallest unit of society, the family is an important part of Korean life and each family member has a different status and duties to perform to maintain harmony in the family. Generally, the father is referred to as the *gajang*, the head of the family, and most domestic work and childcare are performed by the mother (OECD, 2014). Also, when the father comes home from work, he typically asks his children questions such as, "Have you been a good girl?," "Did you obey your mom and older brother?," or "Did you take care of your younger sister?." In other words, children should obey their parents and older siblings and take care of younger siblings to be "good." These examples clearly show the hierarchical relationships and values of Confucianism.

Another example can be shown by events of a first meeting with a Korean (Paxton, 2013). For example, when a Korean mother visits the teacher, she might want to know how old the teacher is. If the mother finds their birth years are similar, she will be delighted and act very friendly to the teacher. Although this could be perplexing to the teacher, it is very common and acceptable in Korean culture because age determines relationships and communication between people in Korea.

Confucian philosophy also influences Koreans' communication patterns. According to Merkin (2009), Koreans are likely to use indirect communication and face-saving strategies because Confucian values include harmony in a group. They prefer not to take a stand or they will obscure a position on an issue so that both they and others can save face. Thus, disagreeing with others, particularly elders, is done in an implicit way that does not make them lose face or undermine the elders' authority. For example, Jiang (2006) compared communication strategies that Koreans and Americans use in press conferences. While Americans more directly refuse questions they are not comfortable with, Koreans avoid answering questions or do not answer sufficiently in order to be polite to the questioner.

Another example can be seen in classroom contexts. When a teacher asks Korean students if they understand the educator's directions, the students tend to say "yes" and do not ask questions even when their facial expressions suggest the opposite. Students feel they are taking a risk of losing their own face by admitting that they did not pay attention to the teacher or that there is a risk of undermining the teacher's authority by pointing out that the instruction was not clear. Thus, Korean educators tend to observe students' facial expressions or ask a question to make sure the students understand their instructions. These indirect communication patterns and face-saving behaviors also demonstrate Confucian values that emphasize harmony and egalitarianism (Merkin, 2009).

Diverse Religions

A variety of religions are practiced and followed by Koreans. According to Statistics Korea (2005), there are over 510 religious organizations in Korea. Although the oldest religion in Korea may be Shamanism, or indigenous nature worship, according to statistics, the two religions most Korean people believe in are Christianity and Buddhism. Forty-seven percent of Korean people do not claim any religion. Among Koreans with religion, 55.1% of them believe in Christianity (34.5% Protestant and 20.6% Roman Catholic) and 43% believe in Buddhism (Statistics Korea, 2005). Buddhism was introduced to Korea in 372 and widely accepted, blending with indigenous nature worship by the 6th century. It was eventually made a national religion during the Goryeo Kingdom period. Christianity was first introduced by Roman Catholic Church missionaries in the 17th century, followed by Protestant missionaries in 1884 (KOCIS, n.d.b). Although the Joseon dynasty persecuted Christianity, after Japanese rule Christian organizations, particularly Protestant, gained popularity rapidly by providing schools /universities, orphanages, and hospitals. Even today, this religion has an influence on Korean education and healthcare.

Because Christianity and Buddhism are the two most influential religions in Korea, both Christmas and Buddha's birthday have been made national holidays. Regardless of religion, people celebrate these days as part of Korean culture. For example, on Christmas Eve, many people buy Christmas presents for family or friends, and children wait for Santa Claus to come with their presents. Also, on Buddha's birthday, people can visit Buddhist temples that are beautifully decorated with lanterns and are open to everyone.

However, this does not mean that Koreans accept these two religions only. All the world's influential religions peacefully coexist with others in Korea (KOCIS, n.d.b). In fact, the South Korean Constitution clearly states that every Korean has freedom of religion and must not be discriminated against based on religious belief or practice (U.S. Department of State, 2014). Since diversity in religions is well respected in Korea, asking about someone's religion is not necessarily offensive or taboo. For example, one native English teacher who worked in Korea wrote that he found it surprising that Korean students often asked him, "What's your religion?" The teacher suggested that educators should not misunderstand or overreact when Korean students ask this question, even though questions about religion might make them uncomfortable. If educators do not want to answer this question, they can just avoid answering it or explain that it is too personal.

Additionally, people in different religious groups practice Korean traditions differently, adapting to their religious traditions and values. For example, an ancestral memorial service, which is an important part of Korean culture, is practiced differently by the followers of different religions. According to tradition influenced by Shamanism, Buddhism, and Confucianism, at midnight on the night before the anniversary of the death of an ancestor, people prepare meals and set them out on tables for their ancestors (Bae, 2007). Then, male descendants pass every dish over burning incense and everyone bows to the table. However, since idol worship is against Christian beliefs, Christians have adapted this ancestral memorial service to fit with their religion. For example, on the eve of the anniversary of the ancestor's death, a family gets together and has Christian worship. They read the Bible, sing Christian songs, and pray for the ancestor.

EDUCATIONAL SYSTEM AND PRACTICES

Historically, education has been highly valued and respected in Korean society under Confucianism's influence. Today, South Korea is well known for its high literacy rate and academic achievement among Organization for Economic Co-operation and Development (OECD) countries. President Barack Obama also praised Korea's academic success, as the country was ranked within the top five countries in global literacy and numeracy tests (Salmon, 2013). In addition, according to an OECD (2015) report, South Korea had the highest rate of young adults with a high school diploma (98%) and tertiary attainment (68%) among the 34 OECD countries in 2014. The following section discusses how students are taught in

Korea, what motivates Korean students, what education means in Korean culture, and Korean parents' views on education.

Educational System

The education system in South Korea consists of 9 years of compulsory and free education: 6 years of elementary school and 3 years of middle school. There are also 5–7 years of noncompulsory and tuitioned education: 3 years in high school and 2–4 years in college or university. Although preschool and kindergarten are not part of formal education, Korea has increased the number of free preschools and kindergartens to support working mothers. Children of ages 3 and 4 years can enter kindergarten before they start formal education at age 7. In South Korea, the academic year starts in early March and finishes in early February, with a break that gives educators and students time to prepare for the next academic year.

Research shows that South Korean students study longer than students in most other countries to meet the high academic standards provided by the national curriculum (Barrett, 1990; Sorenson, 1994). Once students enter school, they are placed in a specific class, called a *ban*, with about 35 other classmates who share the same classroom and homeroom teacher for one year. Classes are taught and assessed based on the academic standards provided by the national curriculum. In elementary school, most subjects except for English are taught by a homeroom teacher who stays with the students in the same classroom, while different subjects are taught by subject-area educators in middle and high schools. Students take a 10-minute break between each 40–50-minute session and a 50–60 minute lunch break. School used to be held 6 days a week, including Saturdays; however, currently students go to school only every other Saturday.

Also worth noting is the mandatory English education that is given from grade 3 to grade 12. Because of the high demand for English education, English was made part of the elementary education curriculum. With rapidly growing industrialization, English language proficiency is highly valued in Korea; thus, if students want to enter or graduate from university or have a good job, they need to take an English language test and have a high score (Spolsky & Sung, 2015). Also, although kindergartens are not part of formal education, many kindergartens include English in their curriculum, and expensive private English kindergartens are very popular.

Educational Practices

Korean educational practices and school culture can be characterized as hierarchical, uniform, and focused on hard work. First of all, the classroom environment in Korea tends to be more hierarchical, teacher-centered, and formal than in American classrooms (Jung & Stinnett, 2005; Suh & Price, 1993). Although corporal punishment has been banned since 2011, educators are still considered as powerful authority figures in the classroom and students are expected to show respect and listen. This results in lecture-based instruction and passive participation in class. Most interaction between the teacher and students in Korean classrooms takes place when the teacher asks students questions that have a correct answer. Students may be reluctant to answer the teacher's questions voluntarily because they might lose face or receive criticism when their answer is incorrect. For this reason, Korean students in U.S. classrooms may feel nervous or reluctant to share their thoughts and opinions during class discussion. Once they understand that everyone in the classroom has a part in the learning process and there is no right or wrong answer, they may feel more willing to participate in class discussion.

Next, uniformity is valued in Korean school culture (Chang, 2010). Although this might sound strange to Americans who value diversity, Koreans' value of uniformity is related to the country's history, Confucian traditions, and the Korean language. Since Korean Confucianism values harmony in a group, being different from other group members is considered as potentially dangerous. For example, in the classroom, if students answer the teacher's questions voluntarily during the lecture, these students are likely to be isolated or excluded from the peer group because standing out from the peer group is considered to be showing off and breaking the conformity of the group (Park, Crystal, & Watanabe, 2003). In fact, the Korean language has a word that means "different" that used to have a second definition, "wrong" (Chang, 2010). Although the second definition is no longer standard in Korean, many people still use the word to mean "wrong." In order to prevent this type of peer pressure, most Korean middle and high schools have school uniforms so that students, regardless of their parents' economic status, feel that they belong to the peer group and can focus on learning.

American education, which highly values diversity, may come as a shock to newcomer Korean students. It is important for educators to help students understand that being different can be fun and that differences make everyone unique and special. In addition, Korean students may benefit from classroom activities that encourage their creativeness, rather than repeating after their teacher and copying the teacher's modeling.

Many Korean parents tell their children that a good education and entering a top university will bring them a good life in the future. Students and parents work hard together to achieve their mutual goal, the student's academic success. Parents provide support in all aspects, spending time, energy, and money, and students are expected to work hard and live up to their parents' expectations. For example, many Korean parents pay expensive tuition to send children to private cram schools after regular classes to practice more or to move ahead of the school curriculum. Salmon (2013) reports that South Korean parents are the "world's second-highest per capita spenders on education" (p. 1), spending 8% of the gross domestic product (GDP). Also, according to Paik (2004), many Korean mothers are the "driving force" (p. 53) behind their children's educations, monitoring their academic progress, homework, attendance, and private schooling. This is crucial because the student's academic success and acceptance to a prestigious university bring honor to the family. In this pursuit, Korean parents might contact educators to ask for more homework (Farver, Kim, & Lee, 1995); they may also exchange information on good tutors, cram schools, and brain food through online communities or workshops to be knowledgeable about educational trends. In return for parents' dedication and sacrifice, students are expected to do their best to have high scores in school and on university entrance exams.

Research shows that Korean students do not only study more in school but also study more outside of school than students in most other countries (Barrett, 1990; Sorenson, 1994). After class, they are likely to study in the library or in evening cram schools that run until midnight or after (although the government has warned cram schools that they should not operate after midnight). Salmon (2013) reports that 75% of Korean children attend evening cram schools. In Korea, it is not particularly strange that students, including elementary students, come home after midnight. In comparison, Korean students and parents in the U.S. may feel that the student workload is much lower and be anxious that they or their children might be behind. Providing some measures that allow parents and students to monitor academic progress, such as online student work portfolios, is likely to make the parents less concerned about the school workload.

IDEAS FOR EDUCATORS

This section introduces several Korean customs and matters of etiquette that are useful for educators to know.

Greetings

The bow is the traditional Korean greeting. Handshakes and hand waves are often used along with bowing, depending on the context. Although bowing can be used with handshakes, it is not appropriate for a younger person to request a handshake from an older person. Hand waves are less formal than bowing; however, educators commonly use hand waves to be friendly with students. Hugs are generally between couples or family members to show affection. If educators want to hug a student, especially one of the opposite gender, they should ask for permission in advance.

Name and Title

Korean etiquette requires the use of a person's title instead of their name. For example, when students call their teacher, Mr. Brown, they call him, "Teacher" or "Brown Teacher." Also, in writing names, educators in American classrooms should be careful not to write Korean students' names in red ink, because Koreans only write of people who are dead in red.

Traditional Dress

The Korean traditional costume is called *hanbok*. *Hanbok* is characterized by "a two piece outfit of either trousers or a skirt, and a robe without pockets and buttons that are closed with strings, belts, or cords" (Brown & Brown, 2006, p. 81). Although Koreans used to wear it every day before Korea was under Japanese rule, today Koreans wear *hanbok* only on special days such as Korean New Year's Day or a wedding ceremony.

Dining

The main staple of the Korean diet is rice, which is served with soup and *kimchi*, "a vegetable side dish which is commonly fermented in a brine of anchovies, ginger, garlic, green onion, and chili pepper" (Brown & Brown, 2006, p. 153). Although Koreans traditionally use a spoon and chopsticks to eat, it is now acceptable to use a fork instead of chopsticks. Most important, people should not pick up their spoon to eat before older people do (KOCIS, 2008). When Koreans are in the classroom, usually the teacher tells the students when to start to eat, and among classmates it is okay for anyone to start to eat first.

Celebrations

The two most important celebrations in Korea are *Chuseok* and New Year's Day celebrations. *Chuseok*, on August 15th in the lunar calendar, is a harvest festival that celebrates the year's harvest, just like Thanksgiving Day in the U.S. On *Chuseok*, all family members gather together and make *songpyeon*, half-moon shaped rice cakes, competing in making the best *songpyeon.* Another important celebration is Lunar New Year's Day. Although Koreans celebrate birthdays, eating *dduk*, a sticky rice cake, they do not become one year older on their birthday; every Korean becomes one year older after every family member eats *ddukguk* for breakfast together on New Year's. Then, children do *sebae*, a New Year bow, to their older parents and relatives and receive good words and gift money from them (KOCIS, n.d.a). Further, family members play the traditional board game called *Yut-nori*. If they play well and win the game, other people tell them they are likely to have a lucky year; if they lose the game, others comfort them by saying they will have a lucky year because they used up all their bad luck by losing this game. These cultural practices can be incorporated into their classrooms in the U.S.; for example, students can play *Yut-nori* with their classmates and teacher and wish each other luck for the coming year.

LANGUAGES AND LITERACIES

Korean students may face challenges while acquiring English in U.S. classrooms because language and literacy practices are different between Korean and English. The following information will help educators better understand Korean language and literacy practices.

Characteristics of the Korean Language

The Korean language is one of the world's oldest languages, one that has been spoken for thousands of years. Currently, *hangul*, the Korean alphabet, is used to represent the Korean language. *Hangul* was first introduced by King Sejong the Great in the 15th century in order to increase the literacy rate in Korea. Before *hangul* was created, people used Chinese characters for writing. *Hangul* is a phonetic alphabet that uses vowels and consonants to represent speech sounds (Kim-Renaud, 1997). In *hangul*, there are 40 letters: 10 pure vowels, 11 compound vowels, 14 basic consonants, and 5 double consonants. Table 19.1 introduces Korean alphabet letters and their sounds. For example, the consonant sound "n" is represented by "ㄴ" while the vowel sound "a" is represented by "ㅏ."

These consonants and vowels are grouped into syllables to represent Korean words. For example, the consonant sound "k" is represented by the letter " ㄱ ," the vowel sound "i" by the letter " ㅣ ," and the consonant sound "m" by the letter " ㅁ ." These three letters, ㄱ , ㅣ , and ㅁ , can be grouped as one syllable block " 김 " with the sound "kim." In this way, Korean sounds are easily predictable in reading; however, there are a

Table 19.1. The Korean *Hangul* Alphabet

21 vowels	Basic consonants	ㄱ ㄴ ㄷ ㄹ ㅁ ㅂ ㅅ ㅇ ㅊ ㅋ ㅌ ㅍ ㅎ
		g,k n d,t r,l m b,p s ng ch k t p h
	Double consonants	ㄲ ㄸ ㅃ ㅆ ㅉ
		kk tt pp ss jj
19 consonants	Pure vowels	ㅏ ㅑ ㅓ ㅕ ㅗ ㅛ ㅜ ㅠ ㅡ ㅣ
		a ya eo yeo o yo u yu eu i
	Compound vowels	ㅐ ㅒ ㅔ ㅖ ㅘ ㅙ ㅝ ㅞ ㅟ ㅢ
		ae yae e ye wa wae wo we wi ui

number of pronunciations that differ from English such as double consonants and some vowels (e.g., ㅓ , "eo" and — , "eu").

Differences Between English and Korean

English and Korean are different in many ways. Following are some of
the major differences.

- Letters are written into square syllable blocks in the order of a consonant (C), a vowel (V), and/or a consonant (optional).
  o 김치 (*kimchi*)

- Honorifics are highly developed—for example, 고마워 (the casual
  form of "thank you"), 고맙습니다 (the honorific form of "thank
  you").
- Sentences in Korean are written in order of subject-object (or others)-verb, for example, I (S) books (O) read (V), while English is
  SVO ("I read books").
- Present, past, and future verbs tenses are conjugated by adding a
  past tense suffix or a future tense suffix directly to the stem of the
  verbs. There are no auxiliary verbs (in English, these are words that
  assist the verb to modify tense, voice, or mood such as "will,"
  "should," and "may.")
- No articles (i.e., "a," "an," "the") exist in Korean.

Challenges for Korean-Speaking Students When Learning English

Because Korean and English have many differences, Korean students may experience difficulties in English learning in terms of grammar and pronunciation, academic writing organization, and vocabulary confusion, as noted below.

Grammar

Students may experience difficulties in learning English grammar because English and Korean differ in the ways that words are put together to make sentences.

- Korean does not have upper and lower case distinctions; students may write "i am hyun gyung," for example.
- There are no articles in Korean, so students may write or say "I have book," or "Book is interesting."
- Irregular past tense verbs (e.g., go/went instead of "goed," eat/ate instead of "eated") may be challenging because these forms do not exist in Korean.
- The third person singular "-s" form also does not exist in Korean (e.g. She give_ a present, he have a present)
- Students may find it difficult to understand present/past perfect tenses. Korean only has simple past, present, and future.
- Learning word spellings in English can be challenging since there are not many exceptions to spelling rules in Korean, but English has many.

Pronunciation and Listening

Differences in sounds between English and Korean may make it difficult for Korean speakers to hear some of the sounds and pronounce others.

- Korean does not have certain sounds such as /f/, /v/ /d/ /z/, /θ/, or clear distinct sounds like /l/ and /r/, which makes it challenging for Koreans to pronounce and distinguish the following sounds:
  o /p/, /f/, and /b/: e.g., pen, fan, bend
  o /r/ and /l/: e.g., rule, letter
  o /v/ and /b/: e.g., very, berry
  o /j/, /ch/, and /z/: e.g., jam, children, zoo
  o /θ/, /s/: e.g. think, sink
- Stress or intonation: Korean students may speak in a monotone.

Academic Writing

Koreans may face challenges when writing academic papers because they may be used to a different way of organizing ideas.

- Students may lay out examples and details before writing a topic sentence.
- Students may express their argument indirectly.

Vocabulary

There are some English words that are confusing to Korean students because there are not two words with the same meaning in Korean.

- Promise vs. appointment (e.g., I have a promise with the doctor).
- Power vs. energy (e.g., I have power to do this; The energy of the car is strong).
- Understand vs. know (e.g., I understand that the book is interesting; I know what you mean).
- Exciting vs. excited (e.g., I am exciting; The game was excited).
- Boring vs. bored (e.g., I am boring; This game is bored).
- Look, see, vs. watch (e.g., I looked at TV last night; I watched you; I see out the window).
- Tell, say, talk, vs. speak (e.g., I said you; She tell loudly; I spoke you to do it).

Useful Phrases in Korean

Using some simple expressions in Korean can be beneficial to building rapport with Korean students. Table 19.2 gives some useful phrases that educators can use.

As presented in this section, it is important for teachers to understand Korean students' language and literacy practices. Through understanding some expressions, educators can guide Korean speaking students to develop their English learning more efficiently and effectively.

IDEAS FOR EDUCATORS

Previous sections in this chapter discuss Korean culture and language and show how they are different from those in America. Based on cultural and linguistic differences between Korea and America, this section discusses

Table 19.2. Useful Expressions in Korean

Korean	Transliteration	English
안녕 ?	*an-NYOung?*	Hello.
안녕하세요 .	*AN-NYOung-ha-se-yo.*	Hello. (Honorific form)
잘가요 .	*CHAL-ga-yo.*	Good bye.
잘지냈어요 ?	*CHAL-ji-net-so-YO?*	How are you?
고마워 .	*KO-ma-wo.*	Thank you.
감사합니다 .	*KAM-sa-HAP-ni-da.*	Thank you. (Honorific form)
잘했어요 .	*CHAL-hat-so-yo.*	Good job.
이름이뭐예요 ?	*Yi-ru-MI-mo-ye-YO?*	What's your name?
제이름은 ~~ 예요	*CHE-yi-ru-MUN ~~ ye-yo.*	My name is ~~.
네 .	*Ne.*	Yes.
아니요 .	*A-ni-yo.*	No.

some practical implications and makes suggestions for educators in the U.S. when they work or communicate with Korean students and their parents.

Communication

There are some instructional strategies that educators can use to communicate with Korean students and parents effectively. First, after giving directions in class, educators can check comprehension using non-yes/no questions. If educators ask, "Do you understand?," Korean students are likely to say "Yes" or nod their heads to be polite or to save face. Thus, instead of asking yes/no questions, educators can ask more specific questions such as "What do you need to do first?" or "What is your role in your group?"

Second, educators can use written interaction as well as oral interaction. For example, educators can provide an activity handout that includes written instructions after explaining the activity orally. Korean students are likely to have better reading skills than oral language skills, so educators can build on students' strengths while addressing their weaknesses. Educators can use this strategy to communicate with parents, too (e.g., parent letters).

Classroom Participation

It is important to build stress-free and safe learning environments to encourage Korean students to participate in classroom discussions. For example, educators can work on building a friendly relationship with Korean students through casual daily conversations and interactive dialogue journals (Woodward, 2001).

Also, educators can use group discussion before whole class discussion to help Korean students. In the Think-Pair-Share strategy (Wright, 2012), before the main classroom discussion, students can pair up and share their ideas quickly. This will make Korean students more willing to share their ideas since friendships between friends or people at the same age tend to be viewed as the only equal relationship in the Confucian hierarchy. In addition, Korean English language learners can practice speaking before the whole class discussion and perhaps feel less shy about speaking in class.

Parent Involvement

Educators can involve Korean students' parents in their children's learning. As the literature notes, Korean parents value parental support and are willing to sacrifice much for their children's learning. In order to involve parents in their child's learning, educators can provide students with interactive homework, assignments that are done with parent participation (Battle-Bailey, 2003).

Additionally, parents can be involved in assessment. For instance, educators can send a parent feedback form that will be completed by parents and included in students' writing portfolios along with peer feedback and teacher feedback forms. This will provide parents with an opportunity to be more involved in their child's education and assessment.

Motivation

As noted in the previous section, Korean school culture encourages students to work hard to win the competition and to live up to the family's or educators' expectations. In other words, students are more likely to work hard to receive rewards or to avoid negative consequences than to study for enjoyment, which suggests that they might be more extrinsically motivated. Although extrinsic motivation is also important and may be transferred to intrinsic motivation in the long run, intrinsic motivation can last longer and make students more self-directed and happier in the classroom. Therefore, educators should use learning activities that can stimulate both intrinsic and extrinsic motivation. For example, since much schoolwork, including classroom activities and exams, can be competitive in nature, educators can offer students choices, such as types of activities or assignments and topics of discussion, presentation, or reading so that they can learn to be in control of their own learning and more internally rewarded. Moreover, engaging them in self-assessment is a good way to make them more intrinsically motivated. While they are engaged in self-assessment of their own work, they can reflect on their weaknesses and strengths and set improvement goals for next time.

Oral Communication

Educators should correct Korean students' speech errors in a way that does not embarrass or intimidate them, preserves face, and does not discourage them from speaking in English. For example, if a Korean student says, "Teacher, I buy apple yesterday," the teacher can correct the errors implicitly by asking/modeling, "You bought apples? How many apples did you buy?"

Also, educators can have one-on-one conference with students. Educators can sit with a Korean student and discuss their frequent errors based on an anecdotal record that the teacher keeps regularly. Although accuracy is important, it is not always essential to maintain conversation. Thus, instead of correcting the errors directly and frequently, educators can ignore some mistakes unless these errors lead to misunderstanding or communication breakdown. If educators correct every speech error students make, this may increase their speech anxiety and they are likely to be frustrated and reluctant to speak in English (Wright, 2015).

Academic Writing

Educators can use graphic organizers to help students practice writing thesis statements. Moreover, introducing good examples before they start writing can be helpful for Korean students. Explicit and consistent feedback with encouragement, during and after the writing class, will increase Korean ELLs' motivation and writing competence.

Reading

Educators can encourage students to read in Korean extensively in class and at home. According to Wright (2015), reading in the first language can influence reading in the second language positively since literacy strategies learned from first language reading experiences can be transferred to second language reading. Reading in Korean is also beneficial for students in order to learn content in depth. Additionally, educators can recommend some English books that are the appropriate level, length, and content for extensive reading.

CONCLUSIONS

Overall, this chapter discusses distinct features of Korean culture and language and provides some practical tips for educators to help them work with Korean students and their parents effectively. However, this chapter does not aim to generalize the whole Korean culture, and this information should not be used to stereotype Korean students and their parents in the U.S. In other words, it is important for educators not to use this information to overgeneralize about Korean students but to use it as a tool to understand where they are from and to build learning environments that embrace their cultural diversity.

ADDITIONAL RESOURCES

Brown, J., & Brown, J. (2006). *China, Japan, Korea: Culture and customs*. North Charleston, SC: BookSurge.

> This book provides in-depth analysis of cultures and customs in China, Japan, and Korea and their cultural similarities and differences.

California Department of Education Bilingual Education Office. (1992). *Handbook for teaching Korean-American Students*. Sacramento, CA: California Department of Education.

> This handbook aims to provide educators and school administrators with insight into educational, sociocultural, and linguistic characteristics of Korean American students.

Haynes, J. (2007). *Getting started with English language learners: How educators can meet the challenge*. Alexandria, VA: Association for Supervision and Curriculum Development.

> This book provides introductory but practical guidelines to help educators and teachers who are beginners at providing instruction for English language learners.

Ro, J. M. (2010). Identities of young Korean English language learners at school: Imposed or achieved? *The Reading Matrix, 10*(1), 1–14. Retrieved from http://www.readingmatrix.com/articles/april_2010/ro.pdf

> Based on Gee's (2000–2001) analytical framework, the author analyzes the constructed identities of two young Korean English language learners in American school environments to gain insight into their academic success and attempts to illustrate current realities of U.S. education and instructional approaches to meet both the academic and affective needs of English language learners.

Yoon, K. K., & Williams, B. (2015). *Two lenses on the Korean ethos: Key cultural concepts and their appearance in cinema*. Jefferson, NC: McFarland.

> This book explains key cultural concepts such as *han* (regret), *jeong* (feeling), and *deok* (virtue) and examines narratives in both South Korean and North Korean movies to discuss how these concepts are expressed in the movies.

TASKS FOR EDUCATORS

1. What might you need to do to help ELLs from Korean-speaking backgrounds learn to use English in your classroom?

2. Interview an ELL student from a Korean-speaking background. Ask the student about linguistic or cultural difficulties they have had in U.S. classrooms.

3. How have your perceptions of Korean students and culture changed after reading this chapter? Discuss.

4. Find a video or audio clip about the Korean education system. Share it with others and discuss what you learned.

REFERENCES

Bae, C. (August, 2007). *Ancestor worship and the challenges it poses to the Christian mission and ministry* (Unpublished doctoral dissertation). University of Pretoria, South Africa. Retrieved from http://repository.up.ac.za/bitstream/handle/2263/25045/Complete.pdf?sequence=10

Barrett, M. J. (1990). The case for more school days. *The Atlantic Monthly, 266*(5), 78–106.

Battle-Bailey, L. (2003). Training educators to design interactive homework. *ERIC Clearinghouse on Teaching and Teacher Education*. Retrieved from http://eric.ed.gov/?id=ED482700

Brown, J., & Brown, J. (2006). *China, Japan, Korea: Culture and customs*. North Charleston, SC: BookSurge.

Chang, S. J. (2010). When East and West meet: An essay on the importance of cultural understanding in global business practice and education. *Journal of International Business and Cultural Studies, 2*, 1–13.

Farver, J. A. M., Kim, Y. K., & Lee, Y. (1995). Cultural differences in Korean and Anglo?American preschoolers' social interaction and play behaviors. *Child Development, 66*(4), 1088–1099.

Fillmore, L. W., & Snow, C. E. (2002). What educators need to know about language. In C. T. Adger, C. E. Snow, & D. Christian (Eds.), *What* educators need to know about language (pp. 7–54). Washington, DC, and McHenry, IL: Center for Applied Linguistics and Delta Systems.

Institute of International Education. (2016). *International students in the United States: 2015–16.* Retrieved from http://www.iie.org/Services/Project-Atlas/United-States/International-Students-In-U.S.#.WCtQzDbrvVh

Jiang, X. (2006). Cross-cultural pragmatic differences in U.S. and Chinese press conferences: The case of the North Korean nuclear crisis. *Discourse & Society, 17,* 237–257.

Johnson, J. E., Christie, J. F., & Yawkey, T. D. (1999). *Play and early childhood development.* (2nd ed.). New York, NY: Longman.

Jung, W., & Stinnett, T. (2005). Comparing judgements of social, behavioural, emotional and school adjustment functioning for Korean, Korean American and Caucasian American children. *School Psychology International, 26*(3), 317–329.

Kim, K. (2012). *Rootless: A chronicle of my life journey.* Bloomington, IN: Author-House.

Kim, W. (2015). *Global pulls on the Korean communities in Sao Paulo and Buenos Aires.* Lanham, MD: Lexington Books.

Kim-Renaud, Y. K. (1997). *The Korean alphabet: Its history and structure.* Honolulu, HI: University of Hawaii Press.

Korean Culture and Information Service (KOCIS). (2008). A Korean style table setting. Retrieved from http://www.korea.net/NewsFocus/Culture/view?articleId=72871

KOCIS. (n.d.a). Festivals. Retrieved from http://www.korea.net/AboutKorea/Korean-Life/Festivals

KOCIS. (n.d.b). Religion. Retrieved from http://www.korea.net/AboutKorea/Korean-Life/Religion

Merkin, R. S. (2009). Cross-cultural communication patterns—Korean and American communication. *Journal of Intercultural Communication, 20.* Retrieved from http://www.immi.se/intercultural/nr20/merkin.htm

Paik, S. J. (2004). Korean and U.S. families, schools, and learning. *International Journal of Educational Research, 41*(1), 71–90.

Park, Y., Crystal, D., & Watanabe, H. (2003). Korean, Japanese, and U.S. students' judgments about peer exclusion: Evidence for diversity. *International Journal of Behavioral Development, 27*(6), 555–565.

Organization for Economic Co-operation and Development (OECD). (2014). *Balancing paid work, unpaid work and leisure.* Retrieved from http://www.oecd.org/gender/data/balancingpaidworkunpaidworkandleisure.htm

OECD. (2015). *Education at a glance 2015: OECD indicators.* Retrieved from http://www.keepeek.com/Digital-Asset-Management/oecd/education/education-at-a-glance-2015/korea_eag-2015-66-en#page1

Paxton, N. (2013). *The rough guide to Korea.* New York, NY: Penguin.

Salmon, A. (December, 2013). OECD education report: Korean educational excellence culturally rooted. *The Telegraph.* Retrieved from http://www.telegraph.co.uk/education/10491188/OECD-education-report-Korean-educational-excellence-culturally-rooted.html

Sorenson, C. (1994). Success and education in South Korea. *Comparative Education Review, 38*(1), 10–35.

Spolsky, B., & Sung, K. (2015). *Secondary school English education in Asia: From policy to practice*. New York, NY: Routledge.

Statistics Korea. (2005). *Statistics of Korea's major religions*. Retrieved from http://kostat.go.kr/portal/english/help/1/index.board?bmode=list&bSeq=20185

Suh, B., & Price, G. E. (1993). The learning styles of gifted adolescents in Korea. In R. Milgram, R. Dunn, & G. Price (Eds.), *Teaching and counseling gifted and talented adolescents: An international learning style perspective* (pp. 175–186). Westport, CT: Praeger.

U.S. Department of State. (2014). *International religious freedom report for 2014*. Retrieved from http://www.state.gov/j/drl/rls/irf/religiousfreedom/index.htm#wrapper

Woodward, T. (2001). *Planning courses and lessons: Designing sequences of work for the language classroom*. Cambridge, UK: Cambridge University Press.

Wright, W. E. (2015). *Foundations for teaching English language learners: Research, theory, and practice* (2nd ed.). Philadelphia, PA: Caslon.

Yoon, K. K., & Williams, B. (2015). *Two lenses on the Korean ethos: Key cultural concepts and their appearance in cinema*. Jefferson, NC: McFarland.

Zong, J., & Batalova, J. (2014, December). Korean Immigrants in the United States. Retrieved from http://www.migrationpolicy.org/article/korean-immigrants-united-states

SECTION 7

AFRICAN REGION

CHAPTER 20

WORKING WITH STUDENTS FROM NORTH AFRICA

Omran Akasha and Mohamed ElHess
Washington State University

Ali Abdullah is a Libyan father of two children, one of whom is a first grade student in a rural town in the U.S. His daughter, Fatima, has faced some challenges in her school due to the differences between Arab and English languages and cultures. At the same time, Abdullah has faced some difficulties trying to keep their family traditions, culture, and religion while in the U.S. One religious obligation for Fatima is to avoid eating meat at lunchtime in school. To make sure she only ate halal *(permissible) foods, Fatima's father clearly stated on the lunch form that was sent by the school that Fatima should not be given any pork or other meat; in other words, Fatima could only eat fish at lunch or something that did not contain meat at all. Part of the problem was that Fatima could not understand the purpose for the restriction because other children in her classroom could eat meat and pork. It was hard for her to understand the idea of* haram *(impermissible) foods based on Islamic law* (shari'a). *To help her, Abdullah visited his daughter's school many times to explain to her teacher some of the challenges that he and Fatima faced, including eating halal and not playing with boys. Abdullah found it very hard to work with the teacher to solve the problems because he discovered that she was not very aware of challenges related to cultural differences. Thus, the teacher could not offer him the support he expected; she only told him that all students would be treated equally, which actually meant that it would be inequitable for Fatima.*

Views From Inside: Languages, Cultures, and Schooling for K–12 Educators
pp. 349–368
349

BACKGROUND

A number of North African Arab families come to the United States each year seeking knowledge, looking for a better life, or fleeing from unstable countries like the Sudan, Egypt, and Libya. As in Fatima's case, North African Arab children and their families could face a number of challenges as they set up lives in the United States because of cultural and linguistic differences. To understand these children better, this chapter looks both at Arab countries in general and more specifically at the six nations that comprise the North African Arab region.

According to Carrasquillo and Rodríguez (2002), Arabs generally live in countries spread in North Africa and in two regions west of Asia (the Gulf States [Chapter 4] and the *Alsham* region [Chapter 5]). Most of them speak Arabic and share a common culture and heritage, but they may differ slightly in political and religious beliefs. However, the majority of Arabs practice one of two forms of Islam (in other words, they are Sunni or Shia); most Arabic-speaking countries consider Islam the main religion and Arabic as the official language. The Arab world, including North Africa (NA), "accounts for just over two-fifths of the total population of the entire Muslim world" (Chuchmuch, 2006). NA countries that are majority Arab include Libya, Egypt, Algeria, Tunisia, Morocco, and Sudan. The North African part (excluding Egypt and Sudan) of the Arab world is known as the Maghreb. Although people in most of the NA countries believe that they are descendants of Arabs, Egyptians prefer to be perceived as descendants of ancient Egyptians (Bassiouney, 2009).

History

The histories of the countries that comprise the North African group are different from each other. For example, after gaining its independence from joint British and Egyptian rule in 1956, Sudan suffered violence and Africa's longest-running civil war, which ended by separating South Sudan from the north in 2011 (BBC News, 2014). Libya, on the other hand, was known in the past by its tenuous relationship with the West, especially the U.S., and it became even worse when Libya was accused of the 1988 U.S. plane bombing over Lockerbie, Scotland, for which a Libyan man was convicted. In 2011, Tunisia, Libya, and Egypt witnessed revolutions that toppled their regimes. Since then, however, these countries have been economically and politically unstable and insecure, resulting in thousands of citizens displaced or persecuted.

One characteristic of North Africa is that it contains the largest subtropical hot desert in the world, the Sahara Desert; this location has impacted the economies of all the NA countries. While Egypt's economy depends mainly on agriculture, tourism, and export, Libya depends primarily on its oil industry. Sudan, which shares the Nile River with Egypt and has been ranked as one of the poorest countries in the world, depends mainly on agriculture (Elbagir & Karimi, 2011). All countries of North Africa, however, suffer from a high unemployment rate, especially among its younger population.

SCHOOLING

According to the latest statistics (Huebler & Lu, 2012), South Sudan has the lowest literacy rate in the world. It is estimated that 15% of the school dropouts between 2008 and 2009 were due to a lack of textbooks and insufficient number of schools and teachers. According to the same report (Huebler & Lu, 2012), Egypt's literacy rate is 92%. However, many Egyptian public schools are overcrowded to the extent that students cannot find desks, and there are insufficient texts and technological resources. In some villages in Egypt, the illiteracy rates are high due to lack of transportation, high poverty rates, and the absence of enough teachers. At the same time, Libya's literacy rate is 99%, one of the highest in Africa. In 1986, a Libyan Ministry of Higher Education resolution stated that English would no longer be part of the curriculum in Libyan educational institutions (Kreiba, 2012). However, English was included back in grades 7–12 and colleges in 1989, and then was gradually added to the elementary curriculum as well. Recent unrest in Libya has caused the closure of many schools and universities, and the future of Libya's education system is unknown.

Arabic is the official language in North Africa, and it is the medium of instruction in both public and private schools. French and English are considered foreign languages and are taught starting in the third grade in public schools and private bilingual schools. In the northwest of Africa—in Morocco, Tunis, and Algeria—however, the French language is still prevalent. Since the French colonization of these three Arab countries (1881–1956), its importance has quite paralleled, and sometimes surpassed, that of Arabic, to the extent that is the main language of instruction in many public and private schools in these countries. In general, people in Algeria, Morocco, and Tunisia prefer to listen to and read newspapers and journals in French (Bassiouney, 2009).

On the other hand, the impact of British colonization on Egypt and Sudan is evident in their systems of education, especially in the instruction of technical subjects such as math and science, but it did not affect the use of Arabic. Arabic in those two countries has maintained its importance and remained the sole language of instruction in public schools, long after Egyptian and Sudanese independence (some private schools provide exceptions). Also in Egypt and Sudan, French and German as foreign languages are taught in both public and private schools. In Libya, there is some use of Italian technical terms due to the fact that Libya was occupied by Italy until 1951.

In Egypt, mixed-gender classrooms can be seen at all grade levels. In other NA countries, such as Libya and Sudan, classrooms are mixed at the elementary and university levels, but not for seventh grade through high school. Textbooks in the Arab world, including NA, focus on Arab and Islamic cultures; therefore, Arab students sometimes have limited exposure to Western cultures and ideas. Arab textbooks also do not address taboo topics such as sex education or homosexuality; even if they are included in the curriculum, some teachers prefer to assign them as homework. Although using technology has countless advantages in improving literacy skills, Arab educators have not integrated it in their classrooms to a large extent (Aradi, 2013).

All schools in NA teach the Islamic faith as part of a mandatory religious class at all levels, and as Egypt has the highest percentage of Christians in North Africa, it offers classes in both the Islamic and Christian faiths. Although all schools provide counseling services for students with educational, social, and behavioral needs, Arabs in general consider their academic or social issues as private matters that should not be shared with strangers. Despite the fact that all NA schools prohibit it, physical punishment is still used on students performing inadequately, to command respect for the teacher, or to maintain classroom discipline; it is even perceived as effective pedagogy (Wasef, 2011). Furthermore, classrooms are teacher-centered learning environments where teachers concentrate on passive and rote learning such as memorization, direct instruction, individual activities, dictation, choral repetition, and drill exercises (Chuchmuch, 2006).

Although NA Arabic-speaking students who come to the U.S. can receive a better education, they may also need extra help and support so that they can fully integrate into the new system socially and academically. In addition to the language barrier, NA Arabic-speaking students could also face some difficulties participating in classroom activities and engaging in classroom discussions in student-centered classrooms. Having this in mind, both parents and their children may need to know how the school system works in the U.S. Thus, giving parents and students an opportunity to participate in workshops or classes about the school, American life, American culture, school culture, and other important factors could help them better understand, and hence learn to work within, the new system. In addition, providing such important information to the new family and making use of a home language interpreter or translated documents could help the children face challenges more successfully.

CULTURE

People

Although the role of Arab scholars during medieval Islamic civilization was very significant in different fields such as medicine, mathematics, geography, and chemistry (Santos & Suleiman, 1993), Arabs and Muslims are not often credited for their contributions that benefit the whole world (Hamada, 1990). For example, Arabic numerals (1, 2, 3, etc.) are one example of a contribution that millions of people use in their daily lives. Further, Mohammed ibn-Musa Al- Khowarizmi, a Persian scholar who published work in Arabic, invented algebra in the 9th century; he also developed algorithms, a quick method of multiplying and dividing numbers (Szalay, 2013). Many other Arabs have made contributions that still have impacts today. In his 2009 speech in Cairo, Egypt, U.S. President Barak Obama clarified some of the Islamic contributions to the world. The president noted that:

> It was Islam ... that carried the light of learning through so many centuries, paving the way for Europe's Renaissance and Enlightenment. It was innovation in Muslim communities that developed the order of algebra; our magnetic compass and tools of navigation; our mastery of pens and printing; our understanding of how disease spreads and how it can be healed. Islamic culture has given us majestic arches and soaring spires; timeless poetry and cherished music; elegant calligraphy and places of peaceful contemplation. (The White House, Office of the Press Secretary, 2009, para. 5)

In other words, Arabs from North Africa have significantly impacted our world. Important Arab scholars include:

- Ibn Khladun (A.D. 1332–1406). Abd al Rahman Ibn Khladun was born in Tunisia. According to Hamada (1990), Ibn Khladun was considered one of the greatest historians and historiographers ever and he is acknowledged as the founder of modern sociology, historiography, and economics. His statue can be found in the capital, Tunis.
- Ibn Battuta (A.D. 1304–1369). Ibn Battuta was born in Morocco and is known for his famous travel book about his extensive travel experiences, *Rihla* (*My Travels*). In this book, he recorded his journeys that included trips to North Africa, Eastern Europe, the Mid-

dle East, south and central Asia, and China. *Rihla* is one of the best resources for information about the ancient world; as Bullis and MacDonald (2000) note, "His descriptions of life in Turkey, Central Asia, East and West Africa, the Maldives, the Malay Peninsula and parts of India are a leading source of contemporary knowledge about those areas, and in some cases, they are the only source" (n.p.).

- Prophet Muhammad (*Peace be upon him*, PBUH). The teachings of the Prophet Muhammad (PBUH), along with the different principles of Islam, impact Arabic and Muslim culture today. The Prophet (PBUH) is one of the most influential figures to Muslims everywhere, whether in North Africa, the Arabian Peninsula, *Alsham*, or elsewhere around the globe. The Prophet (PBUH) was born on the 12th of *Rabi Al Awwal* (based on the lunar calendar) in 570 AD. Before the Prophet Muhammad (PBUH), every part of Arabia was steeped in polytheistic beliefs, slavery, adultery, gambling, and alcohol consumption. Muslims believe that the Prophet Muhammad (PBUH) was sent by God (*Allah*) to change this and teach all humankind about Islam. Unacceptable behaviors were then gradually forbidden. The teachings of the Prophet (PBUH) are followed by millions of Muslims around the globe. Some of his sayings are:
  o "Seeking knowledge is a duty of every Muslim."
  o "God will show no compassion on the one who has no compassion towards all humankind."
  o "He who eats his fill while his neighbor goes without food is not a believer."
  o "Cleanliness is half of the religion" (Council on Islamic Education, 1998).

These edicts form the basis of the Arab Muslim's way of life. They are also part of the educational materials that are used to educate people about good behaviors and manners with family, parents, neighbors, and society.

However, Arabs in one area may interpret the Quran differently from those in other areas, relying on the local clergy's (sheiks') interpretations of the Quran in accordance to the context and time. This issue, unfortunately, may sometimes lead to conflicts among Muslims.

Some North African Muslims also believe in *jinn*—spirits created by God and made from fire. *Jinn* are invisible to the naked eye and are not limited to time and space; therefore, they are more powerful than human beings. The Holy Quran contains a Sura on these creatures (Sura 72: AL-JINN-Juz' 29). In Arabic cultures, some people believe that *jinn* can possess humans' souls, objects, or animals. For instance, one of the prevalent beliefs is that black cats are possessed by *jinn*, and people need to restrain from keeping them. People believe that there are good *jinn* in the world, which are good omens, and bad *jinn*, which cause harm. In case of *jinn* possession and black magic (voodoo), people resort to magicians and clergy to break the spell.

Ethnicity and Tribes

In many Arab countries, people define themselves according to the tribe or family that they belong to. Every Libyan, for example, must belong to a specific tribe that he/she should be loyal to and retain its traditional cultural and moral code. For example, one ethnic group that lived in Africa before the Arabs was the Berbers, known as *Amazigh* (free people) in Arabic. Their descendants reside nowadays in Algeria, Morocco, and Egypt, but the largest populations are in Tunisia, Libya, and Mauritania. The *Amazigh* native language is *Tamazight*, which originates from the ancient Egyptians. As a result of the Muslim conquest and the European colonization of NA, many *Amazighs* speak varieties of Maghrebi (Moroccan) Arabic, French, and Spanish. Tribal affiliation is often the cause of conflict in NA countries.

Traditional Clothes

Dressing modestly and conservatively is essential for both men and women in the six Arab countries in North Africa; thus, wearing loose-fitting clothing in public is the common dress code for that region. In Egypt, for example, the traditional Egyptian garment for men in small towns and villages is the *galabeya*—a long ankle-length garment with long sleeves of different designs and colors, much like the white *dishdasha* in the Gulf countries. Libyan and Sudanese men in villages and small towns wear similar attire for special events and religious celebrations—either a white *galabeya* or a long traditional white knee-length garment with open edges on both sides. However, nowadays in big cities, the majority of men generally wear Western-style clothes such as jeans and shirts or suits in public and in the workplace (but not during Friday prayers or other religious festivals).

To comply with the Islamic clothing code, women in all North African countries typically wear nonrevealing and long loose clothes in order to conceal the contours of their bodies. In many places, women are required to cover their heads with a *hijab*, or headscarf, which completely covers the head and the neck. To Muslim women, the hijab symbolizes modesty and piety. As they reach puberty, girls are obligated, according to Islamic custom, to put on their *hijab* when they go out in public. This also occurs when appearing to strangers, known in Arabic as *ghayr mahram* (males whom women are allowed to marry, such as a cousin or random Muslim male). Women who refrain from wearing the *hijab* are either non-Muslim or do so by their personal voluntary decision.

Acceptable and Unacceptable Behaviors

There are many differences between customs from NA countries and those in the U.S. For example, North African Arabs do not generally

- Hold someone's neck. This is insulting for Egyptians.
- Shake hands with the opposite sex. Different opinions can be found over this issue, so there is no one way to state whether shaking hands with the opposite sex is acceptable. Thus, when meeting with a person of the opposite gender, it is wise to let the other party start first unless you know his/her opinion on shaking.
- Use the left hand. Arabs eat, drink, and shake hands using their right hands, because they consider the left hand unclean. The historical reason for this is that using the left hand is for personal hygiene when going to the bathroom.
- Speak with the same politeness conventions expected in the U.S.; Arab people make requests directly without using terms like "please." Sometimes, when people try to be polite, others tell them not to stand on ceremony, and they may even go so far as being mad at the person for doing that. In the U.S., this apparent lack of politeness may come across as rude or demanding.
- Cross legs when sitting facing other people. This is a sign of disrespect to the other party (Egyptians in particular).
- Keep their hands in their pockets while talking.
- Have the bottom of a shoe face someone else—another sign of disrespect.
- Photograph people without their permission, particularly females.
- Wear shoes when entering a mosque or a house; they are usually left at the door.

Unacceptable behaviors can be slightly different from one place to another; however, being aware of such differences can help teachers when, for example, meeting a family member of an NA Arabic-speaking student, whether at school or at home. Moreover, knowing such behaviors could make a teacher's visit more comfortable and successful. For example, entering a house after leaving shoes at the door could be seen as a sign of respect to the Arab family.

Values and Beliefs

Although there are always exceptions, in general:

- Arabs appreciate social relationships and are willing to greatly inconvenience themselves to please others.
- Arabs greatly value social interdependence.
- Good manners require that one never directly refuses a request—it is good to be agreeable all the time.
- Arabs are known for their hospitality, generosity, and giving gifts.
- Freedom of speech is not valued and transparency is not encouraged.
- Arabs in general reject Western culture, as it is perceived to have lower social and moral standards (Nydell, 2006).
- Interruption is not considered a rude behavior; it signifies engagement in conversation.
- People of the same gender in general tend to stand close while speaking. In fact, the closer the distance, the closer the relation is; holding hands or hugging among people of the same gender is a sign of intimacy and friendship.
- Because many Arabs believe in the power of the evil eye (a cultural, not religious, belief), Muslims tend not to reveal their future plans or their achievements until they have been accomplished.
- Arabs rarely admit to errors if doing so will cause them to lose face (Nydell, 2006).
- Arabs feel that criticism of their work is a personal insult (Nydell, 2006).
- Older people are highly respected and have authority over young people.
- Punctuality is not observed at all; invitations are not set for a specific time. Time is relative in the Arab world. Being late for work, school, or a special event is not considered disrespectful.
- North Africans would rather disguise a problem than bring shame to their family. For NAs, "Family is a person's ultimate refuge" (Nydell, 2006, p. 91).

- In the Arab culture, most Muslims are fatalistic and believe that destiny is foreordained by *Allah*, who makes all decisions. Therefore, people have no responsibility for their own actions. For example, in the classroom context, failing an exam can be attributed to fate rather than academic proficiency.

These values, although very common, have exceptions for individuals based on factors such as background knowledge, education, society, and family. Rather than attributing them to students across the board, teachers can find out more about their particular students. Knowing students' values, teachers can be prepared to support their students based on their specific needs. For example, teachers can highlight a family's values and include them in their lesson. This way, students can share their knowledge and experiences with the class. When language is a barrier to such activity, teachers can include a home activity so the student can receive support and help from their parents or other family members.

Impact of Religion

Islam has five main obligations, known as *arkan* al Islam, "the five pillars of Islam"; described in earlier chapters, these are: (a) declaration of Islamic faith ("there is only one God, *Allah*, and Muhammad is his messenger"), (b) praying five times a day, (c) *zakat*, or giving 2.5% of one's savings to the needy, (d) fasting during *Ramadan*, and (e) making a pilgrimage (*hajj*) to the holy site of Mecca in Saudi Arabia. Like all Muslims, people of North Africa believe that the Islamic holy book, the *Quran*, is the supreme authority in Islam. It shapes and governs all facets of daily life. The *Quran* is also important because it is the directive for Islamic *sharia* law, in which Muslim social actions and values are laid out. To any Muslim, religion is a way of life; in other words, religion and culture are inextricably intertwined. According to Bassiouney (2009), religion in the Arab world is not seen as a matter of individual choice, but as a matter of family and group affiliation; one is born a Muslim, a Jew, or a Christian, and this characteristic is almost identical to one's ethnicity.

Important Days and Holidays

Teachers who are aware of Islamic holy days and holidays might be better able to support their Muslim students in meeting the requirements of these celebrations. The most important days are described below.

Ramadan

Ramadan is the 9th month in the lunar calendar. It celebrates the foundation of the first Muslim city-state, a turning point in Islamic and world history. This month is considered a special month for all Muslims around the world, and it starts and ends on different days each year that are determined by changes in the lunar calendar.

- Muslims fast during the day—from dawn to sunset—for the whole month.
- Before the dawn prayer, families eat *sahoor* (food) to prepare themselves for the next fasting day.
- It is very common in Ramadan to see families visit each other at night.
- It is also common to see Muslim students in middle and high schools fasting during school hours. It is therefore very important to bear in mind any possible challenges the students may face.
- During the last few days of Ramadan, each Muslim family is required to give a determined amount of money as a donation (*zakat*) to the needy, and it should be given before the *Eid-ul-Fitr* prayer that comes immediately after Ramadan.

Eid-ul-Fitr (Festival of Fast-breaking)

Eid-ul-Fitr is defined as "an annual Muslim festival marking the end of Ramadan, involving the exchange of gifts and a festive meal" (Eid-ul-Fitr, 2012).

- It is the first day of *Shawwal*, the 10th month of the lunar calendar.
- In all Arab and Muslim countries in North Africa, *Eid-ul-Fitr* is a 3-day holiday for governmental and educational institutions. In the U.S., this means that Muslim children may miss school.
- *Eid* is a time for buying new clothes for everyone in the family (as well as toys for children) because on the day of *Eid*, everyone should wear new clothes.
- On the day of *Eid*, Muslims gather early in the morning in outdoor locations or mosques to perform the *Eid* prayer.
- After the *Eid* prayer, Muslims usually visit families, neighbors, and friends and give gifts, especially to children.
- Families, friends, and neighbors visit each other during the three days of *Eid* to congratulate each other and share their food.
- Every family offers different types of desserts as a sign of welcome to others.

- All families gather during *Eid*; in most cases they gather in their parents' house.
- The deceased are remembered during *Eid* by their friends and families.

Eid ul Udha

This is the tenth day of *Dhu* al-*Hijjah*, the last month in the lunar calendar. This festival, which comes at the end of the *hajj*, the fifth Pillar of Islam, as mentioned previously, that requires every adult Muslim to travel to and pray in Mecca once during his or her lifetime. *Eid ul Udha* remembers an event in the life of the Prophet Ibrahim (peace be upon him), which is the Arabic name for the biblical Abraham. To all Arabs and Muslims in North African countries, *Eid ul Udha* is a major holiday. Like *Eid-ul-Fitr*, on the day of *Eid* Muslims gather early in the morning in outdoor locations or mosques to perform the *Eid* prayer.

- There is a similar gathering of families and friends and wearing of new clothes.
- A family usually sacrifices a sheep, cow, or goat and has a barbecue; they also donate one-third of the sacrificed meat to the poor and needy as *sadqa* (charity).

Food

As noted in the classroom scenario that began this chapter, eating approved foods is important for Muslims. *Halal* is an Arabic term that is mentioned many times in the *Quran* to give permission to Muslims for doing or eating certain things. The opposite of *halal* is *haram*, which means "forbidden" or not permitted according to *sharia* (law). The rules include:

- Alcohol and pork are totally forbidden (*haram*), so Muslims do not usually eat pork or drink alcohol.
- Although they can eat other kinds of meat like chicken, beef, and lamb, the animals must be ritually slaughtered first.
- Similar to kosher for Jewish people, in Islam *halal* food refers to any meat or other products containing meat that meet the religious requirement.

It is important for Arab and Muslim students that such food issues are taken into account, for example, when having parties in the classroom or school.

LANGUAGE

Arabic has many differences from English. Some of these can cause native Arabic speakers challenges when it comes to learning English.

Characteristic of the Arabic Language

Arabic belongs to the Semitic family of languages, of which Hebrew is also a member.

- It is written and read from right to left.
- It has 28 letters (see Table 20.1).
- It has only 3 vowels (aa, ee, oo)
- It uses verb-subject-object order (e.g., "read (verb) Ahmed (subject) the book (object)."
- It has only one article (e.g., "The book" = "Al ketab").
- It uses words that are written as they are pronounced, so it is common to see Arabs write English words like "knife" as "nif" or "honest" as "onest."

Arabic-speaking students may experience difficulty with the following in English:

- Capitalization: There is no distinction between lower and upper case in Arabic.
- /P/ and /b/ sounds: In Arabic, there is only one letter that represents the /b/ sound (ب), so students may face difficulty in pronouncing the /p/ sound.

Table 20.1. Arabic Alphabet With English Sounds (Starts With the Letter _Alif_ and Ends With _Yaa_)

خ	ح	ج	ث	ت	ب	أ
kha	haa	jiim	thaa	tah	bah	alif
ص	ش	س	ز	ر	ذ	د
saad	shiin	siin	zaay	raa	thaal	daal
ق	ف	غ	ع	ظ	ط	ض
qaaf	faa	ghayn	ayn	thaa	taa	daad
ي	و	ه	ن	م	ل	ك
yaa	waaw	ha	nuun	miim	laam	kaaf

- Articles: The articles "a" and "an" do not exist in Arabic.
- Placing the stress in English: Because stress is regular in Arabic, Arabic speakers may have a problem distinguishing between verbs and nouns with the same root [e.g., PREsent (noun) and presENT (verb)].
- Word order: Nouns precede adjectives in Arabic, so students may mix this up in English. For example, in Arabic *"sayaraton jamila"* is literally translated as "car nice."
- English present perfect tense: This constitutes a problem for Arabic-speaking students because it is marked for present time (e.g., I have eaten today). Arabic students tend to use adverbs of time that denote past time with this verb form due to the Arabic usage (e.g., I have eaten it yesterday) (Mansour, 2011).

The Arabic language, in particular MSA (Modern Standard Arabic), is considered very important to all Muslims because it has a strong bond with religion, culture, and, most important, in reciting and understanding the most sacred text of Islam, the *Quran*. Table 20.2 presents some common Arabic phrases that teachers can learn and use.

As mentioned previously, a number of linguistic differences exist between English and Arabic. Thus, Arabic-speaking students who arrive in the U.S at an older age could have more problems in recognizing the

Table 20.2.   Common Words in Arabic

English	Context	Transliteration	Arabic Phrase
Hello (literally, "peace be upon you")	When you first meet people	AssalAMa'LAIkom	الســـلام عليكـــم
Hello (literally, "peace be upon you, too")	To reply to the Arabic greeting	WaaLAIkomASsa'lam	وعليكـــم الســـلام
Hopefully (literally, "If Allah wills")	To confirm an appointment or any future plan	In'ShAaAllah	إن شـــاء الله
What's your name?		Ma'ISmok? (male); Ma'ISmek? (female)	ماإسمك؟
Good morning		SabAHal'KHEer	صـــباح الخـــير
How are you?		KAefa'HAlok	كيـف حالـك
Okay	To agree with something	'HAder	حاضر
Yes		'NA am	نعـم
No		'Laa	لا

differences. At this stage, students might write and read from right to left, write an English sentence with no or incorrect articles, and use adjectives after nouns as they learned in their first language. To support Arabic-speaking English language learners, teachers might try to give their students more time to process the new language. As Akasha (2013) found, Arabic-speaking students face some difficulties in learning new vocabulary in the mainstream classroom; thus, preparing lessons that include some pictures may enable these students to better connect the lesson to their prior knowledge. Peer support can also be another way to help these students, and this can be done by a native speaker who has the ability to give some support to others and/or a native speaker of Arabic who has already acquired the second language.

IDEAS FOR EDUCATORS

To understand NA Muslim students further, Carter (1999) and Akasha (2013) point out several important issues that teachers and school administrators can consider:

Stereotypes

Muslim students and their families often face negative stereotypes in U.S public schools (Akasha, 2013; Carter, 1999; Jackson, 1995). Teachers should be aware of and carefully address discrimination in the form of name-calling, using media misinformation to denigrate Arab students and their families, and making fun of Arab customs.

Home/School Relations

Muslim parents are not likely to request a meeting with their child's teacher because they want to avoid disturbing the process of teaching and because, as Jackson (1995) argues, Muslim families respect educators and hold them in high esteem. Carter (1999) also notes other factors that may prevent parents from requesting meetings with the teacher, such as the fear of being misunderstood culturally and linguistically. However, parents of Arabic-speaking students welcome teachers if they request a home visit or classroom meeting.

Family Relationships

It is very common in Muslim society to see a Muslim child living within a family community and having close relationships with extended family members. This large family may include siblings, parents, grandparents, aunts, uncles, and others. The family is valued in Islam; there is a special respect for parents and a great respect particularly for mothers. Everyone plays an important role in the family based on their age. Most often the father is the head of the family and the mother looks after the children and home. Moreover, the parents' decisions are almost always respected (Ariza, Lapp, Robison, & Rhone, 2003; Carrasquillo & Rodríguez, 2002; Jackson, 1995). Family relationships can be very important to Arab students, and allowing students to talk and write about important family members can help connect the lesson to students' lives.

Arab/American Peer Relations

American students' lack of knowledge about Muslim students' cultures and religions (and of U.S. customs by Arab students) may cause some misunderstandings with their peers. Carter (1999) notes that Muslim students may appear "different" when displaying signs of their religion, such as wearing a *hijab* (scarf) for female students or fasting during the day in the holy month of *Ramadan*. These characteristics may look "weird" to others if they lack knowledge about Muslim culture. Sharing all students' customs may be one way to ameliorate any discomfort or misunderstanding.

Working in Groups

Talking and working with the opposite sex, particularly for new students and for those who come from segregated schools, could be a challenge for NA Arab students. This needs to be taken into account as it may discourage students from participating in discussions. Teachers may talk to the student and/or the family to make sure the student feels comfortable within his/her small group, particularly when it is mixed-gender. If the new student is not participating or taking part in the classroom discussion, teachers could encourage the student by allowing him/her to choose his/her partners.

Reading and Critical Thinking

The Arab culture has a long history of oral recitation and puts less emphasis on reading other than the *Quran*. Arabic-speaking students learn colloquial Arabic at home, followed by learning the modern standard at school (Abu-Rabia, Share, & Mansour, 2003; Palmer, El-Ashry, Leclere, & Chang, 2007). Abu-Rabia et al. (2003, p. 426) state that "literary Arabic is taught to children at school almost as a second language," and thus, as Palmer et al. (2007) argue, there is a real need for teachers to address issues that affect NA students' reading development. Teachers can invite families to reading workshops to demonstrate the value of reading, and they can also introduce technologies to encourage reading, such as animated videos and audio books.

In addition, Arab learners may lack critical thinking skills; as noted above, rote learning is pivotal to the learning process in their home countries, with little or no focus on creativity. The Arab/Muslim value of not questioning stands in opposition to what students are expected to do in U.S. schools. Thus, teachers can understand the need to model and explain creative and critical thinking tasks and to take into consideration student backgrounds as they do so.

Curricular Issues

Wingfield and Karaman (2001) reported that a member of the American-Arab Anti-Discrimination Committee (ADC) complained about not being taught about Arab cultures in her earlier school days, whereas the curriculum included Jewish culture. This curricular discrimination is also noted by Carter (1999), who argues that there is not equal coverage in the school curriculum. He gives an example of a parent complaining about her child's spelling book that included *Chanukah* (a celebration in Jewish culture), whereas nothing was included about their Islamic culture. Wingfield (2006) also indicates that it is common to see lessons on *Chanukah* or hear Christmas carols in school; however, it is not common to see *Ramadan* and other Muslim holy days noted in the school calendar. Ariza et al. (2003) urge public school teachers to consider their Arabic students by introducing Islamic culture in their curriculum. However, negative or incorrect information about Arabs and Islam can also be taught in schools through materials that have not been appropriately vetted (Britto, 2008). To ensure reliability, teachers can review textbooks for religious and cultural prejudices by consulting members of the target community. The teacher can also invite a family member to the classroom and/or arrange a visit to the community—for example, visiting mosques during Muslim festivals or other daily practices.

CONCLUSIONS

One more thing to be taken into account by teachers can be learned from the following personal experience. The first author of this chapter, Dr. Akasha, was in a teacher education classroom preparing preservice teachers to visit Arab families to learn more about their children, culture, and language. To prepare preservice teachers for the visits, he gave them some tips to help ease their worries and support their success in their first meetings with the families. Interestingly, one of the preservice teachers asked if she could take a gift to the family, and her suggestion was a bottle of wine! Although gifts are fine for a family, a bottle of wine can be a sign of disrespect to the family's values, culture, and religion because alcohol is *haram*. This showed that learning about the family's values and culture ahead of time could be very helpful.

To sum up, this chapter provides information that is important for teachers to know about Arab countries in general and North African Arab countries in particular. The aim is to provide a clear understanding of Arabic cultural and linguistic characteristics in order to support teachers of Arabic-speaking English language learners. Learning about Arab culture is necessary and important in order to create a positive classroom environment. Most important, teachers can also integrate some materials from this chapter into their lesson plans and create classroom activities that are related to their students' background knowledge; this can be very effective and useful for instructing Arabic-speaking and Muslim students.

ADDITIONAL RESOURCES

U.S. Library of Congress (2016). *Middle East and North Africa resources*. Available from https://www.loc.gov/rr/armed/
   Links to everything from *AlJazeera* News to Human Rights Watch. Great teaching resources.
The Qu'ran. (2016). Retrieved from https://quran.com/
   The Islamic holy book verse by verse with audio and translations.
North Africa. (2016). Available from http://allafrica.com/northafrica/
Zurutuza, K. (2016). To be black in Libya. *New Internationalist*. Retrieved from https://newint.org/features/web-exclusive/2016/06/23/to-be-black-in-libya/
   Racism and tribalism in Libya and how it affects the people.

TASKS FOR EDUCATORS

1.   Use this chapter and other resources to answer these questions:
   •   What might the history and education of North African Arab countries mean for students coming into U.S. schools? What should teachers consider?
   •   How do the Prophet's sayings, listed above, compare with your understanding of Islam? Why might your understandings be different from the NA Muslim authors of this chapter?

- How might you address behaviors that are okay for U.S. students but unacceptable for NAs in your classroom?
- Many of the values listed above conflict with traditional U.S. school values. What might this mean for your classroom?
- What might you need to do to help ELLs from Arabic-speaking backgrounds learn to use English in your classroom?

2. Based on the information in the chapter, about what do you need more information concerning Muslim Arab students from North Africa? List three places you might find this information.

3. What are some similarities and differences between what you read in this chapter and what you knew about Muslims/Arabs before you read? Why might that be?

4. Reading is an essential part of education in the U.S. How might you interest Arabic-speaking students in reading more?

REFERENCES

Abu-Rabia, S., Share, D., & Mansour, M. S. (2003). Word recognition and basic cognitive processes among reading-disabled and normal readers in Arabic. *Reading and Writing: An Interdisciplinary Journal, 16*, 423–442.

Akasha, O. (2013). Exploring the challenges facing Arabic-Speaking ESL students and teachers in middle school. *Journal of ELT and Applied Linguistics, 1*(1), 12–31.

Aradi, W. (2013). Education technology usage in Arab higher education. *Tahseen* Counseling. Retrieved from http://tahseen.ae/blog/?tag=educational-technology-usage-in-arab-higher-education

Ariza, E. N., Lapp, S. I., Robison, S., & Rhone, A. (2003, January). Coping with cultures in the classroom. *Proceedings of the Hawaii International Conference on Education*. Mānoa, HI: University of Hawaii.

Bassiouney, R. (2009). *Arabic sociolinguistics*. Edinburgh, UK: Edinburgh University Press.

BBC News. (2014, August 14). *South Sudan profile*. Retrieved from http://www.bbc.com/news/world-africa-14069082

Britto, P. R. (2008). Who am I? Ethnic identity formation of Arab Muslim children in contemporary U.S. society. *Journal of the American Academy of Child & Adolescent Psychiatry, 47*(8), 853–857.

Bullis, D., & MacDonald, N. (2000). From pilgrim to world traveler. *Saudi Aramco World, 51*(4). Retrieved from http://www.saudiaramcoworld.com

Carrasquillo, A. L., & Rodríguez, V. (2002). *Language minority students in the mainstream classroom* (2nd ed.). Bristol, UK: Multilingual Matters Ltd.

Carter, R. B. (1999). Counseling Muslim children in school settings. *Professional School Counseling, 2*(3), 183.

Chuchmuch, S. D. (2006). *Impacts of education and modernization on Arab Muslim society* [Unpublished M.A. Thesis]. Ann Arbor, MI: Michigan State University.

Council on Islamic Education. (1998). *Teaching about Islam and Muslims in public school classrooms* (3rd ed.). Fountain Valley, CA: Council on Islamic Education.

Eid-ul-Fitr. (2012). Dictionary.com. Retrieved from http://www.dictionary.com/browse/eid-ul-fitr

Elbagir, N., & Karimi, F. (2011, July 10). South Sudanese celebrate the birth of their nation. *CNN World*. Retrieved from http://www.cnn.com/2011/WORLD/africa/07/09/sudan.new.nation/

Jackson, M. L. (1995). Counseling youth of Arab ancestry. In C. C. Lee (Ed.), *Counseling for diversity: A guide for school counselors and related professionals* (pp. 41–60). Boston, MA: Allyn & Bacon.

Hamada, L. B. (1990). *Understanding the Arab world*. Nashville, TN: Thomas Nelson Publishers.

Huebler, F., & Lu, W. (2012). *Adult and youth literacy: 1990–2015 analysis of data for 41 selected countries*. UNESCO Institute for Statistics: Canada.

Kreiba, H. (2012, September 25). Learning English in Libya: A long suppressed ambition. *The Tripoli Post*. Retrieved from http://www.tripolipost.com/articledetail.asp?c=5&i=9206

Mansour. A. S. (2011). Difficulties in translation of the English present perfect simple and the past perfect simple into Arabic and some suggested solutions. *Alustath, 200*, 502–521. Retrieved from http://www.iasj.net/iasj?func=fulltext&aId=30087

Nydell, M. (2006). *Understanding Arabs: A guide for modern times*. Yarmouth, ME: Intercultural Press.

The White House, Office of the Press Secretary. (2009). *Remarks by the president on a new beginning*. Retrieved from https://obamawhitehouse.archives.gov/the-press-office/remarks-president-cairo-university-6-04-09

Palmer, B. C., El-Ashry, F., Leclere, J. T., & Chang, S. (2007). Learning from Abdallah: A case study of an Arabic-speaking child in a U.S. school. *The Reading Teacher, 61*(1), 8–17.

Santos, S., & Suleiman, M. (1993). Teaching English to Arabic-speaking students: Cultural and linguistic considerations. In L. Malave (Ed.), *Annual Conference Journal* (pp. 175–180). Washington, DC: National Association for Bilingual Education. Retrieved from http://www.eric.ed.gov/PDFS/ED360865.pdf

Szalay, J. (2013). Who invented zero? *Live Science*. Retrieved from http://www.livescience.com

Wasef, N. H. (2011). *Corporal punishment in schools* [Unpublished M.A. thesis]. The American University in Cairo, School of Global Affairs and Public Policy, Egypt.

Wingfield, M. (2006). Arab Americans: Into the multicultural mainstream. *Equity & Excellence in Education, 39*(3), 253–266. doi: 10.1080/10665680600788453

Wingfield, M., & Karaman, B. (2001). Arab stereotypes and American educators. In E. Lee, D. Menkart, & M. Okazawa-Rey (Eds.), *Beyond heroes and holidays: A practical guide to K-12 anti-racist, multicultural education and staff development* (pp. 132–136). Washington, DC: Network of Educators on the Americas.

CHAPTER 21

NIGERIA

Nathaniel Hunsu
University of Georgia

Olusola Adesope
Washington State University

Jumping onto his bed still in his daywear and shoes, Emeka called out to Kareem, his friend:

Emeka: Can you imagine my embarrassment today!

Kareem: Wetin dey? *(What happened to you?)*

Emeka: Rob invited me, a couple of his American friends, for ice cream to celebrate his girlfriend's birthday.

Kareem: Ehen …

Emeka: I went thinking they'll pay for their guests *(has a bewildered look)* … I was overly disappointed…

Kareem: Ha ha ha … *(Interjects with long ludicrous laughter)*

Emeka: You dey laugh! I was so embarrassed, I ate the most expensive pie and ice cream, and had to pay with my last $10 bill, only reserved for any emergency needs till I get my first pay, when it dawned on me that I was on my own.

Kareem: Uhm … *(Laughs even more)*, wake up friend this is not Nigeria, better prepare to pay when you are so invited, or find a nice way to decline.

Views From Inside: Languages, Cultures, and Schooling for K–12 Educators
pp. 369–382

Emeka: Kai, see as I be *mugun*! *(Imagine how I just fooled myself!)*
Kareem: Man, you're welcome to the world, this is America!

BACKGROUND

Nigeria is a West African country sitting at the extreme corner of the Gulf of Guinea. It shares borders with the Republic of Benin on the west and the Niger Republic on the north, with Cameroon and Lake Chad to the east. The Gulf of Guinea defines its 853 km (530 mile) coastline in the south. Its geographical space is just a little less than one and a half times the size of the state of Texas, but it has slightly more than half the population of the United States. The country enjoys a tropical climate with varying degrees of dry and rainy seasons depending on location. Most Nigerians only know an all-year summer, with gradations in annual rainfall from its coastlines in the south to its savannas and semi-arid regions in the north, and bouts of the gusty *harmattan* winds that blanket its northern states with Saharan dusts late in the dry seasons.

The Nigerian state, its geographical boundaries, and its nomenclature are the product of the territorial ambitions of colonial Great Britain. The nation is an agglomeration of diverse ethnic groups, each with a distinctive cultural identity. Ethnic groups in Nigeria are broadly classified as ethnic "majorities" and ethnic "minorities" (Mustapha, 2006). The country is often loosely classified into three ethnic groups from which comes the term *WaZoBia*—a combination of the word "come" in the languages of the Yoruba, Hausa, and Ibo respectively. The term implies a uniting of Nigeria's people. There are, however, other large "minorities" (e.g., Ijaws, Efik, Nupe, Edo, Kanuri, Fulani) and a myriad of other smaller minority groups. Otite (1990) posits that Nigeria is a country of more than 350 ethnic groups. Even before the colonial era, most ethnic groups had an established form of perennial rulership, often headed by a king. The most successful ethnic groups had vast empires, some spanning beyond the current geographical boundaries of Nigeria; for example, the Kanem-Bornu Empire and the Sokoto caliphate extended to regions within other current western and northern African countries.

Each ethnic group is identified with a particular region of the nation's 356,667-square-mile landmass. Hausa-Fulanis occupy the northern regions, Igbos the southeast, Yorubas the southwest, and other minority groups are identified with other specific geopolitical regions. However, because of the lack of even distribution of social amenities and economic opportunities, people of most ethnic groups live in the country's major commercial cities. Although Nigeria has a few urban and semiurban cities that offer some services comparable to those obtainable in Western cities, most of the country's settlements are rural or semiurban townships.

The nation is endowed with many natural resources—ranking 10th (ahead of the United States) in its proven oil reserve—and it is the 12th largest producer of petroleum (Central Intelligence Agency, 2012). Despite its potential for being a leading global economy, its wealth is hoarded away in the hands of a very few elites—a recent UNICEF report suggests that about 55% of the country's population lives on less than $1.25 per day (UNICEF, 2013).

The prevailing socioeconomic situation in the country is the result of successive poor governance and resource mismanagement. Since independence from Britain in 1960, the country has had a succession of civilian rulers overthrown by disgruntled military juntas. While the military has always used corruption and bad governance as an excuse for usurping civilian rule (Julius-Adeoye, 2011), their regimes have been fraught with ignoble human rights violations, repression of free speech, and misappropriation of public funds. These and other factors have concocted the prevailing socioeconomic morass in the country.

After sustained civil activism and mounting international sanctions, however, the military could no longer retain its grip on governance, paving the way for democratic governance. Since the Fourth Republic was established in 1999, the country has witnessed a mix of economic boost and civil insurgence. The democratic experiment in Nigeria has not delivered its goods for most people, due to poor management. Nigeria has not been able to leverage the power in the diversity of its people. Nigerians are, however, enterprising; riding on the prevailing global information culture, more and more Nigerians are pulling themselves up by their bootstraps in their bid for a better quality of life.

CULTURE

The culture and customs of the Nigerian people are as diverse as the country's ethnic constituencies. However, many of the ethnic cultures share common practices; as a result of interethnic marriages, commerce, and other communal interdependencies, neighboring ethnic groups have borrowed much from each other.

Languages

Nigeria is one of the most linguistically diverse countries in the world (Omotosho, 2014). The *Ethnologue* website posits that Nigeria has 522 distinct living languages (Paul, Simons, & Fennig, 2016). However, the English language has been officially adopted to facilitate cultural and linguistic unity. It is the language of instruction at all levels of schooling. Hausa, Igbo, and Yoruba are major languages spoken in public spheres, depending on the region of the country. Pidgin English is also rampant around the country. Many Nigerian languages, and subsequent cultures associated with them, are in danger of extinction because of the increasing dominance of the English language. More of the younger generations of Nigerians who aspire to break into a higher social class in Nigeria regard speaking English language alone as an indicator of social class (Ohai, 2013). In homes where English speaking is privileged, it is not uncommon for children to grow up not speaking the local language.

Family Life

Nigerians, like people in most of the non-Western world, have a collectivistic cultural orientation. This is reflected in the family structure in most of its ethnic groups, in spite of the strong influence of Western values in recent times. In most ethnic groups, families have a dominant father figure, and extended families are the traditional familial experience of many Nigerians. In the past, families were often a knit of extended families living within a common space. Polygamy was commonly practiced in the past but has significantly waned in recent times due to the influences of Christianity and Western civilization. Besides, the increasing cost of living in modern civilization makes financing polygamy prohibitive, especially in cities.

Family Structure and Customs

In most ethnic groups, the father, as the head of the family, is expected to provide for the family; mothers as housekeepers are dependent on their husbands, although the increasing cost of living has changed this structure significantly. More women are becoming actively engaged in professional careers and local politics. While divorce is not uncommon, most women would rather remain in a marriage in most parts of the country than endure the social stigma that comes with being divorced, even if love and emotional attachment do not exist (Falola, 2001). Children are expected to respect their elders, and children's upbringing is viewed as the collective work of all in some communities. It is considered disrespectful to engage in an argument with an elder, while making direct eye-to-eye contact might be considered rude. In the same vein, it is against the norm for the younger (or junior) to call the elder (or senior) by name. This custom eventually goes beyond families, as not adhering to these norms could mar a good working relationship, and deviants are commonly seen as lacking proper home training. On that note, a Nigerian student would mostly likely refer to her instructor as "Teacher" or "Miss/Mister" and might find the use of first names an "American thing."

Marriage

Marriage ceremonies in Nigeria vary from place to place; however, many ethnic groups have practices in common. In the past, marriages were often arranged for the groom, while a marriage broker often mediated between the contracting parties. In this case, marriage would not necessarily be for love and could be between a girl in her teens and an adult. Modern marriages are more often made between consenting adults. These, however, must still often comply with deeply rooted customs and traditions. Most customs follow a three-stage marriage process: first, an introduction ceremony in which the two families meet. A delegation of elders from the groom's extended family meet with the bride's family to ask for their daughter's hand in marriage. This is followed by an engagement ceremony, which often involves families and friends of the couple. Depending on the ethnic group, the groom brings gifts and dowry items for the traditional engagement ceremony. The amount of the dowry varies from one ethnic group to another and could range from a few items to an exorbitant list of items demanded by the bride's family. The engagement ceremony is then followed by a formal marriage ceremony in a church or mosque to obtain a cleric's blessing. Some few couples choose a court marriage, where the bride and groom are joined by a magistrate.

Religion

Religious affiliation is integral to the culture of the peoples of Nigeria. A recent poll ranked Nigeria second for religiosity on the global index for religiosity and atheism (Gallup International Association, 2012). Many Nigerians hold dearly to religion, especially as a solace in the present time of national socioeconomic hardship, and they see God as hope for provision and protection in the face of increasing economic and social insecurity.

Christianity and Islam are the two major religions—about 48.1% of the population identify with the Christian faith, while 50.4% of the population are Muslim. Some, albeit a shrinking population, still practice other forms of indigenous religions; most ethnic groups had beliefs about gods and worshiped several deities before the arrival of Islam and Christianity in precolonial periods. Some deities are similar across ethnic groups and share features with those found in European mythology. For example, *Sango* is a common deity in Yoruba mythology but is referred to as *Amadioha* among the Igbo people. *Sango* shares features similar with Thor in Norse mythology (Werness, 2003). Indigenous religious practices share such similarities as annual festivals, rituals, and sacrifices. Different types of masquerades are often identified with religions in specific regions across the country.

With the *jihad* campaigns of Usman dan Fodio, a religious teacher and writer, in the early 19th century, most of northern Nigeria was Islamized; missionary activities entrenched Christianity as the major religion in the southern regions of the country (Aguwa, 2005). As a result of the routes of their propagation, the two religions are largely associated with ethnic regions of the country—Hausas in the north are majority Muslims, with Igbos in the south mostly Christians, and Yoruba areas have a blend of the two.

Clothing

Nigerians have a variety of dress styles, and how people are dressed often indicates their ethnicity. These traditional attires are diverse and colorful and depend on taste, the occasion, and social status. Most Nigerian fabrics are patterned and multicolored. Everyday dresses for most city people and office people include Western dress types, while most of the people who live in rural Nigeria dress more simply. For special occasions, men wear *sokoto* (pants), *buba* (blouse), and a traditional cap. Yoruba men complement their attire with a flowing garment (*agbada*) worn over their outfits. Holding a staff to complement an outfit is a mark of status in some other parts of the country when attending social functions. Women, on the other hand, have an assortment of styles for *iro* (wrapper) and *buba* (blouse) and gowns topped with different styles of headgear.

Food

Although a vast assortment of food can be found across the country, most ethnic groups share some very similar food types and eating habits. Nigerian traditional meals often include "solid foods" (local expression of food prepared in a certain way) made from powdered or granulated root and tuber crops like cassava, yam, and plantain. These staple food items have different names depending on the region of the country, but they share a common name when prepared in a certain way (e.g., *gari, fufu, tuwon*). These foods are eaten with one's bare fingers. Locals wash their hands, roll up a morsel mixed with soup and swallow; hence the nickname "swallow" for this style of food. Unlike the Western custom of serving dessert, many Nigerians would *step-down* (as some say) a relished meal with an after-dinner drink of preference (such as palm wine). Foods referred to as "solid," rice, beans, and bread are common household foods. However, many prefer the "solids" with meat or fish garnished with spicy soup. In fact, most Nigerians in Western countries recoil at the casserole, potato, and bread-centered meals of the West and do all they can to eat Nigerian.

Other Customs

Greetings and Etiquette

Most ethnic cultures in Nigeria highly value greetings and good manners. Among the Yorubas, for instance, there are greetings for almost every occasion and event. It is considered spiteful not to greet one's neighbor. Yorubas, for example, would say "*E k'aabo*" (welcome) when you return from an outing, to which the response is "*E ku 'le*" (literally, "good evening"). A younger man greets an elder with a bow to show respect, while younger women greet the elderly by kneeling on one or both knees. Younger men may also prostrate on the ground in some ethnic groups. It is deemed rude for the younger person to extend his hand to an elder for a handshake in many Nigerian cultures. When people meet, greetings are often extended to include inquiries about the general welfare of one's family, his health, and his job. Greeting etiquette is also very important in formal and professional settings—the junior is expected to show respect to his seniors in order to maintain a working relationship, and not greeting one's senior in the morning is a sure sign of lack of respect and might foment trouble. Overseas, Nigerians still value greetings and would appreciate a teacher who not only knows their names but is also concerned enough to stop, greet them, and ask about their welfare.

Haggling

It is common for Nigerians to haggle on the price of commodities in the marketplace, as one might do at a garage sale in the U.S. Unlike in the West, most grocery purchases are made in the common market where wares do not come with price tags. This makes being able to negotiate commodity prices a common and desired trait for Nigerians. It is a brand-new experience for many Nigerian students when they find that they have to scout for sales, deals, or rebates to get a bargain in the American marketplace.

Conflict Resolution

From the perspective of an American, the conversational style of many Nigerians may appear loud and aggressive. This, however, is a way to show that one is passionate about the discussion. Similarly, Nigerians are prone to resolve conflicts by direct confrontation and call their opponent out on hard truth. Unlike Westerners, who may be more inclined to be indirect in dealing with conflicts or dissatisfactions, it is easy to tell when there is relational conflict or dissatisfaction between parties in Nigeria. Shows of displeasures are often open and may be displayed as direct confrontation or an outright boycott.

EDUCATION

There are three notable educational systems in Nigeria: indigenous education, Quranic-schools, and Western education (Country Studies, 2017). Nigerians' attitudes toward or preferences for any of these systems depend on their social exposure or religious convictions. For example, the indigenous system of education often comes in apprenticeship arrangements between a protégé and his/her mentor. This means that a parent may choose to send a daughter to learn tailoring for an agreed-upon period of time, after which she gets her "freedom" to practice. This practice is common among the lower rungs of the society or those who drop out of school because they find formal education too challenging.

Quranic education, in which students study the *Quran*, is common with Nigerian Muslims. Quranic education may be had along with, or exclusive of, Western education, depending on the region of the country and religious convictions. For example, some northern Islamic fundamentalists support the *Almajiri* model of education (a type of Quranic boarding school for the very poor), while some are outright enemies of Western forms of education—for example, the *Boko Haram* Islamic sects.

Western education began through missionary expeditions in Nigeria, and it has since flourished in the country. Today, Nigerians place a very high value on education, partly due to the proliferation of highly skilled jobs and an increasingly harsh economy. Western education is seen as the ticket for social mobility in Nigeria's emerging culture. This thought is well portrayed in a nostalgic Yoruba folk song taught and sung in elementary schools in western Nigeria—"*B'o ba ka'we rę, bàtà rę á dún kokokà*" ("If you study hard, you could wear a prestigious shoe").

Many Nigerians now aspire for education in Western countries as a result years of government neglect of the development of the nation's education system. For some, schooling abroad means earning a certain prestige when they return to Nigeria (this is especially so among the elite), while it is deemed a route to emigrate for others. Although Nigerians have been studying abroad since the early 1900s, there has been an explosion in the desire for foreign education and its accompanying prestige recently. Currently, Nigeria has more students studying overseas than any other African country besides Morocco (Clark & Ausukuya, 2013). In their sojourn abroad, Nigerian students are among the most successful in education. According to a recent U.S. census, about 40% of Nigerians in the U.S. hold a bachelor's degree, 17% hold a master's degree, and 4% hold doctorates—higher than the ratio of U.S. Whites and Asians who hold those degrees (Aziz, 2012). Their fascination with higher education stems from the acknowledgment of the fact that it is the foremost vehicle of social mobility in the Western countries where they sojourn.

Nigerian students coming into American classrooms would already speak the English language, although with varying degrees of accent depending on their ethnicity and linguistic inclination. However, it is not uncommon for some to struggle initially with American accents and language expressions. Many Nigerians new to American classrooms may also be bewildered by the teaching style and struggle with understanding some language expressions and the use of self-expression in White-dominated classrooms. The norm in the classroom experience of a typical student from Nigeria is to see a teacher stand and teach in from of the class. He expects to read for and take an exam at the end of the session. He also expects much of the summative assessment to depend on the final examination. However, what he may get in an American classroom is a constructivist learning model, in which he has to read and discuss his week's readings in class. This becomes even more problematic if the reading material is voluminous and dense. Because he may struggle with his accent and language expression, coupled with the fact that some students in the class may try to avoid working in groups with students of color, the Nigerian student may find the first year of school challenging and overwhelming. However, by being empathetic about what is counted as classroom participation, teachers can do a lot to ease the burden, thus minimizing the student's apprehension and encouraging social integration. Because of their achievement need, most Nigerian immigrant students soon get over the initial culture shock and seek cultural integration.

Nigerian students may also be surprised by the grading system in American schools. The letter grade "A" means a score of 70 in Nigeria, and it takes a lot to convince the teacher to assign that "A." A "B" in Nigeria is considered a prestigious grade, while a "C" is not held in the same disdain as in America. In fact, the letter grade "D," which is equivalent to 45 out of 100, is the passing grade in most Nigerian schools. However, the letter grade "A" in America schools means to score 90 or above and seems to come more easily to students than the Nigerian letter grade "A." For the Nigerian student, America makes learning fun and easy, and they would do their best to reap that "A" letter grade.

IDEAS FOR EDUCATORS

Based on the information provided in this chapter, American teachers of Nigerian students may consider:

- Using educational videos and multimedia aids that vividly illustrate the topic of a class lesson. Using well-designed (or well-illustrated) multimedia instructional material helps people foreign to American culture relate to and understand what they need to learn in their American classroom. The effective use of educational videos may help students to situate a new learning experience within their prior cultural experiences.

- Rethinking the use of examples from popular culture when illustrating a point in the classroom. For example, a reference to American football might lose a Nigerian student's attention because he is unfamiliar with football, which in his mind is what Americans call "soccer."

- Ensuring a positive classroom climate. The Nigerian student is conscious of her foreign status, especially if holding a student visa, and is considerably conversant with America's age-long racial struggles. Such self-consciousness may color student perceptions of relationships with others, impact self-efficacy, and affect her class participation. Teachers may do well to encourage racial intermingling when students work in groups and enjoin students to appreciate people who are culturally different from them. Nigerians would most likely shoulder more group responsibilities and work beyond the call of duty to make themselves respected when working with people of other ethnic groups.

- Explaining cultural differences. For example, when discussing or debating in the classroom, the Nigerian student might appear loud, which might be problematic for other students. In reality, she never meant to appear loud, but that is the nature of friendly expression in the first culture. By being aware of and exploring these differences, the teacher can help avoid prejudice against the student.

- Knowing students' names, monitoring their educational development, and making them know they can succeed in America if they try hard enough can make a very big difference for those students who find themselves experiencing unanticipated challenges after migrating to the U.S. Nigerian immigrant students do appreciate teachers who are passionate about what they teach and clearly care about students' progress.

CONCLUSIONS

We believe that teachers are better equipped to offer instruction when they understand their students' background and cultures. This chapter provides an overview of the major cultures and customs of the Nigerian people. While we acknowledge that an extensive description of Nigeria and the Nigerian people is beyond the scope of this chapter, we believe the chapter sufficiently describes Nigeria to help American teachers relate better with Nigerian students in their classes. Along with the resources noted below, it should also contribute towards their making viable curricular decisions that could impact the climate and culture of their classrooms and lighten the experiences of Nigerian students in their classrooms.

ADDITIONAL RESOURCES

Falola, T., & Heaton, M. (2008). *A history of Nigeria*. Cambridge, UK: Cambridge University Press.
> A leading historian and an expert in Nigerian science and culture combine their expertise to explain Nigeria's recent history.

Onyefulu, I. (2009). *Ikenna* goes to Nigeria (Children return to their roots). Singapore: Frances Lincoln Children's Books.
> An engaging photo-essay about of a young boy who visits his cousins in Nigeria. Includes maps, locations and photos. Appropriate for children in grades K–3.

For Teachers: Nigeria. (2016). Retrieved from http://www.ket.org/artstoolkit/wodm/tour/africa/nigeria/teachers.htm
> Educators might find useful information about Nigeria. For example, how Latin music is connected to Nigerian and African rhythms and instruments.

Cultural Information—Nigeria. (2014). Retrieved from http://www.intercultures.ca/cil-cai/ci-ic-eng.asp?iso=ng
> Global Affairs Canada offers information and links for understanding cultural, political, and religious aspects of Nigeria.

Lemieux, D. (2012). *Nigeria—culture smart!:* The essential guide to customs *and* culture. London, UK: Kuperard.
> A useful guide for visitors who are planning to stay in Nigeria for more than just a few days.

Siollun, M. (2013). *Nigerian history videos*. Retrieved from http://maxsiollun.word-press.com/nigerian-history-videos/
    A variety of videos about Nigerian history.

TASKS FOR EDUCATORS

1. What are some of the challenges that Nigerian students, fluent in English, might experience in U.S. schools?

2. Interview a student or adult from Nigeria. Ask what types of challenges they have in communicating with others in the United States.

3. View the TED Talk, *The Danger of a Single Story* (Adichie, 2009). What did you learn about your "single story" about Nigeria and Nigerian people?

4. Why do you think the speaker in the video in question #3 states that there is never a single story about any place?

REFERENCES

Adichie, C. N. (2009, July). *Chimamanda Ngozi Adichie: The danger of a single story* [Video file]. Retrieved from https://www.ted.com/talks/chimamanda_adichie_the_danger_of_a_single_story?language=en

Aguwa, J. C. (2005). Christianity and Nigerian indigenous culture. In C. J. Korieh & G. U. Nwokeji (Eds.), *Religions, history, and politics in Nigeria* (pp. 14–28). Lanham, MD: United Press of America.

Aziz, N. (2012). *Survey: Nigerians most educated in the U.S.* Retrieved from http://www.bet.com/news/national/2012/03/20/survey-nigerians-most-educated-in-the-u-s.html

Central Intelligence Agency. (2012). Nigeria. *The world factbook.* Retrieved from https://www.cia.gov/library/publications/the-world-factbook/geos/ni.html

Clark, N., & Ausukuya, C. (2013). *Education in Nigeria.* Retrieved from http://wenr.wes.org/2013/07/an-overview-of-education-in-nigeria/

Country Studies. (2017). Nigerian education. Retrieved April 26, 2017, from http://countrystudies.us/nigeria/49.htm

Falola, T. (2001). *Culture and customs of Nigeria.* Westport, CT: Greenwood.

Gallup International Association. (2012). *Global index of religion and atheism* [Press release]. Retrieved from http://sidmennt.is/wp-content/uploads/Gallup-International-um-tr%C3%BA-og-tr%C3%BAleysi-2012.pdf

Julius-Adeoye, R. J. (2011). Nigerian economy, social unrest and the nation's popular drama. *Afro Asian Journal of Social Sciences, 2*(2.3), 1–11.

Mustapha, A. R. (2006). *Ethnic structure, inequality and governance of the public sector in Nigeria* (UNRISD Programme on Democracy, Governance and Human

Rights, Paper No. 24). Geneva, Switzerland: United Nations Research Institute for Social Development.

Ohai, C. (2013, August 8). Gradually, Nigerian languages are dying. *Punch Newspapers*. Retrieved from http://www.punchng.com/feature/gradually-nigerian-languages-are-dying/

Omotosho, K. (2014). *Nigeria: Local languages fight for survival*. Retrieved from http://www.bbc.com/news/blogs-news-from-elsewhere-26432933

Otite, O. (1990). *Ethnic pluralism and ethnicity in Nigeria*. Ibadan, Nigeria: Shaneson C.I.

Paul, L. M., Simons, G. F., & Fennig, C. D. (Eds.). (2016). Nigeria. *Ethnologue: Languages of the world* (19th ed.). Dallas, TX: SIL International.

UNICEF. (2013). Statistics at a glance: Nigeria. Retrieved April 27, 2017, from https://www.unicef.org/infobycountry/nigeria_statistics.html

Werness, H. B. (2003). *The continuum encyclopedia of animal symbolism in world art*. London, UK: Continuum Publishing.

CHAPTER 22

THE DEMOCRATIC REPUBLIC OF THE CONGO

A Case for Hope

Kristen L. Pratt
Washington State University

Rose Lusangi Phambu
Luila Village Ministries

Looking out to the carpet, I (first author) see my students all sitting snuggled in close together, anxiously awaiting the read-aloud we do each day after lunch. I notice my newcomer students looking up at me. They have only been in the U.S. for a couple of weeks and all four are sitting right up front, gazing at me with soulful brown eyes, excited to hear the text and see the images.

All of the students in this class speak languages other than English as their first language. This year there has been a large influx of refugee families who fled from two war-torn countries in the central region of the continent of Africa. The families are sponsored to enter the United States by a U.S.-based religious organization and are placed in low-income housing in the inner-city neighborhood that our school serves.

Each day, we start our reading time with a teacher read-aloud and a mini-focus lesson. Today, we are reading a fictional picture book about a family daring to trek

Views From Inside: Languages, Cultures, and Schooling for K–12 Educators
pp. 383–402

383

out on an adventure across the jungle river, apprehensive about the perilous obstacles awaiting them on their journey. We are using this text as a lesson in story sequencing—what happened first, next, then, and last. While I am reading the text, one of my newcomer students, who speaks Swahili, French, and his tribal language and is learning English, starts to become visibly uneasy and then covers his eyes and asks me in a loud urgent voice to, "Please, Miss, please stop." I return a gaze of puzzlement and confusion, and he proceeds to pull up the sleeve on his shirt to show me an enormous scar he has all the way up his arm. When I ask him to tell me what happened, he becomes animated, using the emerging English he developed during his studies at the refugee camp over the past year. He talks about his real-life experience crossing a river to escape from violence, how an animal in the water had attacked the boat his family was in and he had nearly died. He had been bitten in the process and felt fortunate to have survived the experience. He explains that it is hard for him to hear and see the story because it is too scary and close to his own experience.

As the year goes by, I continue to learn about the complex experiences my students bring to my classroom, working to understand the suffering and struggle as well as the hope and perseverance of the students and their families. I also grow more and more conscious of the importance of implementing culturally affirming as well as culturally sustaining pedagogy (Paris, 2012). I deeply long to have a window into my students' prior educational and life experiences in their home countries. How do the students come to know so many languages? Why is there such a difference in the formal schooling experiences between male and female refugee students? Do the students have school buildings with classrooms or is class hosted outside? Do they have materials such as pencil and paper or books? What type of training do their educators have? What are the classroom experiences around teaching and learning like for both students and educators? What was the educational experience like for their parents? And how can knowing all of this help me be a more effective teacher while supporting my students to be successful personally and academically?

BACKGROUND

The contrast between educational experiences and the direct impact learners' prior experiences have on their engagement with the language and content of school reinforces the need for educators to know: (a) their students' and their parents' countries of origin and a brief history of these countries; (b) their home language(s); (c) the ethnic and cultural groups represented in the home; (d) students' prior schooling experiences and literacy development in both their native languages and English; (e) parents' prior educational experiences; and (f) the family's socioeconomic status. The cultural richness students bring with them to school contributes to developing unique classroom communities, which deeply and profoundly impact students' academic experiences. Students may experience linguistic as well as cultural mismatches between their home culture and that of the school, and those mismatches, when not carefully attended to, can have negative outcomes for students as well as the classroom community as a whole; everyone misses out on the rich exchange of resources. As educators, we are challenged to bridge those apertures, in part through knowing and honoring students' funds of knowledge and then discerning students' educational experiences in light of the political, historical, and social contexts within which education occurred in the students' home countries. In doing so, we bring an informed understanding to students' ways of knowing and offer the most accessible instruction possible.

In this chapter, the authors explore educational experiences as they relate to students and educators in the Democratic Republic of the Congo, or the DRC. Throughout our chapter, we attempt to paint a picture of a representative educational experience for students in the DRC. Just like anywhere, there are varieties of educational experiences, and in writing a chapter like this, there is a risk of overgeneralizing. The DRC is socially, culturally, and economically diverse, with rural and urban experiences that vary widely. However, the majority of children live in rural areas throughout the DRC, and the descriptions below are typical for the average family. We first paint a picture of the political, historical, and social contexts within which education occurs in the DRC. We then share the cultural, economic, and educational experiences of educators as well as students and their families. We end the chapter with suggestions for reaching students who have immigrated to the United States from the DRC.

POLITICS AND EDUCATION—A HISTORY

Appreciating, valuing, and acknowledging the diversity of each country and cultural group on the vast continent of Africa is an enormous undertaking. Africa, in Western contexts, is often referred to as one place and one people, with gross overgeneralizations and stereotypes threatening the understanding of the rich diversity and experience of each unique group. Africa is a continent, not a country, and referring to it as one place only reifies stereotypes and categorizes all people into one group. For example, there are more than 200 ethnic groups and over 250 language and dialectal varieties spoken in the DRC alone. There are five national languages: Lingala, Kikongo, Tshiluba, Swahili, and French. French, the colonizing language of Belgium, is still used in educational and administrative contexts; however, the majority of people speak Lingala and

Kikongo during all other interactions. In fact, if you pass someone and say "*bonjour*," you are immediately identified as an outsider. Lingala and French hold equal national importance among the Congolese, although in many resources, French is listed as the sole official language, which reflects the lasting deleterious impacts of colonization. However, the perseverance of Lingala and Kikongo as national languages also reflects the hopeful perseverance of the Congolese in maintaining a deep connection to their linguistic roots as well as their ancestral heritage and culture.

The DRC is made up of stunning rolling hills, magnificent grasslands, and vast, thriving rivers and lakes, as well as three remarkable mountain ranges with incredibly captivating valleys, which geographically straddle both sides of the equator. The DRC is the third largest country on the continent of Africa, located in central Africa with 25 miles of coastline along the Atlantic Ocean. The country is approximately one quarter the size of the United States and is landlocked on all other sides by nine neighboring counties: Angola, Zambia, Tanzania, Burundi, Rwanda, Uganda, South Sudan, Central African Republic, and the Republic of the Congo. The population of the DRC has grown from 14 million in 1960 to over 60 million in 2010.

In 1885, Belgium, Germany, France, Spain, Portugal, and England conducted the Berlin West Africa Conference. Leaders of these countries boorishly and arbitrarily divided territories on the African continent to be colonized and exploited for natural and human resources. Originally, Congo (modernly called the DRC) was given to King Leopold II himself, rather than the Belgian government, to use for his own personal gain. He cruelly and callously ruled what he incongruously called the *Congo Free State's* government and territory from the distant shores of Brussels, allowing his commanders to viciously sever the limbs of those who were perceived not to meet the unrealistic quotas for rubber production. Through the brutalization and murder of entire villages used as a means of instilling fear and coercing slave labor, he singlehandedly nearly decimated the country. Finally, as a result of international outcry, in 1908 Congo was ceded to the Belgian government by the king and governed as a colony. By the time the Belgian government took over, it is estimated that over 10 million autochthonous (indigenous) people had died as a direct result of severe exploitation, starvation, brutality, and disease (SARUA, 2016).

Between 1900 and 1950, the country was exploited for mineral wealth, including but not limited to copper, rubber, and diamonds. There was a sharp increase in Belgian immigration to the DRC after WWII and with it a harsh divide between social, cultural, economic, and political opportunities for native Congolese and Belgian immigrants. Congolese did not obtain the right to vote on any governing policies until the 1960s (Haskin, 2005). On June 30th, 1960, the Democratic Republic of the

Congo gained independence from Belgium. Four days later there was a military coup in response to the racial disparity of the officers in the army. The coup was followed by five years of political unrest, followed by decades of both civil and international war. Although the DRC maintained an amazing wealth in its natural resources, there existed incredible tensions between the distinct ethnic groups who were forced together when the boundaries of the DRC were so arbitrarily drawn by the colonial nations. Joseph Mobutu led a military coup in 1965 and began the process of establishing a dictatorship and a revitalization of the DRC's precolonial identity. He renamed cities, demanded citizens change their names to traditional names, and even renamed the country the Republic of *Zaire,* meaning "great river." His position as leader persisted for nearly 30 years. In 1997, Laurent Kabila, with the support of Tutsi soldiers who had migrated from neighboring Rwanda fleeing genocide, marched into Kinshasa, the capital city of the DRC, to overthrow the government. Kabila's victory led to the country's name change to the Democratic Republic of Congo, and there has been a struggle for power ever since. The total estimated war-related deaths in the DRC as a result of the internal and international struggle to control the mineral-rich country ranges from 1.6 to 5.4 million (Haskin, 2005).

Understanding the political history of the DRC offers educators in the United States an insider knowledge of the deep and lasting consequences of colonization and the global responsibility for the state of affairs our students experience in the DRC prior to immigrating to the United States. The tyrannical colonizing practices have impacted every aspect of daily life and thus impact students' experiences in our classrooms in relation to cultural, social, and economic notions of capital and power.

EDUCATIONAL CONTEXTS IN THE DRC

Education in the DRC must be understood through the lens of a hopeful, proud, accomplished, and determined people who, in spite of nearly a century of political oppression, turmoil, and destruction, continue to press forward toward creating the country it purposes to be.

Before independence, in an agreement between Belgium and the Vatican, the Catholic Church built schools in the DRC in exchange for land concessions and grants. The missionaries were paid by the government to take over education in an effort to proselytize and fashion a Congolese elite that would serve the interests of the Belgian government. Parents were hesitant to send their children to school because the schools undermined local ways of life through assimilationist practices. The educational system created a metropolitan program, which was in line with the will of the Belgian government. This program was developed to train a small number of native Congolese to become a Congolese elite in order to exercise certain administrative powers that were in agreement with the colonizing vision (World Bank, 2005). The metropolitan program afforded only basic educational training and did not offer advanced educational or professional opportunities. Thus, the few Congolese who were willing and chosen to participate between 1906 and 1960 were trained enough to do entry-level tasks but not enough to do managerial or administrative-level work. It was not until 1954 that the very first native Congolese person was granted admission to university for purposes other than studying religion (World Bank, 2005). The education system created separate and very unequal educational spaces between Congolese and those who had migrated from Belgium. These are powerful examples of the deeply seated, systemically repressive practices carried out during the colonizing tragedy in the DRC that have had lasting impacts.

Owing to extremely oppressive and restrictive educational policies throughout the duration of the colonial occupation, there were only sixteen native Congolese who were afforded an opportunity to obtain college degrees by 1960 (World Bank, 2005). The intentional barring of educational opportunity left the Congolese void of educational experiences when independence was achieved in 1960. Seeing the enormous need for an educated populace, the government created a variety of educational reforms and programs through the newly founded Department of Education. The government obtained financial support from the World Bank through its Education Quality Improvement Project (World Bank, 1969). By 1996, enrollment of students in primary and secondary school had nearly quadrupled. Congolese educators were trained and hired along with Peace Corps volunteer educators from around the world to work in schools across the country. However, by the year 2000, due to war, economic crises, and political tensions, there were still over five million children who were not able to attend school (République Démocratique du Congo, 2005).

As of 2010, there were over 10.5 million students attending primary school and just over 17,000 students attending secondary school (République Démocratique du Congo, 2014). Currently, nearly 52,000,000 people live in the DRC, and 71% of those people live in rural areas around the country. This makes access to adequate schooling challenging. In the rural areas, over 40% of children do not attend school at all (Lygunda, 2013), even though Article 43 of the Constitution states that primary education for children ages six to twelve is free and compulsory. The *Millennium for Development* (OMD) document stated a goal of achieving a primary education for all childreén by 2015, and the Congolese were committed to obtaining this objective (République Démocratique du

Congo, 2014). However, as of 2016, the government had allocated only 3% of federal budget dollars toward education, resulting in per pupil spending falling short of covering the minimum annual cost. The budget shortcomings have resulted in inordinate sacrifices for families and educators, because even though public education is a constitutional right and is legally obligated to be accessible, many students are still not able to attend.

Congolese in the Democratic Republic of the Congo and all around the world are purposed to improving educational opportunities in which all are afforded equal opportunities and for which collaboratively they strive to change the political and educational landscape. Many have worked tirelessly for years to channel resources, both material and human, within the DRC in an effort to improve the quality of life for all. The collective efforts include collaborating with local and international organizations to exchange economic, intellectual, and material resources in an attempt to (a) create clean water reservoirs; (b) buy land and support sustainable farming; (c) teach sustainable trades for commerce; (d) offer educational opportunities through sponsorships, scholarships, and professional development; and (e) collaborate with universities.

After 1974, an acute economic crisis forced Congolese families of privilege who were not involved in the government to leave the DRC and settle in French-speaking countries such as Belgium, France, and Canada. Most remained with close ties to the DRC. Those who were mobile also chose to settle in countries such as South Africa and the United Kingdom in hopes of acquiring greater economic capital to bring back to the DRC. The mobility of many Congolese has created a unique cultural pluralism, integrating a variety of linguistic, cultural, and religious practices into the culture one sees today in the DRC. Expatriates of the DRC have learned and worked in these host countries and have also taken initiatives to lobby and advocate on behalf of fellow countrymen and women to exchange resources and capital while drawing awareness to the pressing issues facing Congolese today.

The Educator

Knowing about schooling experiences through the eyes of an educator in the DRC will enable educators in the United States to bridge experiences for students entering school in the U.S. Educational experiences in the DRC are highly valued and celebrated. Educators are rich with knowledge and impassioned to inspire and affect change through their pupils. Educators in the DRC are kind and loving with students and carry a heavy societal burden to educate the next generation at great personal sacrifice.

Educators in the DRC work tirelessly to creatively educate children with very limited resources, igniting an eagerness to learn and become meaningful contributors to society. Educators working in the DRC are eager to learn about education from around the world in order to share that knowledge within the community.

The majority of educators were born and raised in the areas where they teach. Educators are either educated locally (as in Figure 22.1) or in Kinshasa at the university, but the training is often partial because the profession is not lucrative. The pay is nominal and inconsistent, making it difficult to justify the expense of higher education; thus, many have only completed the sixth grade and have received a small training session before being employed to teach. Educators are tasked with teaching the material outlined by the government, reflecting what will be assessed on the mandated high-stakes annual exams. Just like educators around the world, educators in the DRC desire for their students to be able to solve the problems in their lives, be respectable and considerate persons, and become meaningful contributors to society.

Some of the most profound challenges facing educators in the DRC are the notions of freedom and free speech. To be free to fully express one's thoughts, concerns, and divergences from traditional norms is a luxury that many people around the world, including in the DRC, do not have. Although negotiation is a part of a cultural norm among social equals,

Source: Photo taken by Kristen L. Pratt

Figure 22.1. Teachers in a local village in the DRC receiving professional development training.

negotiation, public petition, and protest are not permitted with authority figures. The notion of relative freedom is complicated and challenging, as the country has been under colonial or dictatorial rule for over a century. Divergent thinking comes with a very real personal risk. The cultural-historical context of the learning environment in the DRC complicates how one understands one's role as a learner and how one sees oneself as having the power to make changes.

For the last two decades, education in the DRC has presented a variety of significant difficulties. As noted above, there have been challenges acquiring well-trained and well-educated instructors and administrators. When there is a qualified educator willing to endure the insecurities and the financial sacrifices embedded in the profession, the financial resources are not available for continuing education, curricular materials, or even adequate space and resources for a classroom. Education in the DRC has been subjected to many reforms through the years, as those vying for political authority alter the education system in order to carry out their political ideals, often for financial gain. Policy changes are needed in the education sector of the DRC if the social and economic conditions are truly going to change. Enhancing preservice training; improving working conditions in schools and classrooms; providing desks, chairs, and material resources such as pencils and paper as well as a curriculum; and consistently providing fair wages to reduce the need for bribes are all keys to cultivating a quality education in the DRC.

For educators in the United States, it is meaningful to understand that students from the DRC are used to their teachers and administrators being involved in their lives on a personal level beyond the academic. It is also prudent to note that the educational norms in the DRC are to offer instruction through a minimum of two, if not three, languages. Further, educators are perceived as the knowers and are expected to directly impart their knowledge to students. Finally, it is judicious to consider that the parents of our students from the DRC who are not involved in daily classroom activities are choosing to respect the educator's perceived position of power and knowledge and desire not to usurp the educator's authority. This choice is not out of a lack of desire to be involved in their child's education; it is very much the opposite. DRC students' parents deeply value education and are intimately involved with their children.

The Student

Although there is a compulsory attendance law in the DRC, in order for students to attend school, the student's parents must pay a fee because the annual federal budget does not cover operating costs. In some cases, particularly in rural areas, parents cannot pay and the children are needed at home, so students are not able to attend school. For the children who are able to attend a typical school in the DRC, they can choose one of two shifts. Class usually takes place in a school building with concrete walls and concrete or dirt floors that are swept clean of debris prior to students' arrival. The classrooms use natural light, depending on daylight to shine through the openings in the walls. Students sit on the floor or on benches in order to be able to maximize the number of students able to fit into each room. There is a green chalkboard with white chalk at the front, and students listen to the teacher lecture. Classroom resources are almost nonexistent. There are so many children in any given class that it is nearly impossible to track the progress of each student; yet educators press on, steadily working to make it better for the generations that follow.

The school day is characteristically from 7:30 a.m. until 12:15 p.m. for shift one, and the second shift is from 12:30 p.m. until 5:15 p.m., with a break for about 20 minutes halfway through each shift. Splitting the school day into two shifts is due to the large number of students, the limited classroom space, the available number of teachers, and the scarce resources. During breaks, students typically go outside to play a game of soccer for the boys and to socialize outside the boundaries of the field for the girls.

The formal educational experience in the DRC is accessible for boys and girls alike. However, there is a strong patriarchal presence where favor, power, and authority are given to males and compliance to this authority by females is expected. Class sizes can be over 60 students in a single classroom, and students are called upon to provide direct, knowledge-level answers to teacher questions. Students experience annual standardized tests required by the government. In order to be promoted to the next level, students must pass this high-stakes assessment.

Primary education in the DRC has a minimum duration of 6 years. Typically students range from ages 6 to 12. At the end of the 6th year, after students have passed their primary assessments, they earn their Certificat d'Etudes Primaries (CEP). Students must pass their primary assessments to earn their certificate, because without this certificate students are not allowed to go on to secondary school. Seventy-five percent of boys and 66% of girls who attend primary education programs earn their CEP. When children graduate from primary school in the 6th grade, there is a huge family and community celebration. The entire community commemorates the achievement with shared meals, music, and festivities. Family members of the graduating student place white talc on their heads (as in Figure 22.2) as a covering to show the community that someone from their family successfully completed primary school. The family

Source: Photo taken by Kristen L. Pratt.

Figure 22.2.   Boys with talc on their heads celebrating and playing games.

members then parade the graduate through the town, singing praises and
rejoicing with noisemakers and jubilance. The festivities begin very early
in the morning and last clear through the night. Very few students go on
to secondary school, so this 6th-grade graduation is seen as a culminating
educational experience.

For many students, this is the end of their formal schooling career and
they must go on to apprentice for the future work they will do; however,
earning the CEP affords students the opportunity to enroll in secondary
school for those with the means to do so. Secondary education is optional
and lasts 5 to 6 years. During the secondary education cycle, students can
do one of two tracks—the long or the short cycle. Only those who choose
the long cycle and pass are allowed to apply for higher educational
opportunities. The long cycle includes both general and technical education and the typical duration is 6 years. The short cycle is technical or
vocational training and lasts for up to 5 years.

It is helpful to consider that DRC students, their parents, and the generations before them have most likely only experienced schooling, if at all, up to the 6th grade. Students are not practiced in calling out answers or speaking without being called upon during class. Students are often not versed in collaborative group work or projects that result in collective performances and grades. When students are asked to generate information, it risks being perceived by the student and their parents as the educator not knowing. These common tasks in American schools can cause a cultural mismatch and frustration as students expect teachers to lecture if they know what they are talking about. Students and their families entering school in the U.S. from the DRC understand schooling as an opportunity for personal empowerment as well as an opportunity for economic and social mobility.

Situating some of the current education challenges helps to frame the educational context students immigrating from the DRC have probably experienced. Unless students are coming from families of privilege, they have very likely been afforded limited access to education and what access they have been afforded has come at a prodigious cost to their families. By the time students arrive in the United States, placing students in U.S. schools according to their chronological age poses complex quandaries that necessitate careful consideration for each individual student.

LANGUAGE AND CULTURE IN THE DRC

Families and communities in the DRC are supportive of their children. Children in the DRC are genuinely esteemed and loved. While the expressions of this love and value may look outwardly different than those expressions of adoration in the United States, children feel an intimate connection as well as an obligation to their families and those within their community. There is a strong sense of giving back to one's community and to adhering to cultural and religious practices.

Lingala

Lingala is one of many African Bantu languages. According to Omniglot (2016), "Lingala was first written by missionaries in about 1900. Today there are various ways to write it, all of which use the Latin alphabet. There is no standard spelling system and literacy in Lingala is low among Lingala speakers" (para. 7). This low literacy rate is a result of DRC history and policies, as noted throughout this chapter. The Lingala alphabet and its pronunciation are reproduced in Figure 22.3.

Vowels

a	e	ɛ	i	o	ɔ	u
[a]	[e]	[ɛ]	[i]	[o]	[ɔ]	[u]

Consonants

b	c	d	f	g	gb	h	k	l	m
[b]	[ʃ]	[d]	[f]	[g]	[gb]	[h]	[k]	[l]	[m]
mb	mp	n	nd	ng	nk	ns	nt	ny	nz
[ᵐb]	[ᵐp]	[n]	[ⁿd]	[ᵑg]	[ᵑk]	[ⁿs]	[ⁿt]	[ɲ]	[ⁿz]
p	r	s	sh	t	v	w	y	z	
[p]	[r]	[s]	[ʃ]	[t]	[v]	[w]	[j]	[z]	

Source: http://www.omniglot.com/writing/lingala.htm

Figure 22.3.   Lingala alphabet and pronunciation.

Lingala also has four tones and many borrowed words from other languages such as French, Spanish, English, and Dutch. Examples of the language include:

- ngáí = me
- wápi = where
- mamá = mother
- litéya = lesson
- nyɔ́nsɔ = all

Body Language

Meetings or gatherings in the DRC are opened with a Lingalese expression, *"Nzambe ampambola bino"* (God bless you all). It is also common for people passing by to warmly greet each other with the Lingalese expression *"mbote"* (Hello) or *"mbote ndeko"* (Hello, friend) and if they are close, one might say *"mbote ndeko nguy"* (Hello, my friend), which indicates a compassion or closeness. People greet each other by shaking hands with the right hand. To show respect of social status, people hold the right forearm with their left hand before shaking hands. Men also use the touching of their foreheads, touching each side once when they are of equal status, to communicate friendship and familiar greeting. Women kiss cheek-to-cheek, touching each side once when greeting other women, also to communicate friendliness or affection. When men and women talk to each other, there is no touching. It is also respectful to cup one hand into the other and extend both hands together with a slight bow to receive a gift or item. It is considered rude to point at a person with the index finger, as this is a frowned-upon gesture. Eye contact is important when talking; however, when children and women are addressed by men they typically look down or away to show respect.

Food

A large majority of the DRC is comprised of small, humble agricultural communities. Large trucks drive through these rural communities each week to purchase agricultural as well as manufactured goods and other products to take into the city of Kinshasa to sell. People work to maintain small plots of land, chiefly for self-sustenance, yet some have limited trade with the city. Food is not necessarily a part of daily life. When food is available, it often is a root or starch, which goes a long way in filling up one's stomach but leaves one wanting for the vitamins and minerals required to help ward off disease and maintain healthy development. Throughout the DRC, the palm tree is significant because it provides three things: (a) wine made from the sap of the tree; (b) materials for roof construction made from the leaves; and (c) palm sauce for meals made from the nuts of the tree. Palm sauce is also used as a cosmetic lotion and as a medicinal herb to heal wounds. However, the primary food for people comes from the cassava plant, a root used in the U.S. to make tapioca (see Figure 22.4 for another way of preparing cassava). In the DRC, the leaves are used as vegetables and the roots of the cassava are steamed to create a bread-like substance eaten with fingers.

Fish and meat are exceptionally expensive and are not a common source of protein for Congolese. People eat small insects such as caterpillars as a source of protein. The economy and food resources in the DRC are becoming increasingly stressed. Trees have been cut down and used for rubber, firewood, charcoal, and construction. As people have cut the trees, the insects have also become difficult to find, leaving many people nutrient-deprived. Deforestation has also resulted in large amounts of land being covered in nutrient-poor sand, which makes successful farming difficult. Innovators have begun exploring how to use the sand to make glass, but this is still in the developmental stage. Vigorous reforms

Source: Photo taken by Kristen L. Pratt.

Figure 22.4.   Cassava root wrapped and
steamed and ready for eating.

in the agricultural sector are needed in order to provide rural communities in the DRC access to adequate food and sustainable economic capital.

Family Life

Family in the DRC has an expansive definition as compared to how people understand the term in the U.S. In the DRC, by definition, everyone is related to everyone because they claim to have the same ancestor. Each village or rural area has a chief. The chief of the village serves as the spiritual leader and holds power over all in the village. He is the owner of all of the land. He is the source of any blessings and his permission is required for guests to enter. After the chief of the village, uncles are the most powerful people in the family because they have to take care of their nieces and nephews and are seen as an ally. The father is considered the head of the house with the final say over matters concerning the home and immediate family, where sons are privileged. The role of mothers and daughters is to provide and prepare food as well as to take care of the small children. Children are not allowed to question adult authority. They are to remain silent, although having children is a sign of wealth. Everyone, regardless of talent, ability, or age, is involved in work for the family's daily survival.

When people are not working, they typically stay home. Between collecting water, finding and preparing the little food available, and tending the children, women of maternal age have very little time for rest. There are places where men can buy drinks, but there is no place for entertainment outside of the major metropolitan areas. In rural DRC, people spend the majority of their time trying to survive and there is little time for leisure. The few times a year where time is made for celebrations are on religious holidays such as Christmas and Easter, when people go to church. At these events, usually people invest what little they have to purchase material and make new clothes to wear to church. These are bright, beautiful, colorful materials created into blouses, skirts, scarves, and trousers. The other celebratory events are dictated by the political calendar and are less consistent. During celebrations music is played and there is dancing in the streets.

This is an important note for educators to understand the familial and daily lives of the typical rural family in the DRC. The daily stresses and demands on families leave little time to think about reading for 20 minutes a night or practicing the times tables. When Congolese students end up in the United States, it has most often been an arduous journey. Even though students may not have a plethora of formal schooling experiences, students bring with them a wealth of linguistic, cultural, and experiential resources that can be essential assets to the classroom community.

IDEAS FOR EDUCATORS

Being curious and sensitive to what we might not know is a great place for teachers to start. People often make broad generalizations about people who are from the continent of Africa and sometimes even consider populations from African countries as homogeneous, which could not be further from the truth. As we become more aware of our own cultural lenses and biases, we can begin to unpack the systemic and lasting impacts of influences we may or may not even be aware of within ourselves that can cause unintended harm. Being mindful of assumptions, biases, and areas of ignorance, we can begin to implement a more culturally sustaining pedagogy within our classrooms. Caringly getting to know our students and their families will help us to be mindful of their experience and to challenge our assumptions. The following ideas can help students from the DRC to be successful in U.S. classrooms.

One way to get to know our students and their families is to ask questions. There are many interpreter/translator services that are willing to come in or do three-way phone calls if needed in order to communicate in one of the many languages our students and their parents speak. Meeting with families early in the year to get to know them, inviting them into your space, or visiting them in their space and being welcoming and caring will open doors for partnerships and success. Questions we might ask our newcomer students and their families include: (a) Where did you live before coming to the United States? What province? What town? Tell me about what it was like there, and let's find it on a map together; (b) What was education like and what were your prior schooling experiences?; (c)

What language(s) do you know?; (d) What are the ethnic and cultural group(s) represented in your home and community?; (e) What were your parents' occupations prior to immigrating?; (f) Tell me about your family; (g) What is your favorite tradition or celebration from your home country?; and (h) What is your favorite food from your home country? We can also gain information and develop cultural and linguistic pluralism within our classroom communities, such as game shows or small groups with questions on a spinner or card where each student spins and answers a question. When we offer our students opportunities to bring the richness and wonder of their home cultures into the classroom, we are creating spaces to engage in a more culturally sustaining pedagogy.

Another activity that educators can do to draw in parents and families from the DRC is to make sure to have dual-language texts, signs, and communications with the home. When sending any communication home it is imperative to be sensitive that communication is written in a language parents can understand. When parents are able to understand the communications sent home, they can readily support what is happening. Additionally, playing culturally familiar music as students enter the classroom is another way to help students connect their home and school cultures.

CONCLUSIONS

It is imperative to develop an awareness of the realities students and their parents face prior to entering the school system in the United States. Being cognizant of our gestures, greetings, and interactions can help make lasting first impressions. Immigrating to a new country is unbelievably challenging; the food is strange, the language is strange, the customs and mannerisms are strange, the rules for protecting one's family and property are strange, and all of that is tied to value notions of right and wrong that are deeply rooted yet ever-changing. Being sensitive to the customs and norms of students and their families comes through being informed and open to there being more than one right way to exist harmoniously in the world.

ADDITIONAL RESOURCES

101 Languages. (2005). Podcast. Retrieved from http://www.101languages.net/fsi-course-downloads/
   An additional online resource to learn Lingala.

Hochschild, A. (1999). *King Leopold's Ghost: A story of greed, terror, and heroism in colonial Africa.* Boston, MA: Houghton-Mifflin.
> An interesting text bringing to life the colonized history of the DRC.
Kasahorow, L. (2013). *Lingala learner's dictionary: Lingala-English, English-Lingala.* Seattle, WA: CreateSpace.
> A Lingala/English dictionary
Lingala Institute. (2006, January 8). 60 Free Lingala lessons on YouTube. Podcast. Retrieved from https://www.youtube.com/playlist?list=PLhAfWjnRD3SocS1Qihrf0gRFmbFoTkwyT
> An online resource to learn Lingala.

TASKS FOR EDUCATORS

1. Compare the lives of students from the DRC with those in other African countries. How are they similar and different? How do they compare to children's lives in other countries around the world?

2. View two or three of the 60 Lingala Lessons on YouTube, referenced above. Practice learning a few words and phrases. Now imagine the reverse, that is, a Lingala speaker trying to learn English. What did you learn from this brief exercise?

3. If critical thinking is not part of the K–12 curriculum in the DRC (see section on "The Educator") how would you help your students from the DRC slowly develop this way of thinking?

RESOURCES

Achberger, J. (2015). Belgian colonial education policy: A poor foundation for stability. *The Ultimate History Project.* Retrieved from http://www.ultimatehistoryproject.com/belgian-congo.html
AfriMAP and the Open Society Initiative for Southern Africa. (2010). *The Democratic Republic of Congo: Effective delivery of public services in the education sector.* Rosebank, South Africa: Open Society Institute Network Publication.
Bender, L. (2010). Innovations in emergency education: The IRC in the Democratic Republic of the Congo. In the EFA Global Monitoring Report, 2011. *The hidden crisis: Armed conflict and education.* Paris, France: UNESCO.
Bloom, B. S. (1956). *Taxonomy of educational objectives, Handbook I: The Cognitive Domain.* New York, NY: David McKay.
Central Intelligence Agency. (2016). *Democratic Republic of the Congo. The World Factbook. Africa.* Retrieved from https://www.cia.gov/library/publications/the-world-factbook/geos/cg.html
Congo (Democratic Republic of the). (2005). *The Constitution of the DRC.* Retrieved from http://www.constitutionnet.org/files/DRC%20-%20Congo%20Constitution.pdf

Education Development Center. (2008). *Improving basic education in the Democratic Republic of the Congo, especially for girls*. Waltham, MA: Author.

Foreign Policy and the Fund for Peace. (2016). *Failed state index*. Retrieved from http://fsi.fundforpeace.org/

Hochschild, A. (1999). *King Leopold's ghost: A story of greed, terror, and heroism in colonial Africa*. New York City, NY: Houghton Mifflin.

Lave, J., & Wenger, E. (1991). *Situated learning: Legitimate peripheral participation*. New York, NY: Cambridge University Press.

McCabe, K. (2011, July 21). *African immigrants in the United States*. Migration Policy Institute. Retrieved from http://www.migrationpolicy.org/article/african-immigrants-united-states#top

Moll, L., Amanti, C., Neff, D., & Gonzalez, N. (1992). Funds of knowledge for teaching: Using a qualitative approach to connect homes and classrooms. *Theory into Practice, 31*(2), 131–141.

Mukenge, T. (2002). *Culture and customs of the Congo: An academic view of Congolese culture*. Westport, CT: Greenwood Press.

Omniglot. (2016). Lingala. Retrieved from http://www.omniglot.com/writing/lingala.htm

Rosenblatt, L. M. (1978). *The reader, the text, and the poem: The transactional theory of the literary work*. Carbondale, IL: Southern Illinois University Press.

Southern African Regional Universities Association, SARUA. (2016). *Democratic Republic of Congo*. Retrieved from http://www.sarua.org/?q=content/congo-0

StateUniversity.com. (2007). *Democratic Congo: History & background*. Retrieved from http://education.stateuniversity.com/pages/358/Democratic-Congo-HISTORY-BACKGROUND.html

Weiss, R. (2012) *A history of resistance in the Congo*. The Social science research council: African futures. Retrieved from http://forums.ssrc.org/african-futures/2012/12/08/african-futures-history-of-resistance-in-congo/

Wright, J. (2015). *Foundations for teaching English language learners: Research, theory, policy, and practice* (2nd ed.). Philadelphia, PA: Caslon Publishing.

REFERENCES

Haskin, J. M. (2005). *The tragic state of the Congo: From decolonization to dictatorship*. New York, NY: Algora Publishing.

Lygunda, F., Li-M. (2013). *Toward a reconstructionist philosophy of missiological education in Francophone Africa: Case of the DR Congo*. Norderstedt, Germany: GRIN, Verlag.

Paris, D. (2012). Culturally sustaining pedagogy: A needed change in stance, terminology, and practice. *Educational Researcher, 41*(3), 93–97.

République Démocratique du Congo. (2005, December). *Draft 3 of the poverty reduction strategy paper*. Ministère du Plan, Kinshasa.

Re?publique Démocratique du Congo. (2014). *Ministère du Plan et Révolution de la Modernité: Annuaire statistique 2014 de la RDC*. Programme des Nations Unies pour le Développement (PNUD) en RD Congo.

World Bank Group. (1969). *Projects—Democratic Republic of Congo: The education quality improvement project, EQUIP.* Retrieved from http://www.worldbank.org/en/country/drc/projects/all?qterm=&lang_exact=English&os=140

World Bank. (2005). *Education in the Democratic Republic of Congo, priorities and options for regeneration.* Retrieved from http://datatopics.worldbank.org/hnp/files/edstats/ZARpub05.pdf

CHAPTER 23

ENGLISH LANGUAGE, LITERACY, AND CULTURE

The Case of Angola

Nicolau N. Manuel
Agostinho Neto University, Angola

Pamela J. Bettis
Washington State University

Mr. Hooks is a well-respected high school social studies teacher in a medium-sized city in the U.S. Midwest. He prides himself on teaching his mostly European American students about cultural and social diversity, and he has initiated a "no bullying" campaign in his school and classrooms, specifically targeting homophobia. He is aware of the gay slurs that have been scribbled on bathroom walls and heard in classrooms and hallways. Many of the spoken comments have been articulated by male athletes at the school, including the football and soccer players. Mr. Hooks has decided to infuse this "no bullying" campaign into his own world history curriculum and by tracing homosexuality throughout history. When one of his new students, a young man named Acklee who just emigrated from Angola, is openly offended by this curriculum, Mr. Hooks contacts the student's parents for a conference. During the meeting, the boy's parents, Mr. and Mrs. Ribas, speak disparag-

Views From Inside: Languages, Cultures, and Schooling for K–12 Educators
pp. 403–414

ingly about individuals who are gay or lesbian, even though homosexuality has been legally protected in Angola since 2013. However, it is not widely accepted due to strong religious resistance and cultural norms. Further, Acklee's parents relate that their son is in total agreement with the sentiments of some of the other soccer players who ridicule the student members of the Gay/Straight Alliance just recently organized at the school. These soccer players are Acklee's new American friends, and he desperately wants to keep them.

BACKGROUND

How might Mr. Hooks talk to Mr. and Mrs. Ribas? How might he talk with Acklee about how problematic this condemnation of homosexuality is in his new country? How does Mr. Hooks juggle the social needs of Acklee, an international student seeking friendships in his new environment, with his own belief in social justice for all? Learning more about the history and culture of Angola may help Mr. Hooks challenge Acklee's homophobia and other culturally based values in a thoughtful manner.

Angola is a country located in the southern part of Africa (sub-Saharan Africa), bordering the south Atlantic Ocean and situated between Namibia to the south, the Democratic Republic of Congo to the north, and Zaire to the east. Angola is a former colony of Portugal and achieved its independence in 1975. According to the 2014 census, the population of Angola is estimated at 24 million inhabitants, of which 43.2% are under 15 years of age (UNESCO, 2016). Portuguese is the official language of the country, but Angola is a multiethnic and multicultural nation with approximately 39 African Bantu languages (Manuel, 2015). Among the major Bantu African languages spoken are Cokwe, Kikongo, Kimbundu, Kwanyama, Ngangela, and Umbundu. This makes Angola an interesting and unique context for language, literacy, and cultural examination.

At its independence in 1975, approximately 85% of the Angolan population was deemed illiterate by traditional Western literacy assessments, although there is a long and rich oral tradition in Angola. After independence, due to the power struggles between the three liberation movements that fought for independence (i.e., MPLA, FNLA, and UNITA), the country witnessed a 30-year civil war that destroyed the country's infrastructure and prevented many children from accessing education and traditional forms of literacy. With the advent of peace in 2002, the country has made great strides towards the improvement of literacy rates and the fulfillment of the millennium literacy and education goals established by UNESCO (UNESCO, 2016). Government statistics indicate that the illiteracy rate has drastically decreased thanks to the efforts of the Angolan government in promoting literacy campaigns and the investments channeled to basic education and literacy. The result is a literacy rate of 73% as of 2014 (SAPO24, n.d.).

Given its geographical location, Angola is a member of the Southern African Development Community (SADC) that comprises 15 member states, namely Angola, Botswana, the Democratic Republic of Congo, Lesotho, Madagascar, Malawi, Mauritius, Mozambique, Namibia, the Seychelles, South Africa, Swaziland, Tanzania, Zambia, and Zimbabwe. Created in 1980, the main goal of SADC is to further regional socioeconomic cooperation and integration as well as political and security cooperation among the various member states. Although English is not the official language of all member states, English has been adopted as the official working language of the SADC. Further, with the recent diversification of the national economy, Angolans have turned to English as the international language of commerce. However, after independence, Angola adopted Portuguese as the medium of instruction in schools, while English and French continue to be taught as foreign languages. Of course, this has a bearing on literacy education, given that the majority of the Angolan population communicates in African languages and has only a partial command of standard Portuguese (Manuel, 2015).

Economically, Angola has depended on natural resources, mainly oil and diamond revenues. More recently, the government has taken corrective measures and has created the conditions for the diversification of the Angolan economy to include more industry and agriculture, which has had a stabilizing effect on the economy. This diversification is still made problematic by the number of landmines and other explosive devices left by the many years of war. The United States and nongovernmental international organizations have contributed to the eradication of these weapons, found particularly in rural parts of the country, to improve social and economic activities. The history of colonialism, globalization in the economy, international efforts to eradicate the landmines, and continued use of traditional African languages have all contributed to a multilinguistic society.

Angola's complicated political history has also shaped the educational systems in Angola. While living in Angola, Acklee's parents had Acklee attend a private religious school where classes were taught in Portuguese, and he studied English as a foreign language. Moreover, Acklee's grandmother lived with the family and spoke mostly Umbundu. Mr. and Mrs. Ribas were willing to take the risk of leaving their Angolan ancestral home due to their politics and desire for their children to live and be educated in the U.S. Although Acklee might not see it as an intellectual strength now, he speaks four languages and can write fluently in Portuguese and English. Acklee hides this fact and does not want any of his new friends to know this about him because he fears that knowledge would only emphasize his differences from the other boys.

CULTURE, RELIGION, AND HISTORY

Given that Angola is an African country in which the overwhelming majority of the population is of Bantu origin, the African Bantu culture constitutes the cornerstone of the majority of the Angolan people's understandings of the world (Altuna, 1985). The term "Bantu" refers to the African civilization characterized by unity of culture and customs of most African people, mainly in the southern part of Africa. For Bantu people in general, and Angolans in particular, language is the ultimate realization of culture. It is through language that people express the richness of their culture as manifested in proverbs, storytelling, epics, myths, and legends. Bantu people express their beliefs through spiritual socialization, which is characterized by the use of what Altuna (1985) refers to as "African magic." According to this view, in Bantu tradition, culture and religion intersect and represent the central aspect of how Bantu understand reality. As Altuna (1985) notes, Bantu magic is a religion that is the necessary expression of African values, logic, and mysticism. For example, in *bakongo* traditional culture, God (*Nzambi Wa Mpungu* in Kikongo) is distinct from the Christian God. Bantu people's beliefs are that the occurrence of social events, including birth and death, depend on the power of the forebears and the ancestors who are the guardians (the gods) of the land and people. In essence, African Bantu religion is a cultural religion and African culture a religious culture.

The nature and character of African religion is epitomized in the story of Beatriz Kimpavita, who was a Bantu and Kongolese prophet who led a messianic movement in the first decade of the 18th century in the territory of the ancient Kingdom of Kongo (now Mbanza Kongo, Angola) (Thornton, 1998). She was burned alive for claiming different spiritual beliefs, maintaining that Jesus and Mary were of Kongolese ancestry, and she chastised the colonialist friars at the time for their lack of attention to this point. Her religious and spiritual movement was very influential in shaping the Bantu people's beliefs and reinforcing the relationship between magic and religion in Bantu culture (Thornton, 1998).

Marriage, Kinship, Sexuality, and Gender Dynamics

The impacts of Portuguese colonization and Christianity have drastically influenced the practices of Bantu culture and religion in most sub-Saharan African countries, including Angola. With the establishment of the Christian diocese of San Salvador by the Portuguese in Mbanza-Kongo (Angola) in 1596, the Bantu cultural and religious practices receded considerably, and Christianity became the most dominant religion within Angola. A striking example of the abandonment of Bantu cultural practices can be observed through the prevalence of interethnic and intertribal marriages and the abandonment of initiation ceremonies. For example, nowadays it may be offensive to ask Angolan learners of English about their ethnic group and even tribe.

However, some cultural and religious practices related to marriages and kinship remain very traditional in southern African countries and in Angola in particular. Although expressed in different linguistic terms, the bride's dues, paid by the groom to the family of the bride, remain one of the most important aspects of the African Bantu culture. While the influence of Western civilization and culture are evident in every domain of Angolan society, issues such as sex and sexuality remain taboo in most Angolan households, mainly in those families where traditional culture remains at the center of social and moral life. For example, it is not acceptable in most social circles to talk about same-sex marriages or homosexuality. Moreover, the Christian religion has had a great influence in shaping African people's view about morality and the notion of what is morally wrong and right. The influence of Christianity is noticeable, for example, in education. Although officially the church is separate from the state, the introduction of the subject of moral education into Angolan schools can be seen as an instance of Christian influence.

Another important aspect related to culture in Angola is about how to behave in public places. It is, for example, normally accepted that two individuals of different genders (male and female) greet each other by kissing on the cheek. It is also normal in Angola to see two men walk along together, holding each other's arms or hands. In contrast, it is highly offensive, for example, to be in public spaces without a shirt or blouse. This holds for both men and women.

There are no cultural taboos regarding mixed-gender classrooms. In Angola, coeducational or mixed gender classrooms can be seen at all grade levels and in higher education. In fact, segregated classrooms are unlawful in Angola. The Angolan Constitution guarantees gender equality in education and literacy and also equal participation in all domains of social life, including politics. Reports indicate that young girls tend to stay out of school for cultural and economic reasons. However, according to the official report from the Ministry of Education, Angola reached primary education gender parity in 2015 (Grilo, 2015).

Learning and the Legacy of Colonialism

Although teaching practices have changed drastically due to educational reform, educators who work with English learners from Angola should be aware that to some extent, Angolan classrooms remain teacher-centered and learners are often expected to mimic textbooks and teachers' views. Rote learning continues as a reality in many schools, so independent tasks in U.S. classrooms that aim to teach critical thinking and critical reflection should be well-planned and graded taking into account Angolan learners' background knowledge.

As mentioned at the outset, multilingualism and the different ethnolinguistic groups who speak different languages are officially recognized in Angola. Surprisingly, many Angolans find it offensive and unethical to speak a language other than Portuguese (a lingua franca and official language in Angola) in public spaces. The reasons for such beliefs and behavior are manifold. First is the persistence of colonial language ideologies and linguistic culture (Schiffman, 1996) in which African languages are regarded as the languages of dogs (Bender, 2004), that is, languages that are not worth learning and speaking because they belong to "uncivilized" people. Second, despite the government's efforts to promote African languages, research has shown that many still regard African languages as symbols of backwardness (Manuel, 2015). Although in recent years the situation has improved significantly, there remains much to do in order to promote the value of African languages.

Angolan Holidays

In terms of festivities, similar to most Christian nations, in Angola Christmas (December 25th) is celebrated and valued nationwide. Other important cultural dates include but are not limited to: Independence Day (November 11th), Carnival Day (February 17th), and All Souls' Day (November 2nd). Educators working with Angolan ELLs might accommodate discussions of holidays and festivities in their classes to encourage critical reflection and boost intercultural awareness on the part of all students.

To recapitulate, culturally speaking, Angola is a mosaic of cultures and languages in which Western civilizations and cultures have considerably influenced social and linguistic practices that shape the practice of language and literacy acquisition, to which we now turn.

LANGUAGES AND LITERACIES

There are many causes of the maintenance of Portuguese as the sole language of literacy and education in Angola; these include the impact of Portuguese colonization on Angola, an encumbered education system that the country inherited from the Portuguese administration, the number of

African languages spoken in Angola, and the lack of extensive research on African languages. More recently, however, the government launched a pilot project and policy that introduces African languages into the education system. This initiative marks an important step towards not only the preservation of African languages but also the promotion of Angolan cultural heritage and identity.

While the use of African languages in schools is a new phenomenon, foreign languages such as English and French have always been in the curriculum in Angola. Although English and French are taught at the secondary school as foreign languages, English has gained much prominence in recent years; this is partly due to the discourse of English as a global language of international communication (Nunan, 2001). Moreover, the prominence of English in Angola can be justified by the presence of many foreign oil companies from the English-speaking world, such as Chevron and British Petroleum. Literacy in the English language is one of the most important prerequisites for employment in most foreign companies, especially those involved in oil. As a result, English language learning and teaching has become one of the most successful businesses in Angola. Of course, apart from its teaching in secondary schools, English is also taught at the higher education level as a subject and as a scientific discipline. For example, at the School of Languages of Agostinho Neto University, the Department of English Language and Literature has graduate and undergraduate programs that provide courses in English linguistics, theories of literature, and literary criticism.

In recent years, there has been a noticeable shift in literacy and language education practices in Angola because of globalization and technological development. Angolan youth have been able to rapidly adapt to some of the major communication innovations of the 21st century, thanks to easy access to cellular phones. According to the World Bank, only 43% of the Angolan population lived in urban areas as of 2014 (World Bank, 2014). At least in the major cities of Angola, technology is used in education, and English language learning in particular, to improve literacy and language acquisition for many children in schools. Although there is still some focus on teacher-centered approaches and rote learning, technology has to some extent helped to improve children's computer literacy, which is crucial for literacy acquisition in the era of technology and communication development. In Angola, 6 out of 10 children own a tablet or a mobile phone with internet access.

It is relevant to stress here that Portuguese is a Romance language and English is Germanic language. As a Romance language, Portuguese is closely related to Spanish. Although different in terms of language family and subgroup, the Portuguese grammatical system has a lot in common with English and many other Indo-European languages (Shepherd,

2007). For example, Portuguese and English have similar parts of speech and both have definite and indefinite articles. These are very important insights for language and literacy acquisition for English language teachers. Awareness of the differences and similarities between English and Portuguese can be helpful for understanding students' struggles as they learn English.

Common learning problems and some of the outstanding characteristics of the Portuguese language are:

- Similar to most Indo-European languages, Portuguese is written from left to right.
- The Portuguese alphabet has 26 letters, as shown in Table 23.1.
- In English, auxiliary verbs (e.g., "do") are critical for forming the interrogative, negative, and empathic forms of speech and tenses of mood and voice. Learners who speak Portuguese often produce faulty interrogative forms due to overgeneralization of the rules, e.g. "*Conheces* a Nicandrova?" (Portuguese), translation: "You know Nicandrova?," instead of "Do you know Nicandrova?"; "*Ele engenheiro?*" (Portuguese), translation: "He is engineer?," in lieu of the correct English structure, "Is he an engineer?."
- In Portuguese, questions are marked by intonation and by the use of auxiliary verbs.
- Word order in Portuguese is somewhat freer than in English—for example, "*Bolos eu gosto*" (Portuguese) for "I like cakes" (or literally, "Cakes I like") in English. The Portuguese has the object at the beginning of the sentence in this example.
- There are many false cognates between Portuguese and English, such as *pretender* (Portuguese) and "pretend" (English). While "pretend" in English means to behave as if something is true, in Portuguese *pretendo* means to intend (for more details see Manuel, 2004; Shepherd, 2007).
- The English and Portuguese vowels are quite different (see the Portuguese alphabet in Table 23.1). Shepherd (2007) notes that there are 12 pure vowels in English and eight schwa /ə/ that can all be nasalized (see Mateus & d'Andrade, 2002 for more insights on the phonology of Portuguese).
- Educators must also be aware that in Angola many learners speak African languages that are very different from English. For example, in Bantu languages spoken in Angola (e.g., Kikongo), prefixes function as members of singular and plural pairs; in other words, plurals are formed through prefixation. For example, knife in Kikongo is /mbéele/ and a small knife is /fi-mbéele/ and *nti* is a tree

Table 23.1.   The Portuguese Alphabet With Sounds

Letters and Their Names									
A	ah	G	gêh	M	êhmee	S	ehsee	Y	epsilon
B	bêh	H	Ah-gah	N	êhnee	T	têh	Z	zêh
C	sêh	I	ee	O	oh	U	oo		
D	dêh	J	sota	P	pêh	V	vêh		
E	eh	K	kah	Q	quê	W	dahblioo		
F	eh fee	L	ehlee	R	Ehreh	X	shes		

(singular), while "trees" is *mi-nti* (plural) (Carter & Makondekwa, 1987). In addition, in many Bantu languages, including Kikongo, nasal sounds occur in the initial position in some words, a characteristic that is not obvious in English (e.g., *ngangu* means wisdom). This may cause difficulties for pronunciation acquisition for Angolan ELLs.

Given the above differences between Portuguese and English grammatical systems, native Portuguese speakers who are learning English may experience difficulties in the following areas:

- Because there are fewer diphthongs in Portuguese, Portuguese learners often tend to confuse the /ɪe/ and /eə/ in English words such as "hear" and "hair" (Shepherd, 2007).

- Given that the final /z/ sound does not occur in spoken Portuguese, learners may have problems with English words such as "rise." Learners tend to replace the sound /z/ with /s/, thus mispronouncing "rise" as "rice."

- Research on the errors and mistakes committed by Portuguese-speaking English language learners in Angola has revealed that learners confuse the use of auxiliaries in English. This is evidenced in learners' confusion of the auxiliaries "do" and "be" in the formation of negative sentences. For example, it is very common for Portuguese-speaking learners to say "I speak not English" or "I am not speak English" or even "I not do speak English." This is due partly to word-for-word translation and the formation of negative structures, which is different in Portuguese (Manuel, 2004).

- Because of the difference in the construction of questions in Portuguese and English, learners with Portuguese as their L1 may ask "He speaks English?" instead of "Does he speak English?"

- Another difficult aspect of the English language that may cause trouble for Portuguese-speaking learners of English is the use of the third person singular (the "-s" inflection). In most cases, learners forget to use the "s" because this feature is absent in Portuguese, as the following example illustrates: *Ele anda devagar* (Portuguese); in English, literally "he walk slowly."

Although most Angolans speak different African languages, the Portuguese language, especially the Angolan variant of Portuguese (AVP) (Manuel, 2015), has become a lingua franca used in most social transactions. As the official language of Angola, and the medium of instruction and literacy, the Portuguese language also has a strong symbolic value. The Portuguese language is the language through which Angolans create a cultural bond, and it is also the language of unity in the diversity of languages and ethnicities that constitute Angola as a nation.

CONCLUSIONS

This chapter provides information that can help teachers to explore Angolan ELLs' cultural backgrounds and to improve the teaching of various language skills that are challenging to English language learners from Portuguese and African Bantu language backgrounds. After the disastrous parent meeting with Acklee's mother and father, Mr. Hooks did the kind of work that he should have completed prior to this first meeting. He learned a few words of Portuguese so that he could be more welcoming, and he read about the history of Angola and some of its religious and cultural beliefs. When he set up a second conference with Acklee's parents, and one with Acklee by himself, Mr. Hooks was much better prepared to discuss the challenges they all faced.

ADDITIONAL RESOURCES

Bunting, E. (2006). *One green apple.* New York, NY: Clarion Books.
  One Green Apple is a children's book about a girl who travels to a new country and feels like an outcast in her new school environment.
Farnsworth, M. (2016). *Consider culture before referral of culturally and linguistically diverse students for special education services.* Retrieved from http://www.colorincolorado.org/article/consider-culture-referral-culturally-and-linguistically-diverse-students-special-education
Onyefulu, I. (2004). *Here comes our bride: An African wedding story.* London, UK: Frances Lincoln Children's Books.

This book depicts African traditions and customs as epitomized in African weddings in Nigeria.

Smith, D. J. (2011). *If the world were a village: A book about the world's peoples.* Toronto, ON: Kids Can Press.

This children's book explores the lives of many villagers around the world. It could help students and teachers understand that life is different in other nations.

TASKS FOR EDUCATORS

1. The story of Dona Beatriz Kimpavita in this chapter reports an instance of colonial atrocities against the Angolan people. How might you use Dona Beatriz Kimpavita's story to promote intercultural communication in your classroom?

2. Having discussed the major language and literacy problems facing Portuguese ELLs, what might you need to do to help them learn to use English in your classroom?

3. How might you help Angolan students understand U.S. culture, particularly when it conflicts with their native culture?

REFERENCES

Altuna, R. R. A. (1985). *Cultura tradicional Bantu.* Luanda, Angola: Secretariado Arquidiocesano de Pastoral.

Bender, G. J. (2004). *Angola under the Portuguese: The myth and the reality.* Berkeley, CA: University of California Press.

Carter, H., & Makondekwa, J. (1987). *Kongo language course: Maloongi makikoongo, a course in the dialect of Zoombo, Northern Angola.* Madison, WI: African Studies Program, University of Wisconsin.

Grilo, L. (2015). Angola: Ensino primário no país já regista paridade de género. [Angola: Country records gender parity in primary education]. Retrieved from http://www.angop.ao/angola/pt_pt/noticias/educacao/2015/2/14/Angola-Ensino-primario-pais-regista-paridade-genero,59428e94-4b2a-4705-9404-0542c11db64f.html

Manuel, N. N. (2004). Cogitation on the misuse of English operators by Mutu-Ya-Kevela secondary school and Puniv learners. Some suggestions for remedy (Unpublished master's thesis). Agostinho Neto University, Luanda, Angola.

Manuel, N. N. (2015). *Language and literacy policies in Sub-Saharan Africa: Towards a bilingual language education policy in Angola.* Retrieved from ProQuest Dissertations (1711730356).

Mateus, M. H., & d'Andrade, E. (2002). *The phonology of Portuguese.* Oxford, UK: Oxford University Press.

Nunan, D. (2001). English as a global language. *TESOL Quarterly, 4*(35), 605–606.

SAPO24. (n.d.). *Número* de *angolanos analfabetos caiu mais* de 68% *desde* 1975. Retrieved from http://24.sapo.pt/article/lusa-sapo-pt_2015_09_08_410499205_numero-de-angolanos-analfabetos-caiu-mais-de-68--desde-1975

Schiffman, H. F. (1996). *Linguistic culture and language policy*. London, UK: Routledge.

Shepherd, D. (2007). Portuguese speakers. In M. Swan & B. Smith (Eds.), *Learner English: A teacher's guide to interference and other problems* (pp. 113–128). Cambridge, UK: Cambridge University Press.

Thornton, J. (1998). *The Kongolese Saint Anthony: Dona Beatnz Kimpa vita and the Antonian mo*. Cambridge, UK: Cambridge University Press.

UNESCO. (2016). *Education and the millennium development goals*. Retrieved from http://www.unesco.org/new/en/education/themes/leading-the-international-agenda/education-for-all/education-and-the-mdgs/

World Bank. (2014). Urban population. Retrieved from http://data.worldbank.org/indicator/SP.URB.TOTL.IN.ZS

SECTION 8

EUROPEAN REGION

CHAPTER 24

A GLIMPSE INTO RUSSIAN HISTORY, CULTURE, AND LANGUAGE

Yuliya Ardasheva
Washington State University

Alexei Kochetov
University of Toronto

Maxim was first exposed to English when his family moved to the United States and he was enrolled in fourth grade in a school near his new home. Now a seventh grader, he does quite well in school (especially in mathematics), earning B's and occasionally A's. To maintain his mother tongue, the family speaks Russian at home, and Maxim often visits his grandparents in Russia. The family's library has books in both languages. Maxim's teachers describe him as "responsible and bright," always eager to volunteer answers, but at times a bit too zealously. The teachers wonder, though, if Maxim truly likes the school and his American teachers, as he rarely smiles at them. The teachers also wonder why Maxim often looks either lost or disinterested (or both) when asked to brainstorm ideas or to work on an assignment in a group. When consulting with the school's ESL specialist during a team meeting, the teachers learned that in Russia, smiling has a slightly different meaning than in the U.S., and that students who have been initiated to schooling within the Russian educational system may place lesser value on—or simply be less familiar with—brainstorming sessions and group work.

Views From Inside: Languages, Cultures, and Schooling for K–12 Educators
pp. 417–433

BACKGROUND

History

Russia takes up a substantial part of Eurasia and—as the name of the landmass suggests—finds itself between Europe and Asia, which represent the two major influences in shaping Russia's history and the mentality of its population. Current European neighbors of Russia include Belarus, Estonia, Finland, Latvia, Lithuania, Norway, Poland, and Ukraine, and those in Asia include Azerbaijan, China, Georgia, Kazakhstan, North Korea, Mongolia, and Japan.

In fact, some historians argue that throughout the course of its history, Russia has made a number of 180-degree turns—at some most critical moments of its development—in terms of pursuing either European or Asian alliances (political, economic) and aspirations (intellectual, philosophical, religious). This duality has contributed to the uniqueness of Russian civilization and is reflected in the double-headed eagle of Byzantium, the symbol of the Russian state, with one of its crowned heads facing the East and the other facing the West. The symbol was adopted as the coat of arms first by the Muscovite tsars, then by the Russian Empire, and it has now been resurrected as the symbol of post-Communist Russia (Chubarov, 2007).

This duality has also caused much intellectual debate—in many respects still ongoing—as to the best path for Russia's future. The 19th century Westernizer/Slavophile controversy exemplified this debate perfectly, with the Westernizers believing that Russia's future depended on Western technologies and the adoption of liberal government, and the Slavophiles holding the Russian civilization as unique and superior to that of the West. The Slavophiles ascribed the uniqueness and superiority of Russian ways to such institutions as the village commune, with decision-making being done by a popular assembly of the heads of the households, and the Orthodox Church, with the authority of the emperor linking the earthly and heavenly orders (Chubarov, 2007; Columbia Encyclopedia, 2015).

Throughout its history, Russia has had several names associated, among other things, with different political systems, none of which have been truly democratic (at least not for meaningfully long periods of time), with highly centralized political power typically concentrated in the hands of one or a few individuals. Believed to have been the first Russian state, the Kievan Rus, or the Grand Principality of Kiev (Kiev is the current capital of Ukraine), emerged in the 9th century, a period of active state-building in Europe (Bartlett, 2006; Chubarov, 2007). In 988, Kievan Rus adopted Christianity as its official state religion, around the same time as

Hungary, Denmark, Norway, and Sweden did. Unlike other European countries, however, Kievan Rus adopted Orthodox Christianity, which was not the religion of the Roman Empire but that of the Byzantine Empire. The conversion to Orthodox Christianity and the concomitant adoption of the Greek-based Cyrillic alphabet solidified Kiev's eastern orientation that dominated until the times of Peter the Great. By the end of the 12th century, Kievan Rus was broken down into smaller feudal principalities. This fragmentation was exploited by the Mongols, who invaded and dominated the territories from 1237 to 1480—a legacy of 240 years that furthered the separation of Russia from Europe.

From Mongol domination, the Grand Principality of Muscovy led by the Rurik dynasty emerged as the new unifying force, absorbing surrounding principalities. This policy of gradual expansion extended to Siberia in the early 17th century under the new Romanov Dynasty (Bartlett, 2006; U.S. Central Intelligence Agency, 2016). Under Peter the Great, considered to be the most influential ruler of the country (1682–1725), Russian territory was extended to the Baltic Sea, providing access to navigable waters and refashioning Russia as a strong military and trade force in Europe. Besides the shifts in external politics, Peter the Great modernized and Westernized Russia, including reforms to civil, military, and religious administration and to the educational system, as well as to social fashions and dress styles, all modeled after the West (Bartlett, 2006; Chubarov, 2007). Expanded and reformed, the country claimed the new title of Russian Empire. Peter's administrative reforms proved stable and lasted in most essential aspects until the fall of the imperial household in 1917; this change was due in part to devastating Russian defeats in the Russo–Japanese War and in World War I, and then to subsequent civil unrest, riots, and revolutions.

As the Communist Soviet Union led by Vladimir Lenin came into being, a wave of massive emigration of Russian aristocrats, professionals, artists, and former imperial officials—more than 2 million—occurred. More than 30,000 of the Russian immigrants made their way to the United States (Library of Congress, 2015). During the years of the Soviet Union (1917–1991), a number of additional waves of Russians immigrated to the United States. First, in the 1930s, a wave of Russian immigrants left the country out of fear of a new world war approaching and to flee the brutal rule of Iosif Stalin (1928–1953). This wave of interwar immigrants brought in the major artists and thinkers of the Russian avant-garde who enriched modernism, the then burgeoning artistic movement in America. These renowned-throughout-the-world artists included, among others, the composer Igor Stravinsky, the novelist Vladimir Nabokov, and the choreographer George Balanchine, whose influence brought "much of 20th century American dance into being" (Library of Congress, 2015, p. 2).

Emerging victorious from World War II in alliance with the United States (1939–1945), the Soviet Union emerged as a global power, expanding both its territory and influence in Eastern Europe and becoming the principal adversary of the United States during the Cold War (1947–1991; U.S. Central Intelligence Agency, 2016). Although during this period the Soviet Union established strict control over emigration (embarrassed by a high percent of people wishing to leave), some defectors, political dissidents, and those judged as "undesirable" by the Soviet state made it to the United States (Library of Congress, 2015). These included the renowned ballet dancer Mikhail Baryshnikov, the Nobel Prize-winning poet Joseph Brodsky, and Alexander Solzhenitsyn, a famous novelist who was fiercely critical of the Soviet regime.

After years of economic stagnation, Mikhail Gorbachev sought to reform the country by introducing *perestroika* (restructuring) and *glasnost* (openness) in the 1990s (Bartlett, 2006; U.S. Central Intelligence Agency, 2016). These reforms inadvertently resulted in the total collapse of the Soviet Union in December 1991, splitting the country into Russia (Russian Federation) and 14 other independent states, and opening the gates for hundreds of thousands of Russians to seek a better future in the United States. This last major wave of Russian immigration gradually subsided as a result of both U.S. immigration policies (seeking to equalize immigration opportunities across countries by creating immigration caps) and increasing economic stability in the Russian Federation. Still, however, the United States remains a very attractive immigration choice for highly educated and entrepreneurial Russians.

RUSSIAN CONTRIBUTIONS TO THE WORLD

Many Russians have made—and continue to make—historic contributions to the world, something that educators of Russian students may easily integrate into their classrooms as illustrative examples of the global nature of our civilization. Below is a list of some prominent Russian scientists and explorers whose biographies and contributions may be investigated as part of student research projects in science, social studies, and mathematics classrooms:

- Mikhail Lomonosov, natural scientist (1711–1765): Invented the first gas barometer; developed methods of exact weighting; brought up the kinetic theory of warmth; developed the method of processing colored glass; proved the organic origin of oils, stone, coal, and amber.

- Dmitri Mendeleev, chemist (1834–1907): Arranged the 63 known elements into a periodic table based on atomic mass (published in *Principles of Chemistry* in 1869).

- Sofia Kovalevskaya, mathematician (1850–1891): The first woman since the physicist Laura Bassi and Maria Gaetana Agnesi to hold a chair at a European university.

- Ivan Pavlov, psychologist (1854–1929): The first Russian Nobel Prize winner in Theoretical Medicine in connection to discoveries in the sphere of blood circulation physiology, digestion, and the central nervous system.

- Yury Gagarin, astronaut (1934–1968): The first man to orbit the earth in a man-made spacecraft.

- Nikolai Basov, physicist (1922–2001): His pioneering work led to the invention of the laser.

More extended lists of prominent Russians across the fields of literature, arts, geography, and others can be found at: tristarmedia.com/bestofrussia/scientists.html and russiapedia.rt.com/prominent-russians.

RUSSIAN CULTURE

Ethnic, Religious, and Linguistic Composition

The population of the Russian Federation—which is about 146 million, less than half of the U.S. population—includes nearly 200 national and/or ethnic groups, with the largest ethnic groups being Russians (78%), followed by Tatars (4%), and Ukrainians, Bashkirs, Chuvash people, and Chechens (about 1% each group, as per the 2010 census; U.S. Central Intelligence Agency, 2016). Other national and/or ethnic groups comprise less than 1% of the population.

Orthodox Christianity, Islam, Judaism, and Buddhism are officially recognized religions in Russia, and the country has large populations of nonpracticing believers and nonbelievers. After over seven decades of Soviet repression of religious freedoms, the number of practicing believers has been on the rise, estimated at about 37% of the population in 2006. Similar to the Unites States, many Russians support the separation of church and state; in 2015, the majority of the population (57%) noted that they wanted to live in a country where religion does not have a major impact on people and where having or not having religious beliefs is a private matter (Russian Public Opinion Research Center, 2015). Educators of students from families practicing the Russian Orthodox religion may find it surprising and important to know that these families celebrate Christmas on January 7th. This is because the Russian Orthodox Church uses the Julian calendar, and January 7th of the Julian calendar corresponds to December 25th of the Gregorian calendar used by most non-Orthodox Christian churches.

Most speakers of minority languages in the Federation—which include over 100 different languages—are bilingual, speaking Russian as an additional language. According to the Ministry of Education and Science of the Russian Federation (2015), speakers of minority languages have the right to receive basic general education in their native languages; this, however, may not be the reality for most speakers of minority languages.

Mainstream Values

Like in American society, shared media exposure and governmental, educational, and economic systems bring about a number of mainstream values shared by most; however, as in every group, there are individuals "who do not conform and are therefore not 'typical' representatives of their group" (Zainuddin, Yahya, Morales-Jones, & Ariza, 2011, p. 20). These Russian mainstream values are summarized and contrasted with American mainstream values in Table 24.1.

Patterns of Communication

When Americans and Russians speak to each other, a "conversational clash" may occur, potentially leading to misunderstandings and misinterpretations. This may be due to Americans and Russians having different conversational patterns characteristic of, respectively, "high-considerateness" versus "high-involvement" cultures (Tannen, 1990 as cited in Zainuddin et al., 2011). It is customary in both cultures to show interest in the conversation, yet this is achieved through the use of different verbal and nonverbal means. That is, Americans who follow a "high-considerateness" conversational pattern speak one person at a time, with no interruptions while others are speaking; interest is shown through attentive listening, nodding, and positive sounds. By contrast, Russians who follow "high-involvement" conversational patterns tend to interrupt more, "expect and are not bothered by people who interrupt them while speaking, and speak louder and quicker" (Zainuddin et al., 2011, p. 30)—all of which indicate that they are paying attention and are invested in keeping

Table 24.1.   American and Russian Mainstream Values Contrasted

Values	American Perspective	Russian Perspective
Progress	Change is the driver of progress.	The tried-and-true ways are foundational.
Time	Time is money and should not be wasted. Schedules are important and are to be observed to the letter (e.g., if the invitation says 2:00 to 4:00, the party will usually end at 4:00).	Time begins when everybody is ready. There is no rush to things; things will take their own pace to happen (e.g., providing the end time for a party may be perceived as rude).
Social Dynamics	Egalitarianism and informality: equality is foundational (*"All men are created equal"*); all enjoy equal rights under the law; an apparent lack of formality and "casual" attitudes (e.g., joking with the boss); "ritual and formality do exist, but are not easy to discern" (Zainuddin et al., 2011, p. 21).	Hierarchy and formality: status, rank, and seniority determine importance (someone is always superior to another); addressing people by formal titles, formal names, and observing formal rituals (language forms and functions are represented in the fixed language forms such as the polite versus informal 'you': *vy* versus *ty*).
Social orientation	Individualism; individual responsibility and acting for one's own good are primary; privacy is honored.	Group orientation*; individuals act for the good of the family and the community; acts bringing dishonor to the family/community disgrace everyone; everybody's business is everyone's.
Material goods	Materialism; "tangible items are more important than intangible ideals" (Zainuddin et al. 2011, p. 21).	Spiritualism and intellectual pursuit; intangible ideals are more important than tangible items. Materialism, however, seems to be on the rise in current Russian society.

Source: Adapted from Zainuddin et al. (2011).
Note: *Despite being group-oriented in personal life, most Russian students will not be comfortable working in groups because this instructional format is not common in the Russian educational system and most school assignments—at all educational levels—are done individually.

the conversation going; however, this may come across as rude to Americans. Additionally, while American culture values small talk, Russians traditionally value silence—"Silence is gold," a Russian saying goes—and may take more time to answer and to get involved in a conversation to begin with.

Smiling is another factor that may contribute to miscommunications among Russians and Americans. In Russia, a smile is the symbol of laughter or of an established friendship or intimacy. So, a smile from a person not belonging to the inner circle of friends and family may be perceived as friendly by Americans but as "unusual, inappropriate, or even suspicious" by a Russian (e.g., perception of being ridiculed/laughed at; perception of violation of established boundaries; Zainuddin et al., 2011, p. 37).

Family Composition and "Nomenclature"

Financially, the Russian family depends on the contributions of all its members, which leads to the mother typically having to work, a small number of children per household, and several generations sharing the same living space (typically a small apartment) to provide care for each other. Traditionally, the father (or the oldest male) is the head of the household, and he will have the last word in major decisions. Although the role of the woman has changed substantially in 20th-century Russia, male domination—both on personal and social levels—still persists (Savenko, 2007).

Each Russian name includes three parts. For example, Olga Vladimirovna Polikarpova can be broken down into:

1. First name: A person's given name (e.g., Olga);
2. Middle name (patronymic): Father's first name + *avna/ovna* for a female (e.g., = Vladimir + *ovna* = Vladimirovna) and + *vich/ovich* for a male (Vladimir + *ovich* = Vladimirovich);
3. Last name: Family name, traditionally that of the husband (e.g., Polikarpova).

Reflecting patriarchal traditions, the last names of females (i.e., a daughter or wife) are the male (father's or husband's) last name + *a*, an equivalent of the English possessive *'s* (e.g., Gorbatchev + *a* = Gorbatcheva). Educators of Russian students may find it interesting to know that the politest way to address a person, especially a person who is older than the speaker, is by their first plus middle (patronymic) name.

Russian Cuisine Over the 12 Time Zones

While a Russian family in a Kaliningrad apartment block sits down to a breakfast of freshly cooked *bliny* (thin pancakes) with fresh butter and jam, fishermen in the Volga Delta take a break from catching sturgeon to make the all-favorite fish soup *ukha*; at the same time, over 3,500 km (2,000 miles) to the northeast, in the small town of Norilsk, filled pasta pockets called *pelmeni*, a favorite Siberian dish, are on the lunch table and, on the Bering Sea shores, a Chukchi family is having a traditional evening meal of dried fish and raw seal liver (Trutter, 2007). Bread appears on the table with most Russian meals; "After all, Russians have long regarded bread and salt not merely as foodstuffs but also as symbols of hospitality and respect for the gifts of nature" (Trutter, 2007, p. 15).

Another Russian staple is called *pirogi*. These are large pockets of dough filled with everything that the garden, the forest, the pond, or the barn can provide (smaller versions are called *pirozhki*). The name comes from the Old Russian word *pir*, a feast or a banquet, probably because in the early days *pirogi* were only made on feast days. You can find *pirogi* filled with cabbage, potatoes, peas, carrots, eggs, berries, poppy seeds, or kasha (cereal porridge). *Pirogi* filled with poultry, game, innards, or ground meat are a particular delicacy. Sweet *pirozhki* filled with fruit, honey, or drained *fromage blanc* (similar to cottage cheese) go well with the ever-present tea (Trutter, 2007). Russian food is traditionally based on a few staples, but everyone manages to cook these staples differently and families can have arguments about whose *bliny* or *pirogi* recipe is the best!

A few cooking habits of Russians, however, are commonly accepted and well respected as they are grounded in Russian history and traditional ways of life. For example, "the slow cooking methods of boiling, brazing, stewing, and baking are determined by the warmth of a Russian stove" (Trutter, 2007, p. 14), the centerpiece of the Russian *izba* (a traditional log house) that provides a continuous source of heat throughout the long months of winter. The liking of salty, sweet, smoked, and dried preserves such as pickled cucumbers, marinated mushrooms, *varenye* (jams and conserves) of wild berries, and dried apples, has its roots in the need for food to keep over the long, cold winter. The wealth of traditional vegetarian recipes—including the all-favorite buckwheat *kasha* and vegetable and mushroom "caviars" (spreads)—is the result of the Russian Orthodox Church requiring that more than half the year be spent in fasting. Because Russians are rarely in a hurry and believe that "if you spend a long time eating, you will have a long life," *zakuski* (small appetizers) serve to extend every meal "by a few delicious moments" (Trutter, 2007, p. 20). Although everyday *zakuski* choices are modest, "the table threatens to collapse under the weight of the *zakuski*" (Trutter, 2007, p. 20) on the days when guests come. Some of the old-time favorites include caviar, sturgeon or pike in aspic, and slow-boiled tongue.

EDUCATION

General education in Russia is free and is usually completed in 11 years (starting from 6–7 years old until 17–18 years old; Nordic Recognition Network, 2005). The school year typically includes 34 weeks, with 27–38 hours of study a week. The school year starts on September 1st and ends at the beginning of June. Foreign language instruction—typically English, French, and German—begins in grade 2 and continues until grade 11. Russian students who have taken English as a foreign language classes (often British English) come to U.S. schools with some initial grammar, vocabulary, and literacy skills. Fluency in spoken English, however, is less likely due to a traditional emphasis on grammar and reading in Russian foreign language education classrooms.

General education in Russia includes three stages: (a) primary general education (grades 1–4); (b) basic general education (basic secondary; grades 5–9), and; (c) secondary complete general education (upper secondary; grades 10–11). The first two stages—primary and basic secondary—are compulsory. Four main types of schools offering general education include:

- General schools: Schools of general education (Grades 1–11; 80% of all schools)
- General schools with intensive learning programs: Schools of general education offering advanced teaching in specific fields (e.g., foreign languages, science, sports, choreography, or music; 15% of all schools; may offer teaching at primary, basic general, and upper secondary levels)
- Gymnasiums: Schools of general education with a focus on humanities (2% of all schools; may offer teaching at primary, basic general, and upper secondary levels)
- Lyceums: Schools of general education with a focus on scientific and technical subjects (3% of all schools; may offer teaching at primary, basic general, and upper secondary levels) (Nordic Recognition Network, 2005, p. 18)

Private schools offering programs similar to those described above are fully financed by parents. Completing the basic general education and passing the exit attestation examination entitles students to admission to one of three options: (a) secondary complete general education, (b) basic vocational education, or (c) middle level professional education.

A number of issues plague Russian education well into the higher education system (Chirikov, 2015). Such issues—which may affect Russian student experiences in U.S. schools—include predominantly teacher-centered instruction that encourages passive learning and memorization (i.e., structured in-class learning such as lecture with little intellectual challenge or problem-solving), minimum teacher–student interaction, and high tolerance for cheating. Yet, as indicated by international comparative studies of educational outcomes, Russian students perform roughly comparable to U.S. students, particularly in mathematics and science, although they score lower than students from leading Asian (e.g., Japan, Korea) and European (e.g., Finland) countries (Amini & Commander, 2011).

U.S. educators may find it unusual that Russians typically begin and end their general education in the same building with the same classmates. Primary general education in core disciplines is typically provided by the same grade 1–5 teacher. Beginning with upper secondary school, core disciplines are taught by subject matter specialists who, unlike in the United States, loop by cohorts. That is, they do not teach a single grade level year after year, but rather teach their subject area to the same cohort of students from grade 6 until graduation, either in grade 9 or in grade 11 (a teacher may work with 2–4 cohorts of students at the same time). As a result, Russian students coming to U.S. schools in upper grades may have difficulty acclimatizing to a new content-area teacher at each grade level in each discipline and to a need to develop a new network of peers when transitioning from middle to high school.

Another interesting fact is the Russian grading system, which is as follows:

5 = excellent (*otlichno*)
4 = good (*khorosho*)
3 = satisfactory (*udovletvoritelno*) = the lowest passing grade
2 = unsatisfactory (*neudovletvoritelno*)
1 = unacceptable (*yedenitsa*; a very rarely used grade) (Ministry of Education and Science of Russian Federation, 2013)

RUSSIAN LANGUAGE

Differences From and Similarities to English

When speaking about Russian we use the term "Greek-based Cyrillic alphabet" rather than "Greek alphabet," because some of the Russian sounds not present in the Greek language were represented with letters from the Hebrew alphabet. The comparison of the English and Russian sound and grammatical systems below is largely based on Jones and Ward (1969) and Timberlake (1993).

Sound System and Pronunciation

Russian has only five vowel sounds, compared to 11 basic vowel sounds in English. Given this, English vowels often present problems for Russian learners. For example, Russian learners of English would normally pronounce the words *beat* and *bit* the same, as *beat*; and they would pronounce both *Luke* and *look* as *Luke*. This is because Russian does not have short ("lax") vowels (as in the English words *bit* and *look*). This can cause some misunderstanding.

Unlike with vowels, Russian is rather heavy on consonants. There are 33 of those, compared to 23 consonants in English. In part, this is because many Russian consonants come in pairs: "hard" (plain) and "soft" (palatalized). The hard consonants are pronounced roughly similar to English ones, while for the soft ones the middle portion of the tongue is raised as it would be for the sound *y* in *yes*. There are, for example, two kinds of *s* in Russian: the hard *s* as in *sok* (juice) and the soft *sy* as in *syok* (whipped). Russian learners of English may transfer this soft quality to English consonants, for example, pronouncing words like *see* and *sit* as "*syee*" and "*syit*." In most cases, however, this should not cause confusion.

Among the consonants that Russian lacks are the English sounds *th* and *w*. Early Russian learners tend to substitute these sounds with *s/z* and *v* respectively, so that the words *this*, *mouth*, and *wine* may be pronounced as *zis*, *mouse*, and *vine*. Further, the Russian *r* sound is a *rolled r* similar to that in Spanish, and some learners may substitute it for the English *r*. Another important difference between the two languages is that Russian consonants *p*, *t*, and *k* lack the puff of air (aspiration) typical of their English counterparts (as in *pet*, *time*, *cap*), and may occasionally sound to an English speaker more like *b*, *d*, *g* (as in *bet*, *dime*, and *gap*). Even more confusingly, Russian *b*, *d*, *g*, *v*, and *z* are pronounced at the end of words as *p*, *t*, *k*, *f*, *s*, so the English words *bed*, *dog*, and *save* in Russian-accented speech would sound the same as *bet*, *dock*, and *safe*. Changes in the opposite direction happen in sequences of consonants, with, for example, McDonalds and Facebook being commonly pronounced more like *magdonalts* and *fazebook*.

Stress (accent) plays an important role in Russian, so that many words with the same sounds differ only in the placement of stress as in *plaCHU* (I pay) and *PLAchu* (I cry). This is comparable to the different stress in English words *IMport* (noun) and *to impORT* (verb), but is certainly more widespread. There are some differences between Russian and English in terms of intonation patterns as well. For example, Russian questions always have a rising intonation, while some English questions (beginning with *wh-* words) tend to be pronounced with a falling intonation. It is not uncommon for Russian learners to pronounce questions like *What is it?* with a rise similar to the question *Is it?*

The Writing System

Russian uses the Cyrillic writing system, which consists of 33 letters. There is a fairly good correspondence between letters and sounds in Russian. Some of the Cyrillic and Roman letters are the same, but may correspond to different sounds (e.g., letter *a* = '*ah*' sound, but letter *p* = '*r*' sound and the letter *b* = '*v*' sound), initially leading to confusion.

The Grammatical System

Russian is well-known for its extensive use of diminutives. Essentially any noun can have a form or multiple forms with a secondary meaning of "little, cute" (e.g., *solntse—solnyshko*: "the sun—the little sun"). First names also have diminutives and are frequently used when addressing children or friends and family members (e.g., *Mariya—Masha, Mashen-yka; Nikolay—Kolya, Kolen-yka*).

Russian lacks the grammatical concept of articles and thus does not differentiate phrases like *a house* and *the house*. This presents a considerable problem for Russian learners who tend to omit articles or overgeneralize either *a* or *the*. Unlike in English, Russian has a grammatical category of gender, with all nouns belonging to either masculine (e.g., *stol*: "table"), feminine (e.g., *kniga*: "book"), or neuter (e.g., *solntse*: "sun") gender. Typically, but not exclusively, feminine nouns end in *–a*, neuter nouns end in *–e* or *–o*, and masculine nouns end in a consonant. This concept is alien to English, but similar to other languages like French and German.

Another challenge for Russian learners is the use of English tenses. That is, unlike in English, Russian verbs lack the grammatical categories of progressive and perfect tenses. This means that sentences '*She writes*' and '*She is writing*' are rendered in Russian in the same way (e.g., *Ona pishet*).

As in English, most Russian nouns have singular and plural forms (*shkola—shkoly*: "school—schools"). The complexity of word endings—the Russian case system has six cases for nouns, adjectives, and prepositions—allows for a relatively free word order in sentences. That is, the sentence "I opened a book" can be said in any of the following ways with essentially the same basic meaning: "I opened a book," "I a book opened," "Opened I a book," and "A book I opened." This may cause some initial problems for Russians learning English, as English relies on a much stricter subject-verb-object word order (rather than on an ending system) to convey the basic meaning of who did what and to whom.

Language in Context

Russian and English also differ considerably in terms of the contextual influences on interpreting meaning (pragmatics). For example, requests made in Russian tend to be more direct, making use of imperatives, as compared to the more standard English indirect requests using interrogative constructions (e.g., "Call me" in Russian rather than "Could you call me?" in English). The greater directness of requests in Russian does not imply lesser politeness; rather, it reflects a more hearer-oriented perspective compared to the speaker-oriented perspective typical of English and of Western cultures in general (Ogiermann, 2009).

Among the commonly used words and phrases that might be helpful in the classroom are the following, with hyphens indicating syllables (stressed vowels are capitalized):

- *dO-brah-ye OO-trah* (good morning)
- *dO-bry dyEny* (good afternoon)
- *pree-vyEt* (hi!)
- *kAHk dee-lAH?* (how are you?)
- *dah-svee-dAh-nee-yah* (good bye)
- *spah-sEE-ba* (thank you)
- *pah-zhAH-loos-tah* (you are welcome)
- *eez-vee-nEE-tye* (excuse me, sorry)
- *hah-rah-shAW* (good)
- *aht-lEEch-nah!* (excellent!)

CONCLUSIONS

This chapter provides a glimpse into Russian culture and language to supply educators with some initial understandings of their Russian students. Being just a brief introduction, this chapter misses on some of the rich Russian traditions, values, and beliefs like art and architecture, the beauty of the basilicas, the strength of Russian people to deal with adversity throughout history, the way that Russian parents give everything to their children, and how loyal they are to those they love. As suggested by the activities below, the missing pieces from this chapter may become classroom projects that would help engage Russian students and their families—one of the strongest assets that educators may draw on—with their schooling in the United States. Going back to the introductory classroom vignette, the educators of Russian students may anticipate that

American communication patterns and school expectations may be the biggest challenges in integrating Russian students. One research-based means of helping ELLs familiarize with both is *Accountable Talk* (Ardasheva, Howell, & Magaña, 2016), an instructional approach that (a) explicitly teaches the how-tos and the whys of school-based norms of behavior and communication, (b) provides scaffolds to support the use of targeted behaviors and communication norms, and (c) develops classroom structures to support the use of the targeted behavior and communication norms. A link included in the Resources section below provides ample information on the approach for the interested educator.

TASKS FOR EDUCATORS

1. Discuss these questions with your colleagues/peers:
   - In your opinion, how different were the experiences of the different waves of Russian immigrants? How may their experiences have impacted younger Russian immigrants attending schools in the United States?
   - In what ways could you, as an educator, minimize potential miscommunications with Russian students and their families due to differences in communication patterns?
   - What are the advantages and the disadvantages of grade-level (United States) versus cohort (Russia) content-area teaching? How can educators capitalize on the schooling that immigrant children may have had in their countries of origin?
2. Develop ways to use the resources listed below to engage your Russian students and their families.
3. Read this book chapter with your Russian students and ask them to write a rebuttal, a review, or an alternative to the chapter.
4. Do a research scavenger hunt on the topics that are missing in the chapter yet are of interest.
5. Conduct a community study by visiting local Russian businesses and community gatherings.
6. Interview Russian families about their histories, beliefs, and values.

ADDITIONAL RESOURCES

Chubarov, A. (2007). All Russias: History section. Retrieved from http://www.allrussias.com/sitemap.asp

The site has a series of short articles dedicated to Russian history, grouped under two large topics: Tsarist Russia and Soviet Russia

Chubarov, A. (2007). Russia from A to Z. Retrieved from http://www.allrussias.com/section_az.asp

The site has a series of short articles on a number of topics dedicated to Russia, such as architecture, folklore, climate, holidays, ethnic minorities, and so on.

Encyclopedia Britannica (2015). Cyrillic alphabet. Retrieved from http://www.britannica.com/topic/Cyrillic-alphabet

The site includes transliterations and approximate pronunciations of Cyrillic letters

CommisceoGlobal (n. d.). Award-winning culture guides: Russia guide. Retrieved from http://www.kwintessential.co.uk/resources/global-etiquette/russia-country-profile.html

The site includes recommendations for meeting, gift giving, dining, business meetings, and so on.

Russiapedia (2005). Prominent Russians: Faces of Russia. Retrieved from http://russiapedia.rt.com/prominent-russians/

The site includes biographies of prominent Russians, including artists, scientists, entertainers, cinematographers, and sportsmen.

Saint-Petersburg.Com. (2001). Petersburgers: Biographies of the city's greatest residents. Retrieved from http://www.saint-petersburg.com/famous-people/

The site includes biographies of prominent Russians, including artists and scientists who lived in St. Petersburg.

Ministry of Education and Science of the Russian Federation (2006). Education in Russia for foreigners: Russian educational system today. Retrieved from http://en.russia.edu.ru/edu/description/sysobr/

The site describes the Russian educational system as well as opportunities for study in Russia for international students.

Institute for Learning: University of Pittsburg (n.d.). Accountable Talk. Retrieved from http://ifl.pitt.edu/index.php/educator_resources/accountable_talk

The site provides extensive resources on Accountable Talk, including the sourcebook [description, research base], podcasts, videos, and so on)

REFERENCES

Amini, C., & Commander, S. (2011). *Educational scores: How does Russia fare?* Bonn, Germany: Institute of the Study of Labor. Retrieved from http://ftp.iza.org/dp6033.pdf

Ardasheva, Y., Howell, P. B., & Magaña, M. V. (2016). Accessing the classroom discourse community through accountable talk: English learners' voices. *TESOL Journal,* 7, 667–699. Retrieved from http://onlinelibrary.wiley.com/doi/10.1002/tesj.237/full.

Bartlett, R. P. (2006). *A history of Russia.* New York, NY: Palgrave Macmillan.

Chirikov, I. (2015). The mystery of Russian students: Poor learning experience, high satisfaction. *Higher Education in Russia and Beyond, 3*, 10–11.

Chubarov, A. (2007). *Russia from A to Z*. Retrieved from http://www.allrussias.com/section_az.asp

Columbia Encyclopedia (6th ed.). (2015). *Slavophiles* and Westernizers. Retrieved from http://www.encyclopedia.com/doc/1E1-Slavophi.html

Jones, D., & Ward, D. (1969). *The phonetics of Russian*. Cambridge, UK: Cambridge University Press.

Library of Congress. (2015). *Immigration: Polish/Russian*. Retrieved from http://www.loc.gov/teachers/classroommaterials/presentationsandactivities/presentations/immigration/polish2.html

Ministry of Education and Science of Russian Federation. (2013). *The marking system*. Retrieved from http://en.russia.edu.ru/edu/description/sysobr/909/

Nordic Recognition Network. (2005). *The system of education in Russia*. Retrieved from http://norric.org/files/education-systems/Ruslandsrapport-feb2005.pdf

Ogiermann, E. (2009). Politeness and in-directness across cultures: A comparison of English, German, Polish and Russian requests. *Journal of Politeness Research, 5*, 189–216.

Russian Public Opinion Research Center. (2015). *Church and society: Together or separately?* Retrieved from http://wciom.ru/index.php?id=236&uid=115295

Savenko, Y. (2007). *Do women have equal rights with men in Russia?* Retrieved from http://humanrightshouse.org/Articles/7821.html

Timberlake, A. (1993). Russian. In B. Comrie & G. G. Corbett (Eds.), *The Slavonic languages* (pp. 827–886). New York, NY: Routledge.

Trutter, M. (Ed.). (2007). *Culinaria Russia: Ukraine Georgia Armenia Azerbaijan*. Cambridge, UK: Ullmann Publishing.

U.S. Central Intelligence Agency. (2016). Central Asia—Russia. *In the world factbook*. Retrieved from https://www.cia.gov/library/publications/the-world-factbook/geos/rs.html

Zainuddin, H., Yahya, N., Morales-Jones, C. A., & Ariza, E. N. (2011). *Fundamentals of teaching English to speakers of other languages in K-12 mainstream classrooms* (3rd ed). Dubuque, IA: Kendall Hunt Publishing.

CHAPTER 25

UKRAINE

Nataliia Borysenko and Petro Borysenko
Kyiv Taras Shevchenko National University

A 10-year old boy from Ukraine, Denny came to the U.S. with his mom under the auspices of an America–Ukrainian project. Denny was quite a sociable kid and he loved Americans and their culture at once. His mom was happy to see his shining eyes and his constant desire to socialize with American children. He loved school and kept telling his mom that American kids were kind and very welcoming. After school he would go outside and watch a bunch of kids playing football, but he never played himself, which was quite strange because he loved sports. When his mom asked Denny why he was not playing, he replied that those kids did not want to play with him because they never invited him to play. Fortunately, Denny's mom was more knowledgeable about American culture and knew that, unlike in Ukraine, he had to express his desire to play the game first. Following his mom's advice, Denny asked the group if he could play with them. He was very excited to hear "Sure!" After that he was never just watching the game, but he was playing it with every-one else.

For a variety of reasons, more and more Ukrainian children are ending up studying in the U.S. In order to engage these children, educators can reach out to them in ways that are culturally and linguistically appropriate and responsive. To do so, it is useful for educators to know the cultural characteristics, assumptions, biases, and stereotypes that Ukrainian students may bring into the classroom. Although it may seem an easy task for American educators to work with Ukrainian students, in reality it may not

Views From Inside: Languages, Cultures, and Schooling for K–12 Educators
pp. 435–452
Copyright © 2018 by Information Age Publishing
All rights of reproduction in any form reserved.

be because common misconceptions and stereotypes may play a role in their conclusions and decisions. The crucial American misconception about Ukraine is that it is a part of Russia, which is quite painful for Ukrainians. This chapter gives an overview of Ukraine and its culture in order to facilitate American educators' understandings of the "soul" of the Ukrainian children they may teach, avoid possible miscommunication, and support the creation of optimal learning environments for Ukrainian children.

BACKGROUND

Geography

Ukraine is an eastern European country. In area, it is the second largest in Europe after the Russian Federation (Russia), and it is the biggest country located completely in Europe. At 233,062 square miles, it is a little bit smaller than the territory of Texas (List of U.S. states and territories by area, 2016).

Ukraine is washed by the Black and Azov Seas and bordered by Moldova and Romania to the south; Hungary, Slovakia, and Poland to the west; Belarus to the north; and Russia to the north and northeast (see Figure 25.1).

Demographics

About 42.5 million people inhabit Ukraine (Demographics of Ukraine, 2016). Of its entire population, almost 78% are of Ukrainian ethnic origin. The largest share of ethnic Ukrainians lives in the western and central regions of the country. In the eastern regions, ethnic Ukrainians make up around 60% of the population. In the Crimea, Ukrainians constitute 24%. Another significant ethnic group in Ukraine is Russians (17%). The residual 5% is made up by Jews, Poles, Germans, Byelorussians, Moldovans, Romanians, Greeks, Hungarians, Steppe and Crimean Tatars, Roma, and Armenians, along with other groups (Ukraine, 2016).

Due to such a variety of cultures existing in Ukraine, Ukrainian children and their parents in general have developed tolerant attitudes towards different cultures. The shared geographical borders and history with some Western countries and Russia, however, have created a deep divide in the Ukrainian population between pro-Western and pro-Russian groups. In light of current conflicts between Russia and Ukraine in the Crimea and other areas, any generalizations about these two countries

Source: Adapted with permission.

Figure 25.1.   Map of Ukraine and surroundings (Savchuk, 2016).

may provoke sad memories for Ukrainian children and their parents and lead to miscommunication with Ukrainian immigrant families. Because representatives of each of these groups come to the U.S., educators in America should not be surprised at the very different views that their Ukrainian students may have. Educators might consider paying attention to interactions among students of Russian/pro-Russian and pro-Western Ukrainian backgrounds. American educators can ask which part of Ukraine their Ukrainian students represent and ensure that those who disagree with their stance on Ukraine's future have effective and diplomatic ways to do so.

History

Ukraine's capital is Kyiv, one of the most ancient cities in Europe, dating back to the end of the 5th century. Older and current pro-Russian sources use another spelling of the capital of Ukraine, *Kiev.* This spelling is not used in Ukraine anymore because it was coined during Soviet times and reflects the Russian pronunciation of this capital, not the Ukrainian one. Due to the latest events in Ukrainian–Russian relations, it is considered politically incorrect to use the old spelling (Embassy of the United States, 2016).

Because of its vast, deeply rich black soil and hard-working people well experienced in agriculture, Ukraine has served as the "breadbasket of Europe" for centuries. These beneficial characteristics, along with the country's geographical location at the crossroads of trade routes between Europe and Asia, helped shape Ukraine's long and complex history.

According to the famous Ukrainian political and public activist Volodymyr Vynnychenko (1880–1951), one should read Ukrainian history only after taking bromine (a kind of tranquilizer used in the early 19th century), as it is filled with misfortune, senselessness, and helplessness. During its statehood periods, the downtrodden and outcast nation had to defend itself in all directions: from Poles, Russians, Tatars, and Swedes. The whole Ukrainian history is a series of nonstop rebellions, wars, conflagrations, famines, invasions, military takeovers, intrigues, quarrels, and betrayals (Vynnychenko, 1980).

Having lived through the tragic years of the *Holodomor* (death by forced starvation; see the memorial in Figure 25.2) of 1932–1933 that took the lives of 28,000 people (Holodomor Facts and History, 2016) and surviving World War II, Ukraine became independent again in 1991 after the Soviet Union collapsed. These historical events forced many Ukrainians to seek safer places to live, and many eventually settled in the United States and Canada. Both Ukrainians living in their native territory and those who emigrated to other countries remember well these major turning points of their history that have been woven into their culture. More recently, Ukrainians have faced additional challenges, including the development of democracy, transition to economic and social independence, and the elimination of corruption at all levels. Above all, Ukraine is a proud nation that values its independence very much.

This history has implications for Ukrainian children at school. For example, people are very supportive of each other because this was and is a crucial condition for Ukrainians to survive and prosper. Therefore, Ukrainian students may share their meals, as well as their assignments, with peers, because in the eyes of the Ukrainian child it is how someone can be supportive. Further, Ukrainian students may easily participate in misbehaviors with their peers and, even if they were just witnesses, Ukrainian children would rather claim guilt or fault than betray their classmates. Teachers can consider withholding punishment until other pedagogical strategies have been employed to reveal the truth.

Source: Photograph by Valery Savchuk, used
with permission.

Figure 25.2.   Holodomor Memorial, Kyiv,
Ukraine.

CULTURE

Ukrainian Identity

Situated on the border of two worlds (Western and Eastern Europe) and not protected by any natural boundaries, Ukraine has always felt the influence of other cultures seeking to devour it in their geopolitical ambitions. This tragic history helped form the nation's worldview, full of contradictions that often influence Ukrainians in observing and perceiving the surrounding environment. For example, national features include adaptability and intelligence, lack of rationality and individualism, a tendency toward indecision in situations that require choice among several options, and firmness in achieving the goal. The majority of Ukrainians would describe themselves as direct, patriotic but skeptical, and hardworking but unorganized. Ukrainians are distinguished by their love of freedom, emotionality, value of family (of which the woman is the heart and charm), adherence to religion, and tolerance towards other nations. The culture of Ukraine is based on the values of farming and bread as the essential treasures in people's lives.

Ukrainians are world-known for their boundless hospitality. They love to invite people to their homes or to visit their relatives and/or friends. Ukrainians always do their best to cook the most festive dishes on these occasions (even if they have to save money for some time to do so) and to feed the guests as soon as they enter their home. If the table does not have enough variety by Ukrainian standards—which means at least 2–3 different entrees, several main courses with at least four side dishes, and some desserts—it will be a great shame for the host.

To thank the Ukrainian host for the delicious meal, besides nice words, Ukrainians expect guests to finish everything on their plates. As soon as the plate is empty, however, the host will start begging the guest to try something else. Their persuasive words (which may be perceived as insisting by Americans) will be supported by multiple attempts to put "just a tiny but very delicious piece of food" on the plate. Assurances by the guest that it is not a tiny piece or that the guest is very full will never work—giving in is often the easiest way to deal with this situation. This situation is based in Ukrainian history, too—throwing food into the garbage can or compost means wasting food, which is one of the most severe sins for a nation that has gone through famine. Any leftovers can be consumed later and/or fed to home-raised animals in the countryside or birds and homeless dogs and cats. Feeding animals and birds, domesticated or wild, is considered helping "our little brothers and sisters," which Ukrainians believe should be protected. However, Ukrainian parties and gatherings are not just about indulging the stomach with yummy food but also about having fun by enjoying light conversation and playing various games.

Traditionally, Ukrainian culture is very family-oriented. It is not unusual for Ukrainians for parents or grandparents to live together with their children or grandchildren, even if the latter have their own families. The older generations help young families raise their children because they believe they know better how to do it. This tradition was a necessity in the past when the majority of Ukrainians lived in villages. The tradition for elders to help their children and grandchildren and support them even financially is still very strong in Ukraine. This is because the incomes of Ukrainian youth and young families are typically so low that it is impossible to buy or rent their own home. In addition, the banking system is still quite undeveloped in terms of loans and mortgages. Rare successful attempts to obtain a mortgage end up with at least 30% annual interest. Thus, when educators in America deal with Ukrainian students and their parents, special attention might be paid to detailed explanations of social programs in the U.S., the banking system, and ways to finance students' education.

Ukrainians value educated people. Taking into consideration that one of the cultural values in Ukraine is education, complete literacy in Ukrainian is essential for every citizen who has finished high school. Ukrainian parents work hard to give their children every opportunity to get a higher education (bachelor's and/or master's degrees). Against a backdrop of the constant growth of unemployment and competition in finding a well-paid (by Ukrainian standards) job, higher education has turned into a "happy lottery ticket." For example, in Ukraine, it is impossible to find a job as a waiter/waitress—even in fast-food restaurants like McDonalds—if you are not a college student or do not have a college degree. This is why parents sacrifice their career and savings to give children the best education they can.

If Ukrainian children have problems in U.S. classrooms with proper behavior or if they do not succeed in their studies, these students may be very surprised if educators discuss these issues with them without involving their parents. This approach is opposite to the Ukrainian one, where the parents of a naughty child are called to school at once. This difference may have two effects: either the Ukrainian child, impressed by being treated like an adult and influenced by other students in the classroom, will change his or her attitude toward school for the better, or the child might feel that acting with impunity is a major feature of the American school. The challenge for U.S. educators would be to find an appropriate pedagogical strategy to make sure that the outcome is positive.

Cultural Characteristics

Typical Ukrainian characteristics and behaviors include the following:

- Ukrainians are brought up to avoid attracting attention to themselves. They usually speak quietly in public to respect the privacy of other people. To sit or lie on the floor in public places is considered inappropriate and may be perceived as that the person violating this rule is drunk. American educators would be advised not to make Ukrainian students sit on the floor during activities until they understand the reason, because these students may perceive it as a humiliation.

- Americans may be surprised that Ukrainians do not typically smile in the street, but in Ukrainian culture, it is a good sign. When Ukrainians look at you and smile, it means they are laughing at you. That is the reason why Ukrainians avoid smiling at strangers—they just do not want to hurt them. But when you are introduced to Ukrainians, you will see sincere smiles on their faces. When students with Ukrainian backgrounds start smiling at their educators after some time, this means that they really like their educators and are eager to show their appreciation.

- In Ukraine, men often carry heavy bags for women, open doors for them, and buy them flowers. Many Ukrainian men try to do their best to please a woman and make a lady feel that she is a "queen." Educators should not be surprised if Ukrainian boys open doors for their female teachers and peers. This is just a gesture of politeness. Further, when a Ukrainian male student brings flowers to his female American educator, he is showing his deep respect to both the woman and the educator. It would be nice for the educator to appreciate this gift and thank the student by emphasizing how beautiful the flowers are.

- Unlike Americans, Ukrainians never stand with their backs toward other people in the elevator. In Ukraine, it is a sign of impoliteness and ignorance. It is not required to look at a person or in his or her eyes, but to face other people sharing a quite small space is a norm of politeness in Ukraine.

- In Ukraine, there is a strict division between street and home footwear. Guests in a Ukrainian home should take their shoes off. Forgetting about it may cause complete incomprehension from the Ukrainian side. It will appear as if the guest does not respect the host. Educators who do home visits should remember to take their shoes off despite "protests" from the Ukrainian family. As compensation, the educator will receive the most welcoming attitude and every word since that minute will be accepted as the law to abide by.

- The majority of Ukrainians love pets. However, pets in Ukrainian culture are treated differently than in the United States. Ukrainians try to create an environment that would be natural for their pets. For example, Ukrainians do not decorate or dress their pets as much as Americans do. They also consider it a sin to spay or neuter their pets. Ukrainians are convinced that appropriate professional training can reduce and even eliminate any challenges caused by the pet's behavior.

- Ukrainian students do not consume food during classroom hours. Nevertheless, Ukrainian children and adults can adapt quickly to food rules in the classroom.
- The tradition of recognizing schools and colleges by school colors (e.g., the "Crimson and Gray") and animal symbols (e.g., the "Cougars" or the "Wildcats") does not exist in Ukraine and may be misinterpreted. At first, students with Ukrainian backgrounds may feel uncomfortable being called, for example, a "Fox" or a "Bear."
- Ukrainians are not shy to express their emotions, and it does not matter if their emotions are positive or negative. Educators in America might need some time to teach Ukrainian students not to reveal their negative emotions by emphasizing politeness norms in the U.S.
- In Ukrainian culture, students' attempts to cheat happen quite often because students perceive cheating as a kind of "problem-solving" activity, unlike in the U.S. Thus, it would be helpful to explain to students with Ukrainian backgrounds how cheating is perceived and punished in the U.S. Even so, these students should be monitored for some time because it is not so easy to get rid of some habits.

Superstitions

Before Christianity invaded Europe, Ukrainians were pagans; superstitions were rudiments of the pagan faith and created "fertile soil" for mystical beliefs in Ukrainians' worldviews (Ukraine Travel Advisor, 2014). For centuries now, pagan traditions have peacefully coexisted with the Orthodox Church in Ukraine. Although most Ukrainians realize that superstitions are just superstitions and have nothing to do with reality, they prefer not to tempt their providence ("just in case ..."). Among the strongest superstitions are the following:

- Like many other cultures, Ukrainians consider it a bad sign when a black cat crosses their way.
- Ukrainians avoid looking at a broken mirror or using broken or chipped tableware so they do not attract bad luck.
- There is a belief that if salt is scattered, it will lead to a big argument.
- Any endeavor on Friday the 13th will never be successful.
- Ukrainians avoid giving something in an entranceway because it may bring misfortune to both persons.

- If someone happens to sit between two persons having the same first names, that person should think about a wish and in some time it will definitely come true.
- The superstitious nature of Ukrainians gave birth to the proverb: "If you want to make God laugh, tell Him about your plans." Thus, if Ukrainians do utter some of their plans and talk about how successful and/or lucky they are, they always spit (pretend more than factually spit) three times over their left shoulder or knock on a wooden item so they do not jinx their future.
- For the same reason, when Ukrainians leave their home or office and suddenly realize that they need to go back and grab something they have forgotten, Ukrainians try to change something in their appearance to keep good luck with them.
- Casual acquaintances should not get embarrassed or upset when not recognizing a Ukrainian whom they have met before, as it is a good sign in Ukrainian culture—the person will definitely become rich in the future.
- Breaking a dish in a Ukrainian host's home is considered a sign of luck for the near future (of course, only if it is not a piece of very expensive dinnerware).
- Coming to a Ukrainian home with flowers shows deep respect to the hosts (at least one of whom should be female), but guests should buy an odd number. Even numbers are brought only for those who have passed away.
- Whistling inside means attracting dark forces, that is why it is unacceptable in Ukrainian culture.
- Unlike in America, it is a very bad sign in Ukrainian culture to celebrate a birthday before the day of birth arrives. The birthday can be celebrated only on the day of birth or after.
- Ukrainian girls try to avoid sitting at the corner of a table so as not to jeopardize their future marriage. According to the belief, a girl will not be wed for a long time if she sits at the corner of a table.
- Being much more superstitious than people of other nations, Ukrainians applaud the airplane crew members after the plane takes off or lands to show their appreciation for making every effort in saving their lives.

Food

Since Ukrainians ancestors had brick furnaces called *pich* for cooking their meals (see Figure 25.3), most of the recipes suggest boiled, steamed,

Source: Photograph by Valery Savchuk, used with permission.

Figure 25.3. Traditional Ukrainian *pich*.

stewed, and baked food. Due to its rich history, Ukrainian cuisine, influenced by Russian, Polish, Turkish, Hungarian, and Romanian cultures, is a mix of vegetables, fruit, meat, fish, and grains. Traditionally, Ukrainian cuisine is cooked with natural, organic ingredients. It is also full of calories, because Ukrainians use much whole milk, sour cream, butter, and many eggs in their cooking and baking.

Dishes usually associated with Ukrainian culture (shown in Figure 25.4) are:

- *Borsch*—a soup of meat, lima beans, and a variety of vegetables served with sour cream (bottom left)
- *Holubtsi (holubTSI)*—cabbage rolls stuffed with meat, rice and vegetables (middle left)
- *Deruny (deruNY)*—potato pancakes served with sour cream (middle right)
- *Pyrohy (pyroHY)*—big buns stuffed with vegetables, fruit, or meat or pyrizhky *(pyrizhKY)*—a smaller version of pyrohy
- *Varenyky (vaREnyky)*—dough dumplings filled with any stuffing one could possibly imagine (top right)
- *Homemade Kovbasa (kovbaSA)*—baked pork sausage (bottom right).

Source: Photograph by Valery Savchuk, used with permission.

Figure 25.4.   Traditional Ukrainian meals.

Ukrainians also love egg dishes. Potatoes, garlic, onions, cabbage, cucumbers, tomatoes, carrots, peppers, beets, and mushrooms are the most common vegetables in traditional Ukrainian cuisine.

A loaf of bread, being the heart of all Ukrainian meals, is an integral part of most Ukrainian ceremonies. When official guests or delegations come to an organization, institution, or company in Ukraine, they are greeted by girls or women carrying a nicely decorated round loaf of bread with salt on its top. It is an ancient welcoming ritual that has several meanings. It shows that Ukrainians are happy to host the guests and are ready to give them everything they can. The "Bread and Salt" ceremony also demonstrates that Ukrainians are ready to help the guests in case they need it and they are ready to share not only a nice experience (the bread), but also challenges (the salt) that may face them. Each of the guests is supposed to break off a piece of bread by hand, touch the salt with the piece of bread, and eat it right away. This means they confirm their peaceful intentions and appreciate the hearty welcome.

FAMOUS UKRAINIANS

Ukrainians are talented people and have made significant contributions to the world. The outstanding people listed below are either ethnic Ukrainians or were born, lived, and/or worked in Ukraine.

- Aeronautical engineer and aircraft pioneer Igor Sikorsky (1889–1972), born in Kyiv, immigrated to the United States in 1919 and formed the Sikorsky Aero Engineering Company in 1923. His company built the first twin-engine plane, the S-29. Sikorsky is also credited with designing the first helicopter (the VS-300, first flown in 1939) and the first large American four-engine clipper (the S-40, which could take off and land on water or land, built in 1931). Sikorsky modified the design into the Sikorsky R-4, which became the world's first mass-produced helicopter in 1942 (Igor Sikorsky, 2016).

- Ukrainian Jew Golda Meir (1898–1978), the 4th Prime Minister of Israel (1969–1974), was born in Kyiv and lived there until she was five (Pidlutsky, 2013).

- A native of Zhytomyr (Ukraine), Sergey Korolev (1906/07–1966) was a founder of Soviet rocketry and astronautics. In 1931, Korolev and his colleague Friedrich Tsander created a public organization for the study of jet propulsion, which later became the state scientific laboratory of missile aircraft design and development. In 1957, Korolev launched into orbit the first-ever artificial Earth satellite (Sergey Korolev, 2015).

- Milla Jovovich, an American actress, model, musician, and fashion designer, was born in Kyiv in 1975. Jovovich immigrated with her parents to the United States when she was five (Milla Yovovych, n.d.).

- Another American actress, Mila Kunis, was born in Chernivtsi, Ukraine in 1983. In 1991, she moved to Los Angeles with her family (Mila Kunis, 2015).

Figure 25.5. Famous Ukrainian boxers (Klitschko brothers, 2016).

- Vitaliy (1971–) and Volodymyr Klitschko (1976–) are Ukrainian athletes (see Figure 25.5), world champions in boxing in the heavy-weight division of all four major professional boxing organizations. The brothers promised their parents that they would never be opponents in the ring (Klitschko Brothers, 2016). The younger brother, Volodymyr, is the fiancé of Hayden Panettiere, an American actress, and is the father of their daughter.

Ukrainians are so proud of these outstanding people that mentioning their names in connection to Ukraine, especially boxers and actresses, may create a special connection between educators and their students with Ukrainian backgrounds.

LANGUAGE

Ukrainian, the only official language in Ukraine, belongs to the Eastern subgroup of the Slavic group of Indo-European languages. It is the second-most widely spoken language of the 12 surviving members of this group. Because of its rich history, the Ukrainian language has several dialects. Basic Ukrainian is the language of such great Ukrainian writers and poets as Taras Shevchenko and Lesia Ukrainka; it is also called the Poltavsky dialect because of the Poltava region that was the birthplace and workplace of Taras Shevchenko.

Ukrainian dialects in western Ukraine were greatly influenced by neighboring European countries such as Poland and Hungary, which occupied part of Ukrainian territory for several decades. The Ukrainian language in the east and south of the country and in the Crimea is highly influenced by the Russian language. In those regions, the Ukrainian language is nicknamed by Ukrainians themselves as Surzhik (*SURzhyk*), which means mixing Ukrainian and Russian words, spiced by some Ukrainian words pronounced with a Russian accent.

There is a constant battle between Ukrainian linguists, who try to add more western Ukrainian dialect words into basic Ukrainian, and those who believe that Poltava's language norms should not be changed. Further, Ukrainian linguists developed the only citation and usage guidelines used in Ukraine and believe that they should be followed by everyone, including students, professors, scholars, and officials. Thus it may be difficult for Ukrainian students to understand and use APA or MLA formatting in their academic papers.

There is also a belief in Ukraine that the Italian and Ukrainian languages are the most melodic ones among functioning languages, and Ukrainians are very proud of that. Tastes differ, but here is the opinion of an American who, when visiting Ukraine, described his perception of the Ukrainian language:

> Ukrainian sounds very strange to me, though interesting. Many Americans consider the French language to be the epitome of grace and perfection. Personally, I like how Ukrainian, German and Russian sounds much more. I think it is because of the directness and the emphases that make certain words stand out, while the French say everything with the same intonation. French is a more feminine language, and Ukrainian sounds strong and masculine. However, Ukrainian women manage to speak very softly, and it is difficult to refuse them anything. Their speech sounds like cats purring. The Ukrainian language may seem difficult to learn and understand, but in reality it is very rich and agreeable. (Shcherbinina, 2014)

Due to its history of being part of the Soviet Union and having the Russian language as official and compulsory for learning for every Soviet citizen, many Ukrainians are bilingual, speaking Ukrainian and Russian. However, a significant portion of the Ukrainian population, especially that which lives in the Eastern Ukrainian industrial cities, does not speak or understand Ukrainian because it vanished during the times of the Soviet Union. Unfortunately, language issues in Ukraine are a subject of constant argument between politicians. It is sad to admit that many Ukrainians take seriously political propaganda about the benefits of legalizing the status of Russian as the second official language or eliminating Ukrainian as an official language. Moreover, many Ukrainians believe that Russian becoming the second official language will solve all of Ukraine's problems and will lead Ukraine to prosperity. Politicians know that this would be the first step towards reintegration with Russia, but the ordinary people do not understand this.

To communicate with Ukrainian students, educators can use the following words and expressions (stressed syllables are in capital letters):

- Greeting words and expressions
  - *ViTAiu!* which means "Hello!"
  - *DObroho zdoROvia!* is a kind of greeting as well. However, literally it means "good health."
  - *Do ZUstrichi!* (See you!)
  - *Do poBAchennia* (Good-bye!)
- As Ukrainians represent a direct culture, the words *tak* (yes) and *ni* (no) are very frequent in everyday use.
- If you want to thank a Ukrainian for something, just say, "*DIAkuiu!*" When you thank a Ukrainian, just expect the answer "*Bud' LAska!*" or "You are welcome!" However, the phrase "*Bud' LAska*" is also used to say "Please!"
- When a Ukrainian tells you "*VYbachte,*" it means he or she is apologizing.
- A cult of food in Ukraine helped shaped two more expressions that Americans do not usually use:
  - When Ukrainians sit at a table for a meal or when they see someone eating they will always say "*SmachNOho!*," wishing you wonderful feelings while you consume the meal.
  - "*Na zdoROvia!*" is a kind of "You are welcome!" when you thank the Ukrainian for the meal cooked for you. However, literally it is translated as "To your health!" This phrase is also used as "Bless you!" when someone has sneezed.

CONCLUSIONS

This chapter gives the reader a glimpse of Ukrainian culture, the culture of a Slavic nation in the European continent. The information provided in this chapter may help American educators understand the Ukrainian soul better and avoid any intercultural misunderstandings.

ADDITIONAL RESOURCES

Jenkala, M. (2007). Read Ukrainian: A reading course for beginners. *Ukrainian-language.org*. Retrieved from http://www.ukrainianlanguage.org.uk/read/
> This site offers a free interactive course to support English speakers in developing their reading skills in Ukrainian. The course consists of twenty units. Each unit embraces a topic presentation, exercises to help learn the material covered by the unit, and texts for reading.

Learn Ukrainian online. (n.d.). *Ukrainian 101*. Retrieved from http://www.101languages.net/ukrainian/
> This website provides free top resources for learning Ukrainian. These include the language survival kit, vocabulary and grammar lessons, Ukrainian keyboard and pronunciation, and the country's travel guide.

Welcome to Ukraine. (n.d.). *Frontier vision technologies, Inc.* Retrieved from http://www.ukraine.org/
> This site gives a glimpse at Ukraine as a European country, its place in the history and culture of the Slavic nation.

TASKS FOR EDUCATORS

1. Consider your responses to these questions:
   - Which features of the Ukrainian national character sound nice to you? Explain your position.
   - What Ukrainian traditions are similar to American ones? Why?
   - What should American educators be aware of when interacting with Ukrainian students and their parents?
2. Compare the information about Ukraine to the chapters on its neighboring countries. What are the similarities and differences in how the authors explain their cultures and languages? Why do you think this might be?
3. How might you address conflicts between Ukrainian students (and their families) with different perspectives on Russia?

REFERENCES

Demographics of Ukraine. (2016, November). *Wikipedia*. Retrieved from https:// en.wikipedia.org/wiki/Demographics_of_Ukraine

Embassy of the United States, Kyiv, Ukraine. (2016, November). The U.S. Department of State. Retrieved from https://ukraine.usembassy.gov/

Holodomor Facts and History. (2016). *Holodomor 1932–1933*. Retrieved from http://www.holodomorct.org/history.html

Igor Sikorsky. (2016, November). *Wikipedia*. Retrieved from https://en.wikipedia .org/wiki/Igor_Sikorsky

Klitschko brothers. (2016, November 11). *Wikipedia*. Retrieved from https:// en.wikipedia.org/wiki/Klitschko_brothers

List of U.S. states and territories by area. (2016, October). *Wikipedia*. Retrieved from https://en.wikipedia.org/wiki/List_of_U.S._states_and_territories _by_area

Mila Kunis. (2015). *Moviestape*. Retrieved from http://moviestape.com/persons/ 1191-mila-kunis.html

Milla Yovovych. (n.d.). *24.SMI*. Retrieved from http://24smi.org/celebrity/978-mila-jovovich.html

Pidlutsky, O. (2013, December 13). Golda Meir: Kyiv's inhabitant who became a myth. *ZN, UA*. Retrieved from http://gazeta.dt.ua/personalities/ golda-meyir-kiyanka-yaka-stala-

Sergei Korolev (2016, November). *Wikipedia*. Retrieved from https://en.wikipedia .org/wiki/Sergei_Korolev

Shcherbinina, M. (2014, June 24). Foreign ears: What foreigners are saying about the Ukrainian language. *Euromaidan Press: News and Views from Ukraine*. Retrieved from http://euromaidanpress.com/2014/06/24/foreign-ears-what-foreigners-are-saying-about-the-ukrainian-language/#arvlbdata

Ukraine. (2016, November). Wikipedia. Retrieved from https://en.wikipedia.org/ wiki/Ukraine

Ukraine Travel Advisor. (2014). Ukraine customs and traditions. Retrieved from http://www.ukraine-travel-advisor.com/ukraine-customs.html

Vynnychenko, V. (1980). *Dairy* (Vol. 1, 1912–1920; H. Kostiuk, Ed.). Edmonton, Canada: Canadian Institute of Ukrainian Studies.

CHAPTER 26

POLAND

Justyna Hjeltness
Washington State University

Maria and Jan Kowalski emigrated with their two children from Poland two years ago. The oldest son Szymon is a third-grade student in a Washington State primary school. Szymon speaks basic English and is the only Polish child at school. As a result, he faces many cultural difficulties regarding his communication with educators and classmates. Since Szymon's parents are busy making a living in their new country, Szymon is mostly left to his own devices when it comes to dealing with school. One of the main problems that Szymon encounters at school is active participation in class. In Poland, education is rather teacher-centered and most children learn by listening to their teacher and taking notes. Frequently, good students are expected to participate quietly by only answering the teacher's questions. For this reason, Szymon, who was always an 'A' student back home, was surprised when his American teacher expressed his concern that Szymon was not an active member of the class and therefore lowered Szymon's grade. In Polish culture, asking multiple questions is looked on as a sign of disrespect and shows a lack of understanding rather than active class involvement as it does in the U.S.

BACKGROUND

Poland is located in Central Europe and shares borders with Germany, the Czech Republic, Slovakia, Ukraine, Belarus, Lithuania, and Russia. Its

Views From Inside: Languages, Cultures, and Schooling for K–12 Educators
pp. 453–467

estimated population is about 38.4 million people. There are also more than 13 million Poles who live abroad. Even though Poland occupies a central location in Europe, it is a very homogenous country. According to Glowny Urzad Statystyczny (2002), over 96% of the people living in Poland are of Polish origin and almost 97% of Poles speak only Polish at home. This homogeneity may be a result of Polish history; due to its central location, Poland has been involved in manifold conflicts in which other countries have tried to take over the Polish land. In order to fend off enemies, Poles have always needed to cooperate and work as one group, which has resulted in cultural uniformity and strong patriotism.

History

In the 18th century, Russia, Austria, and the Kingdom of Prussia partitioned Poland and, as a result, Poland disappeared from the map of the world for 123 years (Lukowski & Zawadzki, 2001). The three countries were trying to force Polish people to adopt new languages and laws compatible with their countries' own policies. However, they were met with significant resistance, and Poland became an independent country in 1918 after World War I (BBC News, 2017). After only two decades of peace, Poland was again at war with Nazi Germany and Communist Russia. During World War II (1939–1945), over 6 million Polish citizens were brutally killed in battles and concentration camps. Polish citizens, however, did not want to surrender to their occupiers, and therefore created a secret state underground. Conspiratorial groups existed all over Europe, but only Poland had its own secret parliament, army, police, ministries, and social services. In order to preserve Poland's cultural and national heritage, the secret Department of Education and Culture hid or rescued many artifacts and significant objects (Ministry of Foreign Affairs Republic of Poland, n.d.). The Department also was able to establish a secret school system by recruiting over 100,000 students and printing Polish textbooks (Ministry of Foreign Affairs Republic of Poland, n.d.).

Due to its resistance and sacrifices, Poland helped win the war against Nazi Germany. However, by 1945 Soviet occupancy had already spread to Poland, and, as a result, Poland was controlled by the Communists. The Communist government tried to eradicate Polish culture by censuring Polish universities and churches. Poles that publicly opposed and protested against the Communist party were arrested and imprisoned. The Communist oppression lasted until the 1980s, when Lech Walesa and the Polish trade union called *Solidarnosc* led a social movement of over 10 million Polish citizens against Soviet political oppression. The movement resulted in semi-democratic elections in 1989, in which Polish citizens chose Lech Walesa as president and removed the Communist party from the government (Burke, 2009). Poland finally became a free country with a democratic government.

Religion

Religion is an important part of the Polish culture. Currently, more than 95% of Poland's inhabitants are Catholic (Glowny Urzad Statystyczny, 2012). Over the centuries of political oppression, religion offered the Polish people hope and a means for cultivating Polish culture. In fact, the above-mentioned success of the trade union *Solidarnosc* can be greatly attributed to the Polish Catholic pope John Paul II. He officially supported the union, which brought a lot of international attention to the movement and weakened the political and social position of the Communist party (Repa, 2005).

Even though Poland is a secular country, Poles officially celebrate most of the important Catholic holidays such as Easter, Christmas, Ascension of Jesus, Assumption of the Virgin Mary, and so on. All government offices and schools are closed during these holidays, and families are given special time to celebrate (Ministry of Labor and Social Policy, 2015). Also, school children begin and end each school year by attending a Catholic mass. It is rare that a student would not go to mass even if they themselves are not particularly religious. One can see crosses in school classrooms and other public areas. A religion class (which only teaches Catholicism) is usually offered at school (Ministry of National Education, 2014). Polish traditions and Catholic religion are intertwined and sometimes difficult to separate.

Emigration

After WWII, many Poles fled the country seeking freedom and economic stability. In fact, about 2 million Poles emigrated to the U.S. during the 1950s and 1960s alone (U.S. Census Bureau, 1999). Nowadays, almost 10 million Polish Americans live in the U.S., mostly on the east coast (DADS, 2016). Polish Americans usually settle in areas with large Polish communities. For example, Chicago has the largest Polish community outside of Poland (Polish American Association, 2004).

CULTURE

National Pride

Due to unduly suffering throughout their history, Poles have a strong sense of national identity and pride. The following Poles have greatly impacted Poland and the rest of the world:

- Nicolaus Copernicus (1473–1643) was an astronomer, physician, Catholic clerk, translator, jurist, governor, military leader and economist. His book *On the Revolutions of the Celestial Spheres* is considered to be "a starting point of modern astronomy" (Lorie, 2008, para. 3). Copernicus is well known for his heliocentric theory that states that the Sun, not the Earth, is the center of the Solar System.
- Marie Skłodowska Curie (1867–1934) is known as "Madame Curie." She was one of the most famous female scientists of all time. So far, she has been the only person who won Nobel Prizes in two different sciences. She is famous for her pioneering work in the field of radioactivity.
- Lech Wałęsa (1943–) is a human rights activist, former President of Poland, and a Nobel Prize laureate. He was a leader of Poland's first trade union, *Solidarnosc*, which helped end Communism in Poland.
- Karol Wojtyła (John Paul II) (1920–2005) was the 264th Pope of the Roman Catholic Church. John Paul II supported the Polish movement against the Communist party in the 1980s. He was well known for his attempts to unite people of different religions. John Paul's Polish upbringing played an important role in his views. He is still an icon of morality and solidarity among Poles. Some of his sayings are:
  o "Humanity should question itself, once more, about the absurd and always unfair phenomenon of war, on whose stage of death and pain only remain standing the negotiating table that could and should have prevented it."
  o "Have no fear of moving into the unknown. Simply step out fearlessly knowing that I am with you, therefore no harm can befall you; all is very, very well. Do this in complete faith and confidence."
  o "The historical experience of socialist countries has sadly demonstrated that collectivism does not do away with alienation but rather increases it, adding to it a lack of basic necessities and economic inefficiency."
  o "When freedom does not have a purpose, when it does not wish to know anything about the rule of law engraved in the hearts of men and women, when it does not listen to the voice of conscience, it turns against humanity and society." (Pope John Paul II, n.d.)

Societal Norms

Even though Poland is increasingly adopting cultural traits from Western cultures, there are still many societal norms that significantly distinguish Poland from other Western countries.

The following information is from the CBOS (2010) Public Opinion Research Center:

- Family, good health, and honesty are the top three most important values among Polish people, whereas material well-being, freedom of expression, and an adventurous life are the least significant values.
- Nearly 65% of Poles claim that homosexuality is wrong and unacceptable, and only 8% consider it normal. Over half of the Polish population strongly rejects public displays of sexual orientation by homosexuals. A vast majority disagrees with gay marriage and gays' rights to adopt children. Additionally, more than two-fifths of Poles state that gays should be banned from certain jobs in education and medicine.
- Fifty-four percent of Polish people claim that divorce is unacceptable.
- Nearly 70% of Poles completely disagree with abortion. Abortion is generally illegal; however, the law allows abortion if pregnancy threatens the mother's life, the fetus is irreparably destroyed, or the pregnancy is a result of an illegal action.
- Only half of Polish students consider cheating during examinations unfair. When it comes to academic dishonesty, Polish students are not always aware of what plagiarism is and how to avoid it. In fact, students frequently feel that they need to cheat in order to be successful in class. This belief is a result of the strict Polish educational system and educators' unrealistic expectations.

In order to help students understand that cheating is dishonest and unacceptable in the U.S., educators might consider providing Polish students with examples of different types of plagiarism and discussing why it is not allowed in the classroom. Also, educators should ensure their Polish students that they will only be assessed on what they practiced in class and that the educator is not there to catch the smallest detail the student has not learned yet.

In order to facilitate the transition of a Polish student into an American classroom, educators can also explicitly discuss freedom of expression as a significant part of the American classroom. In addition, Polish students should be informed about the cultural and religious diversity they will experience in the classroom. Being prepared ahead of time may ease students' transitions and minimize culture shock.

Cuisine

Poles are well known for eating *kielbasa* (garlic-flavored pork sausage), cabbage, potatoes, beets, and barley. Traditional Polish food is usually consumed during holiday seasons for Easter and Christmas. Besides sausage and cabbage, Polish-Americans have added breakfast rolls, *Babka* coffeecake, and potato pancakes to American cuisine (Jones, 2000).

Traditional Costumes

Poles wear traditional clothing to celebrate major Polish festivals. For example, on Pulaski Day (October 11th) each year, up to 100,000 Polish Americans parade in New York. Many of them wear traditional Polish clothing, which consists of a blouse and a petticoat under a colorfully embroidered skirt. Headdresses are also common and often include either a kerchief or stiffened linen (Jones, 2000).

Holidays

Poles mainly celebrate religious holidays such as Christmas and Easter. Polish traditional Christmas Eve (*Wigilia*) starts when the first star appears in the sky. Before dinner, everyone gathers around the table to share a wafer and good wishes. The traditional dinner, which is served on a white cloth with some hay underneath, consists of 12 meatless dishes (e.g. apple pancakes, pierogies, fish, sauerkraut, potato salad) symbolizing the 12 apostles. The tradition says that one needs to try all of the served dishes; otherwise, they will have bad luck for the rest of the year (Jones, 2000). Poles always set an extra chair for an unknown guest since Poles believe that no one should be left alone during Christmas Eve.

Architecture

Poland is famous for its beautiful churches built in the Middle Ages. One of the staples of Polish architecture is St. Mary's Basilica in Krakow, which was built in the late 14th century. The altar of the Basilica was created by Veit Stoss, who was a renowned Gothic sculptor and painter. He spent 12 years carving the 42-foot-high, 36-foot-wide altar in wood, which makes it the biggest Gothic sculpture in the world (Strzala, 2015). The central part of the altar contains lifelike statues of the saints and portrays the Virgin Mary's Quietus. At the top of the altar one can see Mary's Coronation by the Trinity, and the wings of the altar depict relief scenes from the life of the Holy Family (Jurkowlaniec, 2002).

The Gothic-style Basilica has two uneven towers—the taller one is 80 meters high (262 ft.) (Warnke, 2016). Every hour one can hear a traditional Polish anthem called *Hejnał Mariacki* played from the taller tower. A legend has it that *Hejnał Mariacki* saved the city during a Tatar invasion. A trumpeter on the Basilica's tower played *Hejnał Mariacki* and successfully warned the city against the approaching enemy. Unfortunately, the sentry was shot with an arrow and did not complete the anthem. For this reason, to this day *Hejnał Mariacki* is never completed when played.

Idea of *Gospodarz* (Landowner)

The idea of landownership has always been important to Polish people. Some claim that a need for land was the reason why so many Poles emigrated to the U.S. during WWII and Communist times (Jones, 2000). Polish people have a sense of pride in what they own and often stay in the same house/city their entire life. According to CBOS (2010), 65% of Poles permanently live in the city where they were born.

Polish Proverbs

Proverbs oftentimes are a reflection of a culture (Jones, 2000). Polish proverbs include:

- When misfortune knocks at the door, friends are asleep.
- Listen much and speak little.
- If God wills, even a cock will lay an egg.
- He who lends to a friend makes an enemy.
- No fish without bones.

EDUCATION

For Poles, education is extremely important. Almost 18% of Poles have a college degree and the percentage has been increasing steadily over the past decade (Glowny Urzad Statystyczny, 2011). All children in high school already specialize in areas of interest (e.g., science, math, or foreign languages). By the time they graduate, they are expected to take national tests called *matura*, and those who score the highest can attend free public universities. In order to perform well on the national tests, students often participate in tutoring outside of school for many years. Children frequently follow their parents' educational path. In other words, if a student's parent is a doctor or an engineer, it is very likely that they will choose to study medicine or engineering.

Educational System

The Polish K–12 educational system structure is quite similar to that in the U.S. Even though the structure is similar, the instruction style is very different. As described in Szymon's scenario at the start of this chapter, instruction in Poland is teacher-centered, which means that students are rather passive participants. During a regular lesson, a teacher lectures and students are responsible for writing down information. Students typically are responsible for memorizing everything that the teacher has said. Frequently, at the beginning of a lesson, a so-called "questioning" happens. Questioning is an oral form of evaluating students' knowledge during which a teacher asks a student to stand up and publicly answer questions for a grade. Since questioning happens in front of the class, it is rather stressful and often causes students to perform worse than they might on a written test. Unfortunately, questioning is one of the few times during which students actively participate in class. Polish educators are traditional and consider sharing book knowledge with their students as their main job.

LANGUAGES AND LITERACIES

After 70 years, Edward Sapir's profound insights about the nature of language still hold their validity and importance; he noted that "language is a symbolic guide to culture, vocabulary is a very sensitive index of the culture of people and linguistics is of strategic importance for the methodology of social science" (in Wierzbicka, 1997, p.1). There is a close connection between the life of a society and the language it uses. An apparent example from the tangible and visible domain is that of food. It is no coincidence that Polish has special names for cabbage stew (*bigos*), beetroot soup (*barszcz*) and plum jam (*powidło*), whereas English does not—they are staples of the Polish diet (Wierzbicka, 1997). The existence of such language-specific names for different things is something that people of a particular culture are normally aware of. However, there is no one-to-one correspondence between different languages and names of things. Varied meanings of words in different languages convey ways of living and thinking characteristic of a particular culture. They also offer valuable clues to the understanding of culture.

Important Aspects of Polish Language

Directness

Poles tend to be rather direct among friends and family. One can tell how close Polish people are based on the forms of requests they use. For example, an American may ask "Could/may/will you, please," no matter whom they are addressing (a friend or a professor). However, a Polish person would use imperatives with people they know well. For example, a Pole would say "*Przynies* mi *wode*" ("Bring me some water") without using words such as "could"/"may"/"will" or "please." From the American perspective, Polish may show a lack of consideration, inflexibility, and an inclination to be bossy. However, the usage of the imperative mood to perform requests in Polish signals speakers' cordiality (Wierzbicka, 1997). In fact, if one were to use the interrogative form such as "could you," "would you" and so on to request something from a friend, the interlocutor may think that their friendship is over since the speaker does not want to say directly what they need.

In a more formal setting, however, a Polish person would be less direct and would always consider all markers of politeness. For example, a Polish student would use formal language to communicate with teachers. Teachers are considered to be authorities; therefore, a Polish student would never address a teacher in an informal way. In fact, many Polish students are not used to addressing teachers in class since instruction is teacher-centered. Also, Polish K–12 schools do not offer office hours, and therefore children are not given the opportunity to speak to their teachers often.

Grammar

Polish grammar is rather complex and may interfere in some ways with learning English.

- Polish word order is more flexible than in English since nouns, adjectives, and verbs may have many different forms depending on where they are put in a sentence (Sadowska, 2012).
- One of the most frequent mistakes that Polish students of English make is dropping pronouns. For example, a Polish student may say "go home" without mentioning the pronoun "I" because Polish does not require it (*"Ide do domu"*; literally "go to home").
- All nouns have either masculine, feminine, or neuter gender, which often causes difficulties for Polish speakers of English. For instance, a Polish student may say "I like this book. She is interesting." In this case, the student is referring to a book as "she" because a book has feminine gender in Polish.

- Another common grammatical mistake among Polish learners of English is due to the lack of articles such as "a," "an," and "the." Because Polish does not use articles, many Polish students struggle with their usage even at an advanced level of proficiency.
- Polish distinguishes past, present, and future tenses (Feldstein, 2001). Polish learners of English often struggle with English perfect tenses such as present perfect, present perfect progressive, past perfect, and past perfect progressive. For example, a Polish learner of English may say "I am hungry. I didn't eat breakfast yet" rather than "I am hungry. I haven't eaten breakfast yet." This is because Polish has only one simple past tense to talk about past situations.

Polish Alphabet and Pronunciation

Although Polish may seem almost impossible to pronounce, it is largely phonemic, which means that there is a correspondence between letters and phonemes (the way they sound) (Gabryanczyk, 2012). Tables 26.1 and 26.2 provide information about Polish letters and sounds.

Word Stress

Unlike English, Polish has regular word stress, which usually falls on the penultimate syllable (Sadowska, 2012). For this reason, a Polish learner of English may have problems stressing English words and distinguishing English verbs and nouns that share the same root (for example,

Table 26.1. Polish Alphabet and Letter Pronunciation, Single Letters

a (a) as in father	ą (ohN) as in French word 'bon'	b (be) as in boy	c (tse) as in bats	ć (ch'ye) as in cheer	d (de) as in dog
e (e) as in met	ę (ehN) as in French word 'fin'	f (ef) as in fun	g (gye) as in good	h (ha) as in yahoo	i (ee) as in beet
j (yot) as in yes	k (ka) as in kite	l (el) as in last	ł (ew) as English letter 'w'	m (em) as in may	n (en) as in no
ń(en') as in onion	o (o) as in no	ó (oo) as in through	p (pe) as in pan	r (er) as in room	s (es) as in sit
ś(esh') as in sheet	t (te) as in tap	u (oo) as in through	w (voo) as in van	y (yygrek) as in whim	z (zet) as in zoo
ź (z'yet) as in Indonesia	ż (zhet) as in measure				

Source: Sadowska (2012.)

Table 26.2.   Double Letters

ch(kh) as in Johann Sebastian Ba**ch**	ci (ch) as in **ch**eer	cz(ch) as in **ch**air	dz(dz) as in pa**ds**
dʔ(j) as in **j**eans	dż(j) as in **j**am	rz(zhet) same as 'ż' as in mea**s**ure	sz(sh) as in **sh**ow

Source: Sadowska (2012).

Table 26.3.   Common Polish Expressions

Word	*Meaning*	*Pronunciation*
Dzieńdobry	Good morning	(jean DOU-bree)
Cześć	Hi	(CHEshch)
Dowidzenia	Goodbye	(dohveeDZEnia)
Proszę	Please/No problem	(PROsh-eh)
Dziękuję	Thank you	(jenKOOyeh)
Niewiem	I don't know	(NEE-eh VEE-em)
Tak	Yes	(T-AH-K)
Nie	No	(NEE-eh)
Jaksięmasz?	How are you?	(Yah-kshehMAhsh)
Miłegodnia	Have a nice day!	(mee-UEgoDNE-ea)
Nierozumiem	I don't understand	(nEE-ehroh-ZOO-mee-em)
Nazdrowie	Cheers or Bless you	(NAHzdROH-vee-eh)

OBject and obJECT). Table 26.3 presents some words that teachers might learn to support their Polish students.

IDEAS FOR EDUCATORS

Polish Americans and Community Dynamics

Due to large influx of Polish migrants to the United States in the second half of the 20th century, many Poles were faced with intolerance from already "established" Americans (Jones, 2000). Also, the fact that Poles were largely Catholic made Poles' assimilation into American society a lot harder (hence the mocking and racist "Pollock" jokes that were a trend in the past). In fact, most Poles formed close-knit communities in which they could rely on each other's moral and/or financial support. Even though over the last decade Poles have assimilated more into the U.S. culture, they still maintain a strong ethnic identity (Jones, 2000). Lack of complete assimilation by Polish Americans may be visible at schools. Some Polish students may still remember intolerance they were met with and therefore may not want to share more of their personal life with others.

School/Home Relations

There may be certain communication barriers between Polish parents and educators. Many Polish parents are passive during parent–teacher meetings. There is a common belief in Poland that the school is responsible for educating children. Such belief results in parents' infrequent involvement in their children's school life (Christopher, 1996). However, parents' passive participation may also be a result of educators' strong authority. In Poland, parents are not used to addressing educators and may be hesitant to talk to them directly. In fact, creating a close bond between a parent and a teacher may be frowned upon by others in the community. It is very uncommon for the teacher to visit their students' parents at home. In order to help parent–teacher relations, a teacher could communicate and support the idea that parents' input is crucial in education. They might also lead an open discussion about expectations for parent–teacher relations.

Sports at School

Even though Poles enjoy soccer and volleyball, sports are not an important part of K–12 or college education. There are sports teams at schools; however, students do not usually receive scholarships for their athletic achievements. In the U.S., many school events (e.g., the homecoming dance) are organized around sports competitions; however, in Poland that is never the case. In fact, schools that focus on sports would not be considered academic enough for their students to succeed in further education. Polish students in the U.S. may struggle with understanding why U.S. schools put so much focus on sports and may perceive U.S. schools as less demanding academically.

Religion at School

Polish students living in the U.S. may miss some days at school in order to honor their religious holidays. Below is a list of major Catholic and national holidays during which Polish students do not attend school:

- January 1st—Solemnity of Mary
- January 6th—Epiphany

- Maundy Thursday
- Good Friday
- Easter Monday
- May 1st—Labor Day
- May 3rd—Polish Constitution Day and Celebration of Mary the Queen of Poland
- Ascension of Jesus
- Corpus Christi
- All Saints' Day
- November 11th—Polish Independence Day
- December 23–26th—Christmas

CONCLUSIONS

The purpose of this chapter is to provide important insights into Polish culture. Gaining such knowledge will allow educators to create materials and classroom activities that are culturally sensitive and can help Polish students succeed.

ADDITIONAL RESOURCES

Great information on Polish Americans can be found in these resources:

Jones, S. (2000). Polish Americans. *Gale encyclopedia of multicultural America*. Retrieved from http://www.encyclopedia.com/topic/Polish_Americans.aspx
    Helpful site with cultural, historical, and linguistic information about Poland and Polish.
Kmiec, S. (2011). Hundred things every Polish American should do. *Polish American Journal*. Retrieved from http://www.polamjournal.com/Editor-s_Desk/ PAJ_100th/ paj_100th.html
    Ways to explore and reconnect with Polish ancestry.
Ryan, T. (2013, December 5). The Polish education system is no joke. *Thomas B. Fordham Institute: Advancing Educational Excellence*. Retrieved from https:// edexcellence.net/commentary/education-gadfly-daily/flypaper/the-polish-education-system-is-no-joke
    Reflections on today's education written by a teacher who taught in Poland in the 1990s.
TeAchnology. (n.d.). How are K–12 schools different in Poland compared to the U.S.? Retrieved from http://www.teach-nology.com/teachers/employment/esl/ poland/
    Useful article and resources to understand differences between schools in Poland and the U.S.

TASKS FOR EDUCATORS

1. Reflect on these questions:
   * What are the differences between student-centered and teacher-centered approaches to education? From where do the differences stem?
   * How are Polish nationalism and history connected? Why do so many Poles choose to live in close-knit societies in the U.S.?
   * Based on the quotes in this chapter and other information you learned, how might you guess John Paul II's papacy was influenced by his Polish upbringing?
   * What challenges may Polish students face in the U.S.?
   * Based on the proverbs presented in the chapter, can you list any specific characteristics of Polish culture?
2. What aspects of Polish culture mentioned in this chapter surprised you the most? Why?
3. How might you help a Polish student become a more active participant in class?

REFERENCES

Burke, J. (2009). Divided Poland falls out over solidarity. The Guardian. Retrieved from http://www.theguardian.com/world/2009/may/31/poland-communism-twentieth-anniversary

CBOS. (2010). *Mobilnosc i preferencje migracyjne Polakow*. Retrieved from http://www.cbos.pl/SPISKOM.POL/2010/K_026_10.PDF

Christopher, C. J. (1996). *Building parent–teacher communication: An educator's guide*. Lanham, MD: R&L Education.

Data Access and Dissemination Systems (DADS). (2016). *American FactFinder results*. Retrieved from http://factfinder.census.gov/faces/tableservices/jsf/pages/productview.xhtml?src=bkmk

Feldstein, R. F. (2001). A concise Polish grammar. *SEELRC*. Retrieved from http://www.seelrc.org:8080/grammar/mainframe.jsp?nLanguageID=4

Gabryanczyk, D. (2012). *Polish for dummies*. Chichester, UK: Wiley.

Glowny Urzad Statystyczny. (2002). *Ludnosc. Stan i struktura demograficzno-spoleczna. Narodowy Spis Powszechny Ludnosci i Mieszkan*. Warszawa. Retrieved from http://stat.gov.pl/spisy-powszechne/narodowe-spisy-powszechne/narodowy-spis-powszechny-2002/ludnosc-stan-i-struktura-demograficzno-spoleczna-nsp-2002,4,1.html

Glowny Urzad Statystyczny. (2011). *Ludnosc. Stan i struktura demograficzno-spoleczna. Narodowy Spis Powszechny Ludnosci i Mieszkan*. Warszawa. Retrieved from http://stat.gov.pl/cps/rde/xbcr/gus/LUD_ludnosc_stan_str_dem_spo_NSP2011.pdf

Glowny Urzad Statystyczny. (2012). *Statistical yearbook of the Republic of Poland.* Warsaw. Retrieved from http://stat.gov.pl/cps/rde/xbcr/gus/RS_rocznik_statystyczny_rp_2012.pdf

Jones, S. (2000). Polish Americans. *Gale encyclopedia of multicultural America.* Retrieved from http://www.encyclopedia.com/topic/Polish_Americans.aspx

Jurkowlaniec, G. (2002). Wit Stwosz. *Culture.pl.* Retrieved from http://culture.pl/en/artist/wit-stwosz

Lorie, A. (2008, October 3). Famous Poles through the ages. *CNN.* Retrieved from http://www.cnn.com/2008/WORLD/europe/10/03/famous.poles/index.html?_s=PM:WORLD

Lukowski, J., & Zawadzki, H. (2001). *A concise history of Poland.* Cambridge, UK: Cambridge University Press.

Ministry of Foreign Affairs Republic of Poland. (n.d.). *Poland and Poles in the Second World War: Underground army.* Retrieved from https://ww2.pl/underground-army/

Ministry of Labor and Social Policy. (2015). *Dni pracy i dni wolne od pracy.* Retrieved from http://www.mpips.gov.pl/prawo-pracy/ustalanie-i-rozliczanie-czasu-pracy/ustalanie-czasu-pracy/dni-pracy-i-dni-wolne-od-pracy/

Ministry of National Education. (2014). *Informacja w sprawie zasad organizowania nauki i etyki w roku szkolnym* 2014/2015. Retrieved from https://men.gov.pl/ministerstwo/informacje/informacja-w-sprawie-zasad-organizowania-nauki-religii-i-etyki-w-roku-szkolnym-2014-2015.html

Poland profile-timeline. (2017, July 24). *BBC News.* Retrieved from http://www.bbc.com/news/world-europe-17754512

Polish American Association. (2004). *The Polish community in metro Chicago: A community profile of strengths and needs: A census 2000 report.* Retrieved from http://www.robparal.com/downloads/Polish%20Community%20in%20Chicago.pdf

Pope John Paul II. (n.d.). Quotes. *Goodreads.* Retrieved from http://www.goodreads.com/author/quotes/6473881.Pope_John_Paul_II

Repa, J. (2005). Analysis: Solidarity's legacy. *BBC News.* Retrieved from http://news.bbc.co.uk/2/hi/europe/4142268.stm

Sadowska, I. (2012). *Polish: A comprehensive grammar.* New York, NY: Routledge.

Strzala, M. (2015). The Virgin Mary's great altar in Krakow. *Krakow Info.* Retrieved from http://www.krakow-info.com/oltarz.htm

U.S. Census Bureau. (1999). *Historical census statistics on the foreign-born population of the United States: 1850–1990.* Retrieved from http://www.census.gov/population/www/documentation/twps0029/twps0029.html

Warnke, A. (2016). Poland's most beautiful churches (P. Schlosser, trans.). *Culture.pl.* Retrieved from http://culture.pl/en/article/polands-most-beautiful-churches

Wierzbicka, A. (1997). *Understanding cultures through their key words.* New York, NY: Oxford University Press.

SECTION 9

UNITED STATES

CHAPTER 27

CULTURE, LANGUAGE, AND SCHOOLING IN THE U.S.

Joy Egbert
Washington State University

"What are they saying?!," asked my 6-year-old son.
"Well in this part of the country they always call me by my first and second names—Joy Lynn," I replied. "It's the habit, to be a bit more formal."
"But it sounds like 'Jowa Lee-ann'," he commented.
"Yes, and they think we talk strangely, too!" I responded.

BACKGROUND

Most Americans have at least some general knowledge of United States (U.S.) history and culture. However, differences in everything from food to slang can be confusing even for visitors from another region of the country. The premise of this book is that teachers can be more effective if they are aware of the cultures and languages of their students; however, it is also important for teachers to understand their own country and culture so that they can help newcomers to the U.S. to understand the culture to which they are coming. Teachers dealing with American language and culture have to choose not only which dialect(s) of English to teach,

Views From Inside: Languages, Cultures, and Schooling for K–12 Educators
pp. 471–485
Copyright © 2018 by Information Age Publishing

but also which cultural artifacts are important for their students to know. Teachers may have trouble articulating what their own and the broader U.S. cultures consists of, while many immigrant students, who expect to find the United States as portrayed by the media, are surprised and dismayed to find that the U.S. is different from what they expected or hoped. Teachers and students can collaborate to discover how to navigate the cultural, linguistic, and schooling issues that both may face. This chapter presents basic information on these three aspects to serve as a potential starting place for this collaboration.

Demographics

On a first visit to different parts of the United States, even those born here may be surprised at the variety of dialects and differences in culture exhibited in different regions. Because of the scale and diversity of its geography (almost 3.8 million square miles over everything from semi-arid desert to lush rainforest) and the great number of people (316.1 million in 2013, according to the U.S. Census Bureau, 2014), the U.S. varies widely in language and culture. The broader the view from U.S. media that we are exposed to (e.g., movies, YouTube, news outlets), the more we might understand that there are differences not only in major sectors of the U.S. (e.g., the Northeast, South, West Coast, East Coast), but even within regions, states, and, communities. Some people demonstrate their differences (or similarities) by using specific vocabulary or pronunciation (e.g., "Valley" girls, New Yorkers, Hispanic Americans), wearing a certain kind of clothes (such as Goths or Pennsylvania Dutch or Texas cowboys), and others by what they eat, to whom they pray, or any combination of these and other traits. Some writers have called the mix of cultures and languages in the U.S. a "melting pot" (a term attributed to Langwill in 1909), others a "tossed salad" or "cultural mosaic" (Janzen, 1994), but no matter which way you look at it, it can be confusing to figure out how to speak and act even if you are an English-speaking native-born citizen—teachers should consider how much more difficult it can be for English language learners (ELLs) and students from other cultures.

For those who are only familiar with the U.S. they see on TV, its actual demographics might come as a surprise. As noted in Chapter 1, almost 13% of U.S. citizens (who call themselves "Americans") are foreign-born, and 20.5% speak a language other than English at home (U.S. Census, 2014). Of about 49.3 million school children in the U.S. (NCES, 2014), during the 2010-2011 school year 4,693,818 children were enrolled in programs for ELLs (NCES, n.d.). The largest minority group, Hispanics, constituted 16.9% of the total U.S. population in 2012 (U.S. Census,

2014a) and are predicted to comprise 31% of the population, or 128.8 million people, by 2060 (U.S. Census, 2014b). Although the majority of the Hispanic population (65%) is ethnically and linguistically associated with U.S. neighbor Mexico (U.S. Census, 2014b), every country in Central and South America has contributed a share of the Hispanic population in the U.S. Educators can prepare a map with their students that shows different populations across the nation, including a variety of religions, nationalities, and ethnicities; this map can be used as a basis of discussion across the curriculum.

Religion

The majority of Americans who identify with a particular religion describe themselves as Christian (78.4%; Pew Research, 2013), with a growing number of people claiming no affiliation. Other major world and local/native religions, and various sects of each, can be found among the population, and many Americans marry across religious boundaries. Americans consider "freedom of religion," granted by the U.S. Constitution, to be one of their most important rights; however, what this freedom actually entails is a continuing discussion among stakeholders. Christian values, including the "Protestant work ethic" (2013) form the foundation for both personal and legal behaviors in much of the U.S. For example, many stores, banks, and federal agencies are closed on Christian holidays such as Christmas and Easter. However, even though few holidays from other cultures or religions are celebrated in the nation as a whole—with the exceptions of "fun" days such as Mardi Gras and St. Patrick's Day—celebrations of other festivals such as Diwali, Hanukkah, the Lantern Festival, and the harvest can also be found throughout the nation. There is at least one celebration, and sometimes many more, every day of the year. Students can post their own holidays to a large classroom calendar and then interview parents, neighbors, and others to fill in other days. Web sites like *Holidays and Observances Around the World* (https://www.timeanddate.com/holidays/) list festivals from every country and can serve as another resource for all students to learn about the world and how it is reflected in the U.S.

History and Law

The United States is looked upon by much of the world as a young country, but it has experienced a long history of struggle to live up to the ideals presented in its founding Constitution. Many of these same issues, such as civil war, women's suffrage, minority and gay rights, slavery, and poverty have been experienced by immigrants in one form or another and may be used carefully as a common basis for sharing in classrooms.

Although early versions of U.S. history celebrated the discovery of the American continent by Christopher Columbus, more recent narratives have set the record straight by acknowledging both the indigenous Native Americans and other explorers who came before Columbus. In fact, Columbus has been vilified in many accounts, and the "Columbus Day" holiday abandoned, due to the extreme damage to native populations caused by Columbus and his men pursuing their "discovery."

The U.S. declared independence from British colonialism in 1776, famously stating in its Declaration of Independence that "all men are created equal." The main law of the U.S., the Constitution (ratified in 1778), is said to be based in part on the oral constitution of the six Native American Iroquois nations, and it guarantees "peace, equity, and order." The Constitution, with which all other law must agree, outlines the foundation of the three-part governmental system. Throughout U.S. history, debate over who qualifies as one of the "equal men" and what is "equitable" has permeated its system, from discussions of slavery to women's rights to the current controversies surrounding gay marriage and immigration. The Bill of Rights, as an addendum to the Constitution, codifies additional foundation for laws arising from these debates. Regardless of attempts to define specifically who has what rights, the concept of equality has been interpreted in U.S. laws in a variety of ways, with the decisions not always ending up equitable for those who are not native English speakers or who immigrate to the country. A comparison of U.S. laws and government with other countries' can help students understand not only the evolution of these nations and their laws but how differences affect people the world over.

Tolerance of difference varies from place to place and person to person in the U.S. In recent history, one of the biggest impacts on Americans views of "outsiders" was a result of the September 11, 2001 attacks on the U.S. by Al-Qaeda jihadists and the resulting wars and military actions both against and by the U.S. in places like Iraq, Afghanistan, and Pakistan. As a result of these events, many Americans became less willing to travel or to accommodate difference, and federal laws were passed that lessened the civil liberties previously enjoyed by U.S. citizens. Many hate crimes were perpetrated on people identified (sometimes wrongly) as Muslim (Ransford, 2003), and a "culture of fear" or "politics of fear" was claimed by some to have established itself throughout the country (Brzezinski, 2007). To date, the U.S. government claims to be waging a "war on terrorism" and a "war on fear." Certain political figures have thrived on and stirred the controversy even further, questioning the presence of all immigrants to the country and turning some public opinion against new-comers. In some areas, this makes providing services, including education, to immigrants more difficult than it might otherwise be because they may be scared into silence, hoping not to "rock the boat" in any way. On the other hand, these events have galvanized a large segment of the population to look out for and help their immigrant and language minority neighbors and to speak up against racism, discrimination, and acts of violence against difference. Perspectives vary across the U.S.; teachers can examine these and emphasize to their students the importance of communication to conflict awareness and resolution.

Economy

The U.S. has the world's largest economy. Although often perceived as a wealthy country and the "land of opportunity," the U.S. has the largest gap between the very rich and the very poor of any developed nation in the world (Economy of the United States, n.d.). Many immigrants are surprised by how difficult it can be to find a job with a living wage, affordable housing and childcare, and decent schools; this is in addition to the covert prejudice that might come as part of the search. Recently, downturns in the U.S. economy have impacted many families, and many students, both U.S.-born and immigrant, are living in poverty and receiving free or reduced lunch (Aud et al., 2013). Changes in the economy from manufacturing to service have made it more essential than ever that students succeed in school and go on to higher education. Rather than following a path set out by their parents (although some do), U.S. students are encouraged even at school to find a career that is interesting and fulfilling to them. This may cause conflict in ELLs' homes as students do their best to both follow their parents' wishes and be true to their bicultural selves.

Education of ELLs

Bilingual and English as second language education have come in and out of favor since 1839 and the first bilingual education laws. Depending on whether the country was experiencing a backlash against immigration, a desire to assimilate newcomers, or a need for bilinguals in business and politics, programs were designed to either submerge nonnative English speakers in English or to promote the learning or maintenance of two languages through bilingual education. Although laws such as Lau v. Nichols and the Elementary and Secondary Education Act/No Child Left

Behind are meant to ensure that ELLs have equal educational opportunities with native English speakers, the lack of specificity in these laws means that districts and schools do not always provide consistent, evidence-based instruction for all of their ELLs. The current trend in many states is to pass laws to end bilingual education, as California and Arizona have done, and to integrate ELLs into regular classrooms with teachers who have completed some professional development in ELL. Teachers can inform parents of their children's rights under the law and provide a list of resources and services that parents can tap to help their children obtain the services they have a right to.

CULTURE

Even though the U.S. comprises people from every country of the globe and no two locations in the U.S. have exactly the same types of people, places, or characteristics, Americans may identify themselves with adages such as the World War II slogan, "apple pie and Mom," to which "baseball" was eventually added (in TV ads, "Mom" was replaced by "Chevrolet"). It is difficult to describe such a wide range of people specifically, but some general ideas based on both published sources and anecdotes is shared in this section.

Personal Characteristics

The majority White, ethnically Western European, Christian segment of the U.S. population might identify American culture with terms such as these:

- Individual—Americans do not generally live in extended family settings, and children are expected to make their own way in life after high school. This comes from the founding idea of an egalitarian country where everyone is responsible for him or herself. However, this characteristic is changing as more and more graduates return to their parents' homes and support as they look for jobs, have their own children, and try to survive in an up and down economy.
- Patriotic—In the U.S., school children say the Pledge of Allegiance every morning at the start of school. Displays of American flags are common on holidays, and the National Anthem is played before most sporting events.

- Punctual—A meeting set for 9:00 a.m. is expected to start at that time. Being late is typically considered rude and lazy. The saying "time is money" is a reflection of this value.
- Direct—An American saying, "Honesty is the best policy," demonstrates the idea that it is better to be blunt than to distort facts for politeness' sake (Lanier & Davis, 2005). How often this adage is followed, however, is unknown.
- Materialistic—The U.S. has a consumer culture that is evidenced both by the amount of consumption and the amount of garbage (see, for example, Table 27.1). The impacts of this consumption are a variety of environmental, social, and economic issues such as obesity, rising healthcare costs, pollution, and debt.
  o The United States, with less than 5% of the global population, uses about a quarter of the world's fossil fuel resources—burning nearly 25% of the coal, 26% of the oil, and 27% of the world's natural gas.
  o As of 2003, the U.S. had more private cars than licensed drivers, and gas-guzzling sport utility vehicles were among the best-selling vehicles.
  o New houses in the U.S. were 38% bigger in 2002 than in 1975, despite having fewer people per household on average (Worldwide Watch, 2015).

Another American characteristic that might impact English language learners is ethnocentricity. Although "minority" populations can be found in every urban area in the U.S. and in most other parts of the country, Americans are known for being rather insular and having a history of institutional and individual racism. An estimated 26% of Americans can converse socially in a language other than English (McComb, 2001); however, 75% say that all Americans, regardless of origin, should

Table 27.1. The U.S. Consumer

- The United States, with less than 5% of the global population, uses about a quarter of the world's fossil fuel resources—burning up nearly 25% of the coal, 26% of the oil, and 27% of the world's natural gas.
- As of 2003, the United States had more private cars than licensed drivers, and gas-guzzling sport utility vehicles were among the best-selling vehicles.
- New houses in the United States were 38% bigger in 2002 than in 1975, despite having fewer people per household on average.

Source: Worldwide Watch (2015).

speak English (McComb, 2001). The majority of Americans do not speak a foreign language, have not been outside of the United States, and have no first-hand experience with other religions and languages. Teachers have many strategies to help ELLs and students work and learn with Americans who have no experience with other languages and cultures; one such strategy is to include culture facts in every lesson. For example, in a math lesson, the teacher could briefly mention cultures that invented zero or algebra, or in a lesson on genetics the teacher could note the scientists around the world who have contributed to this field. Students could also be asked to discover these contributions as a project.

Surveys from other countries show that the characteristics that Americans find positive about themselves are seen differently from an external view; Johnson (2012) notes that other nations see Americans as always in a hurry; not having an understanding of rank and hierarchy and disrespecting elders; being impolitely blunt; focusing on work over fun; being overly optimistic about the future; wanting to control the world. Others note that Americans seem sarcastic and goal-oriented, that they are very aware of their "personal space," and that, compared to people in many other countries, they are quite informal (ElHess, personal communication, 1/19/15). There is also a perception that the most important value to Americans is freedom of speech.

Of course, within U.S. communities of people who are originally from different countries and cultures, it is possible to find the exact opposite of these typically "American" values. In other words, it is difficult to say that there is only one American culture or what it would be if there was such a thing. However, American textbooks are often written from the Eurocentric point of view and contribute to the hidden curriculum mentioned in Chapter 1. Teachers and students, both native speakers and ELLs, can examine both the information and the presentation of their text as a starting point to examine local and national cultures.

Famous People

In American history, Presidents George Washington and Abraham Lincoln have a number of legends around them that make them heroes; other American heroes are those who have taken up a challenge and not backed down. These include civil and women's rights leaders, explorers, inventors, astronauts, and even politicians. Sports figures are highly revered, as are movie and TV stars, writers, chefs, and even everyday people who make interesting videos and post them on the YouTube web site. The idea coined by the late American artist Andy Warhol, that everyone will have 15 minutes of fame, appears to be becoming more likely as Americans share every thought and event on social media. Social media may be used by teachers to help newcomers understand American culture(s); for students whose cultures do not allow them to use such technologies or who are wary of their pitfalls, teachers can create student teams of users and nonusers.

Food

What constitutes American food varies from region to region. The Midwest is said to live on steak and potatoes, and foods such as Philly cheesesteak, New York bagels, Chicago-style pizza, and New Jersey hoagie sandwiches can actually be found in all major cities, along with an assortment of food from many other cultures and countries. The most common "foreign" or "ethnic" foods are Mexican, Italian, and Chinese, although natives from those countries are quick to let eaters know that these are not the "real" foods but dishes "Americanized" for the U.S. palate. Outsiders might think that fast and/or junk foods such as McDonald's, potato chips, and soda are the national foods, but home-cooked meals are still the most common, and home cooking across the States is very diverse (Joseph, 2012). Cooking in class is not only a great way for students to study vocabulary, measurement, and even chemistry, but it can also serve as a way for students to share their cultures. Having students and their families contribute to creating a recipe book is also a way to accomplish these goals.

CONTRIBUTIONS TO THE WORLD

Like other nations and people, Americans have made many contributions to the world. These include the gramophone, the electric light bulb, the transistor, space travel, ARPANET (precursor to the Internet), Nobelprize winning scientists and writers, and hundreds of other inventions that have changed the world in ways big and small. In addition, American popular culture in the form of Hollywood films, amusement parks, and superheroes is enjoyed by people throughout the world. However, it is important to note that these contributions are often grounded in the contributions of others and borrow heavily not only from other nations and cultures but from the many immigrants to this country, as seen in other chapters in this book.

OTHER CUSTOMS

As noted, previously, it is impossible to list all of the cultural aspects that ELLs might need to know and understand. However, there are some that are commonly experienced, including:

- While in some countries animals are considered untouchable or solely as a food source, in the U.S. ELLs are often surprised to find animals living in homes and considered part of the family. The extent to which some families go to insure the health and well-being of their pets can be astounding even to other Americans! It is important for teachers to consider their students' cultures as they decide on a class pet or invite students and their families to their homes; for example, Muslims do not typically enter homes where dogs are kept in the house, and they may believe that a black cat is in reality a bad *jinn*.

- Although considered dirty and disrespectful to wear inside the home in some cultures, many Americans wear their shoes inside the house, and slippers are rarely provided for guests. Americans do not generally wash their floors every day, either, but children are typically allowed to play on them anyway and their hands are washed when they are done.

- Different from the respectful clapping found at sporting and theater events in some parts of the world, Americans pride themselves on cheering as loudly as possible for their favorites. There are limits, though, such as blowing a horn in someone's ear or screaming to the point that another's ears ring.

- ELLs often wonder why Americans always ask "How are you?" but rarely wait for a reply. It is important that this type of formulaic speech, which really just means "Hi" for many Americans, is explained to students.

Because there is so much to know and specific situations are hard to predict for individual students, providing ELLs with ways to find out about American culture is important—the resources and references from this chapter can be a great starting point.

ENGLISH IN THE U.S.

Although many Americans believe that TV news anchors speak "standard" English, there is actually no such thing (Andrews, 2001). What is standard in one part of the U.S. might be relatively incomprehensible in another. This is due not only to differences in accent but also to variety in word use, speaking pace, and acceptable grammatical patterns (all of which come under the umbrella term "dialect differences"). For example, in some parts of the U.S., "soda" is "pop" or "coke," "candidate" is pronounced "canidate," and a "drinking fountain" might be a "bubbler" (Katz, 2016). If students (and teachers) do not know that "skillet" and "frying pan" are words for the same kitchen utensil in different parts of the U.S., they may end up lacking the means to make "pancakes" (or, rather, "flapjacks"). As Katz (2016) notes, "If American English says anything about us, it's that we have many identities, are many different peoples, and come from all over" (p. 197). By emphasizing the similarities and differences in language use that help shape and express the diversity of American identities, teachers can encourage the exploration and acceptance of a range of languages and cultures in their classrooms.

However, in the U.S., because many teachers have not had advanced language education, they may not really know the rules of the language they speak and write. They may be uncertain about how to explain grammatical and lexical concepts and not have a lot of practice describing various language rules. These teachers may therefore base their instruction on texts that provide a prescriptive view of how language should be used. Rather than try to teach a standard that does not exist, it might be more useful for teachers to think of the types of language that are effective for themselves and their students in the different contexts they may find themselves in. For example, students can speak one way on the playground, perhaps switching between a home language and the social language of their school friends, and another type of language when addressing teachers or applying for a job. A descriptive, rather than prescriptive, approach, can help students use "good" English for the context (Andrews, 2001). Johnson (2012) divides good English into three levels—formal, general/practical, and informal. Students can often link the idea of different levels or types of English to the same idea in their native languages (as demonstrated in other chapters in this book). What is important for teachers and students to know is that there is not one perfect version of English to aspire to; learning English based on context may help some ELLs feel more successful and teachers to experience greater comfort explaining how they use language than using some generic ideal that no one actually uses.

IDEAS FOR EDUCATORS

In addition to suggestions throughout this chapter, recommendations include:

- Teachers of course cannot teach other dialects if they do not know them, but there are plenty of resources to help students be aware of and value them. Teachers and students can explore and share such resources throughout the school year.
- Know your students—are they immigrants? Native-born? Do they live in a native language community and culture? What cultural and linguistic resources do they have access to, both for their first (L1) and second languages (L2)?
- The education systems of many countries do not focus on critical thinking skills like those required of U.S. students. In addition, students from some countries are not expected to ask questions of the teacher during class. Classroom expectations, even those that seem evident, should be taught explicitly.
- Study American cultures. Have ELLs and an American partner choose one not their own and explore it, producing a video, poster, or other product to share with the class.

CONCLUSIONS

All students in the U.S. are English language learners to some extent, and all teachers must therefore teach English. Because language and culture are integrated in so many ways, culture also arises as a necessary part of the curriculum. However, teaching "American culture" is problematic because, like "standard" English, there is really no such thing. Nonetheless, by studying the parts that make up the whole, students and teachers can increase understanding, reduce misunderstandings, and use language that is appropriate for the context. Janzen (1994) notes that teachers are asked

> to infuse pluralist multiculturalism into their courses at the same time that they tell them to produce graduates who are culturally literate in the traditional sense. Additional confusion stems from the reality that teachers must make choices among many topics and curriculum materials, which may take either assimilationist or pluralist perspectives. Take, for example, the western migration of white Americans. Curriculum documents, personal beliefs, and community pressure may demand that [teachers] present white westward migration as a great exploratory achievement that spread civilization from sea to shining sea. James Banks has pointed out, however, that from the perspective of the Lakota [Native American] people, white settlement represented an "age of doom" and "the end of their people." (p. 10)

He continues, "One way to negotiate such a teaching minefield is simple awareness" (p. 10). In line with the ideas presented by Ernst-Slavit in Chapter 1, this means that teachers are aware of their own cultures and language, other cultures and languages, and also of the information they do not have and need to find; more important, they are competent to reflect on and teach language and culture to all students in equitable and pluralist ways.

ADDITIONAL RESOURCES

Datesman, M., Crandall, J., & Kearny, E. (2014). *American ways: An introduction to American culture* (4th ed). White Plains, NY: Pearson Education ESL.

> This texts helps ELLs view culture through a critical lens, using higher-order thinking skills to assess, compare, and discuss as they read and write.

Hickey, W. (2013, June 5). 22 maps that show how Americans speak English totally differently from one another. *Business Insider*. Available from http://www.businessinsider.com/22-maps-that-show-the-deepest-linguistic-conflicts-in-america-2013-6

> Based on a linguistic survey, these maps visualize how individual words are pronounced across the U.S.

Peckham, A. (2012). *Urban dictionary: Freshest street slang defined*. Riverside, NJ: Andrews McMeel Publishing.

> The author of this text publishes his newest slang finds on UrbanDictionary.com. Students and teachers can use this text to understand their peers, references in popular media, and a little bit more about American culture.

TASKS FOR EDUCATORS

1. Watch the *American Tongues* dialect videos available on YouTube. What surprised you? What applications does this information have for your diverse classroom?

2. Create a short video or presentation about the way you and your community express "American culture." What are the artifacts and ideas that comprise it?

3. Read the seminal article by H. Miner (1956), "Body Ritual Among the Nacirema" (*American Anthropologist*, *58*, 503–507 and available on the web). Plan how you might use this same idea of cultural description in your classroom.

4. How does your language use differ depending on the context you are in? How can you explain the differences?

REFERENCES

Andrews, L. (2001). Linguistics for L2 teachers. Mahwah, NJ: Lawrence Erlbaum.

Aud, S., Rathbun, A., Flicker-Wilkinson, S., Kristapovich, P., Wang, X., Zhang, J., Notter, L. (2013). *The condition of education.* NCES. Retrieved from http://nces.ed.gov/pubsearch/pubsinfo.asp?pubid=2013037

Brzezinski, Z. (March 25, 2007). Terrorized by 'war on terror': How a three-word mantra has undermined America. *Washington Post.* Retrieved from http://www.washingtonpost.com/wp-dyn/content/article/2007/03/23/AR2007032301613.html

Economy of the United States. (n.d.). *Wikipedia.* Retrieved from http://en.wikipedia.org/wiki/Economy_of_the_United_States.

Janzen, R. (1994). Melting pot or mosaic? *Educational Leadership, Educating for Diversity, 51*(8), 9–11.

Johnson, L. (2012). *What foreigners need to know about America from A to Z: How to understand crazy American culture, people, government, business, language and more.* Los Angeles, CA: A to Z Publishing.

Joseph, D. (2012, May 10). American food: The 50 greatest dishes. *CNN Travel Website,* International Edition. Retrieved from http://travel.cnn.com/explorations/eat/best-usa-travel/top-50-american-foods-513946

Katz, J. (2016). *Speaking American: How Y'all, youse, and you guys talk: A visual guide.* New York, NY: Houghton Mifflin Harcourt.

Lanier, A., & Davis, J. (2005). *Living in the U.S.A.* (6th ed.). Yarmouth, ME: Intercultural Press.

McComb, C. (2001, April 6). *About one in four Americans can hold a conversation in a second language: Spanish is by far the most frequently spoken second language.* Gallup. Retrieved from http://www.gallup.com/poll/1825/about-one-four-americans-can-hold-conversation-second-language.aspx

NCES. (2013, December). *Digest of education statistics: 2012.* Retrieved from http://nces.ed.gov/programs/digest/d12/

NCES. (n.d.). *Table 47: Number and percentage of public school students participating in programs for English language learners, by state: Selected years, 2002–03 through 2010–11.* Retrieved from http://nces.ed.gov/programs/digest/d12/tables/dt12_047.asp.

Pew Research. (2013). *Religious landscape survey.* Retrieved from http://religions.pewforum.org/reports

Protestant work ethic. (2013). *Wikipedia.* Retrieved from http://en.wikipedia.org/wiki/Protestant_work_ethic

Ransford, M. (October 9, 2003). Many minority groups were victims of hate crimes after 9-11. *Education Redefined.* Ball State University. Retrieved from http://www.bsu.edu/up/article/0,1370,13210-2914-12850,00.html

U.S. Census Bureau. (2014a). *State and County QuickFacts.* Retrieved from http://quickfacts.census.gov/qfd/states/

U.S. Census Bureau. (2014b). *Hispanic Americans by the numbers: From the U.S. Census Bureau.* InfoPlease Database. Retrieved from http://www.infoplease.com/spot/hhmcensus1.html

Worldwatch Institute. (2015). *The state of consumption today.* Retrieved from http://www.worldwatch.org/node/810

ABOUT THE CONTRIBUTORS

Olusola O. Adesope is associate professor of educational psychology at Washington State University. His research focuses on the cognitive and pedagogical underpinnings of learning with computer-based multimedia resources, knowledge representation through interactive concept maps, meta-analysis of empirical research, and investigation of instructional principles and assessments in STEM education.

Raed Alsawaier is a doctoral student in the College of Education at Washington State University. He is interested in gamification and engagement. Raed worked for over 10 years as an educator overseas and in the U.S. Originally from Jordan, he has first-hand experience of the issues relevant to culture and education addressed in his chapter.

Omran Akasha received his PhD from Washington State University–Pullman. He obtained his first degree in English teaching from the University of Sabha, Libya. He joined the University of Sabha as a professor of ESL from 2005 to 2008. His research interests include language and culture and technology in the classroom.

Tariq Akmal is currently the department chair of teaching and learning at Washington State University. Born in Pakistan of American and Pakistani parents, he spent his childhood in Lahore before moving to the U.S. for college. He grew up speaking three languages at home while straddling American and Pakistani cultures.

Eric Ambroso is a doctoral student in the educational policy and evaluation program in the Mary Lou Fulton Teachers College at Arizona State University. His research interests include multicultural education, refugee/asylee education, and language policies in the United States. Eric has taught ESL/EFL in Italy, South Korea, Vietnam, and Washington State.

Yuliya Ardasheva is assistant professor in ESL/bilingual education. She is a native speaker of Russian who learned English by attending an ESL school for adults. Yuliya taught foreign/second languages in a variety of settings, including K–12 experiences and tutoring of young and adult language learners. She now teaches education courses at Washington State University–Tri-Cities.

Brenda L. Barrio is an assistant professor of special education at Washington State University whose work focuses on addressing the disproportionality of culturally and linguistically diverse students in special education. Most of these efforts focus on teacher preparation programs, bilingual special education, culturally responsive practices, and mild to moderate disabilities.

Pam Bettis is a faculty member in the cultural studies and social thought in education doctoral program at Washington State University. She works at the intersection of gender, culture, and schooling and employs critical theoretical frameworks to understand how dominant discourses operate in the lives of youth.

Shampa Biswas, a native of Bangladesh, is a PhD candidate in language, literacy, and technology at Washington State University. Her research focuses on graduate writing support. She has developed a model for graduate writing support according to the perceptions of graduate students. Her vision is to serve as an advocate to promote graduate writing support through creating a collaborative graduate writing organization.

Nataliia Borysenko is associate professor of the Institute of Philology at Kyiv Taras Shevchenko National University and a Fulbright Fellow at Washington State University. Her research interests focus on the use of technology in English language teaching and learning and intercultural communication.

Petro Borysenko is an associate professor in the Institute of Philology at Kyiv Taras Shevchenko National University. He is also an adjunct professor at Pereiaslav-Khmelnytsky Hryhoriy Skovoroda State Pedagogical University. His research interests cover pragmatics of political discourse and cultural aspects of language learning.

Elsie Candelaria Sosa is currently assistant professor in the graduate studies department of the College of Education at the University of Puerto Rico–Río Piedras (UPRRP). She completed her doctoral studies at

UPRRP. Her research interests include language variation and change, pragmatics, and the teaching of grammar.

Gladys R. Capella Noya is full professor in the graduate studies department of the College of Education at the University of Puerto Rico–Río Piedras. She completed her doctoral studies at the Harvard Graduate School of Education. Her research interests include learning environments, curriculum and culture, and democratic education.

Ai-Chia Chang, a native of Taiwan, is a clinical assistant professor at Washington State University's language, literacy, and technology program. She teaches courses in ESL and bilingual education and instructional technologies. Her research interests include computer-assisted language learning and technology-supported teaching and learning. She is currently exploring the benefits of the use of Internet resources and social networking sites for language learning.

Joy Egbert is professor of education at Washington State University–Pullman. She specializes in ELL and education technology. She is an award-winning researcher, teacher, and grant writer, and she has published widely on teacher education and computer-assisted language learning. She is currently the editor of *TESOL Journal*.

Mohamed El-Hess is adjunct faculty in the College of Education at Washington State University. He teaches courses in the English language learners (ELL) endorsement. His research interests include student engagement, creative and critical thinking, and addressing the needs of culturally and linguistically diverse learners.

Abir El Shaban is a PhD candidate in the language, literacy, and technology program at Washington State University. Her research interests focus on multiculturalism, teacher education, innovation, and diffusing the use of education technology among language and K–12 teachers. El Shaban thrives to engage students in technology-enhanced language learning environments.

Gisela Ernst-Slavit, a native of Peru, is a professor of education and ESL at Washington State University Vancouver. Her research, guided by ethnographic and sociolinguistic perspectives, focuses on language pedagogy and teacher education in culturally and linguistically diverse settings. She has authored or coauthored 10 books and about 80 articles.

David Herman is a doctoral candidate in Washington State University's language, literacy, and technology program. He has taught English to speakers of other languages in Washington State, China, and Taiwan. He recently returned from a year in Taiwan training Fulbright English teaching assistants. David's research interests include computer-assisted language learning, online education, and language teacher development.

Justyna Hjeltness is an ESL instructor at Washington State University. She has been teaching English to students from all over the world since 2012. Justyna grew up in Poland and is an English language learner herself. She is particularly interested in using metacognitive strategies in second language learning.

Romella Husain, a special education teacher with 22 years of teaching experience, currently teaches at Poolesville High School in Maryland. She grew up in the Eastern U.S., speaks two languages at home, and has two sons and a daughter. She draws on these roles to inform aspects of this chapter.

Leslie Huff spent nearly 10 years teaching in the Japanese education system. Her experience in Japan includes teaching preschool through graduate school classes. She earned her PhD in language and literacy education and spent 6 years teaching in educator preparation programs. Leslie currently works developing education policy in Washington State.

Nathaniel Hunsu obtained a PhD in educational psychology with an emphasis in learning and instruction. His research emphasis is on how students process textual information for conceptual change in STEM education. Nathaniel holds a B.S. in electronic and computer engineering from Lagos State University, Nigeria, and a project management master's degree from Sunderland University, England. He is currently an assistant professor at the University of Georgia.

Alexei Kochetov is an associate professor in linguistics. A native speaker of Russian, he teaches linguistics and phonetics at the University of Toronto. Alexei's research examines speech production across languages, including the acquisition of English pronunciation by language learners and the English influence on Russian spoken in Canada.

Hyun-Gyung Lee, a native of Korea, obtained her PhD at Washington State University, where she is currently an adjunct professor. Her major research interests are L2 learner engagement, CALL, ESL/EFL curriculum development, and cross-cultural communication. She is also interested in teaching Korean as a foreign language. She has published and presented on these topics in a number of international forums.

Saeun Lee is a doctoral student in language, literacy, and technology at Washington State University. She completed a master's degree from Indiana University of Pennsylvania and a bachelor's degree from Kumamoto, Japan. Her research interests are second language acquisition, language education and curriculum development. She was born in Korea and moved to Japan while still in school. She is passionate to spread Korean and Japanese languages and cultures to others.

Nicolau N. Manuel is assistant professor of English language and cultural studies at Agostinho Neto University, Angola. His work focuses on cross-linguistic and cross-cultural influences in ESL/EFL contexts. Most of these efforts concentrate on promoting best practices for teaching English language learners and effective bilingual education policies.

Sandra Mercuri is a teacher educator and educational consultant with 20 years of experience in the field of bilingual education and ESL. Her research area includes dual language curriculum, the development of the academic language of science, and the effect of professional development and coaching on teachers of English learners.

María Isabel Morales recently obtained her doctoral degree from the cultural studies and social thought in education program at Washington State University. Dr. Morales' research interests emanate from her lived experiences as a first-generation college student and 1.5 generation immigrant from Michoacán, México.

Rani Muthukrishnan is a graduate student in language, literacy and technology at Washington State University whose work focuses on ecoliteracy and sustainability in preK–12. Ecoliteracy recognizes the holistic and inclusive ways of transacting with nature.

Sandra I. Musanti is associate professor in the bilingual and literacy studies department at the University of Texas Rio Grande Valley. She has extensive experience in teacher education in Argentina and the United States. Her research explores issues of language, culture, and identity in bilingual teacher preparation and development.

Nguyễn Thị Thu Điệp is working as a center manager at an international language center in Hoi An, Vietnam. Her daily work is intensively involved with language and culture. She believes that the best way to learn a language is through interacting with the culture underneath it.

Desirée Pallais investigates cross-language and cross-cultural aspects of teaching and learning, as part of doctoral studies at the University of Texas–Austin. In her native Nicaragua, she founded an innovative school, supported large-scale curriculum reform, and presented at a literacy conference, and she participates in several education initiatives.

Rose Lusangi Phambu was born in the Democratic Republic of Congo. She holds a BS in biochemistry, MA in religious arts, and a doctorate of ministry with a major in missions from Kingdom Bible College, Virginia. Rose is the founder and president of Luila Village Ministries, which supports medical, educational, and vocational training for people across the DRC.

Adriana Picoral is a PhD student in second language acquisition and teaching at the University of Arizona. She has taught additional languages in a number of contexts, from young learners in Brazil to undocumented adult immigrants in New Jersey. Her research interests include teacher training and multiliteracies.

Kristen L. Pratt is a PhD candidate and instructor in the College of Education at Washington State University. Her research explores the intersection of language and literacy education within culturally and linguistically diverse communities through the intertextuality of macro language education policies in local contexts using ethnographic and sociolinguistic perspectives.

Rana Raddawi is an associate professor at American University of Sharjah, United Arab Emirates. She teaches in the master of TESOL program in the department of English in addition to intercultural communication, ESP, and EAP. She has mastered five languages: English, Arabic, French, Portuguese, and Turkish. She is the editor of *Intercultural Communication with Arabs*.

Sayeeda Rahman is a lecturer of English and applied linguistics at the American International University Bangladesh. She worked as an adjunct faculty at the Institute of Modern Languages, University of Dhaka. She currently works as a teacher in the community program, Let's Talk Conversational Classes, in Pullman, Washington.

Eliane Rubinstein-Avila is professor of language and literacy at the University of Arizona. Her work focuses on the education of immigrant students (bilingual education and the acquisition of English as an additional language) and on conducting qualitative research. Her single and co-authored articles are published in national and international academic journals.

Seyed Abdollah Shahrokni, a native of Iran, is a doctoral student majoring in language, literacy, and technology at Washington State University. His research focuses on computer-assisted language learning (CALL), with an emphasis on learning environments. Also, he is currently the managing editor of *TESL-EJ* and administrative assistant of *TESOL Journal*.

Raihan Sharif is assistant professor of English at Jahangirnagar University. He is a Fulbright Scholar in the department of critical culture, gender, and race studies, program in American studies, Washington State University, an editor of Heathwood's *Journal of Critical Theory*, and a teaching scholar at the Cooperative Institute for Transnational Studies.

Jacqueline Tanner has a master's degree from the University of Pittsburgh. As a teaching fellow at the University of Siegen in Germany, she gained exposure to the Arab culture, which triggered her interest in tailoring a learning environment to fit the needs of all ELLs. Jackie has spent the last 30 years teaching students of different ages from all over the globe in a variety of settings.

Sreejith Thankappan is a graduate student in the College of Education at Washington State University. He intends to specialize in computer-assisted language learning (CALL). He is interested in creating a useful framework that will assist teachers in achieving curricular and content objectives in rural areas in India.

Ilana Umansky is assistant professor in the College of Education at the University of Oregon. Her work focuses on understanding and improving educational opportunity among immigrant students, particularly those from Latin America. She has lived and worked in Nicaragua and studied the Nicaraguan education system.

Congcong Wang is the associate lead of the Chinese Language Teachers Association–EdTech SIG, the editor-in-chief of the *Handbook of Research on Foreign Language Education in the Digital Age*, the translator/co-producer of the documentary *The Confucius Village*, and a faculty member in languages and literatures at the University of Northern Iowa.

Tingting Wang is a lecturer of East Asian studies at Princeton University whose work focuses on integrating student engagement principles into Chinese as a foreign language curriculum design. Most of these efforts focus on the Chinese as a foreign language teacher preparation program and computer-assisted language learning.

Jeom Ja Yeo earned her PhD in language, literacy, and culture at the University of Washington. Her research interests include immigration, race, and ethnicity, second language acquisition (SLA), multicultural education, and World Englishes. She teaches courses in teaching English to speakers of other languages (TESOL) and K–12 ELL education.

CPSIA information can be obtained
at www.ICGtesting.com
Printed in the USA
LVHW080750060821
694086LV00002B/2